AFTER THE LUFTWAFFE'S LAST BIG ATTACK WHILE BRITAIN
STILL STOOD ALONE

The front of the fire-gutted building at No. 23 Queen Victoria Street, in the City, collapsing after the raid of May 10, 1941. This was the last big air attack on London before the German Army began its assault on Russia.

Fr.   *Reproduced by permission of the Commissioner of Police for the City of London*

THE
ROYAL AIR FORCE
IN THE WORLD WAR

BY

CAPTAIN NORMAN MACMILLAN M.C. A.F.C.

AUTHOR OF
"INTO THE BLUE" "THE CHOSEN INSTRUMENT" "AIR STRATEGY"

VOLUME II
May 1940–May 1941

THE BATTLES OF
HOLLAND
BELGIUM
FRANCE
BRITAIN

GEORGE G. HARRAP & CO. LTD.
LONDON   TORONTO   BOMBAY   SYDNEY

First published 1944
by GEORGE G. HARRAP & CO. LTD.
182 High Holborn, London, W.C. 1

Copyright. All rights reserved

BOOK
PRODUCTION
WAR ECONOMY
STANDARD

Composed in Plantin type and printed by The Riverside Press, Edinburgh

Made in Great Britain

Contents

NOTE

To provide space for an adequate description of the work of the Royal Air Force throughout the period covered by this volume it has been necessary to rearrange the contents originally proposed to be included herein.

Volume III will contain the narrative of the war against Germany and Italy up to the liberation of North Africa.

Illustrations

Maps and Diagrams

CHAPTER I

Stage for Blitzkrieg

§ 1

The Listening-posts

WHEN four of a formation of five Battle bombers, co-operating with the French during the limited offensive against the Saar, were shot down by fifteen Messerschmitt 109's in a fight over Saarbrücken,[1] Nos. 1 and 73 Fighter squadrons of the Royal Air Force were ordered to fly from Norrent, near Saint-Omer, to Vassincourt aerodrome near Bar-le-Duc, and Etain-Rouvres aerodrome near Verdun, to give assistance to the British bombers. With that flight thirty Hurricane fighters were struck off the strength of the Air Component of the British Expeditionary Force and taken on the strength of the Advanced Air Striking Force, which had possessed no fighters.

It is extravagant to use short-range fighters for standing patrols. With only two squadrons to a sector it is impossible. Ground intelligence was therefore essential to enable the fighters to guard their sector.

An observer screen, similar to those in the defence sectors of the United Kingdom, was established to provide rapid information of all enemy aircraft crossing that section of the French frontier behind which the two Hurricane squadrons operated. The Royal Air Force manned listening-posts on top of some of the forts of the Maginot Line; through repeater stations west of Metz the wireless operators linked up with the headquarters of the Advanced Air Striking Force at the Château Polignac, near Rheims (the peace-time home of the head of Pommery, for whose firm Ribbentrop had been a champagne salesman, and where the German Foreign Minister had often stayed), the 67th (Fighter) Wing at Bussy-la-Côte, and the squadron operations-rooms.

The men of the listening-posts were cut off from their British comrades. They lived with the French troops below ground in the forts. Before the war they were civilians, men who had made a hobby of wireless. One of them came from the architectural department of an Essex municipality. Just before war broke out a policeman touched

---

[1] See Vol. I, p. 152, for a description of this action.

him on the shoulder. He received his mobilization orders. He was given uniform. Before long he was beginning to learn French in the Maginot Line. He had one British companion. In ones and twos other Britishers were strung out along the line of forts. For seven months the men manning these posts had the loneliest job in the Royal Air Force. In Metz a flight lieutenant and an army subaltern were the only permanent representatives of the British forces.

§ 2

Attack at Dawn

During the prolonged lull there were two crises—the first when it was reliably learned that a German attack on Holland was planned to take place on November 12, 1939, and the second in January 1940 when secret documents fell into Belgian hands after the forced landing of a German aeroplane within Belgium.

On November 7, 1939, Queen Wilhelmina and King Leopold dispatched telegrams to the heads of the States of Great Britain, France, and Germany, renewing their offer of mediation, first made on August 28, 1939. That crisis blew over, and the German attack, if it had been really intended—the Germans were adept at the tactics of *Nervenkrieg*—did not take place.

The documents taken in Belgium constituted a threat to Holland, France, and Britain, and the military authorities of these countries were informed of the contents; it was thought that the capture of the documents might precipitate an attack; but this crisis too passed. Then on May 4, 1940, the Netherlands Government unexpectedly learned that Holland might be attacked by Germany within a few days.

In the evening of May 9 a report reached Brussels from the Belgian military attaché in Berlin; its import was that the Germans intended to attack Belgium on the following day. At about the same time the Dutch Intelligence service reported: "To-morrow at dawn."

The shadows of the sunset lengthened, and guns began to fire from the Maginot Line and the opposing portion of the Siegfried Line. Their thunder rolled faintly back to Metz.

Darkness fell over Eastern Belgium, and the Belgian frontier guards heard, coming from the German side of the frontier, an unusual noise of voices, footsteps, running motors, and moving traffic.

An hour later—at about eleven o'clock—the Luxemburg authorities were informed that Nazis living within the Grand Duchy had been warned; presently clashes between the police and Nazis occurred when Luxemburg fifth-columnists tried to remove the barriers from the road-blocks that faced the German frontier.

The uneasy night passed.

Dawn had scarcely flushed the sky when, without ultimatum, with no declaration of war, the German Air Force heavily bombed the Dutch aerodromes of Rotterdam-Waalhaven, Amsterdam-Schiphol, Bergen, and de Kooy. With the lesson of the German attack upon Norway impressed upon the minds of the Dutch Air Force commanders, the hangars were empty. The aircraft were dispersed around the aerodromes and about satellite landing-grounds which had been hastily constructed; few aircraft were damaged by bombs, but many were put out of action by machine-gun fire from the air before they could take off.

Dawn brought more bombers and the promise of a perfect morning. As Nature lightened the sky above The Hague, the seat of government of the Netherlands, the Luftwaffe darkened it, and bombed barracks on the outskirts of the town. Two hours passed, and at six o'clock more German aircraft swept down upon the Dutch capital; they raked the streets with machine-gun fire, and scattered leaflets whose contents urged the people to lay down arms, or, alternatively, face destruction; the edges of these leaflets were over-printed in orange, national colour of the Dutch people, who are governed by a constitutional monarchy under the house of Orange-Nassau.

Simultaneously, and equally without provocation, ultimatum, or declaration of war, a powerful German air force bombed and machine-gunned Belgian aerodromes, railway stations, and communication centres. The Belgian Army Air Force, four regiments strong, was taken by surprise, and lost more than half its aircraft on the ground. At 5.17 A.M. sirens wailed in Brussels. Bombs fell on Evere aerodrome, around the Schaerbeek railway junction, and on several other parts of the city. This raid caused many deaths in Brussels. The Belgian Government declared the capital an open town, and stated that there were no troops there.

Under cover of these and other air attacks German ground forces began, at dawn on May 10, 1940, to attack along the whole German frontier from Longwy to the North Sea. Strong pressure was exerted at many points in Holland, Belgium, and Luxemburg. The Maginot Line was left alone. This ingenious fortified line jutted out, like a salient, towards Southern Germany; but it was tragically immobile, impotent to stem the tide of battle that surged past it to the north. In the evidence at the Riom trial, begun in France on February 19, 1942, it was alleged that the best French troops were in and behind the Maginot Line, and that the greatest tank concentrations were also there. No doubt the Germans were aware of the French dispositions, for German espionage had been very active in the area behind the Maginot Line during the eight quiet months of war.

At about 6 A.M. on May 10, 1940, the Dutch and Belgian Ministers in Paris and London, acting on the telegraphed instructions of their respective Governments, made the first appeal to the Allies for aid. They asked, especially, for help in the air. They were immediately informed that the Allies would assist them to the utmost of their ability. Unfortunately, air assistance was the direction in which least help could be immediately given.

§ 3

The Prepared Way

Before the World War began the German Air Force constructed a chain of aerodromes and landing-grounds facing the frontiers of Holland and Belgium, and close to the territories of both States. This action was noted. Nothing was done about it. Nothing could be done about it, because a state—in this case Germany—had the right to build aerodromes and landing-grounds anywhere within its territory, and could be prevented from doing so only by force. The Versailles Treaty was already dead when these advanced jumping-off points for the Luftwaffe were under construction from 1936 onward.

At the outbreak of war in 1939 Holland and Belgium declared their neutrality, in continuation of the policies adopted by each country before the war.

After the conquest of Poland German troops were transferred to the Western Front. The strength of the military forces facing westward continually increased. The ever-augmenting divisions rose to one hundred and six, one hundred and twenty, one hundred and forty. Along the Polish demarcation line agreed by Germany and Russia, the troops of these two States faced one another, the pact of non-aggression keeping the dogs of war still leashed. In South-eastern Europe, where the frontiers of Hungary, Germany's ally, abutted upon Yugoslavia and Rumania, there were German troops, but their numbers were fewer, perhaps twenty divisions.

After the seizure of Denmark and during the conquest of Southern and Central Norway the number of divisions massed in Western Germany was further increased.

The documents taken in Belgium from the German aircraft which forced-landed on January 10, 1940, at Mechelen-sur-Meuse contained instructions to the Commander of the 2nd Air Fleet of the Luftwaffe. They were carried by a Staff Major, who was flying to the headquarters of the 22nd Infantry Division at Cologne—a division specially trained for landing from the air—to discuss the details of these secret instructions, which outlined plans for the German Western Army to attack between the North Sea and the Moselle. There were to be: the strongest possible air support in the Belgo-Luxemburg region; seizure of Dutch territory; attack by the whole of the 3rd German Air Fleet to prevent the French Air Force from taking part in the land operations, and later to prevent the French armies from moving north-east from their concentration areas. The X Aviation Corps was to co-operate with German naval forces and concentrate principally against the British naval forces. German home defence against air attack was to protect, primarily, the ground and war-industries organizations. Air reconnaissance was to cover the whole area west of the line Le Havre-Orleans-Bourges-Lyon-Geneva and north-west and west of the line Frisian Islands-Amsterdam-Antwerp-Brussels-Nivelles (including the islands and towns), to discover the disposition of the opposing air forces in Northern France and Belgium and to watch the concentration areas of the British Army and detect as quickly as possible any movement towards Belgium in the direction of Brussels-Ghent.

A landing of the German VII Aviation Division, assisted by part of the VIII Corps, was to support, in co-operation with the 6th Army, the advance of the land forces detailed to attack the fortified line and the streams of the basin of the Meuse, with the object of destroying the Belgian Army to the west of that region.

Fighter squadrons were to obtain command of the air over the area of attack of the 6th Army.

The German staff recognized that the chief threat to the work of the VII Aviation Division lay in the arrival of French mobile troops from the line Maubeuge-Hirson-Fumay only twenty-five miles away. To prevent this intervention, large forces of German bombing aircraft were to be engaged against French concentrations in the area indicated, and against all lines of communication between the French troops and the area of the German attack.

The air division was to be protected over its routes, parachute area, and landing area by the continuous operation of strong formations of heavy and light types of fighters. Fighting area was to be only 70 miles from the frontier, and flight over enemy territory to be only 125 miles.

The actual German attack, when it came, was similar in character. But there were no prior staff discussions between the Dutch and Belgian military authorities and those of France and Britain.

13

The neutrality of Belgium was guaranteed by the three great belligerent Powers, each of whom had promised assistance in the event of attack. In Belgium it was thought that the Germans secretly hoped that France and Britain would undertake preventive intervention on behalf of Belgium, when the German armies would have at once attacked.

From 1914 to 1936 the Belgian General Staff had maintained close contact with the French General Staff, but the policy of absolute neutrality adopted by Belgium on October 14, 1936, in the declaration by King Leopold to the Council of Ministers, ended this contact.

For the Belgian attitude it was claimed that it united the Belgian people, who would otherwise have been rent by faction. And in Belgium it was further thought that in the state then existing of France and Britain as military Powers, other action might have advanced the course of history by a few weeks or months, but would not have changed it—a sad reflection with which no one has a right to quarrel.

After the capture of the documents the Belgians increased their strength in the east by transferring part of their forces from the west. The Germans alleged this to be a threat against the Reich, and held it up as justification for their assault. Officially they declared that their attack was to forestall the invasion of Belgium, Holland, and Luxemburg by Great Britain and France—a characteristically Teutonic perversion. *Qui s'excuse s'accuse.*

Dutch neutrality was proverbial. The pretext for the German invasion of the Netherlands was the allegation that British naval forces were preparing to make a landing on the Dutch coast, a charge equally absurd. Always the criminal seeks to allay his mental conception of himself as the perpetrator of an act of crime; the German militarist is no exception.

Belgium and the Netherlands rejected the German Government's demand, presented through the Ambassadors of the Reich several hours after the German attack began, to cease resistance and make contact with the German High Command. The Ministers of both monarchies refused to have their states taken into protective custody by Germany. Their armies accepted the challenge, and the fight was on.

§ 4

Britain's Place

From its arrival in France the British Expeditionary Force was under the command of the French generalissimo, General Gamelin; but the

THE FATE OF ROTTERDAM

The photograph shows the destruction caused in the open city of Rotterdam by the bombing of the Luftwaffe on May 14, 1940, after the Royal Dutch Air Force was destroyed. More than a square mile of the centre of the city was systematically wrecked, and the main shopping centre was devastated. The walls of the principal church, the Groote Kerk, still stand, as does the old windmill on the Oostplein.

Photo "The Times"

A TRAGIC SCENE AT SAINT-NAZAIRE

As the Cunard-White Star liner *Lancastria* sinks after a dive-bombing attack, survivors swarm down the sides and swim in the water behind the screw. The dive-bomber that hit the ship was shot down by a Hurricane of No. 1 squadron.

Photo Associated Press

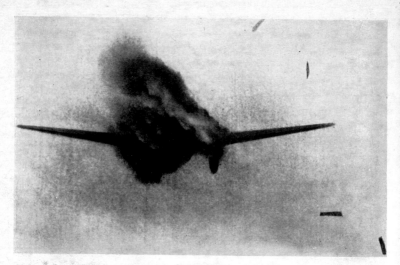

A HEINKEL BOMBER ON FIRE

This photograph of a Heinkel bomber on fire and breaking up in the air was taken by the
camera synchronized with the guns of a Hurricane of Fighter Command.

[*P.* 26]

LOW-LEVEL ATTACK

Battle bombers attack a German horse-drawn transport column. German soldiers
run for cover across the fields to the right.

[*P.* 41]

Chapter II

The Battle of Holland

§ 1

Attack without Warning

FROM two o'clock in the morning of May 10, 1940, Dutch wireless stations announced repeatedly that aeroplanes were traversing Netherlands territory from east to west. They were German aircraft dropping magnetic mines in Dutch rivers and harbour entrances. Before four o'clock the first bombs fell on aerodromes and barracks in Fortress Holland. At five o'clock incendiary bombs fell on the northern part of The Hague (in a later raid that morning a bomb destroyed a maternity hospital, killing and injuring nurses, mothers, and babies); high-explosive bombs were aimed at the headquarters of the naval staff.

Parachute troops were then dropped to attack The Hague, Delft, Zandvoord, The Hook, Ymuiden, Eindhoven, Dordrecht, and Rotterdam-Waalhaven aerodrome.[1] This overhead penetration of the Dutch defences (which were largely dependent upon the flooding of the low-lying lands) proved to be the key which opened the door to the swift downfall of Holland; its success was accelerated by Dutch Nazis, who helped to increase a confusion already serious.

Part of Waalhaven aerodrome was quickly captured by the paratroops, who removed the obstacles placed upon the airfield, and Junkers 52 air transports then began to land troops and equipment. This was a serious threat, because men and material could be concentrated more rapidly by transport aircraft than by parachutes.

The Dutch Air Force possessed 248 aeroplanes. Those that survived the first bombing and machine-gunning were heavily outnumbered in the air, and were driven down and destroyed by waves of German aircraft. (By May 13 ten Dutch aircraft were left, and by nightfall

---

[1] Russia was the first country to experiment with air-borne troops. During the Russian manœuvres of 1936, 1200 fully equipped infantrymen, 150 machine-guns, and 18 field-guns were transported by air and dropped 100 miles behind the opposing front lines by parachute. Germany was the first country to use air-borne troops in war, and the first really big-scale use of such troops was made against Holland and Belgium. They played a large part in the swift overrunning of these two countries.

that day these too were destroyed.) Dutch troops defending the aerodromes were mercilessly machine-gunned from the air and suffered heavy losses.

By five o'clock in the morning of May 10 the three aerodromes of Ypenburg, Ockenburg, and Walkenburg, all near The Hague, were in German hands, and German air transports began to land troops.

More German aircraft landed on the gently sloping beach at Scheveningen, near The Hague, at Katwijk, and at Wassenaar, and disemplaned troops. Seaplanes alighted on canals, docks, and rivers, mostly in the neighbourhood of Rotterdam.

The German general von Sponeck had orders to take The Hague on the first day of the attack. He failed to do so. He and the horse on which he was to have made his triumphal entry into The Hague were killed when the aeroplane in which both were travelling was shot down. More than a hundred other German aeroplanes were brought down by the Dutch Air Force and anti-aircraft artillery on that first day of war in the Netherlands.

German troops were rapidly formed up around the seat of government and the Royal Palace. As in Norway, the attempt was made to end the war prematurely by the capture of the sovereign and the governing Ministers of the Crown. Both bombs and parachutists fell in the Palace grounds. The parachutists were killed by the Palace guards.

A second bombing attack was made against the centre of the capital at 10 A.M. But The Hague held out. The parachutists were mopped up by the Dutch troops responsible for the defences in the west of Holland. Early that afternoon more parachutists landed around The Hague; they were followed during the night and in the morning of the second day by others. All were mopped up by the Dutch troops; they never succeeded in capturing the Dutch capital.

The Dutch Navy engaged the troop-transport aircraft landing along the coast and destroyed them, but at Rotterdam the situation was serious. This open, commercial city was a focal point in the German air attack. It became the scene of bitter fighting. German air-borne troops, repeating the tactics employed in Norway, fetched guns and ammunition from a ship lying in the harbour and flying the Swedish flag.

The Germans' first objective was the aerodrome of Waalhaven; their second the bridges in Rotterdam, the main bridges across the river Meuse (Maas in Dutch) and especially the Moerdijk bridge, the principal transport link between Rotterdam and Antwerp. German troops rushed in on seaplanes took the Meuse bridges by surprise. These bridges changed hands more than once. Many of the German

18

GERMAN INVASION
OF THE
NETHERLANDS
May 10th - 14th 1940

Aerodromes △ German Air-borne ⊗ Troops landed
Defence Lines —•—•—•—
German attacks ◀━━━

air-borne troops wore uniforms indistinguishable from Dutch uniforms except under the closest scrutiny. Parachutists descended as police-men, postmen, tramwaymen, civilians; even German women who had been maidservants in Holland came down from the air to act as guides to the soldiers. The Moerdijk bridge was taken by disguised troops before the demolition charges could be blown.

The Netherlands Army had no artillery to spare for this (to Dutch minds) undreamt-of area for fighting, but a Dutch warship shelled Waalhaven aerodrome, the nodal point for German reinforcements, until the ship was sunk by dive-bombers. Another Dutch destroyer and British destroyers were asked not to proceed up-river because of magnetic mines. The German method of attack had been well planned.

Waalhaven aerodrome changed hands many times. The Germans bombed it. The Dutch bombed it. At the request of the Dutch, Bomber Command bombed it on three consecutive nights. (When the Dutch were down to their last aircraft the pilot announced his intention of dropping his bombs on Waalhaven, knowing well he would never return.) But when the landing area became unusable German aircraft landed on the car parking-grounds of a near-by football stadium.

After four days of fighting Rotterdam was still uncaptured. Then the Luftwaffe bombed the centre of the city. They met no opposition. The Dutch fighters were all destroyed. Immune from interference, the Luftwaffe groups of heavy bombers dropped heavy high-explosive and incendiary bombs. Not a house in the city centre stood intact. Thirty thousand persons, with scarce a soldier among them, perished in the space of half an hour in Rotterdam on May 14. Imperishably this deed is written in the annals of the Luftwaffe. It was done because Dutch soldiers were too brave. . . .

Meanwhile, along the frontier, the Dutch Army had met the full force of the German war machine. In the flat country of the provinces of Gröningen, Drenthe, and Friesland, the Dutch Army could do no more than retard the enemy advance. After destroying the harbour of Delfzijl (opposite Emden) they fought a delaying action to the Zuiderzee dyke, a position they could hold, and which the Germans did not capture. Held up at the dyke, the Germans attempted to cross the Zuiderzee. Dutch warships, joined by mine-sweepers, armed river-craft and motor-boats carrying machine-guns, together with French and British motor-torpedo-boats, fought the first battle in the Zuiderzee since 1578, and denied the crossing to the German troops, in spite of German air support which caused Dutch naval losses. Farther south, where the attack upon the provinces of Limburg and Brabant opened an avenue for subsequent attack upon Belgium and France, the German Air Force possessed great numerical superiority; their mastery in the air covered the advance of their armoured and motorized divisions.

The German Army moved westward along the whole Dutch frontier. The defence-line of the Meuse had to be abandoned, but German losses in crossing the Meuse and the canal connecting the Meuse and Waal rivers were heavy. Four German armoured trains were destroyed; one fell into the Meuse while crossing the bridge near Venlo at the moment the bridge was blown. But not all the bridges were destroyed. . . .

20

A second stand was made on the Yssel river on May 13. There the main defence-line of Fortress Holland was situated, protected by floods. Against this position the Germans threw low-flying aircraft, flame-thrower tanks, and gun-tanks. The troops garrisoning Western Holland, who should (in theory) have come to the aid of the defence of the main position, were still engaged with air-borne enemy troops. The Dutch informed the Allies that without adequate and immediate assistance they could not hold out. But the resources of the Allies were stretched equally to their limit. General Winkelman, the Dutch Commander-in-Chief, was given by his Government, in the evening of May 13, authority to make the necessary military decision according to the situation.

On May 14 the Dutch were again forced back. The German advance reached Rotterdam. Ancient and picturesque Utrecht was threatened with the same fate. The losses of the Dutch Army were estimated to be 100,000, a quarter of the whole effective strength. General Winkelman ordered the main Dutch forces holding the water-line to the north (whose position was then turned) to cease resistance; surrounded by millions of non-combatants, who could not be evacu-ated from the fighting zones, it was the only decision he could take in the face of overwhelming odds.

Queen Wilhelmina arrived in London on May 13 with the Princess Juliana and her children. Prince Bernhard, who accompanied them, returned at once to Holland. The Netherlands Ministers for Foreign Affairs and the Colonies were already in London. On May 14, in spite of many attempts to bomb and sink the British destroyer in which they sailed, the other members of the Netherlands Cabinet arrived in England; many had to leave their wives and families behind.

In the province of Zeeland, the most westerly province of Holland, composed principally of islands, the struggle continued. There Prince Bernhard fought with his troops. French soldiers, and the British Navy, gave aid. The medieval town hall and abbey of Middelburg were destroyed. German pressure grew stronger. At the last moment pupils of an army flying-school, barely fledgelings, took off and landed on French airfields. Before May was out Zeeland, last of the Netherlands provinces to fall, was under the Prussian heel.

But the Netherlands Government lived on in spite of the German occupation of Holland. The Netherlands forces who got away joined those of the Allies in the struggle against Hitler's Reich.

Royal Air Force Aid to Holland

When the blow fell there was no proper Intelligence link between the outraged Netherlands and those upon whom her Government called for help. On the first day of the attack the Netherlands Foreign and Colonial Ministers flew to England in a Dutch seaplane to maintain direct contact with the British Government, but this did not provide the military Intelligence from the field of operations which was essential to assure the correct application of air intervention. Nevertheless, the messages which flowed in to the war-room of the Air Ministry in London began to build up the pattern of the German design for attack upon Holland; but the swift changes of occupation of several key-points as they were captured by German parachutists, retaken by Dutch troops, and recaptured by fresh waves of Nazi-doctrinated German youth, created a picture alternately clear and incomprehensible. One thing stood out above all others: that the weight of the German air attack was overwhelming. Those who had underestimated the size of the Luftwaffe were dumbfounded; these men had done an ill-service to the Royal Air Force and the British people.

The first support to Holland from the Royal Air Force based in the United Kingdom took the form of attacks by fighters and bombers against German aircraft on the Dutch beaches and Rotterdam-Waalhaven aerodrome.

Blenheim long-range fighters and bombers attacked nine Junkers 52 troop-transports on the beach eight miles north of The Hague. The bombers attacked first. Their high-explosive bombs burst among the aircraft. One Junkers was lifted off the ground to fall back in flames; another burst into flames where it stood. Down came the six Blenheims diving in line astern from 5000 feet, sighting their front gun-batteries of four machine-guns, and flattening out low above the beach. Skimming at fifty feet, they unleashed the whip-lash of 18,000 rounds of ammunition. Four more transports were destroyed, and the remaining three riddled with bullets. German machine-gunners fired at the Blenheims flashing low above them, and brought one of the British fighters down; it forced-landed on the beach; the other five circled round and watched, and saw the crew get out, apparently uninjured, before they turned for home.

Shortly after three o'clock Waalhaven aerodrome was attacked. Bombers and Blenheim fighters were employed on this raid. The hangars were ablaze when the British aircraft arrived over the aerodrome, and the attacks were concentrated against large numbers of German aircraft, including fifty air transports which were dispersed along the sides of the landing-field. Bomb-hits were seen, until the smoke from the bursts became so dense that close observation became impossible. The only opposition came from the guns of stationary aircraft. It was ineffective. But German fighters were overhead, and combats took place.

The pilot and air gunner of one of six Blenheims that attacked Waalhaven were awarded the Distinguished Flying Cross and the Distinguished Flying Medal. After diving and destroying a Junkers 52 in company with the formation-leader this pilot, Flying Officer Norman Hayes, climbed and rejoined his formation. Twelve Messerschmitt 110's attacked the Blenheim. Corporal G. H. Holmes told his pilot, Hayes, how to fly to avoid the fire of the Messerschmitts. Hayes, bunched in the nose of the Blenheim between the two engine-nacelles, could not see the German fighters. But presently he saw a Junkers 52, and swinging his own damaged aircraft towards it, gave it a burst. It went down with its port engine ablaze. Before he got home he charged three Heinkel 111's and forced them to break formation; Holmes, suffering from petrol-fumes escaping from a burst tank, continued to give accurate information to his pilot throughout the action, and this enabled the pilot to evade enemy fire and reach his base safely. So these two Londoners brought honour to No. 600 (City of London) squadron, in which they flew as members of the Auxiliary Air Force.

That afternoon the Royal Air Force was asked to bomb Ypenburg aerodrome after it was taken by German parachutists. A force of Beaufort bombers was dispatched. Just as the force was due to arrive above the aerodrome news reached England that the aerodrome had been retaken by Dutch troops. It was too late to stop the bombers. . . .

Leading a formation of three aircraft towards Ypenburg was Flight Lieutenant H. L. Smeddle. A large number of Messerschmitt 110's attacked his formation when it was about two miles from Ypenburg. Two of the three aircraft were forced to retire. Smeddle flew on alone until a cannon-shell, bursting in his cockpit, wounded him and his observer. A second shell exploding in the rear of the aircraft wounded the air gunner and wrecked the wireless apparatus. Yet Smeddle threw off the enemy attack, and, with his compass and wireless both gone, brought his aircraft home. For his courage in saving his aircraft and the lives of his crew this short-service commissioned officer from Shildon, County Durham, was awarded the Distinguished Flying Cross.

Other attacks were made that day. Four Blenheims were lost.

During the succeeding night thirty-six Wellington bombers attacked Waalhaven aerodrome. As the first wave of bombers approached Rotterdam shortly after nine o'clock they were guided by its lights, which were visible many miles out to sea. Machine-guns and multiple pom-poms opened fire on the Wellingtons from around the aerodrome and alongside an adjacent dock, but nearly a hundred bombs were dropped on the aerodrome and buildings. During the attack the lights of the city were abruptly cut off. For almost forty-five minutes the bombs fell, setting buildings alight and starting fires on three sides of the aerodrome where aircraft were parked.

The lights came on again suddenly at ten o'clock after the bombers left, and guided a second wave towards the objective, flying at a different height. These bombers also scored hits on the aerodrome.

Shortly before midnight the first of a third wave began an attack which continued for nearly an hour. Buildings were hit and aircraft set alight. The retaliatory fire from the ground weakened. Slight machine-gun fire alone greeted the fourth wave, which arrived about an hour after the third wave had ended its attack. The Wellingtons glided low, dropping salvos of bombs which straddled the hangars, caused six enemy aircraft to burst into flames, damaged a road and a railway, fired a group of buildings in a corner of the aerodrome, and exploded a dump.

This was the most intensive air bombardment of any objective that had ever been made in a single night by the Royal Air Force. (Two years later, on May 31, 1942, a force of 1047 bombers bombed the city of Cologne during the space of ninety minutes.)

The Royal Air Force lost no aircraft in these night operations. On the ravaged aerodrome of Waalhaven, where drifting smoke drew a veil above the ruined buildings and the bomb-pits on the field, fires were raging, and twenty multi-engined enemy aircraft were blazing fiercely along the west side of the landing-ground.

When dawn came on the second day of the attack on Holland at least fifty enemy aircraft were known to have been destroyed and many more put out of action or seriously damaged either in the air or on the ground by all sections of the Royal Air Force. *Per contra*, some twenty British aircraft were missing. For the Air Force that was a heartening token of relative efficiency. The only sorrow was over the mourning of good men gone. But not all were dead. Some had escaped capture when, their aircraft shot down, they descended by parachute; others had crawled out of their aircraft on the ground, alive; some of these men came back.

Blenheim fighters went into action over Holland again on May 11. One attacked a Junkers air transport and set its port engine smoking, but had to break off the attack when the air gunner reported a Messerschmitt 110 on their own tail. The sergeant observer reported:

Incendiary bullets of a yellowish colour hit our machine, one burning my sleeve. Bullets came into the cabin, and there was a loud bang behind my feet. Pieces resembling burnt paper flew about. I assumed an explosive bullet or cannon-shell hit us. Flames spread inside the machine, and I opened the escape-hatch and went out backwards, but my parachute caught on the rear side of the hatch-opening. I hung with my head underneath the machine. The parachute suddenly became loose. I think the pilot, a squadron leader, kicked it clear. My parachute opened with about thirty feet to spare, and I landed in a field near Rotterdam docks. Some Dutch folks took me across the waterway to the main part of the town, where I was taken to hospital, suffering a cut on the head and burns on my left hand.

Hurricane fighters were over Holland for the first time that day. One pilot said, "There was thick smoke over Rotterdam and The Hague and we could see fires. My section of three aircraft was suddenly attacked by Messerschmitts a little north of Rotterdam. Eight came in for the first attack. A dog-fight developed. I got on to the tail of one and gave him all I had. Then I stalled and lost sight of him. The next thing I saw was a parachute coming down near where the Messerschmitt had been."

A sergeant pilot, outmanœuvring a Messerschmitt who got on his tail, 'gave him' all his ammunition, and saw the Messerschmitt spin in flames to the ground.

A third pilot followed his enemy down to ground-level in a running fight and saw him crumple up fifteen miles south of The Hague. Another British pilot used all his ammunition to send one Messerschmitt spinning down, found two more on his tail, dived until he was close to the surface of a canal, flew along it, and got away unscathed.

All together, that day, fifty Hurricanes, operating from British aerodromes, shot down twenty German aircraft over Holland, including sixteen air transports. Success came to the British fighters from the start. In their training, and in the manœuvrability of their aircraft, they outmatched the German pilots and machines. The bullet jets from their eight Browning machine-guns cut like buzz-saws through the structures of the opposing aircraft; for although the Germans had mounted cannon-guns on their fighters, they had omitted adequate armour. The British score against the Luftwaffe mounted into hundreds during the period of fighting across the North Sea and the English Channel, while the average British losses in aircraft sorties during this period were 5 per cent. In these British fighter pilots, who had seen little fighting—some had seen none—during the long 'phoney' months of waiting for the German offensive to begin, confidence was born, as it had been already born in the pilots of the two Fighter squadrons of the Advanced Air Striking Force following their known achievements. Uncertainty vanished. The worth of British fighter aircraft was established.

But German pressure was too great to be stopped by forces employing weapons less numerous than theirs. With the Dutch aerodromes in German hands almost from the first light of the first day, it was impossible for Royal Air Force short-range Spitfires and Hurricanes to operate against the enemy close to the German frontier. Aerodromes in the United Kingdom were twice as far from the Dutch coast as the German fighter area was from the eastern frontier of Holland; this gave a great advantage to the German aircraft co-operating with the advancing troops, for those enemy aircraft could not be engaged by the high-performance British fighters. The combined air forces of the five Allies then fighting were too small for the size of the Luftwaffe. The Royal Air Force, striving to make up for the inadequacy of the air arms of the four nations allied to Britain, was simultaneously fighting over Norway, Holland, Belgium, and France.

So, in the beginning, the Luftwaffe had numerical superiority, and it was impossible, even locally, to wrest from it its mastery of the air, because its overwhelming numbers filled all the gaps which were mown among its aircraft. The commanders of the Luftwaffe disregarded losses. Transport aircraft were crash-landed when that course was necessary; they landed across wind, down wind, anyhow, to speed up the landing of troops and supplies. Hitler had said that this German generation would have to be sacrificed if necessary; he had encouraged early marriages with State dowries to produce the future German generation prior to the holocaust; now the blood was being let upon the altar of pagan German pride. Obediently the Germans laid themselves upon the altar when bidden by their Führer; copiously their blood was to flow; what mattered it to them that the full red stream mingled with the blood of innocents? As in former wars, fields were to be drenched with blood, deserts stained, roads discoloured, and rivers dyed; but in this war the cities were to be fouled with coagulating streams of blood, and blood was to fall from the heavens to the earth as fighting soared with ever-increasing fury into the skies. . . .

During the night following May 11 bombing attacks were made against troop concentrations and military traffic on roads and railways in Germany and close to the Dutch frontier. Whitley bombers

26

attacked enemy concentrations and enemy troops advancing towards the frontier of Holland between the Rhine and the Meuse.

The air crews saw the lights of long columns of transport on almost every important road. As with the columns that converged on Lübeck for the attack upon Norway, the Germans ignored blackout restrictions, preferring freedom of movement and speed to secrecy, once movement began. In many areas searchlights, working on mobile platforms, came into action against the British night raiders who harassed the enemy columns. Against the masses of troops that Germany had ordered into movement the small forces of British bombers then available for counter-effort were like gnats straining to incapacitate an elephant. But bombs hit the bridge over the Rhine near Wesel, and railway and road-junctions and bridges at Aldekirk, Geldern, Rees, and Goch, and fell among lines of traffic.

Next day the Defiant went into action for the first time. This two-seater fighter had no front gun; instead, four machine-guns were mounted in a rotatable power-turret manned by a gunner stationed immediately behind the pilot's cockpit; these guns could sweep the whole upper hemisphere of sky, and, by tilting the aircraft, could be fired downward. The tactical handling of this aircraft demanded close co-operation between pilot and gunner. More than in any other aeroplane of fighting type, success in air combat in the Defiant depended upon the team-work of the crew of two. In other respects the Defiant was very much like a Hurricane, but not quite so fast, not so rocketing in climb, not so aloof in ceiling.

The Defiant squadron was on patrol near The Hague. It had been there for some time before a Junkers 88 was sighted out to sea trying to bomb three British ships. Squadron Leader P. A. Hunter, leading two other Defiants, swung out to sea to the attack. The Junkers turned towards the coast to escape, but was cut off. It dived, but Hunter outmanœuvred the German pilot, and the Defiant's air gunner scored hits. The Junkers reached the coast, flew low over three fields with smoke pouring from its port engine, and then crashed in a field where cows were grazing. A Spitfire which accompanied the Defiants forced a Heinkel 111 down into a crash-landing amid a cloud of dust and smoke; like the Junkers, the Heinkel had been attempting a bombing attack over the sea.

Reconnaissance aircraft flying over Holland saw that the damage done to the aerodromes by British bombing had forced the enemy to use emergency landing-fields and that this was causing the Luftwaffe considerable losses in aircraft due to accidents. On one landing-ground alone fourteen troop-transports out of sixteen were seen to be damaged.

Coastal Command aircraft on reconnaisaance that day reported wrecked and burnt-out aircraft at The Hague and Rotterdam. Their crews saw the ground around both places flecked with white spots— the parachutes that had been left where they fell by German para- troops. These British aircraft attacked enemy patrol vessels, and shot down several fighters. Coastal Command Blenheims approached Flushing in the evening and engaged Heinkel and Junkers bombers which were attacking an ammunition ship in the harbour. A dog-fight fought between 300 feet and 5000 feet lasted for ten minutes and drove the German aircraft away from their prey. In the course of this engagement a Blenheim pilot saw salvos of bombs burst in the Channel about a hundred yards from the jetty. He looked up. A mile above him more Heinkels and Junkers circled the sky, bombing without interference of any kind. One of their bombs burst in the town, but most fell into the water. Flushing was crowded with motor- cars, lorries, carts; there were obstructions across all the roads, except one.

At dusk Beauforts and Swordfish swooped on Waalhaven aerodrome and took the Germans by surprise. The aerodrome was almost hidden in the smoke-drift from the fires burning in Rotterdam city. But their bombs started new fires in aerodrome buildings, struck the railway-lines along the airfield boundary, and pitted the landing- ground. This attack lasted for twenty minutes.

During the night more British bombs fell on Waalhaven.

Next day—Monday—three Coastal Command Blenheims outfought six Messerschmitt 110's and four Junkers 88's. Keeping their machines in close formation, the Royal Air Force crews drove off the enemy with 7000 rounds of ammunition and sent one Messerschmitt crashing into the sea. The fight ended when clouds enveloped the aircraft.

During daylight that day, and later, under cover of darkness, British bombers maintained their attacks against enemy road and rail approaches to the battlefields. Visibility was poor, and flying conditions were bad, yet considerable damage was wrought in the enemy lines of com- munication. German columns stretched along the roads that crossed the Dutch province of Brabant; some of these roads were blocked by Bomber Command. The night-bombing Whitleys and Hampdens— whose crews dropped parachute flares to light up the landscape before dropping their bombs—were met by heavy anti-aircraft fire; their main targets were railway bridges in Holland.

The Dutch were strategically outmanœuvred, and tactically over- whelmed. The German war machine rolled rapidly over the Nether- lands and crushed resistance by sheer power. The Allies did not possess the weight of weapons to enable them to halt the tide of Teuton mechanization that surged in a flood towards the seaboard, nor did they own one single surprise weapon which might have brought confusion upon the German horde. Indeed, all the novelty lay with the attackers; they had developed old weapons and devised new ones—tanks, armed motor-cycles and sidecars, mobile anti-aircraft guns and searchlights, mobile artillery, fighters, and bombers in numbers which enabled all losses to be instantly replaced; they possessed the only specialized dive-bombers, great numbers of paratroops, air-borne divisions carried in air transports and towed gliders and equipped with suitable light guns and mortars, heavy and light machine-guns, tommy-guns, pistols, and hand-grenades. None of the Allies had made equivalent preparation to create diversion and arouse confusion behind the German front. The German design for attack in 1940 was based upon the assault of areas and the advance of columns. The Allied defence was keyed to fronts, the methods of 1914–18 but little altered. When the fronts were pierced the defence scheme was broken. And the frontal defences were soon weakened by the overhead penetration of the German air-borne divisions.

It cannot be said that the Allies were blameless. The German method was not unique. It was a method of war which had been spoken of and written about, freely enough, by men who were, among the Allies, regarded as military heretics. The Germans had merely taken all ideas, and fashioned them to the needs of their own militant intentions. Credit (if there be credit in what they did) must be given to them for their assiduity in applying themselves to the development of a national machine for the destruction of non-German ideas of the way to live. And there can be no exceptions among Germans, except among those who openly opposed the policy of the Nazi war machine, because the organization was too thorough, too vast in its growth, for it to have been possible that there were any Germans honestly unaware of the intended outcome of the tremendous drive of industry which was developed under Hitler during his six years and a half of tempestuous reign before Britain and France were compelled to declare war upon the Third Reich. But, if credit must be apportioned to Germany, how shall the debit be applied to the Allies? To the corruption that existed in French upper circles, and that ran, like a disease, down to the least important among Government servants, who were notoriously underpaid, but who enjoyed perquisites of office in lieu of proper wages? To the sloth-like habit of mind of the British people, and to the inability of British politicians to dissociate what they wanted to see from what was really happening under their very eyes?

Escape from Holland

The peculiar nature of the fighting in the rear areas of Holland brought strange adventures to Royal Air Force crews who, in the course of their flights and fights, were brought to ground on the Continent.
Here is the tale of the pilot of a Defiant:

The formation with which I was flying encountered seven Junkers 87's south-west of Rotterdam. I got into position on one of them and my rear gunner shot it down. Another Junkers 87 which was coming up behind us was also shot down. Then about twenty-seven Messerschmitt 109's joined in the combat, and I heard my air gunner [1] give a cheer, and I think this meant that he had got a 109 which had been trying to get on my tail.

My starboard tank caught fire and a stream of bullets came from the rear and shot away the dashboard and part of the control column. I lost control for some time, but eventually managed to turn the aircraft on its back. I baled out when the flames were coming right up to the cockpit.

I landed on an island south-west of Dordrecht among some tall reeds.

I explored the island, which appeared to be uninhabited, and then went towards a house two miles away. I had to swim two channels each approximately a hundred yards wide. The house was empty. I found a small boat and rowed for about two hundred yards until I came to a high dyke. I climbed this and saw another house, from which a farm labourer and his wife came to meet me. I managed to make them understand that I was English by showing them the tunic I was carrying over my arm.

The farm labourer rowed me to another island from which we were able to communicate with the nearest Dutch military post. He then carried me on the back of his bicycle until we met a party of Dutch soldiers with whom I found another Royal Air Force pilot who had taken to his parachute.

My brother-pilot and I were taken to a place called Sleewyk. There we were interrogated by Dutch Intelligence officers who seemed to think we were German—by this time I had lost most of my uniform. After being detained for some time in a room with some civilians we were marched to a boat and taken across to Gorinchem, which, apparently, had just been bombed. We were escorted by two guards and interrogated at police headquarters by a police officer who could speak good English.

We explained that we were British airmen, but were not believed when we said that we could not speak Dutch. We were taken to a military barrack and questioned by another Intelligence officer. He took us by car to The Hague. On the way we ran into a large motorized column of Dutch soldiers. They searched the party in the car and discovered that the Intelligence officer, our escort, was a Fascist.

---

[1] This air gunner was immediately afterwards killed.

At this point I thought we were all going to be shot out of hand. But eventually we were taken on to The Hague, where we at last managed to persuade a Dutch officer that our story was true. We were put on board a boat bound for England.

Another aircraft forced-landed in Holland with both petrol-tanks ablaze. The pilot and air gunner got out, but they were seen from a German post some way off. German armoured cars rushed towards them. A Dutch family whose home was close at hand hid the two Britishers in their cellar. Germans arrived and began to search the house. One enemy soldier even opened the cellar door, looked in, failed to see them, and shut the door again. The two fliers crouched in the shadow of the cellar for four hours, while their enemies remained in the house. When, for a brief period, the Germans left the house the two hunted men, wrapped in civilian overcoats given to them by the courageous Dutch people, got out and lay in a ditch two hundred yards away until the soldiers, returned, again left.

Sweating under the overcoats in the May warmth, the British airmen moved carefully across country, avoiding occasional German troops. They reached a river. The gunner could not swim; the pilot could. They stuck together, walking along the bank to find a bridge. When they came to it Germans mounted guard at the other end. The guard shouted to them in German. Ignoring these shouts, the two Britishers walked slowly on for a few yards, then sat by the bank. This threw the Germans off the trail of anything of a military nature: the two men must be what they seemed, a couple of slow-witted Dutchmen. Half an hour later the Britishers rose, and, returning whence they had come, stopped opposite a house. Again they sat, to watch the house, gazing longingly at a boat moored by the opposite bank. Seeing no evidence of troops, they whistled to attract attention. The people of the house appeared. By signs the two men made their wishes known, and were rowed across the river and told how to reach Dutch troops four miles away. With these troops they retreated to Antwerp; thence they sailed to England in a British destroyer.

Chapter III

The Battle of Belgium

§ I

The Gliders Come

MAY 10 was but ten minutes old when Belgian General Head-quarters gave the alarm, and Belgian troops took up their war stations for the third time since mobilization.

Along the south-eastern part of the Netherlands (sometimes called the Maastricht appendix, which lies like a sandwich between Germany and Belgium) the common frontier of Holland and Belgium follows the Meuse, until, near the south end of the appendix, opposite the town of Maastricht, it suddenly curves to the west, in a re-entrant, away from the river. There, just within the Belgian frontier, runs the Albert Canal, spanned by the three bridges of Vroenhoven, Veldwezelt, and Briedgen. The peculiar configuration of this frontier territory made it impossible for the Belgians to place outposts in front of their forward defensive positions; this danger area was therefore protected by the permanent fort of Eben-Emael, built between the two wars. The artillery in this fort could sweep the bridges and their approaches with enfilade fire, and it was thought that it was strong enough to maintain prolonged resistance.

But here the Germans carried out a novel and daring *coup*, whose tactical surprise achieved success. From the first moment of the German offensive the Luftwaffe bombed the whole of this sector incessantly, while troops carried in gliders landed behind the canal bridges. It was the first time in the history of war that glider-borne troops had been used; with the silence of the flight of strigiformes, they alighted in the dark, undetected. A few gliders landed on the roof of the fort; their crews damaged its defensive armament by means of explosives. Parachutists dropped all round. Under cover of an air bombardment they entered the breaches and began to destroy the galleries.

(It has been suggested that German workmen engaged on the building of the Albert Canal married Belgian girls and settled in the neighbour-hood, grew endives which are forced in limestones caves found in the hills surrounding the Jeker valley, carried explosives into the caves in the guise of fertilizers, tunnelled under the fort, and, at the moment of the assault by the German Army and Luftwaffe, blew up parts of the fort from below; and that paratroops entered through these breaches.)

When the fort was out of action glider-borne troops, reinforced by paratroops, attacked from the rear the Belgian detachments guarding the bridges and succeeded in capturing them.

Belgian troops retook the bridge at Briedgen and destroyed it. But German troops established bridgeheads at Vroenhoven and Veldwezelt, where their artillery and fighter aircraft prevented the Belgians from restoring the situation. On May 11 twelve Belgian aircraft attacked Vroenhoven bridge with bombs; eleven were brought down.

German mechanized forces and motorized troops poured across the Albert Canal by the two bridges. The Belgian 7th Infantry Division was forced to withdraw from this sector, and the whole fortified area of Eben-Emael fell in thirty-six hours. Panzer divisions thrust through the gap, threatening the whole Albert Canal position and the fortified town of Liège.

In the night of May 11 the Belgian High Command withdrew its troops from the Albert Canal-Meuse front to the main defence positions of the Antwerp-Namur line. The British Expeditionary Force reached the Wavre-Louvain section of this line on May 12.

§ 2

"For Valour"

The Army has its regiments, with names, and many affectionate diminutives; these inspire those who serve. The Navy names not alone her ships, but even the stations on the shore. The Air Force, the arm that sweeps ubiquitously over land and sea across the skies, gave its units plain numbers to distinguish one from another; later the word 'Bomber,' or 'Fighter,' or 'Army Co-operation,' or 'Torpedo Bomber,' or 'Communications' was put in brackets between the number and the word 'Squadron'; with the formation of the Auxiliary Air Force, in 1925, a territorial designation was given to the volunteer units, so: (County of Kent); and, as one last gesture of distinction, each squadron was given a crest and motto.

The crest of No. 12 (Bomber) squadron is a fox's mask; its motto is "Leads the field." Crest and motto were given to the squadron when it was the sole unit of the Royal Air Force equipped with the Fox bomber, which, during the first decade after the Great War, was faster than contemporaneous service fighters: marking, by its speed, an important advance in the technical equipment of the Royal Air Force.

On May 12, 1940, No. 12 squadron was at Amifontaine aerodrome in the Department of the Aisne, behind Hirson, in France. It was the squadron of the Advanced Air Striking Force nearest to the Vroenhoven and Veldwezelt bridges of the Albert Canal. And that morning the commanding officer of the squadron received orders to destroy these bridges. He called for volunteers from his flying crews. Not a man held back. Lots were drawn to decide the crews to make the attack.

Already that morning a squadron of Blenheims had attacked the bridges, where they found the enemy had strong anti-aircraft defences. The Blenheims attacked from 3000 feet against heavier shelling than any of the crews had ever imagined to be possible. Black bursts of fire completely surrounded them. They made their runs upon the target singly from several directions to defeat the gunners. "Below, the bridges could be seen standing out quite clearly in the sunlight," said the leader of the formation, "and, despite the fierceness of the A.A., we got in some pretty good shots. Soon you could not see the bridges for smoke. A few minutes after we had dropped our bombs the ground batteries stopped firing at us, and then the fighters, which had been holding off until the guns closed down, started in. The fight which followed lasted for twenty minutes. We immediately shot one down."

By radio telephone the Blenheims' leader ordered his formation to re-form. They closed together and drove the fighters off with concentrated machine-gun fire. But four of the Blenheims were lost, and each machine of the eight which returned was hit.

The bridges were still usable.

Six Battle bombers of No. 12 squadron, led by Flying Officer D. E. Garland with Sergeant Thomas Gray as his observer, set out for the objective. Garland, born at Ballinacor, Wicklow, Eire, and educated at Cardinal Vaughan School, Kensington, had entered the Royal Air Force in July 1937 with a short-service commission as an Acting Pilot Officer. He was one month under twenty-two years of age when he took off to bomb the Albert Canal bridges. His companions called him "Judy"—a nickname derived from the contemporaneously successful Hollywood film actress, Judy Garland.

Sergeant Gray was twenty-six, a Wiltshire man, from the rolling downs of Devizes. He was fifteen when he entered the Royal Air Force as an apprentice, and was promoted Sergeant in January 1939.

Three Battles were to attack each bridge; but one machine had to return almost at once with engine trouble. The five bombers flew

34

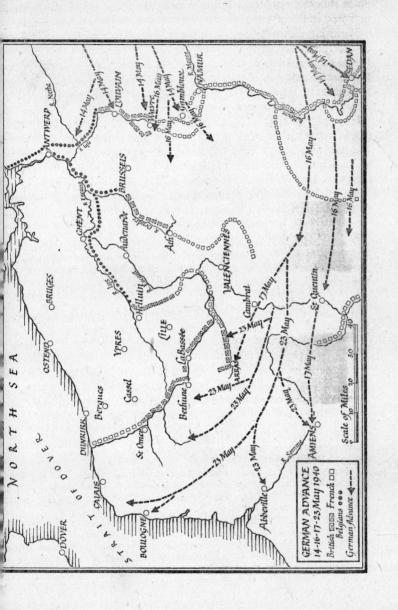

GERMAN ADVANCE
14·16·17·23 May 1940
British □□□ French ▨▨ Belgians ●●● German Advance ---▶

on in two sections, each section escorted by three Hurricane fighters, north-eastward into the shining light of a glorious May morning.

Eight Hurricane fighters from No. 1 squadron flew direct to the area of the canal bridges to clear the air for the bombers a few minutes before the Battles were due to arrive. Leading the eight fighters was Squadron Leader P. J. H. Halahan, the Irish-born, Cranwell College-trained officer (nicknamed "The Bull") who commanded No. 1. About a hundred German fighters were over the target. Fighting was fierce, deadly, brief. The Hurricanes shot down ten German fighters (six Messerschmitt 109's, three Arados, and one Heinkel 112). Halahan was shot down to a forced-landing in Belgium, another pilot leaped in his parachute, a third nursed his badly hit Hurricane back to Vassincourt aerodrome; the other five got back safely.

The Battles had about a hundred miles to fly. Sergeant Mansell, who flew as observer in one of the bombers, said:

> From our preparations you might have thought we were off on a journey across miles of uncharted land. We are always thorough in plotting our routes, but the vital importance of this raid made us even more careful. It was essential that we should not waste any time in finding the bridges.
>
> When we were about twenty miles from our target thirty Messerschmitts tried to intercept us, but we continued on our course while the three fighters waded in to the attack. The odds were ten to one against us, but several of those Messerschmitts were brought down. Nearing our target we met more enemy fighters.
>
> The barrage was terrific, the worst I have ever struck, and we saw the flight of three bombers, now returning home, caught in the thick of the enemy's fire. All three were lost.
>
> The big bridge looked badly knocked about. It was sagging in the middle. It had been hit by the bombs dropped by the three bombers ahead of us.
>
> When we delivered our attack we were about six thousand feet up. We dived to two thousand feet, one aircraft close behind the other, and dropped our load. Looking down, we saw that our bridge now sagged in the middle also.
>
> We turned for home. The barrage was waiting for us. It was even worse than before, and soon our aircraft began to show signs of heavy damage. When our fuel-tanks were pierced the pilot [1] gave orders to abandon aircraft. The rear gunner jumped first. We saw no more of him. [2] Then I jumped. We were near Liège. As I came near the ground I saw a reception committee waiting for me. Hundreds of people were pointing at me from the streets below. The mob was angry. They were shouting and waving their fists.
>
> I landed in a small cottage back-garden. Before I had time to dis-

---

[1] Pilot Officer T. D. H. Davy.
[2] He wrenched a thigh, but succeeded in returning to the Allied lines.

entangle myself from my gear the crowd rushed into the next-door garden and dragged me over the fence shouting, "Sale boche!"

I shouted back, "Je suis anglais."

But either they did not believe me or did not understand my French. They dragged me into the street. Men and women held my arms and an angry old man prepared to shoot me.

Again I shouted, "Anglais! Anglais!"

Somebody must have thought it just possible that I was telling the truth. The old man was prevailed upon to hand me over to the police. On the way to the police station burly women kept trying to hit me. Then, out of the blue, I was spoken to in English by a Belgian woman who offered to act as my interpreter. She persuaded the police to send me to the commandant of the Liège fortress. He believed my story, offered me hospitality, gave me a bicycle and a map, and put me on the road to Namur.

Pilot Officer Davy reached Brussels and landed. His bomber burst into flames. He and his crew were the only survivors. Davy said that the Battles were attacked by a large number of enemy fighters after they had released their bombs on the target.

Four Battles were lost. Twelve out of fifteen men died; but the bridges were broken. General Georges sent this personal message to No. 12 squadron: "Messieurs, je vous remercie." In the 47th Royal Air Force list of awards for gallantry in the World War the King conferred the Victoria Cross posthumously on Flying Officer Garland and Sergeant Gray. Part of the official citation reads:

> Much of the success of this vital operation must be attributed to the formation-leader, Flying Officer Garland, and to the coolness and resource of Sergeant Gray, who in most difficult conditions navigated Flying Officer Garland's aircraft in such a manner that the whole formation was able successfully to attack the target in spite of subsequent heavy losses. Flying Officer Garland and Sergeant Gray did not return.

These were the first awards of the Victoria Cross to members of the Royal Air Force in the World War.

§ 3

Too Few to fill the Breaches

Many opportunities were offered to the Royal Air Force on May 12 to impede the enemy advance, but Lord Gort, in his dispatches, states that "such opportunities were of a fleeting character, since the enemy established strong anti-aircraft defences soon after his arrival, particularly in towns at which roads converged. Tactical reconnaissance became virtually impossible without fighter support, and

37

the demands made on the fighter group of the Air Component were extremely heavy."

From the beginning of the German invasion of the Low Countries and France, British fighters battled everywhere against tremendous odds. By the evening of the third day the fighter strength of the Air Component was reduced to about fifty aircraft. During those three days' fighting the British Air Forces in France destroyed 101 enemy aircraft (mostly fighters) and lost 78 of their own machines. Lord Gort had already asked for four more Fighter squadrons from England.

The first reinforcement squadron arrived in France on May 10. Five more squadrons followed. Owing to the situation which developed at Sedan, three of these squadrons—Nos. 17, 242, and 501—were added to the Advanced Air Striking Force to operate on the French front, while three squadrons—Nos. 3, 79, and 504—joined the Air Component to fight on the British front.[1] These squadrons were all equipped with Hurricane fighters, but not all their machines were of standard type; some Hurricanes had fixed-pitch wooden airscrews, some had two-pitch metal airscrews, some had constant-speed airscrews, each improvement giving better take-off, climb, speed, and ceiling than the earlier model possessed; all the Hurricanes had eight machine-guns.

No. 607 (County of Durham) and 615 (County of Surrey) Auxiliary Air Force squadrons, which had been with the Air Component from the beginning, were due to receive Hurricanes to replace their four-gun Gladiators. The Surrey squadron had begun to re-equip when the German attack began, and some of the pilots were making their first flight in a Hurricane when they went into action against the Luftwaffe. Except for these few Gladiators, the fighters of the British Air Forces in France fought the Luftwaffe as a Hurricane-equipped force.

The twelve squadrons in France did not comprise the total Royal Air Force fighter strength operating against the invader. Squadrons based in England fought over Holland and Belgium. Later they fought over France. Some flew out to French aerodromes daily, but returned to England at dusk: a precaution which enabled the aircraft to be serviced overnight, permitted the pilots better rest, and prevented the possibility of loss of pilots and aircraft if the aerodromes were overrun by Panzer units during darkness.

The Fighter squadrons of the Air Component did not have to move

---

[1] Nos. 3, 17, and 79 squadrons were all regular R.A.F. units; they had fought in the Great War. No. 242 was a Canadian squadron. Nos. 501 and 504 were Auxiliary Air Force squadrons from the counties of Gloucester and Nottingham respectively; 504 squadron was in France from May 12 to 22, 1940.

forward when the British Expeditionary Force advanced into Belgium. Their aerodromes were close to the frontier,[1] and they were conveniently placed for air operations.

The work of all fighters in France fell into three main categories. These were, first, to provide escort for British bomber and reconnaissance aircraft; second, to intercept enemy bombers and fighters; and third, to attack the surface forces of the enemy, and, less frequently, to scout to locate the position of enemy forces.

But sometimes the bombers had to attack objectives situated far beyond the range of the fighters, and then they had to go alone and fight their own way to the target area.

On May 13, while the French Seventh Army under General Giraud fell back from its positions south-west of Breda and on the islands of Zuid Beveland and Walcheren in conformity with the general pressure upon all the Allied armies, a German motorized column pushed on in the attempt to cut off the French troops from the Allied line in front of Antwerp. It appeared that the Germans might succeed, and No. 226 squadron was detailed to block the road approaches in front of the German forces. There were two roads that the Germans might take, so the tiny force of seven Battles was divided into two flights, one of three and the other of four aircraft. They flew to Antwerp, selected their different roadways, and flew along them at tree-top height until they each reached the village which was their respective target. There the job was one of demolition to block the road. The flight of three found their village deserted and quickly bombed houses on both sides of the road from a low level; the wreckage fell across the street. The flight of four Battles found civilians in their village, so the leader flew around to allow the people time to get to safety before he gave the signal to bomb. Then, picking a factory on one side of the road-junction and a tall house on the other, they released their bombs and caused the road-block that was needed. This, a task that formerly would have fallen upon the Royal Engineers—if they had been able to get there in time, which in this case was impossible—was a new duty for the Royal Air Force; the obstructions guarded the open right flank of the French Seventh Army, and assisted this French force to retire safely to the Antwerp line, which, being shorter, permitted part of the Seventh Army to be transferred along the line to the right, where the main German threat against the French was in course of development.

Who has not seen children playing on the seashore sands, building dams to stop the oncoming tide, seeing a breach made in one place and rushing there to build it up, only to find another breach elsewhere, until

[1] See map at p. 144, Vol. I.

the irresistible impulses of the waves at last break through simultaneously at a dozen different points and defy all the efforts of the builders of the dam to stay the tide? So it was with the tide of war that swept across Europe during May 1940. First one point of the defence gave way, then another, until the Teuton tide swept all before it to the seaboard. That vast tidal wave of soldiery, munitioned and equipped with all the skill of twentieth-century science, could not be held back by nations who were inadequately equipped and organized to meet its power. And so, as the storm gathered force, and the waves fell furiously against one part of the defence-line after another, aircraft were sent out by day and night, in sortie after sortie, in vain attempts to fill the breaches in the bursting dam.

Then it was apparent how pitifully small were the air forces at the command of the Allies. Five Battles to bomb the Albert Canal bridges! Seven Battles to block the roads and help the extrication of the French Seventh Army! These two squadrons received the thanks of General Georges and the French High Command; No. 12 gained two posthumous Victoria Crosses, No. 226 received congratulatory telegrams from the Chief of the Air Staff and the C.-in-C. British Air Forces in France. So, with this in mind, for one brief moment let us turn back to November 28, 1934; the scene is the stately, dim-lit chamber of the House of Commons; the Lord President is at the table speaking: "His Majesty's Government are determined in no conditions to accept any position of inferiority with regard to what air force may be raised in Germany in the future. . . ." Thus spake the Right Honourable Stanley Baldwin. His words are writ in Hansard. But after the first few days of fighting in the vain attempt to stem the German advance, Flight Lieutenant E. J. "Cobber" Kain (who gained the Distinguished Flying Cross and died in a flying accident in France) said simply, "In future we are not going to take on any odds over four to one."

When the German attack began the Advanced Air Striking Force possessed six Battle squadrons and four Blenheim squadrons.[1] Blenheims at first concentrated their attacks against the bridges across the Meuse within the Maastricht area (and after the fall of Fort Eben-Emael against troops moving forward along the road to Tongres), while Battles bombed enemy columns advancing through Luxemburg.

On May 11 the flight leader of a section of No. 12 squadron's Battles saw crowds of refugees—mainly women, children, and old people—streaming along the Luxemburg roads towards France, all carrying

[1] Squadrons 103 and 105 had been re-equipped with Blenheims in place of Battles.

bundles of personal belongings. Suddenly the Battles came under intense fire from machine-guns and pom-poms from a German motor-cycle-and-sidecar detachment which was moving forward behind the refugees. The Battles flew on through the barrage, and located their target, a mechanized column south of Luxemburg city; they dived low, dropped their bombs, then machine-gunned the German soldiers, who tried to take cover. A second section from the same squadron followed up the attack; one of their bombs fell in the middle of a line of forty or fifty lorries. The crews saw other lorries piled up and wrecked by the bombing of the first section. Farther away, two other Battle flights bombed an enemy column of all arms moving westward across the north-west corner of the German-Luxemburg frontier.

After the attack one of the section leaders had to forced-land with a leaking petrol-tank. As the aeroplane touched the ground it caught fire. Flames arose from the bomb-aimer's trap. The pilot, Flight Lieutenant William Simpson, trapped in his cockpit, was enveloped in flames. Without a thought for their own safety his observer, Sergeant E. N. Odell, and wireless operator-air gunner, Corporal R. T. Tomlinson, who had escaped from the bomber, went into the flames and pulled the pilot clear before the Battle exploded. And Tomlinson had taken, and brought back with him, valuable photographs of the convoy and the bombing. All three members of the crew were decorated for their gallant action (the pilot with the Distinguished Flying Cross and the sergeant and corporal with the Distinguished Flying Medal), the first instance in this war of a triple decoration for an air crew.

When reports were received that large German concentrations were moving forward through Maastricht Blenheims were dispatched to find the leading enemy column and delay its advance. The required column was found on the road leading to Tongres. Nearly five miles long, it was composed of small tanks, armoured cars, and motor transports, all moving forward steadily at about twenty to twenty-five miles an hour. The vehicles were closely bunched at the rear end of the column, but near its head they gradually thinned out, until, towards Tongres, the tanks were some twenty yards apart. Nine Blenheims broke formation to allow of individual approach. One after another they attacked in quick succession from different directions, diving to within a thousand feet of the ground. Their larger high-explosive bombs tore craters in the road surface, and wrecked vehicles, while their smaller bombs caused casualties among the personnel. The first bomber brought the head of the column to a halt. When the last Blenheim had unloaded its bombs the whole column was stopped in confusion, with the roadway blocked by damaged cars and overturned transports.

German fighters appeared as the Blenheims turned away. One Blenheim was engaged by four Messerschmitt 109's, and in the engagement the air gunner was severely wounded. The sergeant observer immediately removed his flying-kit and parachute (thereby sacrificing his chance of escape if compelled to abandon aircraft) and crawled through the fuselage to the wounded gunner, got him out of his gun-station, began to operate the rear gun, and forced the enemy to break off the attack. When all was quiet he gave a hand to the wounded gunner, then crawled forward to his own cockpit and assisted in the navigation of the aeroplane back to base. For this action he received the Distinguished Flying Medal.

During this period the aircraft of the Advanced Air Striking Force operated by day. The night bombing of strategic targets calculated to delay the German advance was carried out by Bomber Command from bases in the United Kingdom. There was, at first, some lack of agreement between the French High Command and the British Air Staff over the method of employment of the air forces at the disposal of the Allies. The French view was rather like the earlier British Government view in regard to the bombing of naval targets. Nothing was to be done which might endanger enemy civilian life and property. Even after the German attack on France and the Low Countries began the French remained averse to the bombing of objectives within Germany or to the bombing of German troops on the move within their own territory. The key to the widening of bombing policy was to remain in German hands; they were to be responsible for opening the gateway to terror bombing. This policy explains the Allied target selection during the opening phase of the defence of Belgium and France. The British heavy bombers did not go into action until the second day of the German advance. By that time the utter ruthlessness of German bombing policy was already demonstrated in Holland, Belgium, and France. German bombing, ruthless though it was, followed a definite plan to achieve specific objects; and before considering the Allied air defence further it is desirable to understand the German operational scheme in its broad aspect.

§ 4

The New Technique

The German plan for air attack was carried out in much the way that had been proposed in the documents captured in Belgium.[1] That plan referred to one part of the front, except for reconnaissance duties. But,

[1] See pp. 12–13.

if bombing and reconnaissance are regarded as interchangeable terms, the scheme immediately becomes clear. And, as the German High Command can have entertained little doubt about the ability of the German Army to break through the defences of the Allies, the object of reconnaissance must have been as much to establish the focal points where bombing pressure was to be applied as to discover the areas wherein Allied resistance was to be expected. In order to gain the maximum initial advantage, it was desirable (to the German High Command) to conceal, until the last moment, the intention behind the employment of the German bomber force. The disclosures made in Poland and Norway failed to alter the British and French points of view. Even after the further warnings given by the methods of attack against Holland, Belgium, France, and Britain, the United States were shocked and astonished at the Japanese assault upon Pearl Harbour on December 7, 1941. Man evidently does not comprehend until the catalyst is used against himself.

During the first three days of the attack the German object was to beat down air opposition. The purpose was to secure control of the air. The Dutch and Belgian Air Forces were quickly wiped out, principally by attacks on aerodromes. Aerodromes in France were simultaneously attacked. In this period railways and factories were also bombed, but it was noticeable that roads were left untouched. The German forward movement plan was based upon road supply lines.

Attacks against aerodromes and factories then diminished in scale, and the Luftwaffe was employed primarily against military formations and transport. This was the period of decisive battle, from the beginning of the break-through to the capitulation of the Belgian Army. There followed an intense concentration against the defences within the Dunkirk perimeter and the embarkation organization. After the escape of the British Army and part of the French Army from the beaches, the Luftwaffe returned to strategic operations against industrial France, bombing in and about the capital, the great cities of Central and Southern France, and the main lines of communication throughout the country. Here the intention was to disorganize and terrorize. It succeeded. The railways and roads were choked with refugees. French national life came almost to a standstill. Thereafter the Luftwaffe swung back to become again the spearhead of the Army. It had done its fell work across the broad lands of France. There remained but the rout of the French armies to the south-west and to the south-east. The Maginot Line was still intact, but its flank had been turned. Mobile forces had triumphed over static defences. A new technique of war had succeeded on the grand scale.

The Allied fighter air forces were too small to break up the German air attacks. The German bomber formations were heavily escorted by fighters, and the Royal Air Force Fighter squadrons were forced by the tactical conditions to engage the fighters far more frequently than the bombers. Often the German bombers turned back—sometimes after jettisoning their bombs—when their fighter escort was scattered; but sometimes they pressed on while the fighter-versus-fighter battle raged in the sky above them. And so the proportion of fighters destroyed by the pilots of the Royal Air Force exceeded that of bombers. Gallant actions were of hourly occurrence during the hectic fighting in the air against the German hordes. Parachutes saved pilots' lives and enabled them to return to their stations and in new mounts take the air again. They fought until they fell asleep, exhausted by the strain of flying high, breathing oxygen, the queer loads of acrobatic flight upon their bodies as they turned and twisted in the dog-fights, the merciless demands upon sight, sanity, and self-love. Fighter pilots fought during the sixteen hours of daylight; during the eight hours of deep twilight and darkness they ate, bathed (when they got a chance), snatched a few hours' sleep, provided guards against paratroops, took shelter against night bombers, manned machine-guns, often never took their clothes off, and made shift as best they might to be ready for the calls that the dawning day would bring fresh upon them.

But the tide of war rolled mercilessly onwards as they darted about the skies, trying desperately to hold up the relentless flood. Not once did they whimper at their insufficiency. Instead, invective poured forth upon the endless hordes the Hun launched into the skies of Belgium and France.

§ 5

The Gaps in the Bombers

By May 13 the German attack against Belgium had penetrated as far as a line running through Haeles, along the line of the river Gette to Namur, and from there to the south had reached the line of the Meuse where pressure was felt in the area around Sedan on French soil; there the German armies directed their main effort against the French while maintaining their firm pressure on the Anglo-Belgian front. The German thrust breached the line of the French Ninth Army between Sedan and Dinant, crossed the Meuse river at two places, and the Panzer divisions were thrown into the opening. It was quickly apparent that this was to become the decisive thrust, delivered, logically enough, at the hinge-point of the Allied forward right wheel into

Belgium—a manœuvre which had been permitted by the German High Command without air resistance. This manœuvre was a move the Germans had apparently expected. The blow in the region of Sedan was their strategic answer.

General Giraud, who had commanded the French Seventh Army which had withdrawn from Holland to Antwerp, was transferred to command the French Ninth Army.

Royal Air Force bombers escorted by fighters went into action in co-operation with the French forces. The Germans crossed the Meuse at Mouzon and Sedan. The first attack was made by six Battles soon after dawn. These aircraft all got back, one with a wounded pilot. About two and a half hours later four Battles attacked and hit a pontoon bridge near Sedan; these aircraft also returned safely. French bombers then attacked the bridges. These forces were too small to deal an effective blow against so powerful an enemy. A larger force was organized, and shortly after three o'clock in the afternoon sixty-seven Battles took off to attack bridges between Mouzon and Sedan.

This force of Battles met strong enemy resistance. The Germans had brought up powerful anti-aircraft defences, and German fighters were thick over the all-important crossings. So numerous were the German fighters that it was impossible for the small forces of British fighters to drive them off. During the desperate engagement which developed around the Battles these aircraft destroyed two permanent bridges and two pontoon bridges. Fighters and anti-aircraft gunfire brought down fifteen enemy aircraft. But the Battles lost heavily in the action, and thirty-five—more than half the force—were lost.

Altogether, a hundred and fifty British and French aircraft took part in this operation. In addition to the destruction of bridges, tank and troop concentrations were broken up, and roads were blocked. But against an army organized, as the German Army was, for a great offensive, these actions were merely temporary set-backs. They could not stop the invaders. More bridges were thrown across the river by the enemy and he came on, disregarding losses.

It was from the first the German policy to concentrate force at the decisive points, and to strike the hardest possible blow from the outset. It is difficult to understand why the Allied air attack against this German advance near Sedan was made in such puny numbers in the early morning of May 14. These formations of six and four Battles were quite incompetent to deal with a situation so intense as that created by the German crossing of the strategically important river Meuse, the principal bulwark of defence against the invasion of France west of the Maginot Line. This striking evidence of the different outlook of

45

the Germans and the Allies on the value of air-power may explain why Anglo-French air defence was so neglected in the years that preceded the outbreak of the Second World War. These puny forces, incapable of halting the German drive, were useful to the enemy, for they warned him of the need to provide cover against further air attack—a hint of which the German responsible commanders were not slow to avail themselves. In an official publication it was subsequently written: "At first it seemed possible to destroy the bridges they were using with a comparatively small force of aircraft." Yet the maximum air force it was possible for the Allies to concentrate against the Sedan area was not enough to halt the German drive. Moreover, ground forces were required to follow up the breaking of the bridges from the air. But the French Ninth Army was smashed and already in disorder. On May 16 General Giraud was captured by the Germans and flown to Germany. (He escaped from captivity in 1942, and returned to France, whence he was taken by a British submarine and flying boat to Algeria. There, after the assassination of Admiral Darlan, he became chief of the French colonies in North and West Africa. After the Anglo-American landing in Algeria in November 1942 and the United Nations' subsequent victory in Tunisia the French Committee of National Liberation was formed by the union of the forces under Generals de Gaulle and Giraud. The former became president of the Committee and the latter became head of all French armed forces. The French Committee of National Liberation was recognized by the Governments of Great Britain, the United States, and Russia in August 1943.)

So speedy was the German exploitation of their success that air support was at first the only form of assistance that could be given to the French Ninth Army. Bomb raids by Blenheims and Battles continued. The bombers of the Advanced Air Striking Force paid dearly for the gallant effort they made during the few days when the dent in the Allied line near Sedan became the focal point for air action by their force, while the bombers of the Air Component struck at other parts of the front, as did Bomber squadrons based in the United Kingdom. In the first five days of the attack the Advanced Air Striking Force lost 75 out of 135 serviceable bombers. The crews of some of these aircraft returned. Six crews of the thirty-five Battles shot down during the big attack on the Sedan-Mouzon bridges came back; one pilot died on the way, another got back with double wounds. This is the tale of the sergeant observer and rear gunner whose pilot died.

As they approached the German lines near Sedan their aircraft flew into devastating anti-aircraft fire. Their Battle was hit, and one of the pilot's hands was shot away. But the young pilot officer flew on until he came right over his objective. There he dropped his full load of bombs. Several direct hits were observed; the column of enemy troops below was temporarily disorganized. The pilot turned to fly back to base. As he turned another shell struck the bomber. Badly damaged, the aircraft was incapable of further flight. The injured pilot swooped down, swerved violently to avoid a high-tension overhead electric cable, and brought off a successful forced-landing on the east side of the Meuse. They were down in No Man's Land.

The observer lifted the pilot from the cockpit and dressed his wounds with the emergency dressing. Then, aiding the pilot in every way they could, he and the rear gunner set out across the fields, westward towards the French lines. Darkness fell. They reached the outskirts of a wood. Suddenly, close to them, they heard orders shouted in German. They turned off in another direction, undetected. Finding a barn, they entered it to spend the night. The pilot was by now delirious with the agony of pain. The sergeant gave him morphia injections. The night passed.

In the barn was a small hand-cart. When morning came the two airmen placed the wounded pilot on the hand-cart and pushed on westward until their progress was balked by the river Meuse. They searched for a way across, but could find none. Weary with fatigue and lack of food, they lay hiding on the river's bank. There the pilot officer died.

The gunner went out alone to seek a way across the river. He found a partially demolished bridge, and then returned to the sergeant. In the night, with the Germans close at hand on either side, they clambered across the rickety bridge, and on the farther side came to a French outpost. An American volunteer ambulance picked them up and drove them back to their own squadron.

Another pilot, Sergeant A. N. Spear, who came from Marylebone, London, had entered the Royal Air Force as an apprentice in 1927 at the age of sixteen. In May 1940, after dropping his bombs successfully on the enemy, he was attacked by a number of Messerschmitt fighters. The tail of his aircraft was shot away. The sergeant pilot ordered his crew to jump. After they had abandoned the aircraft he prepared to jump, but was thrown out. Nevertheless, he came down safely in enemy territory by parachute. He was repeatedly fired on by the enemy, but luck was with him, and he escaped wounds. He found a horse, mounted, and rode west, swam a canal, and at length came back to his squadron. For his determination and pluck, and his flying gallantry, he was awarded the Distinguished Flying Medal.

But the aeroplanes fell faster than the Royal Air Force could replace them. And still the call came for the bombing of the 'bulge'—as the initial break in the French line was euphemistically described. No. 226 squadron, at Rheims aerodrome, was badly hit. On May 15 the commanding officer, Squadron Leader C. E. S. Lockett, went out on a raid, and did not return. Flight Lieutenant R. G. Hurst received orders to send out all the squadron's Battles to bomb the bulge. There were none to send. There were still a few pilots; but no aeroplanes. Charles Gardner [1] reported seeing Hurst, walking about the empty aerodrome, saying, "Bomb the b——, bomb the b——, but for Christ's sake what with?"

§ 6

The Gap on the Ground

May 15 passed quietly on the British front except for an attack against the 3rd Division north-west of Louvain, where a British counter-attack restored the line to its original position. But there was considerable enemy bombing of Tournai and other towns behind our lines. This bombing caused further movements of refugees along the roads; the French had closed their frontier to pedestrian and horse-drawn traffic. The Belgian refugees flooded westward towards the coast.

On the following day "it became clear," wrote General Gort in his dispatches, "that a prolonged defence of the Dyle position"—that was the Wavre-Louvain section of the line held by the British Expeditionary Force—"was impracticable. The French First Army on my right were unlikely to make good the ground lost on the previous day, notwithstanding the support I had given them in the air and on the ground, and a further withdrawal seemed likely to be forced on them by events in the South.

"On the other hand there had been no serious attack on the Belgian positions on my left. . . ."

Very early on May 16 General Gort sent a representative to General Billotte, the French general who was co-ordinating the movements of British, French, and Belgian forces, asking if he intended to withdraw and asking for immediate information. About ten o'clock in the morning Lord Gort received orders from General Billotte to begin to withdraw that night to the line of the river Escaut. And that night the retreat which was to end in the lifting from the beaches of Dunkirk began.

General Gamelin, the Commander-in-Chief of the Allied Armies,

[1] *A.A.S.F.* (Hutchinson).

had reached the decision to withdraw in the evening of May 15, owing to the serious situation brought about by the German penetration at Sedan, which threatened to envelop the whole of the Allied troops in Belgium. The retreat meant the abandonment of the powerfully organized Belgian position between Antwerp and Namur before any real resistance had been made, and the occupation, in its stead, of an improvised position behind the Escaut.

The Belgian forts around Liège and Namur served as strong points, and by their stand delayed the enemy advance. The first fort did not fall until May 17, and the last was still holding out on May 28 when the Belgian Army capitulated.

Early in the morning of May 17 a gap of at least twenty miles existed in the Allied line south of the Forêt de Mormal; there ten German Panzer divisions were engaged, and against them there was no organized resistance at the gap.

That day twelve Blenheim bombers were sent from an English station to attack German tanks and troops near Gembloux, between Namur and Wavre. Shortly before reaching the target the squadron, flying in two formations of six aircraft each, encountered accurate, concentrated anti-aircraft gunfire which caused them to open formation. Thereupon they were set upon by Messerschmitt 109's, who shot down ten Blenheims. Another Blenheim fell to the gunfire. One escaped. But some of the men who manned the fallen aircraft returned. Some were picked up wounded. One flew back to England from Paris in an air liner; another returned as a passenger in an Anson flying on ferry services between Amiens and England.

On May 17 nine Hurricanes shot down ten Junkers dive-bombers without loss to themselves. On May 18 enemy air action grew fiercer on the British front, and fighter support was required continuously during daylight to enable British reconnaissance aircraft to carry out their duties and to deter German bombers from attacking our positions. German aircraft attacked the columns of refugees moving along the roads. The German bombers were supported by strong fighter protection. Our fighters were active over France and Belgium. Near Brussels five Hurricanes met twelve Heinkel bombers returning from a raid, and in a fifty-miles' fight shot down from three to six Heinkels— there was no time to count the crashes in the mêlée. A second, larger Hurricane patrol met two Heinkels and shot one down. A third fighter patrol, meeting vastly superior numbers of German aircraft, waded in and shot down a Heinkel 111, a Henschel 126 Army Reconnaissance aeroplane, a Junkers 88 dive-bomber, and a Messerschmitt 109 fighter; they hit a number of other aircraft. Later eleven Hurricanes attacked seventeen Messerschmitt 110's, shot down six, and damaged three more, without loss to themselves. These five patrols destroyed from twenty to thirty enemy aircraft for a loss of three British machines.

During these actions the small and depleted Belgian Air Force gave direct support to the Allies. In the defence of their country the Belgian airmen showed prodigious courage, and continued to do so afterwards as part of the air forces of the United Nations associated with the Royal Air Force. In one case a Belgian major was taking off from his aerodrome when he was attacked by a German fighter, and very serious damage was inflicted on his aircraft. It was obvious to the major that a crash was imminent. Without a moment's hesitation he swung his damaged aircraft round and charged the German fighter. From the interlocked aircraft a tangled mass of wreckage fell to the ground. Out of it, alone, limped the Belgian major, unhurt, save for a sprained ankle. His opponent was dead.

The actions of Allied fighters enabled the bombers of the Royal Air Force to attack enemy columns, tanks, roads, and bridges, and harass the enemy advance. Many attacks were delivered from a low level.

During this whirlwind campaign, fought in the air at speeds three times greater than those of the Great War, the strain on the air crews was terrific; but it would have been a thousand times more onerous if these air crews, like their predecessors of the Great War, had had to fly with no means of escape from their damaged aircraft. The increase in gun-power, the use of glycol-coolant in the liquid-cooled engines, the larger-size petrol- and oil-tanks needed for the bigger engines, all made the vulnerability of aircraft greater in spite of increased speed of flight. But whereas, in the Great War, the destruction of an aircraft almost invariably meant the destruction of its crew, the subsequent universal adoption of the parachute introduced a means frequently to dissociate human tragedy from the destruction of the machine. Man was not only master of the air machine, but able also to discard it when he had no further use for it.

No doubt there were escape thrills for the German pilots who fought the Allies. Indeed, judging by the relative scales of aircraft lost, the Germans ought to have had more thrills. But the German pilots had this advantage: their armies were advancing, and thus they had good hope of rescue even if they could only hide themselves for a few days; the Allied pilots, on the other hand, had to get back from the oncoming forces of the enemy, and sometimes to pass through the lines of the foe. Fortunately, the war was of a kind which technical writers describe as 'fluid,' by which they mean that there was not a continuous front (like that of the great trench-barrier of the later stages of the Great War in France); and this type of warfare enabled the safely landed air crews to dodge their way across the intervening territory until they came into contact with Allied troops. Escapes happened to single pilots who had descended from fighters, and to complete air crews who had dropped from their stricken bombers. It was extraordinary how many of these followers of Blanchard, the first parachutist, were not captured by the enemy. If the refugees were a hindrance to the fighting forces on the ground, they were a blessing to the fugitive airmen who were seeking to escape from the clutches of the Germans.

One fighter pilot, trudging along after landing by parachute in Belgium, met a Belgian civilian who told the pilot he was in great danger because the Germans were very near. The pilot borrowed civilian clothes and went on with his Belgian companion. Presently they were overtaken by a column of German tanks. The enemy column pulled up at the side of the road. Putting a bold face on the dangerous situation, the pilot strolled over to the other side of the road, and by signs indicated that he was tired—as he no doubt was—and wanted a lift. The German soldiers cheerfully assented, and the pilot climbed in. He travelled westward for about twenty miles in the enemy tank, then left the column at a small *estaminet*, where he rested. He sat talking to the owner. There was a knock at the door. German soldiers were outside.

The owner of the *estaminet* pushed the pilot into the back room and told him to get away while he kept the Germans talking in the front of the *estaminet*. The pilot climbed through a window into a yard, crept down a lane, and returned to the main road some miles farther on. Thence he began to hitch-hike westward. At last he reached the British area. But his troubles were not over. He was arrested as a suspicious character. Finally, still protesting, he was taken to the headquarters of the Air Component of the British Expeditionary Force, where he saw the Air Officer Commanding, Air Vice-Marshal C. H. B. Blount, who personally vouched for him, and sent him back to his squadron.

German pom-pom shells shot part of the rudder control off a bomber just before it reached the main road along which a German mechanized column was passing. But the pilot carried out his allotted task. A few minutes after releasing the bombs the aircraft was again hit by a shell, which put the starboard engine out of action. The port engine was failing, too, but skilful piloting prevented the bomber from entering a steep dive. Soon it was apparent that it would be necessary to abandon aircraft.

A sergeant left the bomber first. He landed in the top of a tree. "After getting rid of my gear," he said,

> it took me about twenty minutes to climb down the tree, which must have been taller than the beanstalk that Jack climbed. It was pitch dark under the trees as I began to make my way through the wood. I fell down a bank, and found myself lying beside a river. It was too dark to move on, so I waited until dawn before starting off towards the west. On the way I met a couple of Belgian peasants who were on their way to join the Army. We kept company for about eight miles, though German reconnaissance aircraft did their best to part us by coming down low and machine-gunning the road. Then we met some French soldiers, who at once arrested me and marched me to their headquarters, where I soon convinced them that I was not a German parachutist.

The corporal who jumped second fell through a greenhouse, but his thick flying-clothes prevented him from suffering serious injury. He met some Belgian farmers who gave him hot coffee and then led him to the nearest military post.

The pilot came down in a small clearing in a wood. He trudged on foot to the nearest village. A French soldier challenged him.

> A rifle [he said] was stuck in my back, and I was ordered to raise my hands. In my best French I then said, "Je suis un aviateur anglais," but the soldier was not satisfied until a French officer who spoke English arrived on the scene. The officer escorted me to his headquarters, where I was introduced to his general. A few hours later I was on my way back to my squadron.

Sometimes it was possible to bring the aeroplane back. On one occasion a flight lieutenant was returning to base alone after engaging enemy bombers when he was attacked by six German fighters, but got away from them with a holed engine. He soon realized that he would be unable to reach base.

He landed in a field, and got some peasants who were working near to help him to cover his aircraft with branches pulled from trees. He had just time to hide in a ditch when German bombers came overhead. "I thought they had spotted my aircraft for certain," said the pilot. "They kept cruising round for about ten minutes, coming quite low, and all the time I expected them to open up with machine-gun fire. But the camouflage must have been quite good, for they finally flew away."

The pilot came out of the ditch and began to examine the engine. He found two small holes, but otherwise the aircraft was undamaged. He walked to the nearest town and called at a garage, where he got motor-car petrol and oil, and persuaded several men to act as porters

He bought a packet of chewing-gum at a grocer's. Then they all went back to the field.

"I chewed the gum a bit to get it tacky," said the pilot, "and then plugged the holes. It set very well. I got the petrol and oil put in, and then took off, and so home."

The enemy Panzer and motorized forces rolled on across France. More came through the gap. By the afternoon of May 18 some of the enemy had reached Péronne. The Allies' backward move engulfed the Royal Air Force. On May 18 the Air Component moved one of their main operational aerodromes from Poix [1] to Abbeville; in the evening of May 19, with five German Panzer divisions in the area, the Air Component was forced to abandon Abbeville aerodrome. Air Vice-Marshal Blount then moved his headquarters to England. The Air Component maintained an advanced landing-ground at Merville until May 22. From May 21 until the evacuation from Dunkirk arrangements for air co-operation with the British Expeditionary Force were made by the War Office and the Air Ministry in London. Air liaison centre in England was at Hawkinge aerodrome, Kent; targets were selected in accordance with telephone or telegraphic requests from the Expeditionary Force (while communications remained) and information received from the Royal Air Force and other sources.

On May 19 General Weygand superseded General Gamelin as Allied Commander-in-Chief in all theatres of war. But already it was too late to save a situation which had been created, not during ten days of combat, but during the preceding twenty years, and most urgently during the preceding seven. When war began in September 1939 the British Army possessed one cruiser-tank. The British Air Force possessed a quarter of the numerical strength of the Luftwaffe. And while the German Army and Air Force could be concentrated, the British Army and Air Force were dispersed about an Empire greater in dimensions than any the world had ever seen. French conceptions of modern war were no less faulty. The gallant little army of Belgium was not equipped lavishly as was the huge German Army, nor could it ever be so equipped. The Allied failure was determined before the action just as surely as was the German victory. The appointment of General Weygand, the procedure of swopping horses in mid-stream, could not cure the deep-seated cancer of ill-preparedness, and the evil of faulty cohesion in the Allied line of defence.

General Gort early realized the threat to the northern armies, and took steps on May 19 to guard the flank along the canal-lines running inland from the sea, through Saint-Omer and La Bassée to the line of

[1] See map at p. 144, Vol. I.

the Escaut river. By May 20 the gap in the French line extended from Valenciennes to Longwy. On May 21 Allied communications across the Somme were severed, and the northern armies were separated from those to the south. The bulk of the British Expeditionary Force was cut off from its base areas at Le Havre, Cherbourg, Brest, Nantes, and Saint-Nazaire by the severance of the lines of communication. The Germans maintained heavy pressure against the Belgian Army in Belgium, which the attempt to close the gap in the South could do nothing to ease; indeed, it caused a lengthening in the Belgian line, along which the Belgian troops held up the German advance while the attempt to fill the gap was made.

§ 7

Evacuation of the Air Component

The Air Component of the British Expeditionary Force was forced to evacuate its aerodromes early because they lay in the path of the German advance across France. Lysanders that had spotted for the British gunners in Belgium flew back to England; Blenheims that had bombed the advancing German columns went, too; the fighters were last to leave.

Ground crews of the squadrons went to Boulogne by road, and the Royal Navy took charge of their crossing to England. The records of the Air Component, packed into wooden cases, were loaded on to the deck of a destroyer. More and more men and munitions were crowded on to the deck; the cases were dumped overboard into the sea after the destroyer left port, and the records were unfortunately lost, much to the detriment of the history of the Air Component.

In the swift evacuation of the aerodromes there could be no possibility of moving everything that had been accumulated. Such things as private luggage and tool-kits had to be discarded. Best uniforms were worn, and older ones left behind.

After the Lysanders left, fighters were asked to make reconnaissance flights. They had already made unavailing attacks against German tanks near Arras, being shot up by the German ground defences in the process of proving that rifle-calibre machine-gun bullets were useless against the armour of tanks.

Untrained in the practice of reconnaissance flying, the Hurricanes' pilots flew low until a stream of bullets and pom-pom shells soared up from the ground, and then they knew that they had crossed the positions of the German advanced troops. In revenge they swept low and retaliated with their eight machine-guns against the wearers of the field-grey uniforms who fired at them.

The old men, women, and children who lived in the areas towards which the Germans advanced evacuated their homes. The pilots of Air Component Fighter squadrons were left in a desolated countryside; Army units came to take over defence-posts. Squadron after squadron left to fly to English aerodromes designated in their orders. Some of the fighters escorted transport aeroplanes that carried passengers and valuable cargo across the Channel to safety in the sea-girt land of Britain.

At this period Pilot Officer L. A. Strange won a bar to the Distinguished Flying Cross which he had won in the Great War. Louis Strange learned to fly at Hendon civil aerodrome in 1913. In 1914 he was mobilized in the Royal Flying Corps Special Reserve of Officers and went to France with No. 5 squadron, R.F.C. When the Great War ended he was a lieutenant-colonel in the Royal Air Force and had won the Distinguished Service Order, the Military Cross, and the Distinguished Flying Cross. In the years that followed he farmed, then engaged in civil aviation. At the age of forty-nine he joined the Royal Air Force as a pilot officer in the Royal Air Force Volunteer Reserve. It was the spring of 1940. Again he went to Hendon, the old sporting-flying London aerodrome which had been for many years a R.A.F. station.

A number of R.A.F. communication aircraft were then in France to meet the requirements of hard-pressed squadrons. Sometimes extremely rapid evacuation had to be carried out, but it was not always possible to get pilots at a moment's notice. Aircraftmen could not be taken off operations to carry out repairs. So small detachments had to be sent from England to effect repairs and, when necessary, fly the repaired aircraft back.

When Merville was the only advanced landing-ground left in France to the Air Component Pilot Officer Strange was detailed to proceed there to act as ground-control officer during the arrival and departure of aircraft carrying food supplies.

He left England one fine morning as a passenger in a civil aircraft; his pilot was a well-known civilian pilot. When they were over France they saw the pathetic streams of refugees cluttering up the roads below. Over wooded country near Saint-Omer popping noises interrupted their conversation. They thought they were passing over French rifle- and machine-gun practice ranges. But when tracer bullets began to shriek past them, and the pops became nasty sharp cracks, they carefully scanned the area below and saw about a dozen German tanks under trees on a roadway outside a village, their black swastikas plainly visible in a white circle on their brown-and-green camouflaged top decks.

The unarmed British civil aircraft swooped over the tanks; as it crossed the tree-tops the German tank crews hurriedly drew camouflage netting over their markings. German troops dived from motor vehicles into ditches and began firing at the aircraft, which flew still lower and hurried on.

A small fleet of civil air transports quickly unloaded their cargo of food and ammunition at Merville aerodrome and left for England. The R.A.F. personnel settled down to the job of servicing Hurricane fighters they had come to rescue. Soon the first Hurricane was away, in spite of its bullet-riddled condition. The second repair took longer. While the repair crew worked a British pilot landed beside them by parachute after a desperate fight high above their heads. He was offered the second Hurricane, and by midday was off to rejoin his squadron.

For lunch the repair squad had chicken-stew, with lots of vegetables, made by a sergeant of a North-country regiment, who, with ten men from the Sunderland district, had become detached from his unit after a scrap with German troops. The sergeant was in fine form. The war, he said, was "just his cup of tea."

Refugees wandered up and down the road, responsive to the direction from which the sound of the nearest gunfire and sniping seemed to come. The repair party worked under heavy bombing and machine-gun fire. The sergeant joined the Bren-gun carrier section, and had a crack at Heinkels and Messerschmitts whenever they came near.

The only means of communication between England and Merville was by written messages dropped by aircraft in message-bags. Tiger-Moth trainers and Autogiros floated slowly round the sky on message-carrying flights, in much the same way that had helped the police to handle traffic on Derby Day; they were unarmed and 250 miles an hour slower than the Messerschmitt fighters that bestrode the sky above them.

The third Hurricane was just ready when an aeroplane detached itself from a dog-fight, streaked down towards Merville aerodrome, and dropped a message-bag. The message ordered Strange to fly the next serviceable Hurricane to England before nightfall.

Strange had never flown a Hurricane, but he went off in grand style, throbbed gently into top gear, retarded the boost, retracted the wheels, and set course for home. He felt not a care in the world for he was engrossed in flying a strange type of aeroplane.

He flew low. Tracer bullets began to flash down upon him from the hillsides. He shot up to about 8000 feet to get out of them, and sailed into a pattern of noisy, black anti-aircraft shell-bursts. The shell-smoke attracted the attention of the leader of a *Kette* (flight) of Messerschmitt fighters, who instantly dived to the attack.

Strange's guns were not in action, for there had been no time to get them serviceable. He was unarmed, and alone, against six of the enemy. The Messerschmitt leader's first burst hit the Hurricane. Strange side-slipped inward to get out of the stream of bullets, and skidded into line with the burst of fire from the German number two. The "strips these two tore off" shook him more than the efforts of the guns. He wondered what the other four Messerschmitts above and behind him might be up to.

Again he was streaking along just above the ground.

The chase went on up a village street, down a château drive, once almost through the château front door, until, suddenly, after twisting down a wooded valley through which a stream flowed, the Hurricane came out above sand-dunes and a moment later was over the sea. The British fleet off Boulogne opened up on the pack of Messerschmitts. One salvo was enough for them. Strange climbed in leisurely fashion, thankfully; and, perhaps a little regretfully, looked back at the smoke of battle round Calais and Boulogne, which drew weird shadows from the misty red light of the setting sun, in strange contrast to the quiet peacefulness of the Isle of Thanet towards which he flew.

The French armies south of the gap were then stretched along a line running almost straight across France from the end of the Maginot Line to Abbeville. The Franco-Belgo-British forces north of the gap had fallen back to Ghent and the river Scheldt. Their line ran through Tournai to Valenciennes; there it was bent back into the north flank of the gap, running westward just north of Arras and Saint-Pol. Immediately to the north-west of Saint-Pol the Allied northern flank ceased to exist. The Germans, who had already passed Doullens in the centre of the gap, rushed swiftly forward, swept round the exposed flank, and reached the coast. The French, British, and Belgian forces north of the Somme were cut off and surrounded. Attempts to re-establish contact between the separated armies failed.

With their backs to the North Sea, the defence perimeter of the forces cut off in Flanders continually contracted under tremendous German pressure. The Belgian forces staggered under terrific punishment, but held their line. Then, on May 26, came a break between the British and Belgian armies. The Belgians were forced northward, away from the British. Refugees filled the ever-constricting area held by Belgian arms, crowding the roads, blocking the mobility of the fighting forces. The Belgians had nowhere to go; they could retreat no farther; King Leopold capitulated to save needless slaughter.

57

Chapter IV

The Battle of France

§ I

Break-through

FRENCH cavalry, advancing into Belgium and Luxemburg in front of the French Second Army on the first day of the German offensive, retired in face of heavy pressure, which also drove in the Belgian outposts.

While the Belgian Army fought a delaying action back from Eastern Belgium the British Expeditionary Force advanced with the French First Army on its right and the French Seventh Army on its left. The French Seventh Army advanced into Holland; when the Dutch Army laid down its arms on May 15 this army withdrew to the neighbourhood of Antwerp. These two French armies, the British Army, and the Belgian Army occupied the main defensive position line covering Antwerp, thence running south through Louvain and Wavre to Namur, thus covering Brussels. Simultaneously the French Ninth Army advanced into position on the Meuse between Namur and Mézières, while the French Second Army, holding the partly fortified line behind the river Meuse from Mézières to the Maginot Line, formed the pivot upon which the forward right wheel into Belgium hinged.

On May 12 information was received that the Germans were developing a thrust with at least two armoured divisions against the Ninth Army. At 7 A.M. on May 13 the attack was delivered at Houx, where only advanced troops were in position, and the Germans infiltrated into the Meuse valley between Yvoir and Givet. The French Ninth Army was hard pressed in the area between the rivers Sambre and Meuse by German divisions attacking between Namur and Sedan, and the French Seventh Army sent some of its divisions across the line to its assistance.

But spring came early that year, and the weather remained mostly dry. Quick to seize any advantage offered to them, the Germans profited by the low water-levels to drive swiftly through the natural obstacle of the Ardennes valleys. Their overwhelming pressure carried them across the Meuse between Sedan and Mézières. At 5 P.M. on May 13, 1940,

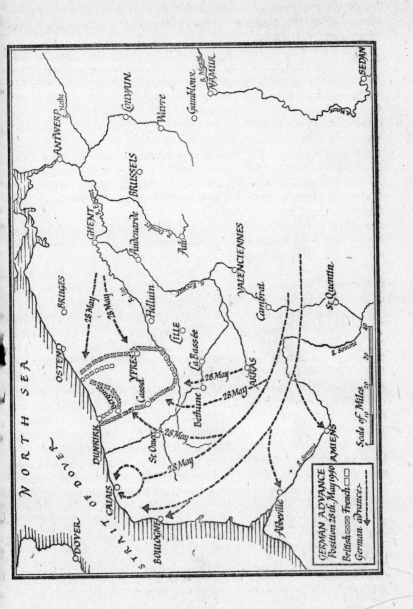

GERMAN ADVANCE
Position 28th. May 1940
British ⊠ French □
German advance :- - -

Scale of Miles
0 10 20 30 40

Sedan fell to a powerful German attack supported by artillery and aircraft, and into this breach the German command threw a concentration of armoured divisions.

At the Riom trial [1] Edouard Daladier, who was Prime Minister and War Minister of France when the war began, said in evidence that in September 1939 France possessed 2500 tanks against Germany's 7000, and that by the beginning of May 1940 the French tank strength was raised to 3600. The Germans attacked with a tank strength about equal to the French total. But, said M. Daladier, General Georges [2] was bitterly antagonistic to the idea of tank divisions, and the French tanks were dispersed in groups and could not be concentrated for the great thrust which might have brought victory. During the Battle of France, said M. Daladier, French crack troops held the Maginot Line; twenty divisions were kept idle behind it; while the divisions that fought in the North were second-rate. Even the Maginot Line was not properly appreciated by the staff, the former Premier alleged, or they would have utilized its resisting power to enable them to concentrate all their forces at a strategic point.

There is evidence to show that French military policy was inadequately defined, and that French politics were schismatic in face of the politico-militarist cohesion of the third German Reich.

France had no cause to fight for. Her people were mostly apathetic. They did not want war. It was forced upon them. In Britain it was not greatly different. But France was unfortunate. It was her fate that of the two great allies she took the first shock of the German military blow. By absorbing that shock France, together with Belgium and Holland, cushioned the blow against Britain, and paved the way for the eventual come-back of the United Nations. It was not until France fell, and the German armies had rolled over the whole face of Western Europe, that the people of Britain awoke to the reality of the time. Then, but not until then, did Britain have a cause to fight for. No longer was it a nebulous war into which the British people had been brought through a belated agreement to guarantee Poland. The initiating causes of the war were forgotten. Instead they regarded the

[1] At Riom, a little town not far from Vichy, the Pétain Government of Unoccupied France indicted on February 17, 1942, in a State trial members of earlier French Governments, who had been held as State prisoners at Bourrasol. The men indicted in this French State 'war guilt' trial were Edouard Daladier and Léon Blum, former Premiers; Pierre Cot and Guy La Chambre, former Air Ministers; generalissimo General Gamelin and former Army Controller General Jacomet. Pierre Cot was tried in his absence in the United States. Trials of Paul Reynaud, Mandel, and others were to follow.

[2] General Georges was Assistant Chief of Staff before the war, and was the General Commanding the Armies of the North-east in the war.

war as a crusade for the liberation of peoples enslaved by German despots, sometimes—but not always—assisted by renegades who sought opportunity to acquire power which they might never have gained in other circumstances: renegades called quislings, from the surname of the Norwegian who first gave his services to Germany as a puppet-governor of his fellow-citizens. Out of the débâcle in Europe emerged the opposite types, the de Gaullists, men—ay, and women —who, like General de Gaulle, rallied to the British and Allied cause, raising their own armies, manning their own ships and aircraft to swell the forces which fought back from the beleaguered isles of Britain and Northern Ireland to restore what German lust and European credulity and duplicity had sacrificed.

So it came about that the Royal Air Force became an international air force, possessing squadrons manned by Poles, Czechs, Belgians, Dutch, Norwegians, French, and Americans. The last, voluntarily giving their services to humanity, formed, before they were taken over by their own United States Army Air Force on September 29, 1942, the personnel of Nos. 71, 121, and 133 Eagle squadrons of Fighter Command, Royal Air Force, for eighteen months. During that time they destroyed 73½ enemy aircraft, the half being part of a Dornier shared with a British squadron. The senior squadron, No. 71, shot down forty-one of the total destroyed by the three squadrons. There were, of course, American volunteer pilots fighting in the Royal Air Force before No. 71 squadron was formed early in 1941 following upon the idea first conceived by Charles Sweeney, a well-known American who had been resident for some years in London, and who had already done much for France. Born in San Francisco, Charles Sweeney trained at America's equivalent of Britain's Sandhurst, the West Point Military Academy, and fought in wars in Mexico, Venezuela, and Honduras, before the beginning of the Great War found him in Paris; there, with a few other Americans, he organized the group of his fellow-countrymen who joined the French Foreign Legion, and some of whom later formed themselves into the Lafayette Escadrille which fought with the French Army air force in the 1914–18 war. Sweeney entered the Legion as a private of the line. Twice wounded, and frequently decorated, he became colonel, the highest army rank France accords to foreigners. In 1925 he re-formed the Lafayette Escadrille to fight Abd-el-Krim's Riff insurgents in Morocco.

In June 1940, before France collapsed, Charles Sweeney went to America to bring the idea of the Royal Air Force Eagle squadron into being, and subsequently became its Honorary Commanding Officer with the rank of group captain.

In preliminary talks No. 71 squadron was spoken of in various ways. The first official British reference to an 'Eagle' squadron was contained in a note written by Sir Hugh Seely, M.P., Parliamentary Private Secretary to the Secretary of State for Air, Sir Archibald Sinclair, wherein the final proposals were put forward. From then on Eagle Fighter Squadron was the official title, and, the *modus operandi* settled, some thirty-odd United States pilots volunteered to form themselves into a regular squadron of the Royal Air Force.

The feathered head of an American Indian had been the badge of the Lafayette Escadrille. The badge chosen for the Royal Air Force American squadron was an eagle with spread wings pointing upward, an eagle quite distinctive from the official American eagle shown on the national insignia of the United States. The design of the badge was the work of the Americans themselves, and was accepted by the Air Ministry and approved by the King.

The three Eagle Fighter squadrons left the command of Air Chief Marshal Sir Sholto Douglas, Air Officer Commanding-in-Chief Fighter Command, on September 29, 1942, to pass to that of Major-General Carl Spaatz, Commanding the United States Army Eighth Air Force, wherein they served under the direct command of Brigadier-General F. O'D. Hunter, Commanding General Fighter Command, United States Army Eighth Air Force.

But in France, during the fateful months of May and June 1940, there were only the French and British Air Forces to defend the land of France against the Luftwaffe, the French assisted by a small number of Czech and Polish pilots who, escaping to France, had joined the French Air Force. The aircraft available for the duties imposed upon those air forces were too few to stem the swollen flood of Nazi air superiority.

The President of the Court of the Riom Trial said on March 4, 1942, that in September 1939 France possessed only 510 fighter aeroplanes, of which 442 were of modern design; 390 bombers, none modern; 170 reconnaissance aircraft, of which 52 were modern; and 340 observation balloons, none modern. At that time Germany had 10,000 modern aircraft. M. Guy La Chambre, who held the post of French Air Minister until March 1940, said that before the war production was at the rate of about thirty-five aeroplanes a month; only about fifty bombers existed when mobilization was ordered, with 142 other bombing aircraft which were, in effect, merely reconnaissance aircraft. When he left the post of Air Minister in March 1940, 249 bombers had been delivered, but the High Command had decided that they must be modified and modernized, and in February 1940 there were only thirty-five bombers. M. La Chambre said that there had been hostility in French aeronautical circles on the question of ordering from the United States (he blamed M. Marcel Bloch, the aircraft manufacturer), but during his administration 850 American fighters and 715 bombers were ordered. During one month of the war French aircraft production rose to 300 aeroplanes. M. La Chambre claimed that he delivered 3300 aircraft between January 1939 and March 1940. When mobilization was ordered France had 1470 aeroplanes in service against the 1748 planned to be ready at that time. The former Air Minister also said that when France surrendered to Germany in June 1940 she had 2500 aeroplanes which had never been used, out of a total of 3500 available.

General Besson, who before the war had a command first in the Ardennes, then in the Alps, and finally led the army which covered Alsace and the Jura, said that in the Ardennes there were no important defensive works, and that the troops between Mézières and Givet (where the initial German break-through took place) were insufficient. In May 1940 it was possible for France to put into the field 115 divisions, 24 of which were in North Africa, and 15 in the Levant, leaving 76 for Metropolitan France. "If we add the British and Polish divisions we arrive at a total of 102 divisions on the north-eastern front against 140 German divisions. Perhaps we might have been able to defend ourselves on our own frontier, but we ought not to have gone into Belgium, for our material was insufficient. The most appalling inferiority was the insufficiency of our air force."

In Rheims—the headquarters of the Royal Air Force Advanced Air Striking Force, and the centre around which the ten Bomber squadrons and two Fighter squadrons of that force had been disposed for many months—the banshee of the air-raid sirens seldom ceased. Bombers flew low over the city, machine-gunning the streets, attempting to bomb the bridge over the Vesle canal, without success, but killing many civilians in the process. They tried to put the British aircraft out of action by bombing the British-occupied aerodromes. Rheims-Champagne aerodrome, Mourmelon, Rouvres, Amifontaine, and Berry-au-Bac were all heavily bombed; the town of Betheniville was almost destroyed; Dorniers aimed 1000-lb. bombs at the Château Polignac, the headquarters of Air Vice-Marshal P. H. L. Playfair, Officer Commanding the Advanced Air Striking Force, but though they flew at a low height, and were uninterrupted by fighters or anti-aircraft gunfire, they missed their targets and succeeded only in erupting huge fountains of earth in the grounds.

Liart and Hirson, two key-towns lying on the German line of attack, were heavily bombed. Many civilians were killed in both places. The French aerodrome at Mézières was attacked and pitted with bomb-holes. Rethel was flattened out. Châlons was in ruins. Revigny was badly hit. Laon was heavily bombed.

The German air strategy was planned to attack aerodromes, railway junctions, and towns, to blast a way through for the ground forces, which, based upon road lines of communication, and possessing large forces of tanks, armoured fighting vehicles, lorry-borne infantry, armed motor-cycle-and-sidecar detachments, mobile anti-aircraft guns, mobile large guns and mortars, used the roads and the road-bridges (and when these were destroyed by Allied sappers the German engineers were fully equipped for swift military bridge-building) so that the German armed forces could move rapidly forward as soon as the transverse defence-lines were pierced. The strategy was more successful even than the Germans hoped. The overrunning of France was achieved in less time than had been calculated. The French system of defence in line failed to offer adequate resistance to these tactics of attack, and within a few days the German advanced forces were speeding across the French countryside with as much freedom as pre-war peace-time motorists. The countryside provided the petrol and oil for the German war machines. They filled their tanks from French petrol-pumps and pushed on. The mechanized and motorized hordes swept across France as once horsemen swept across enemy territory, living on the land they advanced through, requisitioning, commandeering—a process which in a conquering army, ripe with the lust of victory, is removed from stealing only by use of the camouflage of terminology.

There was cunning in the German technique. Saboteurs, in uniforms and in mufti, were dropped in advance of the approaching host. In places boys were dropped by parachute or disemplaned from aircraft which had landed in open fields; these boys ran forward into the villages, shouting to the villagers in colloquial French that the Boches were almost upon the village, and telling the people to get away before it was too late. The women, the children, the old men, the unwanted in war who had been left behind at home in the ebb of the Martian tide, stampeded, unaware that the strange youth who shouted was not French but German, taking no time for rational thought to decide where they would proceed, allowing reason to pass from their minds, and finding in its place panic and the urge to fly before the oncoming horror of the German troops who, twice before in seventy years, had desecrated the land of France. Piling what few belongings they could take, upon hand-carts, into perambulators, tying up bundles in sheets, giving a helping arm to the aged and infirm, they turned out of their cottages

and homes and began the trudge westward, the blind, locust-like fligh
that developed into the migration of millions. And, as French troops
moved forward to defend the land, they met the westward surge of the
human tide of their own country-folks, and were disorganized by the
press of humanity. Everything was chaos. Down upon the lines of
struggling people swept the aircraft with black crosses on their wings and
fuselages, and bearing the sign of a fylfot upon their rudders, manned
by youths who had been trained to believe that to execute the orders
of their masters was the pinnacle-point of knight-errantry. These
fanatical young men flew over the pitiful crowds of refugees and
spattered them with machine-gun bullets and cannon-shells, pock-
marked the line of their passage with bomb-bursts, and no doubt
laughed as Vittorio Mussolini, the dictator's son, laughed four years
before when he saw helpless Abyssinian tribesmen on the ground below
his wings "open up like a flowering rose" when his bombs burst
among their defenceless bodies.

Some of the Germans' many thousands of aircraft were needed to
guard the eastern frontiers, uneasily facing Russia, holding down
Czechoslovakia and Poland, suppressing Austria, threatening Hungary,
Yugoslavia, and Rumania. About 3500 first-line aircraft were loosed
against Holland, Belgium, and France simultaneously. They crossed
the skies in great formations. The British fighter pilots in France,
operating in sections of three Hurricanes, or perhaps in a flight of six,
and rarely in squadron strength of from nine to fifteen aircraft, saw
them, their wings glinting in the sunshine, high up, low down, in formations of fifty, eighty, at a time; bombers, with fighters above and below
them, or sometimes, with the audacity of their known superiority in
numbers, operating without escort.

We have already seen, from evidence given at Riom, how low French
air strength was in Metropolitan France; even to add Britain's total
air strength to it—and this was impossible, for Britain had many
defence commitments where air forces had to be retained outside
France—could not give the Allies semi-parity with Germany. Twenty-
four British squadrons were on French soil when the German attack
began: Army Co-operation, Bomber, and Fighter aircraft; about
300 machines all together. (In addition, the British Expeditionary
Force possessed light aeroplanes—called the Taylorcraft Auster—
that flew from small fields to serve as eyes for Army units and spot for
the guns. These little high-wing monoplanes were unarmed two-
seaters, flown mostly by R.A.F.-trained Army pilots who belonged to
Army Air Observation Post Squadrons. When attacked, Auster pilots
had to evade enemy fighters by turning in small circles so that the heavy

Messerschmitts could not follow them, until British fighters, called up by radio, came to the rescue.) There were 135 Battle and Blenheim bombers in the Advanced Air Striking Force. These were thrown into the full heat of the Battle of France.

During the initial part of the German advance it seemed that Rheims must quickly fall. The German thrust was headed directly towards the cathedral city. Late in the night of May 15 the decision was taken for the Advanced Air Striking Force to retire. But the German advance curved like a scythe-blade abruptly away from Rheims, by-passed the city, and sped towards the Channel coast. That was a function of German strategy which could not have been foretold except through accurate Intelligence, which appears at that period of the war, as during the period preceding the outbreak of hostilities, to have been a weakness on the Allied side. This first retirement of the Advanced Air Striking Force was executed hurriedly; it was by no means a perfect operation; probably few retirements ever are perfect. Some of the units were inadequately prepared for a hurried departure. Just before the retreat began the Luftwaffe bombed the headquarters transport park at Rheims, and the R.A.F. lost a considerable proportion of its transport; that made matters more difficult. It was certainly unexpected that within a week of the beginning of the German offensive it would be necessary to begin a big withdrawal, for no one had credited the German armies with such a rapid advance, nor the French with such a swift breakdown. But Rheims remained in Allied hands for almost another month, and the French occupied some of the vacated aerodromes for several days after the R.A.F. left them.

During the night the Advanced Air Striking Force began to retire from the Rheims area, and the Germans crossed the river Meuse. Next day the Germans reached the river Aisne. Battles and Blenheims continued to pound the advancing enemy forces, bombing troop concentrations, armoured fighting vehicles, and transport convoys.

From bases in England Bomber Command dispatched Wellington, Hampden, and Whitley bombers by night to bomb railway junctions, railway marshalling-yards, oil-dumps, trains, communication congestion-points, river crossings. The French High Command asked for and received the closest possible support from Bomber Command. As the battle developed the night attacks became more and more a direct assault upon the enemy, concentrated mainly upon the rear areas, behind the fighting zone, where German concentrations were to be found. Save for the attack upon Sylt in the night of March 19, 1940, the bombs that fell upon the railway antennæ of the railway junction of München-Gladbach in the night of May 11 were the first to fall upon German soil, and they were the first to fall upon the German mainland. These bombs were the first of a long succession of bombs which were to grow in number and size in a campaign whose intensity and continuity of purpose had been undreamed of in German military philosophy.

(From June 6, 1918, until November 10, 1918, the Independent Air Force dropped 550 tons of bombs on German soil. By contrast, the bombing of the Second World War increased in scale until in the night of November 22, 1943, during the second major attack in the Battle of Berlin, a total of 2300 tons of high-explosive and incendiary bombs was dropped on the Reich capital in the space of thirty minutes.)

In that whirlwind campaign when the German armies sped across France, and the French were poorly armed with bomber aircraft, Bomber Command of the Royal Air Force in the United Kingdom was able to muster no greater a force than 100 night bombers for its work. That does not mean that this figure represented the full first-line strength of Bomber Command; it does mean that with the strength available it was not possible to maintain a striking force of greater size. That was one measure of British lack of preparation for the struggle which began in 1939. The relative power of the opposing air forces was so disproportionate at that time that the employment of Allied air-power in whatever form could not redress the adverse balance which had been struck upon the ground. There was no other force available in the United Kingdom to send to the aid of France. All we had to spare was already there, to the full commitment made by the British Government: 400,000 men (and their equipment), most of them, at the time when the bombs began to fall on German soil, in process of being cut off from the main French armies and forced into the roads that led to the evacuation which brought so many back to Britain, but left their arms, accoutrements, equipment, guns, lorries, light tanks, and what else besides, behind as spoil for the Germans to take over. In a speech at Swansea on August 22, 1942, Sir Archibald Sinclair, Secretary of State for Air, said:

> Our preparations for the struggle against the armed might of Nazi power had been inadequate. In the air, our Metropolitan Air Force was outnumbered by the German Air Force by four to one. At sea, our small craft were all too few to cope with the submarine menace. On land, we had fewer divisions to send to France than we had in 1914. For our tanks we had not two-pounder or six-pounder guns, but nothing heavier than machine-guns.

The one armoured division which was raised by May 1940 never reached Lord Gort. In his dispatches the Commander of the British Expeditionary Force wrote:

The prospect of securing the reinforcement of the Armoured Division had likewise become remote. I had been advised that two Armoured Brigades of this division would disembark at Havre on 16th May, and were to concentrate at Bolbec, and I had therefore sent instructions by the hand of a staff officer to the Commander (Major-General R. Evans). He was to move the leading brigade on disembarkation with all speed to secure the crossings of the Somme west of Amiens, from Picquigny to Pont Rémy, both inclusive, with a view to the concentration of the remaining brigade behind the Somme and the move of his division to join the main body of the B.E.F. However, in the meantime, orders had been issued locally to concentrate the Division south of the Seine, and the plan to cross the Somme and join the B.E.F. proved impossible to execute. The division therefore remained in the Lines of Communication Area and never came under my effective command.

German armoured forces advanced westward down the valley of the Somme towards Abbeville, and via Hesdin and Montreuil towards the Channel Ports, a movement which the gallant defenders of the first Battle of Ypres had prevented in October 1914. In 1940 new methods of mobile warfare (first invented by the British, and strategically developed in theory by the French) were employed by the German Wehrmacht to achieve what was denied to them twenty-six years before. On May 20 the Welsh Guards delayed the approach of German tanks upon Arras from the direction of Cambrai. General Gort made a request for strong bomber support to the Air Ministry through the War Office, and on the following night a large number of heavy bombers attacked roads and bridges in the neighbourhood of Cambrai and Le Cateau; bridges spanning the Sambre and Oise were hit, a train at Hirson derailed, and an ammunition-dump at Nouvion blown up. During daylight the Advanced Air Striking Force kept up pressure upon the advancing enemy, bombing columns of tanks and motorized infantry near Berneuil and Puisieux, Abbeville and Hesdin, on the Amiens-Doullens road, and at Ribecourt. Their work was shared by Blenheims operating from England, who, arriving on May 22 in the dusk over a German mechanized division, dropped twelve 250-lb. and seventy-two 40-lb. bombs and obliterated the centre of the column. The British counter-attack launched southward from Arras in the afternoon of May 21, planned by Major-General Franklyn and so called Frankforce, and directed by Major-General Martel, was supported only by light armoured vehicles of the 1st Army Tank Brigade and the French 1st Light Mechanized Division. It gained the objectives for the day against strong opposition, but failed to cut across the corridor to effect a junction with the main French and minor British forces to the south, weathered heavy dive-bombing attacks during the evening, held its ground during May 22, found itself being hemmed in on May 23, and in the evening of that day was withdrawn by Lord Gort. The defence of Arras was ended; by that time there were but twenty-eight tanks left in the 1st Army Tank Brigade. But this delaying action around Arras was valuable in permitting time to organize the defence of the south-western flank of the British Expeditionary Force along the line of canals from the Escaut river to La Bassée, Saint-Omer, and the sea. This line of canals provided the only obstacle to the German tanks which moved continuously forward along the corridor extending from Sedan almost to the Channel.

§ 2

Political Changes

The withdrawal from Central Norway had created dissatisfaction in political circles, and brought to a head discontent which had been simmering in the Labour Party against the leadership of Mr Neville Chamberlain. On May 8 a Labour vote of censure was defeated by a majority of only 81. Several Government supporters voted in the minority of 200. Before Chamberlain could recover his loss of prestige by negotiations to strengthen the war direction there came the invasion of Holland, Belgium, Luxemburg, and France. It was not to be expected that the German attack upon the Low Countries and France could commence with such fury without political repercussions. Mr Neville Chamberlain was greeted in the House of Commons with stony silence. Unaccustomed to the coldness of the atmosphere, he looked around him and said, "I have friends in this House." But nowhere did he find an answer, a reassurance. Suddenly he found that terrible moment arrive, which fortunately few men ever know, when he was utterly alone, when no one came to his side and vowed to stand with him or to follow him. Neville Chamberlain—the "Man of Munich," he had been called—could not at first believe it. But it was true.

Yet, if we were unprepared for the assault which came in 1940, how much worse would have been the fate of Britain if that assault had been sprung in 1938, at the time of Munich? Then, indeed, the war might have been won by Germany within a year, so far as the Western Powers were concerned. Perhaps, in time to come, it will be attributed to Neville Chamberlain that by the respite he secured at Munich and Godesberg he succeeded in tipping the scales just sufficiently in the favour of the people who were long after to be called the United Nations to prevent the possibility of a German victory, even if that achievement was the consequence and not the intention of the Munich Agreement.

On May 10, 1940, Neville Chamberlain resigned his office as Prime Minister of Great Britain. Mr Winston Spencer Churchill assumed office in succession. The Labour Party, which had steadfastly opposed the Government which Chamberlain represented, was willing to be represented in a reconstructed Government headed by Mr Churchill. Neville Chamberlain accepted office within the Government as Lord President of the Council. He refused the honours which might have been his for the asking. He died on November 9, 1940, his last months being a brief and unemotional postscript to his political career.

Mr Winston Churchill moved from Admiralty House to 10 Downing Street. Next door, at No. 11, Sir Kingsley Wood was to take up residence as Chancellor of the Exchequer, and into his place as Air Minister came the Liberal leader Sir Archibald Sinclair, landowner from the North of Scotland, thereafter described by a Labour member, Mr Emanuel Shinwell, as "the Laird of the Air." Mr A. V. Alexander, a former First Lord of the Admiralty in the Labour Administration, succeeded to Mr Churchill's chair in the Admiralty Board room. Mr Anthony Eden became Secretary of State for War, and Lord Beaverbrook Minister of the newly created Ministry of Aircraft Production. On Whit Monday Mr Churchill addressed an enthusiastic House of Commons whose members had been summoned secretly by telegram. He received a vote of confidence from both Chambers. In the historic words of Garibaldi the Prime Minister said: "I have nothing to offer but blood and toil and tears and sweat."

In France M. Paul Reynaud became Prime Minister and War Minister; M. Daladier took over the Ministry of Foreign Affairs; Marshal Pétain became Vice-Premier.

§ 3

The Bombers at Work

A British bomber returning from a night attack on German troop concentrations was hit by a shell which put the port engine out of action. The twenty-year-old pilot officer, captain of the aircraft, tried to maintain height, but was at last forced to attempt a landing.

It was a thick black night [he said], and I thought we were a few miles out to sea from the coast. I was just preparing to pull off a tricky landing on the water when, in the nick of time, I saw a stretch of sand and made straight for it. The moment we touched ground the aircraft swung violently to the left and two of the crew, still thinking we were landing on the water, actually launched the rubber dinghy and jumped for it. When we realized we were safely down on the beach we burned all our maps and papers, in case we were in enemy territory, and sat down to wait for the dawn.

Instead of the dawn, a group of about twenty men, each armed with a rifle and bayonet, loomed up out of the darkness and advanced on us with far from friendly expressions. They turned out to be French coastguards, and the leader, singling me out, put his bayonet against my stomach and said, "Allemand!"

I was the only one of our chaps who could speak French. I promptly answered, "Non. Anglais," and tried a reassuring sort of smile. The only result was that the bayonet pressed a little closer to my skin.

We had to think quickly, and though our arms were all up in the "Kamerad" position I took a chance, said "Excusez-moi!" and carefully lowered one arm to open my flying-suit and show my R.A.F. wings badge. Pointing to it, I said, "Air—Ah—Eff" very slowly and distinctly. That seemed to relieve the tension a bit, and when the coastguards had flashed their torches on our wrecked aircraft and seen the British markings all was well. We shook hands all round, and they insisted upon taking us up to their hut and lighthouse about a mile and a half away, where we had a wash and a first-rate breakfast. When we had had a rest our 'hosts' escorted us to a near-by village and stood us all an *aperitif* and an excellent lunch before seeing us off to the nearest aerodrome.

The bombers that took part in the early night operations against the German invaders of the Low Countries and France encountered no opposition from enemy fighter aircraft, but the ground anti-aircraft defences were both strong and active. There were large numbers of searchlights and heavy gunfire. Broadcast instructions were issued from German radio stations, telling the people to observe the blackout regulations in the interests of the whole nation which "must be spared any damage from the air." The British crews were given specific military objectives and instructed that bombs were not to be dropped indiscriminately.

The aircraft allocated to the British Air Forces in France Command, and subdivided into the Air Component and the Advanced Air Striking Force, acted under the orders of the Army Commanders in the Field, who themselves were subject to the French High Command. The medium bombers based in Britain—Blenheims—were employed on missions of a similar kind. The heavy bombers based in Britain— Wellingtons, Hampdens, and Whitleys—all of which were subsequently to become medium bombers with the introduction of the much heavier Stirling, Halifax, and Lancaster types, operated solely at night against targets selected by the joint Franco-British staff under orders from the French High Command. The French High Command wanted all bombing effort to be directed to support the armies in the field to resist German invasion. The types of target allocated to the heavy bombers altered as the battle developed. The first targets lay between the Rhine and the eastern frontiers of Holland and Belgium, and were mainly concerned with transportation on railways, and oil-depots; the second general series of targets, still devoted to transportation, was applied to specific crossings of rivers and other points of rail and road concentration; the third series of targets, and the one finally considered to be most important by the French High Command, was concerned with areas where reconnaissance established that there was congestion behind the German front line.

East of the Rhine, direct hits were registered on main roads, *autobahn* roads, railway junctions and lines, bridge-road approaches, military encampments, and mechanized columns. One operation made in the night of May 15 by Wellington and Whitley bombers was in direct support of Allied infantry countering an enemy attack in the neighbourhood of Turnhout and Dinant.

Oil-storage depots were an important part of the targets for Bomber Command, for there was at that time a theory that oil was the scarcest commodity in the German war supplies. In the night of May 17 oil-storage tanks at Hamburg and Bremen were bombed, and further attacks extended southward to Sedan, including enemy aerodromes, troop columns, and road and rail junctions. Opposition came from massed searchlights, anti-aircraft batteries, balloon barrages, and occasional enemy fighters. A few of the bombers failed to find their targets and returned with their load of bombs. The oil-depots at Bremen were attacked in relays for five hours, and more than 300 high-explosive and incendiary bombs were dropped on them; the terrific explosion from a direct hit sent vast sheets of flame to a height of nearly 2000 feet. One sergeant pilot said, "It so lit up the sky that even at 10,000 feet one could have read the smallest print. A huge black mushroom of smoke spread over the town." The captain of one of the force of Hampdens that raided Hamburg said:

We could see the barrage all round us. It seemed to be just one continual stream that might almost have been coming from several hundred hose-pipes. But we managed to keep a straight course at the right moment and to drop our bombs with accuracy.

When we arrived over our objectives we saw an enormous fire blazing. The flames were so brilliant that they lit up the sky and countryside for about fifty miles all round. When we left there were two more fires burning—right on the target.

Some of the petroleum-depots were located by the earliest bombers to arrive over Hamburg by means of parachute flares. Fires started

72

with incendiary bombs spread rapidly and helped to guide the following aircraft. Vast clouds of acrid black smoke—proof of the oil-base nature of the fires—rolled slowly over Hamburg when the last of the raiders left the neighbourhood of the city, indicating destruction which innumerable searchlights, intense anti-aircraft gunfire, and a balloon barrage had been unable to prevent.

The method of bombing at that period of the war is well illustrated by this raid on Hamburg. The bombers were dispatched singly, at intervals, squadron by squadron launching a succession of 'waves.' Perhaps the use of the term 'waves' (although then current) was wrong; the resultant effect in the sky was more like a series of dots, widely spaced, forming a number of more or less rhythmic lines of separate aircraft moving through the moonlit sky from England towards their selected targets in Germany. The procedure in bombing was deliberate. It was then the intention to make bombing a precision operation, and an attempt was made to make the bomb approximate to the accuracy of the shell fired from a gun. Indeed, that was the one way to get a reasonable effect from the relatively small force of bombers available. The test of war and the growth of fire-power were to impose different methods upon the aircraft of Bomber Command as the war proceeded.

Thus we find, in that first raid on Hamburg, one bomber captain reporting, "By the light of the moon we were able to get a clear view of our target. We did a slow run up, took our time about it, dropped our bombs, and came home unmolested."

The crew of another Hampden arrived over their target to find it already on fire. The pilot circled round for nearly five minutes "to be quite sure that he had arrived at the right address." Then, satisfied of his position, he launched his attack and saw a number of small fires break out and quickly develop into one large blaze.

In this manner the raid continued from ten o'clock on Friday night until dawn on Saturday morning. No casualties were incurred by the bomber crews, and all the aircraft returned safely from the operation. No aircraft were lost that night. One Whitley was hit by a light-calibre shell; it damaged the wireless compartment, but injured no member of the crew. The captain of a Hampden saw a Messerschmitt 110 night fighter below him and to the right. He dived and turned and brought the enemy aircraft into point-blank range. A burst of bullets from the Hampden's rear gun struck one engine of the Messerschmitt, and the fighter disappeared from view in a shower of sparks. Another German fighter closed in on a Wellington, only to be engaged at close range by the twin machine-guns in the bomber's front and rear turrets, firing in turn. Streams of tracer bullets appeared to enter the fighter's fuselage. The German pilot broke off the combat abruptly, and dived into the clouds.

The targets for the night included (in addition to the major targets at Bremen and Hamburg) aerodromes, railway-lines, and road- and rail-bridges across the Meuse and in the occupied areas of Belgium and France. At Namur bombs burst on a rail-bridge over the Meuse; four direct hits were made on a road-bridge, whose eastern span was seen to collapse. South of Namur heavy bombs were dropped on a bridge across the Sambre river, and three bursts straddled the target. A road-bridge over the Meuse at Dinant collapsed after being hit. Crews were guided to their target here by moonlight reflecting from the curving river. West of Givet one bomber attacked a mechanized column ten to twelve miles long on the Beauraing road, and after releasing its bombs dived to within 700 feet and opened fire with machine-guns upon the enemy. Other bombers bombed the road and a railway-line near it. Searchlights which blinded the crews made it difficult for them to pin-point their targets, and one pilot reported tersely, "Searchlights south of Namur which interfered with the bombing were machine-gunned."

Night after night these operations were continued from the bases of Bomber Command in England. Oil-storage tanks were bombed at Misburg, a few miles from Hanover, in the night of May 18; the attack began shortly before midnight and continued for about two hours during which heavy explosive and incendiary bombs were dropped. The opposition of guns placed around the target was never fierce enough to interfere with the development of the bombing. On May 19 the night attacks were directed against railways, stations, and bridges south of Brussels. The railway-bridge at Roux received a direct hit. The permanent way and rolling stock were damaged. Troop and tank concentrations in the Aisne sector were attacked. Near Sedan a lorry-park was set on fire. Two of our bombers failed to return that night.

On the morning of May 20 Blenheims attacked armoured vehicles in the Arras-Cambrai area; during the afternoon the scene of attack shifted with the flow of the ground forces to the Arras-Bapaume area. In the succeeding night a large force of bombers attacked troop concentrations in the Cambrai-Saint-Quentin-Le Cateau area. A successful attack was made on enemy troops in the Nuvion forest, north of the Aisne river. Oil-tanks in Rotterdam were bombed and set on fire. On the following day both fighter and bomber aircraft were continuously engaged in operations over a wide and confused fighting front in Belgium and France.

During these operations long columns of mechanized units were harassed and often disorganized, and at places roads and bridges in the path of the advancing German armies were bombed and destroyed. Near a village off one of the main roads leading to Cambrai one section of Blenheims attacked a mile-long procession of motor transport; nearer Cambrai another section attacked motorized units which were protected by pom-poms and light guns on mobile platforms. All the German columns were accompanied by anti-aircraft units.

In the district of Bapaume, cross-roads and important railway-lines were temporarily made unusable.

Wellington bombers concentrated on a triangular area between Cambrai, Saint-Quentin, and Hirson, searching systematically in the light of a full moon for troops and transport on the move, and troop concentrations taking cover in woods and forests. A raging fire spread over a wide area of Nuvion forest. Machine-gun posts in the open spaces of the forest were attacked and silenced. One Wellington passing over the Raismes forest bombed the remains of an ammunition-dump and completed its destruction. Near Le Cateau a convoy of heavy lorries received bombs at the head and centre of the convoy, and was then swept by machine-gun fire from one Wellington. The railway junction and station at Wassigny received four hits. Two bombs destroyed a canal-bridge near Guise, a stationary train outside Le Cateau was hit twice, motor vehicles passing through the Forest of Mormal were attacked. Shadows thrown on the roads by the trees made it difficult for air crews to identify all targets. One pilot made five close investigations before deciding that what he saw were the shadows of poplar-trees and not troops.

Whitley and Hampden bombers concentrated south-east of Cambrai bombed important cross-roads, and a bridge over the Oise at Mont d'Origny was left sagging in the middle until the carriage-way almost touched the water.

In the night of May 21 objectives included railway junctions, marshalling-yards, and bridges lying over a wide area radiating eastward across Germany from Aachen (Aix-la-Chapelle); and in the immediate rear of the battle area, roads and bridges across the Meuse in the region of Namur and Dinant were attacked.

At the time these attacks were described in official bulletins as "repeated," "heavy," "vigorous," and as made with "strong forces" —all adjectives which must be reconciled with the comparatively small-scale force which was then available. Often a target, even an important one, was allotted to a single aircraft, for the simple reason that targets were so numerous and aircraft, in comparison, so few, that what could be done had to be the deciding factor, and not what was necessary to achieve complete results. There is no doubt that the measure of air support accorded to the armies during the fighting retreat after the German break-through at Sedan was full; the limit was the measure, not the spirit.

It was reported that from the air the head of the German advance presented, at times, a picture of utter chaos. Often bombing was made impossible because of the difficulty of identifying enemy columns among the streams of refugees overtaken by the rapid German advance. On one road, reconnoitred at a height of a thousand feet, some forty to fifty green-painted German lorries were seen hopelessly intermingled with pedestrians, ambulances, civilian cars, tradesmen's vans, and bicycles. A few miles away a road-bridge over a river was packed with civilian transport making a precarious way around a gaping bomb-hole almost in the centre of the carriage-way. But at other points, where enemy troops had drawn ahead of the civilian traffic, bombing objectives were clearly defined. A convoy of armoured lorries, three miles long, was bombed by two low-flying Blenheims, and fires were seen to break out among the vehicles immediately after the attack. Another Blenheim overshot its convoy target, but saw its bombs register a direct hit on an enemy tank standing in a field close by. Fast-moving columns of light-armoured fighting vehicles, escorted by a strong force of motor-cycle combinations, were intercepted on a main road north of Abbeville and many direct hits were observed on the closely packed vehicles; explosions were seen to break out. A long column of armoured vehicles, partially hidden in a wood near Abbeville, was bombed by eleven Blenheims which dropped more than 150 bombs upon and around it.

During daylight fighter aircraft from England were engaged in protective patrols for the British bombers operating over Belgium and the North of France.

During the night of May 21 anti-aircraft gunners on the East Coast of England failed to get a recognition signal from an approaching air-craft, and opened fire. It was a Hampden bomber, crippled by German gunners. The crew, all except the pilot, had baled out over Germany. Single-handed, the pilot nursed the Hampden across the North Sea, fighting to maintain height for mile after mile. As he crossed the English coast a searchlight picked up the aircraft. The pilot was 'all in.' The bomber was in no condition to make a safe landing. The pilot said, "Well, thank God, that's England, anyway," opened his door, and stepped out into the night at the very moment that the gunners opened fire. The pilot floated down to a safe landing on a road, where he was able to establish his identity.

During the night of May 22 four heavy bombs from a Hampden hit an ammunition train at Geldern, a German town near the Dutch frontier. "We were about 2000 feet up when we first saw the train standing in a yard," said the navigator-bomb-aimer. "We made a level attack, dropping four high-explosive and fourteen incendiary bombs. Almost immediately the train burst into flames and blew up. The whole train just went sky-high. While it was burning we made a couple of fairly wide circuits around it and counted eighteen explosions, all more violent than anything our bombs could have produced."

Another Hampden sighted two supply-trains standing on the main railway-lines ten miles east of Liège. The pilot reported:

> I did a steep left-hand turn to get a good view of the train, and then climbed another thousand feet to drop my parachute flare. This lit up the target for about three minutes. We then turned round and did the first of six runs over the longest train. Our first bomb landed on the right bank of the line. The second was a direct hit on the rear truck. The third landed on the left embankment. I then decided to drop two bombs together. Both went crashing through the centre of the train, and there was a terrific blast of smoke and flame. We dropped another parachute flare which pierced the cloud of smoke and dust and showed wreckage lying all over the place.

Another aircraft, crossing Holland, made a detour on its way to Germany to drop a heavy bomb on the main runway of The Hague aerodrome. Behind the Belgian battlefield three Wellingtons made direct hits on cross-roads at Gembloux, the adjoining railway-track, and railway-lines at Yvoir and Binche, at the last-named hitting a road-bridge crossing the line. Whitley bombers attacked similar targets near Hirson and Givet. "We were over the target area at Hirson for over an hour before we attacked," said one of the Whitley pilots, "and by that time were quite sure of our target. We opened up with a couple of heavyweights which burst right on the railway junction, and followed those up with a salvo of six more bombs which fell on the railway-line itself."

Farther south, between Valenciennes and Dinant, Wellingtons attacked columns of mechanized forces and lorries.

On May 24 Fleet Air Arm aircraft based in Britain attacked German tanks near the Channel coast, setting three on fire and putting others out of action. Coastal Command co-operated on the morning of May 25 with an attack on the oil-depots at Rotterdam. They sank an enemy motor-torpedo-boat off the Dutch coast.

Day after day the work of destruction went on. Night after night the heavy bombers attacked. The very monotony of the types of target which were attacked day after day and night after night shows that

77

it was impossible by these methods with the available force to hold up the rolling tide of Prussian might. The tale unfolded relentlessly to the climacteric of Dunkirk, that heroic evacuation which is at the same time a story of an army—nay, a nation—unprovided with the weapons of war; indeed, the frightful paradox of war is that the greatest deeds of heroism are accomplished when the odds are overwhelming, but it is seldom that the responsibility for these overwhelming odds can be charged to those who have to face the consequences with their valour.

By May 24 Blenheim bombers were locating and bombing German motorized units on the coast-roads near Boulogne. The Blenheims kept up an almost continuous series of sorties from early morning until nightfall. British home-based fighters were by then encountering strong enemy bomber formations with large fighter escorts, and many air fights were fought over the low-lying sand-dune and chalk-cliff coastline of Northern France. Some of the home-based heavy bombers were deflected that night to attack targets around the area wherein the British Expeditionary Force was contracting its periphery, but the small-scale nature of these attacks is well illustrated in the following Air Ministry account:

> The attack on the aerodrome at Flushing began shortly after midnight, and in the first raid a salvo of high-explosive bombs fell close enough to the hangars to cause considerable damage. Ten minutes later another aircraft arriving on the scene inflicted further damage round the eastern boundary of the aerodrome. Incendiaries were also scattered over the target area, and many fires were started. The captain of a third bomber, flying over Flushing two hours later, reported that buildings on the aerodrome were still burning fiercely. The bridges over the canal which links the river Maas to the Rhine at Zaltbommel were bombed from a low altitude, and both were badly damaged.

Nevertheless, these single, solitary raiding bombers which cruised the night skies of Western Europe sometimes achieved an amazing local success. In the night of May 24 a British bomber approached North Geldern station, a few miles from German soil, and its crew saw a troop-train steaming into the station, where a goods train was already standing. A parachute flare was dropped. About ten machine-guns opened fire at the bomber from the roof of the troop-train. A member of the bomber's crew said, "We met and ran through a curtain of green tracer bullets to drop a salvo of bombs. The noise was deafening. We thought we had blown ourselves up. Later we saw large bits of carriage and truck flying about in all directions. The wreckage soon caught fire, and in a very short time the whole place was ablaze. As every nook and cranny of the town seemed to have an anti-aircraft gun we wasted no time in getting way."

The anti-aircraft gunfire encountered by the night bombers became steadily heavier as the German armies advanced and consolidated their gains. During one attack the pilot of a bomber heard loud, cheerful laughter in the headphones of his intercommunication telephone; it came from the air gunner in the rear turret. Shells were bursting all round them. As the pilot took violent evasive action he asked the gunner, "What on earth are you laughing at? I can't see anything funny in this." "Well," came the reply, "isn't it funny to think that all that stuff is meant for us?" Laughter is sometimes the reaction to the first doses of shellfire.

The attack on railway lines of communication continued night after night in accordance with the requirements of the Joint Staff. In the night of May 24 a train was wrecked ten miles west of Düren, and railway junctions at Jemelle and Libremont were bombed. One bomber attacked a train on a viaduct near Namur. The pilot of the bomber reported the moonlight visibility to be so clear that he could count the arches of the viaduct. The first two bombs fell short. The next four, dropped in a salvo, scored a direct hit on the train and on the foot of the viaduct. "Afterwards," said the pilot, "we again circled the scene and observed that only the front half of the train was left." Twenty minutes earlier this same aircraft had bombed lorries west of Namur. "We dropped four bombs which burst in the middle of them," the pilot reported. And before that a road and railway crossing was bombed to stop the progress of a train seen travelling near Namur.

At Louvain the railway junction was set on fire by a low-level attack. At Audenghen two bombs hit a bridge and others straddled important cross-roads. Between these two places German road convoys were bombed and machine-gunned. Elsewhere one convoy was halted three miles from La Capelle; a bomb burst in the middle of the column; when the railway junction at Saint-Quentin was attacked four heavy bombs fell directly on the track; part of the road between Jülich and Grevenbroich was made unusable.

One Whitley was detailed to bomb a bridge over the Oise. Owing to bad visibility the pilot came down to 300 feet to locate the target; he did so successfully, but while flying low through a heavy barrage of anti-aircraft fire one of the engines was badly hit; in spite of the damage the pilot managed to climb to 3000 feet and carried out his attack. He then attempted to reach the French lines, and got as far as Amiens—which was occupied by the Germans that night—when the damaged engine caught fire and the crew of five had to bale out.

They landed by parachute in the dark. When light came three of the crew met, joined the stream of refugees, made their way to the coast, and got home to England. A fourth member of the crew reached home singly, but the fifth was missing.

The second pilot of this Whitley was a pilot officer. A fortnight later he was promoted to be captain of his own aircraft, and his first raid over Germany as captain was successful. On the next raid, shortly after leaving his base, one of the crew accidentally let off a flare inside the bomber. Thinking the aircraft was on fire, the captain gave the order to abandon aircraft. But before himself leaving he had a good look round, and decided to stay on board ; he succeeded in landing safely at the nearest aerodrome with his full load of bombs.

But his adventures were not over. He went out again, four nights after the flare incident; this time one of his engines was damaged by anti-aircraft fire and the oil-pressure fell to zero. He throttled down that engine and got back to an aerodrome in Britain on the other one. When coming in to land he tried to use the failing engine to assist his approach (to avoid the offset pull from one engine), but the defective engine immediately caught fire. He managed to get to the ground safely.

A week later his wireless burnt out before he reached the enemy coast, and he had to return; but on the following night his task was completed successfully. Next night he went out to attack a target in the Ruhr. While attempting to run up to the target he was caught by enemy searchlights and anti-aircraft fire. He was unable to complete his attack, and sheered off to the north to an alternative target. During this run-up a Messerschmitt 109 attacked, wounded the wireless operator and the observer, and cut the intercommunication system. Not realizing what had happened, the pilot continued his run-up.

About four minutes later [he said] another attack was delivered, and immediately I turned violently to port and saw a Messerschmitt 109 in a steep dive, having been shot down by the rear gunner. I then continued my run-up and bombed the blast furnace with one stick, but had to jettison the remaining bombs owing to the starboard engine catching fire. The fire was put out with the engine extinguisher, but on attempting to use the engine again it immediately caught fire and was therefore switched off. Nursing my port engine, I reached the Dutch coast at 2000 feet and there gave all my crew the option of abandoning aircraft or carrying on, explaining the grave risk of a landing in the sea. All members of the crew decided to carry on, saying: "Last time you told us to jump you got the machine down safely. We're not going to jump now!"

They got back to the coast of Kent as dawn was breaking.

It will be realized how closely these night raids by aircraft flying singly to bomb targets by precision bombing conformed to the methods tried out in the pre-war exercises.[1] It will be understood, too, that damage of the nature inflicted over widely scattered areas on pin-point targets, while causing trouble to the advancing German armies, was similar to the action of a few mosquitoes attacking an elephant. The German staff, too, had foreseen that bridges would be a target selected for destruction from the air, and ample supplies of material and well-trained troops were in the field to repair destruction of this kind rapidly. Indeed, unless the destruction of bridges and railway junctions were succeeded by attacks to prevent work from being carried out upon the damaged points, it proved that repairs or replacements good enough to meet the transport requirements of the German armies were fairly easily and comparatively swiftly carried out. A round-the-clock offensive against the vital traffic arteries and their junctions was impossible, because the long-range bombers able to carry heavy loads of bombs were all night bombers and were employed only at night during this period of the war; the day bombers were employed in close support of the land units actually in contact with the enemy; the numbers of both types of bomber were too few to deal effective blows at every part of the tremendous area of the operations. All that could be expected of the available force of aircraft was done. That was to help to slow up the German advance and thus to enable the retreat of the Allied armies to be made in an orderly manner.

Without evidence from the German side it is impossible to assess how great was the part played by the Royal Air Force in making the retreat to Dunkirk possible, but there can be no doubt that without the air assistance which was given the result of that retreat might have been very different. And in the relative effect of heavy bomber dealing strategic blows at night, day bomber pounding away at the tactical targets by day, and fighter aircraft protecting the ground forces from excessive enemy air attack, it is difficult to apportion more merit to one than to another. The marvel was that the energy of the air effort remained cohesive throughout the whole action; it was never dispersed; and for that valuable contribution to the eventual outcome of the war the ability to base the largest proportion of the aircraft (and all the night bombers) in Britain was largely responsible. For the Germans, intent upon their immediate objectives, confined their air attacks to strategic and tactical objectives in France, and permitted the Royal Air Force in Britain to operate unimpeded by the stress of circumstances that had to be countered by the Advanced Air Striking Force throughout its retreat before the advancing enemy.

[1] See Vol. I, pp. 66–74.

As the Germans advanced to the Channel coast, the tactical targets selected for the day bombers became ever more widely separated from the strategic targets of the night bombers. In the broad stretch of countryside between the two target zones the Germans were able to consolidate the forces brought through the rear target zone and deploy them for attack within the forward target zone. The lesson learned here was that inferior air-power used against advancing enemy land forces, especially when the enemy is in greater strength and more heavily armed, cannot constitute a holding force, but can only slow down the rate of advance, and inflict casualties among the enemy. If greater air-power had been available to the Allies before the Battle of France it could not have prevented the defeat of France, because of the faulty strategy, disposition of forces, lack of cohesion between the four Allies, and insufficiency of the mechanized forces in the field everywhere. When the ratio of four to one against the Royal Air Force is added to the other factors militating against successful defence, the rapid course of the battle and the prostration of France in six weeks is revealed as a triumph of inevitability. The French and British armies were mobilized in August 1939. The German Army was mobilized in March 1935.[1] Nothing that the air could do could alter that discrepancy in political preparedness. Excess air strength over Germany might have restrained the leader of the Third Reich from precipitating war; it would have delayed the defeat of France; it is impossible to say more, for air-power is primarily an offensive power, and its full strokes are most advantageous, not in retreat, but in advance.

Already the German advance dictated the work of the Royal Air Force. By May 25 the day bombers were forced to concentrate their attacks against pontoon and road bridges crossing the river Lys, over which German reinforcements were reaching the Belgian battle-front, and against mechanized columns moving towards Boulogne. In the morning a long column of supply lorries was located on a main road near Boulogne. It was continuously attacked for fifteen minutes by a force of bombers; nearly two hundred bombs were dropped, the heavier bombs from a height, the smaller bombs from as low as ninety feet. Messerschmitt 109 fighters tried to intercept the Blenheims; they were fought off, and one was crashed and another badly damaged. Large bodies of troops, massing in a town in the German rear of the battlefield, were heavily bombed.

During the succeeding night heavy bombers were engaged against targets in the Rhineland and in the rear of the battlefield. Among objectives hit were an ammunition- and petrol-dump, a bridge, troop-

[1] See Vol. I, pp. 18–19.

and goods trains, two aerodromes, and motor vehicles. During the night Blenheims from Britain and Battles from France attacked targets within the fighting area, including armoured vehicles, ammunition-dumps, and artillery. Two heavy and four medium bombers were lost.

During the following night, in addition to attacks against similar targets, the aerodromes at Flushing, Evere-Brussels, Deurne-Antwerp, Venlo, and Charleroi were attacked. The attacks continued, and on May 29 it was possible to report that "the enemy's advance has been considerably harassed and impeded by these attacks."

The men who made the bomber attacks were coached before starting on their perilous journeys. At every Bomber Command aerodrome was a briefing-room where air crews attended before a raid. The pilots and navigators sat in rows. In front of them, on a small platform, were a table and chair, on the wall behind the table a screen, and at the far end of the room a magic lantern. When the crews took their places the Intelligence Officer mounted the platform and explained in great detail the object of the forthcoming raid. Then the room was darkened, and slides were thrown upon the screen, made from photographs some-times obtained by reconnaissance aircraft, showing perhaps an oil-refinery, an aerodrome, a hydrogenation plant, a section of the Kiel Canal, or an enemy warship; and upon the projected picture the Intelligence Officer pointed out detail, while the watching men listened eagerly, for the difference between success and failure might hang upon what they were told and understood. Each pilot and navigator already possessed a photograph of his target, and upon this they wrote notes which might help them later. At the end of the briefing the Intelligence Officer asked for questions. Some he would answer personally. Others concerning the practical side of the operation were answered by the Station Commander, who had taken his place at the back of the room. Positions of anti-aircraft guns, searchlights, balloon barrages, were discussed, until there were no more questions and the crews were ready to set out on their missions primed with precise, up-to-date, and expert knowledge.

But everything on Royal Air Force stations was not always serious. Sometimes comedy was present. On one occasion an Orderly Room flight sergeant made arrangements for a leading aircraftman-storekeeper to see the Commanding Officer. The storekeeper complained of bad treatment he alleged he had received at the hands of an N.C.O., but he was unable to put his case plainly and was apt to ramble in his statement.

"It's no good talking like that," said the C.O. "You must give me something concrete."

"Sorry, sir," replied the storekeeper, "but that's not an Air Force issue."

§ 4

Battle of the Channel Ports

In the afternoon of May 21 a German column of all arms approached Boulogne, from which the rear elements of G.H.Q. had been evacuated to Wimereux the day before owing to enemy bombing. British bomber support was at once asked for; enemy tanks were located at Hesdin and Fruges and bombed, but no good targets were found on the coast road.

Already it was becoming clear that bomber attacks against tanks were not entirely satisfactory. The tank was, by its very construction, an air-raid shelter, and nothing short of a direct hit could be relied upon to do destructive damage. At that time no British aircraft were armed with heavier weapons than machine-guns firing rifle-calibre ammunition : these were useless against armoured vehicles, except for the chance of a lucky shot passing through a raised visor.

A detachment of Royal Marines was landed at Boulogne. On May 22, in the early morning, two battalions of the 20th Guards Brigade and an anti-tank battery followed them to the port. By the evening of that day the German advanced forces were less than nine miles from Calais, and Boulogne was isolated; both ports were out of action; the greater part of the British Railhead Mechanical Transport Companies was captured. The decision to maintain the British Expeditionary Force through the northern ports was taken on May 21 when the headquarters of a Base Sub-area was established at Dunkirk, together with a section of the Quartermaster-General's staff, in close touch with British and French naval authorities. Rail communications were precarious. There were but three days' supplies in the forward area. The force north of the gap required a daily lift of all supplies amounting to 2000 tons. With transport facilities steadily contracting all about them, the B.E.F. was placed on half-rations on May 23.

The air fighting over the French coast between Boulogne and Ostend grew fiercer every day as the Germans strove to defeat and capture the British Expeditionary Force. A Miles Master two-seater training aircraft had been sent across the Channel to rescue a squadron leader from Calais-Marck aerodrome, where he had been shot down. Two Spitfires of No. 54 squadron escorted it. The little cavalcade was attacked by twelve Messerschmitts when taking off at Calais, but the two Spitfires counter-attacked and destroyed one Messerschmitt each.

84

shared in the destruction of another, probably destroyed a fourth, and damaged two others. The Master was undamaged. For his share in that fight Flight Lieutenant A. C. Deere was awarded the D.F.C. Two days later he was one of a section of three fighters on patrol over the Channel. They met two Junkers 88's and destroyed one. Deere, pulling out of his dive attack, saw the second Junkers right in his gun-sight, pressed the fire-button, and shot the German bomber into the sea. (Three years later, as a wing commander, he was the leader of the Biggin Hill fighter wing when it claimed its one thousandth victim, and was awarded the D.S.O. to add to the D.F.C. and Bar which he already held; by that time his personal score had risen to $20\frac{1}{2}$ enemy aircraft destroyed.)

On May 23, between Calais and Boulogne, No. 92 squadron, re-formed in October 1939, went into its first engagement and destroyed at least ten enemy aircraft. The British squadron's commanding officer was shot down in this, his first, fight. Many months afterwards his 'combat report' was received by the squadron in his own hand-writing—from a prisoner-of-war camp in Germany. The squadron leader wrote:

I was shot down by Messerschmitt 110's, but managed to get two of them first. As soon as the battle started about four or five of the Messerschmitts fell on me and, oh, boy, did I start dodging! My first I got with a full deflection shot underneath. He went down in a long glide with his port engine pouring smoke. I went into a spin as two others were firing at me from my aft quarter. I only did one turn of the spin and pulled out left and up. I then saw a Messer-schmitt below me and trying to fire up at me, so I went head-on at him, and he came head-on at me. We were both firing, and every-thing was red flashes. I know I killed the pilot, because suddenly he pulled right up at me and missed me by inches. I went over the top of him and as I turned I saw him rear right up in a stall and go down with his engine smoking. I hadn't got long to watch, but he was out of control and half on his back. My engine was badly shot up and caught fire. My machine was pouring glycol. I don't quite know what happened, but I turned things off and was out of control for a while but got straight at about 5000 feet.

I shut everything off and the fire went out and I glided down. There was a lot of glycol, and I could not see anything much, but I turned the petrol on again and tried to make Saint-Inglevert aerodrome. The engine ran for a little while and then everything seized and a lot of smoke and fumes came into the cockpit. I reckoned it was time to bale out, and opened and undid everything. However, there appeared to be no fire, so I decided to land, undercarriage up. This I did successfully and only took a knock on the nose. When I hit, the old girl burst into flames and, as you can imagine, I moved pretty quickly.

I landed just to the east of Boulogne and, of course, imagined I had come down in friendly territory. The machine was blazing, but I had a look at it and could see some pretty hefty holes.

After I landed I sat by my machine and when a motor-bike came down the road I thought it was French. It wasn't, and there was nothing to be done about it. Thereafter I had a long journey here. This is an Air Force Camp, where we are treated very well indeed.

Dunkirk was subjected to constant air raids. Its water-supply was destroyed. Working under almost intolerable strain, stevedore battalions worked in the port unloading supplies until May 26, when all the quays and cranes were put out of action. Thereafter supplies could be landed only on the beaches. The delivery of ammunition, water, and supplies continued irregularly until May 30, carried in lighters which arrived to embark troops.

On May 23 Calais was isolated. During the succeeding night Boulogne was evacuated under the orders of the War Office. For a brief interval it was proposed to abandon Calais, but finally Brigadier Claude Nicholson, in command, received orders from General Sir Edmund Ironside, the Chief of the Imperial General Staff, to remain. The original garrison had been reinforced by the 30th Infantry Brigade, 3rd Battalion Royal Tank Regiment (with both cruiser- and light tanks), and an anti-tank battery of the Royal Artillery; German reconnaissance aircraft had observed the crossing of their first transports to Calais on May 22. The defence of Calais was a grim affair which engaged two German Panzer divisions for four days and prevented them from interfering with a vital part of the withdrawal of the main body of the British Expeditionary Force upon Dunkirk.

At first air bombing was not severe, for oil-tanks west of Calais town had been set on fire, and the black smoke from their burning hung over the defenders and screened them from the German bombers. Gunfire was then more trying. The Brigadier wanted a bomber force to attack the enemy batteries and enemy troops in immediate reserve. He wanted guns, but it was then too late to get heavier guns over to him. Two destroyers gave support whenever possible.

Gradually the perimeter defences were driven in. Ammunition became precious; men became weary. At about eight o'clock on May 26 Brigadier Nicholson refused a German demand to surrender, although the enemy by then held most of Calais, and what was British-held was under shell and machine-gun fire, while food and water were scarce.

Part of the end of the stand of Calais is told by Eric Linklater in the official publication *The Defence of Calais* thus:

At nine o'clock [on Sunday, May 26] the general bombardment began again; and now the German artillery was reinforced from the air.

The dive-bombers came. From ten o'clock, or a little before, there was almost incessant low-level bombing till some time in the afternoon, and the damage it did was enormous. The bombers came in nearly continuous relay to attack the inner town, the Citadel, and the docks. For a long time there were always three squadrons [a German squadron was nine machines] of the enemy overhead; one squadron bombing, another circling and waiting to attack, the third returning for more bomb-loads. New fires broke out, and our defensive positions fell in ruins. The narrow streets were filled with the debris of shattered houses. . . . Bren guns were almost our only defence against the Luftwaffe, and they, no matter how valiantly used, were insufficient.

. . . The air bombardment did not drive the defence underground, did not defeat it. The enemy had to send in his infantry and tanks and mortars. When the bombers had done their share, the enemy used his medium tanks for close fighting. . . . Tanks were advancing, German machine-gunners were enfilading the streets. . . .

Very early in the morning of May 27 some Army Co-operation planes appeared overhead, and were met by German anti-aircraft fire. They circled the town, and dropped packages of food and ammunition. But they had come too late, and the supplies fell into alien hands. . . . Air reconnaissance at noon could find no British troops in the town. The defence of Calais had come to an end. . . .

It does not seem that any attempt to reinforce the garrison would have been justified. The German attack was delivered with such strength and speed that, by the time reinforcements were ready, a major operation would have been necessary to put them ashore.

The conditions of the defence within a perimeter of about eight miles may have made the possibility of reinforcement by air-borne troops impossible, because they would have been under enemy fire during their descent by parachute. But even if the conditions had rendered such method of reinforcement possible the operation could not have been carried out, because there was no air-borne unit in the British defence services, and many months were to pass before the first British paratroops were to be launched in action from the skies. These descended in Southern Italy in a small band during the night of February 10, 1941, charged with the duty of sabotaging Italian rail communications. But our first real full-scale employment of para-troops occurred during the Battle of El Alamein in October 1942, and in the Anglo-American landings in North Africa in November 1942 and the subsequent attack upon Tunisia. The significance of American and Russian air-borne troop experiments during pre-war manœuvres was lost upon every nation but the German, who employed highly trained air-borne troops from the beginning of their campaign to introduce the element of tactical surprise, and who, later, also employed an air-borne tank division equipped with 12-ton tanks to reinforce the troops in Tunisia during the advance of the British First Army from Algeria.

But if British military education in war-time is slow it is also thorough, although the price that has to be paid for it is often costly, in men, material, and treasure. Brigadier Nicholson died as a prisoner in 1943.

§ 5

Dunkirk

The German attack upon the forces north of the gap and held in Flanders now appeared as a pincer movement, whose southern prong was directed against Dunkirk from the south-west, and whose northern arm was aimed at the Belgian front. There was a serious risk that the Belgian armies' right flank might be separated from the British left flank in the neighbourhood of Menin and thus force the Belgian armies to withdraw in a northerly rather than in a westerly direction.

At this period preparations were in hand to meet the requirements of the Weygand plan, which was, in effect, to execute a counter-offensive on a large scale, by a combined force comprising units of the French, British, and Belgian armies. The plan existed as an idea, rather than as a fully organized and worked-out movement. It was the embodiment of the obvious, without the means to carry it out. According to the plan, the French First Army and the B.E.F. and the Belgian Cavalry Corps were to attack south-west about eight divisions strong, while the newly formed Third French Army Group was to attack northward from Amiens to Péronne, and a new cavalry corps assembling south of the Somme near Neufchâtel was to attack on the line of the Somme west of Amiens in touch with the British armoured division on their left.

In point·of fact, none of the armies north of the gap could afford the troops required to execute the southerly attack because they were all sorely needed to serve as reserves to parry the strong German thrusts which were being launched in Flanders. The troops which were to provide the northerly striking force were unorganized for the purpose, and before they could do anything the situation in Flanders had so deteriorated as to make the attack in a southerly direction a pure gambler's throw. Lord Gort decided instead to consolidate his own peri-meter position and proceed to execute the retirement upon Dunkirk.[1]

[1] In his second dispatch, General Viscount Gort, C.-in-C. B.E.F., stated: "I fully appreciated the importance of attacking early before the enemy could bring up his infantry in strength, but facts had to be faced. The 5th and 50th Divisions [earmarked for the attack southward] were on this day (May 23) still closely engaged with the enemy, and 2nd, 44th, and 48th Divisions would not become available for a further 48 hours, since the French and the Belgians, though they had arranged their relief, could not complete it earlier. The

On May 22 Mr Churchill visited Paris and conferred with M. Reynaud and General Weygand. On May 23 Lord Gort received a copy of a telegram from Mr Churchill to M. Reynaud:

> Strong enemy armoured forces have cut communications of Northern Armies. Salvation of these Armies can only be obtained by immediate execution of Weygand's plan. I demand that French Commanders in North and South Belgian G.Q.G. [Grande Quartier Général (G.H.Q. Allied Armies, under General Weygand)] be given most stringent orders to carry this out and turn defeat into victory. Time vital as supplies are short.

---

ammunition immediately available to the B.E.F. was of the order of 300 rounds per gun, and with communications cut with the main base the prospect of receiving any further supply was remote.

"The French light mechanized divisions and our own armoured units had already suffered serious losses in tanks which could not be replaced. Such information as I had received of the Belgian cavalry did not lead me to take an optimistic view of the prospect of their being able to engage, at short notice, in a battle forty miles away and on French soil.

"Experience had already shown the vital importance of close co-ordination of the allied armies in any operation. General Billotte had been appointed the co-ordinator at the conference at Mons on May 12, but in practice, the measure of co-ordination fell far short of what was required if the movements of the three allied armies were to be properly controlled.

"Except for the issue of orders to retire from the Dyle (obtained only after I had sent Major-General Eastwood to General Billotte's headquarters to represent my views), I received no written orders from the French First Group of Armies, though at the meetings between General Billotte and myself which took place from time to time, we always found ourselves in complete agreement. Unfortunately, however, General Billotte had been seriously, and, as it turned out, fatally injured in a motor accident returning from the conference which he and I had attended at Ypres on the night of May 21. General Blanchard succeeded him in command of the French First Group of Armies, and presumably succeeded to the function of co-ordination, although this was never officially confirmed.

"I telegraphed to the Secretary of State pointing out that co-ordination was essential with armies of three different nations, and that I personally could not undertake any measure of co-ordination in the forthcoming operations as I was already actively engaged on my Eastern and Southern fronts and also threatened on my Lines of Communication.

"Nevertheless, I saw General Blanchard and proposed to him that to implement our part of the Weygand plan, we should stage an attack southward with two British divisions, one French division, and the French Cavalry Corps. So far as we were concerned the attack could not take place till the 26th at the earliest owing to the reliefs which were in progress, and the need to assemble 5th and 50th Divisions. I also asked General Blanchard to inquire from G.Q.G. how such an operation could be synchronized with the attack from the line of the Somme which was said to be in process of preparation. These negotiations, as will be seen, were later continued by Sir Ronald Adam on my behalf. I emphasized, both to the Secretary of State and to General Blanchard, that the principal effort must come from the south, and that the operation of the northern forces could be nothing more than a sortie.

"I never received any information from any source as to the exact location of our own or enemy forces on the far side of the gap; nor did I receive any details or timings of any proposed attack from that direction."

On May 24 Mr Churchill again conferred with M. Reynaud and Weygand in Paris. Mr Eden, Secretary of State for War, sent the following telegram to Lord Gort:

> Both [Churchill and Reynaud] are convinced that Weygand's plan is still capable of execution and only in its execution [is there] hope of restoring the situation. Weygand reports French VII Army is advancing successfully and has captured Péronne, Albert, and Amiens. While realizing fully dangers and difficulties of your position which has been explained to Weygand it is essential that you should make every endeavour to co-operate in his plan. Should however situation on your communications make this at any time impossible you should inform us so that we can inform French and make Naval and Air arrangements to assist you should you have to withdraw on the northern coast.

It was later learned that Weygand's information that Péronne, Albert, and Amiens had been recaptured was inaccurate.

General Gort visited General Blanchard at his headquarters at Attiches early in the morning of May 26 "at a moment when the enemy was attacking at Carvin and had penetrated the front of a North African Division near Bois d'Epinoy." Lord Gort found that General Blanchard also feared the collapse of the Belgian Army and felt that the time for a counter-attack southward was past, and had already decided that the situation on both flanks made it necessary to withdraw. "With this decision," stated Lord Gort, "there vanished the last opportunity for a sortie."

General Gort returned from General Blanchard's headquarters at about 10.30 A.M. and found a telegram from the Secretary of State for War, Mr Eden:

> I have had information all of which goes to show that French offensive from Somme cannot be made in sufficient strength to hold any prospect of functioning with your Allies in the North. Should this prove to be the case you will be faced with a situation in which the safety of the B.E.F. will predominate. In such conditions only course open to you may be to fight your way back to West where all beaches and ports east of Gravelines will be used for embarkation. Navy will provide fleet of ships and small boats and R.A.F. would give full support. As withdrawal may have to begin very early preliminary plans should be urgently prepared. . . . Prime Minister is seeing M. Reynaud to-morrow afternoon when whole situation will be clarified including attitude of French to the possible move. . . .

Later in the day the following telegram came from the War Office:

> . . . Prime Minister had conversation M. Reynaud this afternoon. Latter fully explained to him the situation and resources of French Army. It is clear that it will not be possible for French to deliver

attack on the South in sufficient strength to enable them to effect junction with Northern Armies. In these circumstances no course open to you but to fall back upon coast. . . . M. Reynaud communicating General Weygand and latter will no doubt issue orders in this sense forthwith. You are now authorized to operate towards coast forthwith in conjunction with French and Belgian Armies.

General Gort made arrangements for the shortening of the perimeter-line of 128 miles held by British and French forces (97 miles of which were held by the B.E.F.) to 70 miles, but there was the possibility that the stretch of 25 miles between Ypres and the sea held by Belgian troops might have to be occupied by British troops. Shortly after 11 P.M. on May 27 General Gort learned from the French General Koeltz that the King of the Belgians had asked for an armistice from midnight that night, and the British Commander-in-Chief found himself faced with an open gap, by then twenty miles wide, between Ypres and the sea. For the first time the streams of refugees on the roads assisted the Allies by holding back the German forces which were free to move forward to the gap after the Belgian cessation of fighting at four o'clock in the morning of May 28. The War Office telegram informing General Gort of the Belgian capitulation was received at British headquarters at 1.30 A.M. on May 28. The enemy was forestalled in the occupation of the part of the perimeter left vacant by the Belgian 'cease fire,' at first solely by a troop of the 12th Lancers, followed by troops of various units collected for the purpose, then by troops of the 12th Infantry Brigade and Corps Artillery, and finally by the 4th Division. In the afternoon of May 28 General Gort moved his headquarters from Houtkerque to La Panne.

The action of the Belgian Commander-in-Chief, King Leopold, was foreshadowed in a note sent on May 26 by General Michiels, Chief of Staff of the Belgian Army, to General Neissens, head of the Belgian Mission with G.H.Q., which read, in part, as follows:

To-day, May 26, the Belgian Army is being attacked with extreme violence on the front Menin-Nevele [eight miles west of Ghent], and since the battle is now spreading to the whole of the area of Eecloo, the lack of Belgian reserves makes it impossible to extend our boundaries . . . farther to the right. We must therefore, with regret, say that we have no longer any forces available to fill the gap in the direction of Ypres. As regards the withdrawal to the Yser the idea must be ruled out since it would destroy our fighting units more quickly than the battle now in progress, and this without loss to the enemy.

The Belgian Army fought to the end and to the limit of its resistance. Its capitulation was the one way to avoid final and cruel, unnecessary and unavailing slaughter. Its fate, and the blows it absorbed, played a notable part in the extrication of the British Expeditionary Force, which lay within the arms of the pincers and yet eluded the closing jaws.

La Panne was in direct telephonic communication with London. Arriving there in the afternoon of May 28, Lord Gort received reports from Sir Ronald Adam and the Quarter-Master-General. No ships could be unloaded at Dunkirk. Few wounded could be evacuated. There was no water in Dunkirk and but little on the beaches. Naval plans were not in full operation, but about 10,000 men had been taken off, chiefly from Dunkirk, during the last two days. Owing to a misunderstanding, the personnel of some anti-aircraft units had been embarked. About 20,000 men were waiting on the beaches, and the area was congested with French and Belgian troops, transport, and refugees. The opinion of Sir Ronald Adam and the Q.M.G. was that, given a reasonable measure of immunity from air attack, troops could gradually be evacuated and supplies landed. But if intensive enemy air attack continued the beaches might easily become a shambles within the next forty-eight hours.

Lord Gort communicated the gist of this report to the Chief of the Imperial General Staff, Sir John Dill, who had succeeded Sir Edmund Ironside on May 26, and asked for Government policy in the event of a crisis. The answer, by telegram, was:

> If you are cut from all communication from us and all evacuation from Dunkirk and beaches had, in your judgment, been finally prevented after every attempt to reopen it had failed you would become sole judge of when it was impossible to inflict further damage to enemy.

General Weygand telegraphed to Lord Gort on the same day, appealing personally to ensure that in any counter-attacks the British Army took a vigorous part, adding that the situation made it essential to hit hard.

On May 29 the Germans began to shell Dunkirk. The beaches were constantly bombed. But the arrangements made by the Royal Navy for the re-embarkation of the troops were beginning to operate. At this period Lord Gort reported:

> I realized how heavy was the demand to be made on the Royal Air Force for the remainder of the operation, and how impossible it would be to expect that they could succeed completely in preventing air action on the beaches. Yet they did succeed in intercepting a large part of the enemy attacks, and those which arrived, though at times serious, were never able to impede our embarkation for long.

R.A.F. over Dunkirk

There is in the British people a quality of stoicism which endures the pressure of adverse circumstance with patience. That quality has acted like an amulet for centuries; from it springs the Continental saying that the British know not when they are defeated. That saying strikes at the very root of the difference between the British race and their Continental neighbours and enemies; for the latter regard defeat as a physical condition, whereas the British look upon triumph or disaster as of the spirit, to be regarded physically, as Kipling says, as "two impostors." In this spirit the troops waiting their turn for embarkation remained upon the open beaches : long lines and scattered groups of tired, patient men, in whom hope never died, from whom the thought of defeat was absent, and who knew that over the sea was England, and that England would not let them down. Behind them, along the perimeter, were the rearguards, many of whom died that those in front might live and sail home. Water was scarce in the last days, for the enemy bombed the Dunkirk water-works, and inundations from opened canal sluice-gates allowed brackish water to enter wells.

The British held the perimeter from Bergues along the line of the canals to Furnes and Nieuport. All bridges, except that at Nieuport, were blown up before the enemy reached them. French troops held the western part of the perimeter from Bergues to Mardyck. On the gently shelving beach there were no piers or quays outside Dunkirk. It was a holiday beach transformed; there were no pleasure-seekers at Malo-les-Bains, Bray-Dunes, La Panne, or Coxyde; but, ironically enough, the strangest assortment of holiday boats came to the beach to lend a hand in the grim carnival of war.

Over this small congested area of France and Belgium the Royal Air Force fought its first Homeric battle with the Luftwaffe, a fight different from those which had preceded it over the fields of France and Belgium. Those battles had been fought as actions incidental to the swaying tide of war, now here, again there, over the hills, rivers, towns, villages, poplar-lined roads, and unfenced fields of France and Belgium, as the sweep of war's ground-swell surged; this was a battle of position, an action waged to deny to the enemy a definite air space. It was the first true contest between the British and German Air Forces. And its issue marked the movement of the tide of air war.

For the Air Officer Commanding-in-Chief, Fighter Command, the period of Dunkirk was the most anxious of the war.

93

There were no aerodromes on the Continent suitable for the use of fighters operating for the protection of the troops awaiting embarkation. After the evacuation of Merville landing-ground on May 22, the R.A.F. had to conduct their fighter operations over the northern, and largest, part of the B.E.F. from aerodromes in South-eastern England. Five aerodromes—Manston (Margate), Deal, Dover, Hawkinge, and Lympne—faced the narrows of the English Channel at the Dover Strait, and the nearest of these to Dunkirk was forty-five miles across the water, in a flying line. But the Royal Air Force was ready to meet the occasion, to rise supreme over the difficulties of broken communications, and to press back the German airmen who sought to break the spirit of the British soldier. It has been suggested that the withdrawal from Dunkirk was a demonstration of the failure of air-power, because the Luftwaffe could not prevent the operation. But that suggestion was made before the Battle of Britain. The withdrawal of the British Expeditionary Force from Dunkirk might have been achieved with greater losses, or perhaps have altogether failed, in the days before air-power became a vital factor in war. No one will ever know. Certain it is that the German High Command, with the aid of the Luftwaffe, expected to encompass the complete defeat of the British within their perimeter and on the beaches of the Pas de Calais and Belgium. They failed to do so. The Luftwaffe quailed before the fighters of the R.A.F. And if the German Air Force failed in its task it was because the British Air Force did not fail. In the Dunkirk operation the R.A.F. inflicted its first defeat upon the Luftwaffe, and this, in large measure, ensured the success of the withdrawal.

It was said at the time, by our soldiers, that they could not understand what the R.A.F. were doing when bombs fell among their ranks. Many said they saw little of the action of British aircraft in the sky. How could they? From Dunkirk to Nieuport is $17\frac{1}{2}$ miles, Dunkirk to Bergues but six. British fighters could flash across the area in a fraction over a minute, and pass along its whole length in three minutes. Often their passage would carry them to right or left of the perimeter. For the object of the fighters was not to patrol above the British troops, but to prevent the aircraft of the enemy from reaching the perimeter. The air fighting had to be fought outside the perimeter enclosing the troops if it were to have the desired effect of affording protection to the soldiers within. To meet the German aircraft only one minute before they reached position for high-level bombing from a height of 10,000 feet, the British fighters had to be seven miles outside the cordon. Air fights over Roulers took place but five minutes away when measured at the flying speed of German bombers, but its distance from Furnes was 22 miles in a straight line; Lille, 31½ miles distant, was but seven minutes' time-interval from Hondschoote; Saint-Omer, less than four minutes' flight away, was 17½ miles from Bergues. Small wonder that the British soldiers saw little of what the Royal Air Force did to help them at Dunkirk. The soldiers saw what the Navy did, and what those who manned the small boats did. To the soldier seeing is believing, and the Navy earned the soldiers' gratitude; but it should never be forgotten that the Navy acted under the protection of the fighters of the Royal Air Force, and of the Fleet Air Arm. This is what the Commander-in-Chief of the B.E.F. reported: "The embarkation of the Force would have been well-nigh impossible but for the fighter protection afforded."

During nine days, from May 26 to June 3 inclusive, 377 enemy aircraft were destroyed and shot down for a loss of 87 British aircraft. That was the statistical contribution of the Royal Air Force to Dunkirk. But the collaboration of the air force did not end with fighting. Bombers attacked enemy positions by day and night, easing the pressure from enemy ground forces against the British soldiers. Air actions are imponderable contributions to circumstances such as those affecting the surrounded force whose only link with Britain was a moving bridge of small boats. This was the first great rearguard air action in history. The successful extrication of 186,587 British, 123,095 French soldiers, with 6981 more carried in hospital ships from the face of the most powerfully armed enemy force that has ever ravaged the Continent, is proof of the value of rearguard action in the air.

The greatest proportion of the men rescued were taken off from the East Pier of Dunkirk, a wooden groyne which carried a five-feet wooden pathway, and alongside which smaller boats could come. The main basin was obstructed by sunken wrecks, and the dock area was hot with the heat of fired warehouses and fuel-tanks. Over this scene of destruction and of war-weary, waiting men flew their comrades-in-arms of the fighter and bomber aircraft.

The bombers were concerned with the ground targets, which normally are the affair of the ground forces. Wellington bombers flew every night from May 27 to June 4, placing a curtain of bombs around Dunkirk to deter the enemy ground pressure and reduce his artillery fire. Bomber Command responded not only to the calls of the Army within the perimeter, but to those of the Royal Navy operating on the waters, close inshore, within range of the German gunners.

But the evacuation from Dunkirk was the concern of every fighting unit which could be spared from other tasks. The Fleet Air Arm of the Navy flew in support of the ships, and Coastal Command of the

Royal Air Force patrolled overhead to protect the ferry service of deliverance that plied the Channel.

Near the end of May Flight Lieutenant W. H. Biddell, leading a flight of Hudsons of No. 206 squadron of Coastal Command, saw a flight of Fleet Air Arm Skua fighter-bombers being attacked by eleven Messerschmitt 109's. The Hudson is not a fighter aircraft, but without hesitation Biddell flew to the aid of the Skuas: his air gunner, Leading Aircraftman W. D. Caulfield, maintained a steady and accurate fire and severely damaged at least one Messerschmitt. A wireless operator in the flight, Leading Aircraftman K. S. Freeman, immediately left his wireless-post and manned one of the side Lewis guns. A cannon-shell struck the aircraft and wounded Freeman in the leg in two places, but he continued to fire at the enemy, and the determination and concentrated fire of the flight of three Hudsons drove the Messerschmitts off.

Early in June three Hudsons of No. 220 squadron of Coastal Command were on patrol over the shipping when about forty Junkers 87 dive-bombers attempted to interfere with the evacuation. The Hudsons, led by Flying Officer R. N. Selley with Flying Officer H. A. Haarhoff as his rear gunner, attacked. Selley shot down two Stukas with his front guns, then manœuvred his aircraft and enabled Haarhoff to destroy another and damage two more severely. Two more Stukas fell to the front gun of Pilot Officer R. J. Jouault.

The odds were always weighted against the British air patrols. Another patrol of three Coastal Command aircraft was attacked by nine Messerschmitt 109 fighters near Dunkirk. Pilot Officer P. W. Peters immediately turned to the attack, and he and his air gunner, Acting Corporal L. G. Smith, and navigator, Sergeant D. C. Spencer, all opened fire upon the German fighters; each of the two rear gunners destroyed a Messerschmitt and severely damaged another. In the fight Peters lost touch with the two other British aircraft, who had returned to their base, and he continued his patrol alone. One of the other aircraft shot down another Messerschmitt to the gun of Leading Aircraftman L. S. Dillnutt. One of the wireless operators was shot in the foot; suffering great pain, he continued to pass messages reporting the sinking of a destroyer, refusing morphia so that he might retain the full use of his faculties until his services were no longer required. These men came from Purley, Durban, Amiens, Southport, Canterbury, Northwich (Cheshire), Tunbridge Wells, Leeds, and London; the oldest was thirty and the youngest nineteen; some came straight from college into the R.A.F., others entered as boys, one came from the Territorial Army, one was a caretaker and another an electrical worker

EVACUATION FROM DUNKIRK

British and French troops on the dunes at Dunkirk wait to be picked up by the rescue vessels and brought back to England.

[P. 96]

Photo "The Times"

FLYING OFFICER B. J. WICKS

Flying Officer Wicks, of No. 56 squadron, is here seen in the disguise in which he escaped after coming down behind the German lines in Belgium.

[P. 106]

before they joined the Royal Air Force. The officers won Distinguished Flying Crosses and the airmen Distinguished Flying Medals in these actions.

But, more than any other aircraft, the fighters were the salvation of the evacuating hosts from the port and beaches of Dunkirk. While the evacuation continued between 200 and 300 flights were made from British aerodromes by fighters every day, and of these aircraft every seventh machine shot down a German aircraft, while only 5 per cent. failed to return. Before the war began Air Chief Marshal Sir Hugh Dowding, Commander-in-Chief Fighter Command, had given his dictum that the crippling rate of loss in aircraft was not below 10 per cent. Fighter Command operated over Dunkirk with a safety factor in its favour. Had the Command disposed of more aircraft than it did the whole course of the war might have been altered in those early days. But that was not to be.

The Dunkirk patrols went out from No. 11 Group of Fighter Command under Air Vice-Marshal Keith Rodney Park, M.C., D.F.C., who had graduated both from the Air Staff College and the College of Imperial Defence. Before the war he was the Senior Air Staff Officer at the headquarters of Fighter Command. Just after the war began he became ill, underwent a serious operation, and upon recovery became the commander of No. 11 Group. The sector covered by this Fighter group was the South-eastern area of England, concerned largely with the Fighter defence of London. The group was later to bear the brunt of the fighting in the Battle of Britain. For his services in the world's first great air battle, Park was made a Companion of the Order of the Bath; subsequently, while Air Officer Commanding Malta during the period in which occurred the Battle of El Alamein, he was knighted in the second class of the Order of the British Empire. During the Battle of Britain he put into practice those concepts of air defence which he had formed during the months of study at staff colleges, and which he had helped to shape under Sir Hugh Dowding at Fighter Command headquarters. He came from New Zealand, and was lean, tall, sinewy, a pilot who himself flew the machines his younger pilots flew, although he was, at forty-eight, more than twice the age of many of them. He flew over the beaches of Dunkirk to see for himself the position of the British troops. Once he was forced down by a British fighter who suspected that the Hurricane he was flying might be piloted by a German. During the defence of London he flew more than 100 hours, mainly in his own Hurricane. Younger pilots respect such seniors. How different he was from Göring, who, although younger than Park, now never flew as pilot because his paunch was so distended that he was unable to get the stick back to enable him to land.

Here, in his own words, is the story of one of the men Park commanded, Flight Lieutenant M. N. Crossley, of No. 32 squadron. This squadron was first formed at Netheravon, on Salisbury Plain, in January 1916. It served in France and Belgium during the Great War, when its pilots flew De Havilland 2 single-seater pusher fighters with 100-h.p. rotary engines and a single Lewis machine-gun mounted on a universal joint so that the pilot could aim it at his enemy without the necessity to point the nose of the machine (although the machine-gun could be clipped so that it was held firm should the pilot decide to manœuvre the machine instead of waggling the gun). On this type of aircraft Major Lanoe Hawker, V.C., met the Baron Manfred von Richthofen and was killed because he would not (and, indeed, perhaps could not) get away from the red Albatross with two guns and faster speed. The squadron was disbanded under the economy axe in December 1919, to be re-formed at Kenley in April 1923. In 1940 it was equipped with 1030-h.p., 335-m.p.h., eight-gun Hurricanes.

This is Crossley's story :

When the Germans invaded Holland and Belgium no one in 32 squadron had even seen a German aircraft, much less been in action against one. We'd had plenty of flying, but it wasn't much different from peace-time flying. Like a lot of others, we were just waiting to get our chance. We didn't have to wait much longer.

We were on patrol over the Dutch and Belgian coast on Sunday, May 19, when we ran slap into a bunch of Messerschmitt 109 fighters convoying German bombers. We attacked the Messerschmitts and got six definitely; perhaps another three.

I was just looking round—one is always looking round on these patrols—when I saw a rough-and-tumble starting up between other members of the squadron and the Messerschmitts. As I turned to join in I saw four Messerschmitts. One of them flew right across my sights. I just blazed away for a split second, saw bits fall from his tail and then he was lost to sight. That's the one I wasn't sure about.

Then, as I was about to follow him down and make sure, I saw out of the corner of my eye another Messerschmitt trying to get on my tail. I pulled the stick back a little, and swept up and round towards him. He was only about 200 feet above me when I opened fire. Immediately I saw petrol stream from his two tanks, one under each wing. I swept under him, turned, and then saw him burst into flames before reaching the ground. But without that extra bit of luck it might have been me.

I didn't get a chance to attack the bombers beneath. One of our sergeant pilots did. He went down and got one. It was a Dornier 215.

Then another pilot, who broke away from the main action because he thought he was short of ammunition, lost sight of the rest of the squadron and made a bee-line for home. At least, that's what he meant to do.   Actually, he must have misread his map, for after about twenty minutes' flying he found himself over strange, well-wooded country. Obviously, it was Germany.   So he went below the clouds to reconnoitre.   Suddenly he saw three Messerschmitt 110's coming at him.

He flew straight towards them.   The two outside ones swerved away to avoid colliding.   The middle one apparently did not see the Hurricane approaching, and, keeping straight on, received the full blast of eight guns as our man opened fire.   The 110 simply disintegrated.   Our man bolted for home then.   He was glad to get away that time, as he really had finished his ammunition.   He was lucky.

Yes, but not so lucky as the sergeant-pilot who, after shooting down a Henschel Army Co-operation aircraft, was caught by anti-aircraft fire and made a forced landing.   He came down behind the German lines, walked ten miles, and then came to a canal which was guarded on the opposite bank by British troops.   They told him how to get across—by going some distance up the canal and getting over a makeshift bridge—and then helped him to get a car into Calais.   It wasn't long before he was back with his squadron, on the job.

Recently I have been up twice a day on patrols over France and Belgium.   But that doesn't mean that we are in action every time.   My last patrol was only the day before yesterday.   We spotted two Junkers 88's when we were patrolling between Calais and Dunkirk.   I got one, and one of the other fellows the other.   They were bombers—but most of our scraps have been with other fighters.   So far, we've brought down fifteen that we are sure of, and probably another five.   Two of our pilots have failed to return.   But we know that one of them is safe as a prisoner of war.   Of course, there are other Fighter squadrons that have been doing better than we have.   Altogether, we seem to be getting down an average of about forty a day.

These fights over Northern France began even before the evacuation f the Air Component of the B.E.F.   The fury of the fighting rose eadily as the pilots, many of whom had never fired their guns in anger til a fortnight before, and some of whom were going into their first ;hts now, became accustomed to the changed technique of real war place of exercises.

One Hurricane fighter pilot sighted a suspicious-looking aircraft over he French coast, and detached himself from his squadron to inspect t.   It turned out to be French, and the British pilot swung back hrough the clouds to rejoin his formation.   Suddenly twenty bombers lew out of the cloud.   At first the British pilot mistook them for Blenheims—a mistake that was made several times in the early days of he fighting.   A moment later he was sure they were Heinkel 111's eading for England.   He turned and gave chase, and caught up with hem as they flew over Calais.   Sighting on one, he pressed his firebutton at a range of fifty yards.   The bomber's undercarriage dropped; hick smoke came from its starboard engine; no answering fire came

99

from its guns. The pilot gave the rest of his ammunition to another Heinkel at the same range. Smoke poured from its port engine; the Heinkel rear gunner fired back at the British aeroplane. The Hurricane's ammunition was almost exhausted when a Messerschmitt 110 attacked him. The British pilot swerved away, escaped, and got back safely to his base, with his aircraft undamaged.

Different was the tale of Pilot Officer Ward, a New Zealander flying Hurricanes. His aircraft was badly damaged before he set course for England. The gun-sights were gone. Compass, oil-temperature and pressure-gauges alone worked. His guns were loaded with ordinary ball-cartridge; there were no tracer bullets to enable him to check his line of fire, and he was without incendiary ammunition. The starboard petrol-tank was leaking. There was a risk of fire. Ward decided to land on a French aerodrome to refuel his other tank before continuing his journey home. The aerodrome lay close to a town, part of which was in flames, but he glided down. At 5000 feet he saw two Dornier 215's begin a dive-bombing attack on the aerodrome he intended to use. He dived on to the tail of one of the bombers and gave it two short bursts, hitting it despite his absence of gun-sights. The second Dornier tried to escape into the clouds, followed by the Hurricane blazing away with its eight machine-guns. For the moment the sky was clear, and Ward prepared again to land. Then he was attacked by a bunch of Messerschmitts. Unable to cope with all of them single-handed, he circled the town for ten minutes, firing occasional bursts first at one and then at another. At last he got down. The starboard tank was spurting petrol, and the men on the ground refused to fill his tanks because they regarded it as suicidal for him to go up in the damaged machine. The pilot then took a bayonet and opened out the holes in his leaking tank, allowed all the fuel to escape, and had his port tank filled. It contained just enough fuel to scrape home, but none to spare for a fight. There were fifty rounds left in each machine-gun, enough for a three-seconds burst. Ward took off.

"With only that small amount of ammunition I was almost helpless," he said later. "It was just my luck to run into another formation of six Messerschmitts when I was practically out of petrol. I gave the leader a burst as he came head-on for me (I'm sure I hit him), and I dived down past him towards the ground. After that I just 'put my skates on' for home. It was good fun, that flight, but what would I have given for more ammunition to deal with the Messerschmitts!"

On examination at base the Hurricane was found to have bullet-holes in fuselage, wings, and tail. The escape of the pilot was providential.

when the gun-sights immediately in front of him were shot away. But Ward was not superstitious. His Hurricane bore a coat of arms of his own designing—a shield, quartered, bearing a broken hand-mirror, a hand holding a match lighting three cigarettes, a man walking under a ladder, the figure 13, and under the shield, for motto: *So what the hell*. The device had not been passed by the College of Heralds.

On May 22 No. 11 Fighter group shot down twenty-seven German aircraft and riddled ten more with machine-gun bullets. Six British fighters failed to return, but the pilot of one machine which crashed in France escaped unhurt and reached England safely. That day eight Hurricanes attacked thirty-five Junkers 87 dive-bombers which were about to bomb a target near Arras from 1200 feet. Six of the Stukas were destroyed. Six other Hurricanes attacked twenty Messerschmitt 109's over Hazebrouck and shot down two, coming out of the fight without damage. Over Saint-Omer ten Hurricanes destroyed four of a formation of fifteen Messerschmitt 109's. Twenty-four Junkers 87's bombing roads and railway stations near Hazebrouck were set upon by eleven Hurricanes; four Stukas were destroyed, and possibly three more whose fate could not be observed during the mêlée. Another fighter patrol engaged several Henschel 126 Army Co-operation aircraft, shot down six, forced a seventh to land, and machine-gunned it on the ground. A squadron of Blenheim fighters shot down three Heinkel 111 bombers and damaged a fourth over Northern France.

On May 24 eleven Spitfires of No. 54 squadron patrolled the French coast during the afternoon and met a much larger force of German aircraft. Without loss the Spitfires shot down eleven German aircraft and seriously damaged three others.

During the morning of May 26 a continuous air battle was fought over the French coast between Calais and Dunkirk. British pilots reported that " the sky was filled with aircraft." A squadron leader spoke of " large masses of Messerschmitt 109's." Between 5.30 and 9.30 A.M. R.A.F. fighter pilots shot down at least twenty German bombers and fighters and put another twenty out of action, for a loss of five of their own machines. Fighting occurred at various heights. One British squadron surprised twenty Messerschmitt 110's at 17,000 feet over Calais, approached them from out of the sun, and broke up the defensive circles, which the Nazi fighters flying 110's favoured when attacked, before the German pilots had time properly to form them. Five of these Messerschmitts were put out of action. Ninety minutes later, on another patrol, the same R.A.F. squadron destroyed five more Messerschmitts, damaged five, and knocked down an Army Co-operation aircraft. Another fight began at 10,000 feet when Spitfires attacked a formation of Junkers 87 dive-bombers, shot down five, damaged three more, and sent the remainder hedge-hopping in all directions over French fields before their escort of Messerschmitts could arrive. Another Spitfire squadron caught a formation of Junkers 88's trying to bomb ships; the Spitfires destroyed five escorting Messerschmitt 110's and one bomber, bringing the squadron score to thirty-two enemy aircraft destroyed in less than three days.

The toll of aircraft shot down daily by the fighters of the Royal Air Force rose as the intensity of the fighting around the area of Dunkirk increased. On May 29 fifty-two German aircraft were shot down, twenty-five bombers among them, while seventeen others were seriously damaged. Ten British fighter aircraft failed to return that day, but one of the pilots, wounded, got back.

Some of the fighter pilots returned with tales of strange adventure. One squadron leader attacked two enemy fighters and shot both down, but while doing so was himself shot up by other enemy fighters who had pounced down from a higher altitude. His wind-shield was covered with thick black oil. With his vision blinded, his aircraft swayed wildly, then began to fall, turning and turning. The squadron leader decided to bale out as the aircraft turned upside down in its course. Twice he failed to get away. Then he realized that in the excitement of the moment he had not undone his shoulder-straps. The third time (luckily there was enough height to allow for a third chance) he got out, pulled the rip-cord of his parachute, and began to float earthward. The German pilots flew past his parachute, trying to machine-gun him. The shots passed close to him, but failed to hit him or his parachute in spite of the closeness of the Messerschmitts. He landed in a part of Belgium still held by Allied troops, made his way back to his unit, and was in the air once more a few hours later.

Another pilot came down in enemy-held territory. He was arrested and taken to the nearest village, where he was placed in a small court-yard among a crowd of Belgian civilians. At half-hourly intervals groups of the civilians were ordered out, summarily questioned, placed against a wall, and shot. A German officer in charge of the firing-squad told the pilot, " It will be your turn soon." The pilot protested that he was an officer in uniform who had landed behind the German lines as the result of an air combat. The German officer shrugged his shoulders and said, "You are a spy or a *franc-tireur*, like all these others."

A small closed window overlooked the courtyard. The pilot edged over to it. Amid the momentary confusion of the departure of the next group of civilian victims he made a flying leap through the window.

He landed on all fours outside with only a slight cut on the cheek from the splintering glass, got up, raced round the corner of the outer wall, dashed through a garden, and got clear away from the village, without a single shot being fired at him by the surprised Germans.

He spent the night on top of a haystack. Next day he mingled with refugees and was given a lift in a Dutch car. In the afternoon of the second day he got over the French border and reached Lille, which was held by the French until May 31.

The Defiant squadron created a record on May 29, and made the main contribution to the bag of enemy aircraft shot down. Led by Squadron Leader P. A. Hunter, the twelve Defiants went into action over the French and Belgian coast. They met more German fighters and dive-bombers than they could count, on their first, after-lunch patrol. They first sighted seven Messerschmitt 109's, attacked immediately, and shot down one. This fight had scarcely finished when four more Nazi fighters dived at them out of the sun, firing a stream of cannon-shells as they came. One of the Defiants was hit and its ailerons were shot away, and other parts of its surface began to look like a colander; its air gunner baled out over Belgium; the pilot turned for home and reached his Kentish aerodrome safely in a quite remarkable flight. The Defiants drove off the Messerschmitts without further losses on either side. The Defiant crews next saw two formations of nine Heinkel 111's attempting to bomb Dunkirk; before they could wade in Hurricanes had attacked, and all the Heinkels' bombs fell in the sea. The Defiants turned to look for further quarry. Circling above them was a crowd of Messerschmitt 110 twin-engined fighters, a type which went into production in the spring of 1939, about the same time as the Defiants. In the ensuing dog-fight sixteen of the German fighters were destroyed. The 110's were escorting Stuka dive-bombers; thirty or forty Stukas attempted to bomb Dunkirk; one of these Junkers 87's was destroyed by the Defiants. Not until all their ammunition was expended did the Defiants turn for home.

Later in the afternoon No. 25 squadron again patrolled over the Dunkirk area. This time German fighters were remarkably absent, but there were large numbers of dive-bombers. The Defiants attacked. Eighteen Junkers 87's fell to their turreted batteries of four machine-guns. One pilot, Flight Lieutenant N. G. Cooke, flew right underneath the Stukas, and his air gunner, Corporal A. Lippett, firing point-blank into their bellies, shot down five in succession. The Stuka pilots jettisoned their bombs and scattered in all directions in a panic. Two more may possibly have fallen as they went. Most of the ammunition carried by the Defiants was used up in this combat, but they had enough left to shoot down a Junkers 88 which they encountered foolhardily flying by itself.

Altogether, with only the loss of the missing air gunner, the squadron shot down thirty-seven (and possibly thirty-nine) enemy aircraft, of four different kinds, during that one day, bringing its total of victories to fifty in three days. Unfortunately, on the following day the pilot whose Defiant had shot down the five Junkers 87's failed to come back from a patrol over Dunkirk. The phenomenal luck of the Defiants could not last long. It was partly due to the element of surprise. The machine looked much like a Hurricane in flight. No doubt the German pilots thought that the Defiant could fire only straight ahead, like the Hurricane. It did not take them long to understand their mistake. May 29 was the Defiants' best day. It was a record that stood in 1942 still unbeaten by any other squadron.

On May 31, fifty-six enemy aircraft were destroyed or seriously damaged, and sixteen R.A.F. aircraft failed to come back from their task of screening the evacuation. Next day the air fighting over Dunkirk reached its climax. Hurricanes and Spitfires were above the evacuation area all day. At dawn on June 1 ten enemy fighters were shot down for the loss of one British aircraft. Huge formations of Nazi bombers, escorted by fighters, flew over the target area in successive waves for four hours. From the air the sea looked thick with craft of every kind, but, when the German bombers attempted to bomb, Hurricanes and Spitfires attacked and drove them off, and most of their bombs fell wide into the sea. Junkers, Heinkels, Dorniers, and Messerschmitts crashed into the sea after their bombs. Thirty-two fighters were certainly destroyed. One Spitfire squadron destroyed twelve German bombers and fighters in one short action, and in another patrol later in the day destroyed another six. Two Fighter squadrons destroyed twenty-three Messerschmitt fighters. By seven o'clock that Saturday evening seventy-eight German bombers and fighters had been destroyed or severely damaged, a new record for the R.A.F. in one day. Sixteen British fighters were missing. The Luftwaffe paid a heavy price for the damage it inflicted, and it could not prevent the evacuation.

What of the pilots of that small, heroic force, who returned again and again into the fight, so that by their efforts and their challenge to the risks they ran they might give their quota to the salvation of the thousands of men below who could not defend themselves against the bloodthirsty Luftwaffe? What were these men like? In mufti there was little to distinguish them from their fellows of equal age, for flying was still too young to have bred a special type comparable to the man of the sea. Perhaps there was a keenness of eye noticeable in their glance, a quickness in their way of doing things, for all were men graded by the doctors of the Royal Air Force as suitable for fighter pilots on account of physical fitness and satisfactory co-ordination of brain, hands, feet, and eyes. But these attributes became alive during flight. They might remain dormant on the ground. Some of the boys might even have appeared to be lazy, because they knew how to relax when given the opportunity. The truth is that an air pilot, especially a fighter pilot, really comes to life only in the air, when the exhilaration of flight calls forth the spirit that loves flying, and the handling of the powerful machine at his command brings out the natural aptitude of a fine physique. In their combat reports all the pilots betrayed a quality of directness when describing what happened in a fight. The following examples illustrate this well.

A Spitfire pilot who dived after a Dornier 17 from 5000 feet and pressed home his attack, although the spinner of his airscrew had been hit by a bullet and his windscreen covered with oil, said simply, "I continued to attack below tree-level."

A Hurricane pilot wrote, "The Messerschmitt 110 dived vertically to ground-line. I followed him down and he was within twenty feet of ground, chasing round a chimney-pot."

Another pilot wrote, "When I last saw the enemy he was staggering over a wood."

Even when things went wrong the tenor of the reports remained as imperturbable. Here are two examples: "My machine was hit from behind by machine-gun fire and four cannon-shells. The last cannon-shell hit my port tank, and the Hurricane caught fire. I used my parachute and made a delayed drop from 6000 feet to about 1500 feet. When my parachute opened I was fired on by troops with rifles. Four holes were made in the parachute's canopy."

One pilot destroyed a Junkers 88 after his wings had been hit by cannon-shells fired from Messerschmitt 110's. Again the Messerschmitts attacked. He wrote, "I received direct hits with cannon-fire and then dived to the ground and found my base engine temperature was now registering 145 degrees, and fumes coming from the engine. I switched off to prevent being overcome by the fumes. Made forced landing. . . ."

But for sheer insouciance, the squadron leader whose squadron shot down seven Junkers 87's and damaged three more takes top place with this sentence in his report: "All the Junkers seemed very surprised to see us; they were obviously not expecting an attack, as we were some distance behind the line."

The fate of victims was always put in terse language. One pilot wrote, "I saw the fuselage tear up. The rear gunner was lying helpless in the cockpit." Another reported, "My windscreen was smothered with oil, so that I could only see another aircraft by the flames which just showed through the oil." Wrote a third, "I then saw the complete tail of the enemy aircraft break off, this aircraft rolling over and diving out of its formation vertically. Another Messerschmitt blew up and disintegrated." And a fourth, "I immediately turned round steeply, as the Messerschmitt had passed quickly by, and saw the machine a mass of flames, diving towards the ground-haze."

Some of the pilots whose machines were shot down in combat returned to England in the boats with the troops. One pilot of No. 111 squadron whose Hurricane was shot up by Messerschmitts managed to forced-land on the beach. Carrying his parachute, he walked fifteen miles to Dunkirk, crossed to Folkestone in a paddle-steamer, rejoined his squadron (the first to be equipped with Hurricanes before the war), and was out on patrol again next day.

During the peak fighting of June 1 one British fighter pilot ran out of ammunition and then found himself close to a German bomber. He manœuvred on to the bomber's tail and began to stunt. His manœuvres forced the German pilot downward in the effort to avoid the swooping fighter. At last, near the ground, the German pilot stalled in a turn, and crashed. Not a shot had been fired at him.

Unwittingly, the fighter pilots of the R.A.F. saved one of their own comrades of No. 56 squadron by the very violence of their battle in the air. Ten days earlier, on May 22, Flying Officer B. J. Wicks was forced down by enemy fighters near the Belgian frontier from a fight in which he had shot down several German aircraft in his Hurricane. He had been posted missing and given up for lost, his kit packed up, and his car sold.

When Wicks found he was still a free man after coming down he quickly realized that he would have to get rid of his uniform if he were to succeed in escaping, for he was far behind the German lines. Fortunately for himself, he spoke French. He found a Belgian who was willing to lend him some clothes. ('Lend' is a curious term in this case.) They were a battered old hat, pipe-like trousers six inches too short for him, a dirty grey jacket, and an ancient light grey overcoat. He kept his regulation blue shirt, but wore an old collar with his own black tie. Thus disguised, he passed himself off to Belgians as a Frenchman, to Frenchmen as a Belgian, and to Germans as a Belgian refugee.

"Most of the Belgians with whom I travelled guessed that I was English," Wicks said, "but they did not give me away. I was advised to talk as little as possible when Germans appeared, for they told me that my French had a terrible English accent."

Once he borrowed a motor-car to drive Belgian refugees through the German lines. When they had gone only a few miles the car was held up by German soldiers. The soldiers took the car, and the flying officer's pilgrimage continued on foot.

"I got a lot of food from German soldiers on the way," he said. "I lived for days on boiled eggs, coffee, and water. Occasionally I called at a farmhouse or country cottage to seek shelter."

He spent his nights in cattle-sheds and outhouses, always aware that his identity might be discovered by the numerous German troops who often questioned him and the other refugees with whom he travelled in company. His disguise as a Belgian peasant seemed less satisfactory when the Belgian Army capitulated and he found the Belgian refugees moving back towards their Belgian homes. "I tagged myself on to parties of French peasants," he said. After ten anxious days he neared the perimeter around Dunkirk.

I owe my final escape to the Royal Air Force [said Flying Officer Wicks]. I was on the outskirts of Dunkirk, and I had to pass through the German-patrolled area at the back of the town. Every few hundred yards the Germans had sentries posted along the roads, so that it was impossible for anyone to get by. But one day there was a terrific aerial battle. I could see Hurricanes and Messerschmitts and Heinkels and Spitfires doing their stuff. It was a thrilling show, and the sentries thought so too. They were looking skyward when I slipped through.

He crawled through long grass for more than a mile, unseen by the sentries engrossed in the spectacle in the sky. His was the first recorded escape of its kind under air cover, an incident which opens new possibilities for the passage of spies under a timed diversion overhead. His progression on all fours brought him to a canal.

When I reached the canal I called across to a group of French soldiers [he said] and crossed the canal in a small boat. I was, of course, arrested by the French on suspicion. The guard passed me on to the lieutenant, and the lieutenant to a major, and so, up the scale, until I was put before a general. I told him who I was, and where I came from, and eventually I was passed on to the British authorities in Dunkirk. There again I was suspected, though I was treated extremely well. A naval commander took charge of me, and I was technically under arrest until I had been brought to England in a motor-torpedo-boat, questioned at the Admiralty and later at the Air Ministry, where my identity was finally established. People who saw me in London must have thought I was either a spy or a fifth-columnist or something like that. They looked at me very strangely.

On the twelfth day after his forced landing Flying Officer Wicks was back with No. 56 squadron on its aerodrome in Essex. He fought in the Battle of Britain. Twenty months later, wearing the D.F.C. ribbon, he was leading a Spitfire squadron with the rank of squadron leader.

The damage done by the German bombs on the beaches of Dunkirk was not deadly. Their aim was too often marred by the attacks of British fighters flying, sometimes singly, sometimes in a flight of three, less often in squadron formation, rarely in a wing formation of two and, at least once, three squadrons. The British pilots tackled odds as great as seventy to one, and took a toll of German aircraft five times heavier than their own losses. And the bombs that hit the sand sank in and burst with less effect than they would have had on harder ground, where the radius of their destructive force would have been greater.

The German Air Force tried all methods of attack—dive-bombing men on shore and ships on the water, high-level bombing, machine-gunning, and the firing of cannon-guns whose shells exploded on contact; they dropped magnetic mines in front of the harbour-mouth and in the shallow channels that the ships had to use as they plied the Channel. Damage to ships there certainly was, and casualties to men; a hospital ship was bravely sunk by the Germans in daylight, and bombs were dropped on La Panne after the British troops had evacuated it. Troops boarded their boats, some carrying Bren guns which they tied to the rigging to use as anti-aircraft guns. Troops fired Bren guns and rifles at the aircraft as they swooped down upon them. And so the work of evacuation went on below while the scarcely never-ending fight continued in the skies above. German forces moving in upon the Allied forces within the perimeter were delayed by rearguard actions fought with the courage for which British infantrymen and artillery-men have long been famed; German tanks were held up by the floods from opened canal sluice-gates that softened the land, and by bombs that fell upon them. British bombers dropped more than sixty tons of bombs on German forces closing upon the perimeter from the eastward in the evening of May 31; one squadron dropped eight tons on Germans approaching Furnes; ten tons fell on tanks closing on Cassel.

The ground staff of the R.A.F. worked day and night to make the work of the air crews possible. "Keep the fans turning" was their cry. By their efforts Hurricane, Spitfire, and Defiant pilots flew more than two million miles to and fro across the Channel. At any one of the Fighter stations co-operating in the work, aircraft made an average of 150 landings a day to be refuelled, rearmed, and doctored. Servicing flights worked in shifts round the 24-hour clock. Here was no normal routine of familiar squadrons coming in to their home station. The ground crews never knew from day to day how many fighters might be landing or taking off from any aerodrome. One day might send them a couple of squadrons, the next a hundred aircraft or more. Fitters and riggers specialized in emergency repairs, making aircraft they could repair on the spot ready for another sortie, patching up the more badly damaged aircraft to enable them to be flown back to the repair depot. As soon as a squadron landed from an engagement across the Channel the pilots tumbled out of their cockpits to report, the ground crews took over, filling tanks, reloading guns, checking the structure and wireless set, examining guns, and making the detailed inspection without which no aeroplane normally takes the air. Ammunition was expended so rapidly in sortie after sortie that special parties were organized to make up the cartridge-belts for the eight guns of the single-seater fighters. These are belts in which detachable light-metal links connect cartridge-cases one with another so that the belt is flexible yet accurate in spacing from round to round, thus ensuring smooth and continuous operation of the gun as long as the air-pressure is maintained and the pilot thumbs the fire-button; and as the cartridges feed into the block to be fired at the rate of 1200 a minute from each gun, the belts disintegrate so that empty cartridge-cases and belt-links are thrown out by the ejectors after their work is done. Willing hands made light of all work. A Blenheim fighter with its tailplane and port elevator badly shot up as part of the damage caused by anti-aircraft gunfire was turned about and ready to go into action in little more than twelve hours after it landed. At one station, cooks—who get little enough credit for the work they do in stoking the human boiler—lent all but three of their number for maintenance work, and worked manfully to feed the entire staff, officers and men, of a whole squadron—no light task.

Vice-Admiral Sir Bertram Ramsay, K.C.B., M.V.O., the officer in command of Operation Dynamo—the code-name given to the evacuation operation, which was planned in Dynamo Room in the Casemates in Dover—addressed the following message to the Commanders-in Chief of Fighter, Bosmber, and Coastal Command of the R.A.F. on June 4:

> I and the forces under my command who have been engaged on the evacuation of the Allied Armies owe a deep debt of gratitude to the Royal Air Force for the support and protection which they have given to us. We are fully conscious of the severe strain these operations have imposed on all taking part and we are filled with admiration for the courage and devotion of our comrades in the air.

Air Chief Marshal Sir Cyril Newall, Chief of the Air Staff, sent the following signal in reply:

On behalf of Fighter, Bomber, and Coastal Commands I thank you most deeply for your message. For their part, our squadrons, together with the squadrons of the Fleet Air Arm who so gallantly assisted them, have seen with admiration the tireless and undaunted efforts of the forces under your Command in the face of the most severe difficulties. On their behalf, I express to you my warmest congratulations on the magnificent success which you have achieved.

Dunkirk was the answer to the German High Command announcement on May 25 that "the ring around the British, French, and Belgian Armies has been definitely closed." It was not closed on the seaward side, the side which it was the duty of the Luftwaffe to seal; and even on the landward side, as we have observed, it was possible for a British flying officer, disguised as a Belgian peasant, to pass through the circumference of the ring. Dunkirk was the first demonstration of the lack of German thoroughness, the first exposure of the over-cocksureness of Nazi Germany, and at the same time the evidence that British flexibility and inability to admit defeat were as strong in 1940 as they had ever been.

§ 7

South of the Gap

When the curtain rose on the war in the West at dawn on May 10 No. 1 squadron had scored twenty-six victories over the German Luftwaffe, and No. 73 squadron had scored thirty. No. 1 was the first squadron to arrive in France; it flew back to Britain on June 18 with a score of 155 victories. No. 73 squadron, the second Fighter unit to reach France, and No. 242 squadron were the last to leave, a quarter of an hour after No. 1. No. 73 squadron's score of victories was then 100 enemy aircraft destroyed, with only two pilots killed in action. No. 242 squadron had shot down more than thirty. No. 1 squadron, whose motto is *In omnibus princeps*, had lived up to that proud description; Pilot Officer P. W. O. Mould, one of the squadron's pilots, on October 30, 1939, found a Dornier at 18,000 feet over Toul and shot it down in flames, drawing first blood in France. Mould, born at Hallaton, Uppingham, in 1917, enlisted in the R.A.F. as an aircraft apprentice in 1934, was awarded a Cranwell Cadetship in 1937, and obtained his commission in 1939; when, on July 14, 1940, he was awarded the Distinguished Flying Cross he had added six more to his original victory.

It would be almost invidious to pick out heroes among the gallant company of young men who were the pilots of these two squadrons; and, in any case, it would be unfair to the pilots of the squadrons of

110

the Air Component, to the air crews of the Bomber and Army Co-operation squadrons, and to the pilots of the Fighter squadrons which were sent to France after the battle was locked on May 10, 1940. But one human touch must be mentioned. Air Marshal Arthur S. Barratt, the Air Officer Commanding-in-Chief of the British Air Forces in France, wanted to establish the superiority of British fighters over Germany's latest type, the twin-engined Messerschmitt 110; he offered a dinner in Paris with himself as host to the first pilot who brought down a Messerschmitt 110 on the Western Front. The luck fell to No. 1 squadron, in March 1940.

At 25,000 feet, patrolling north-east of Metz, Flight Lieutenant P. R. Walker led a section of three Hurricanes, with Flying Officer W. H. Stratton and Sergeant A. V. Clowes in formation behind him. Clowes saw the specks in the sky first. He called up his leader by radio telephone. Walker instantly turned and headed towards the specks above the clouds. Presently he could distinguish three machines coming straight towards them 500 feet below. As he drew nearer he recognized them as Messerschmitt 110's. Then he saw six more behind. It was a German squadron in sections of three in line astern heading west near Bozanville, just behind the Maginot Line. Over Bozanville Walker called "Tally ho!" over the radio to his comrades. They gave an answering assent in the same words, and Walker attacked. At the same instant the German pilots saw the Hurricanes, and swept over in a steep right turn to get on the tails of the British machines. Walker banked hard to the right, and got on the tail of one of the Messerschmitts. His first bursts were wild shots at the manoeuvring German machine. Then his aim steadied and he got a better burst. The German pilot half rolled and dived towards the clouds. Walker followed him down to 18,000 feet. The German machine was faster in the dive, but the Hurricane caught up when the Messerschmitt pulled out and stall-turned, with a faint wisp of smoke coming from his port engine. The fight began again. Walker was now able to follow the German's manoeuvres with ease. The Messerschmitt, dodging in and out of clouds, then gave up evasive tactics. Both his engines were smoking heavily. His port engine had nearly stopped. The aircraft were now at 3000 feet above the front. Both had used up all their ammunition, and Walker, breaking away, saw the Messerschmitt gliding towards its own lines. He did not see its end. Others did. The Messerschmitt was later found in small pieces; its pilot escaped by baling out. Stratton attacked a Messerschmitt, which may have been the same one or another, but he was uncertain of the result. Clowes shot at two of the enemy, and was also uncertain of the effect of his shooting. But two of the enemy were destroyed. This is typical of many first fights. The pilots are so engrossed in their attack, and concentration becomes so intense, that few men are able to keep a full record in their memories of all that happens. Their reports are fragmentary. Often an enemy is destroyed, and the destroyer is ignorant of the end of his victim. But in this case, although the pilots were unable to report the final result of their attack, the evidence was undeniably scattered on the soil of France.

Air Marshal Barratt invited Walker next day to dine with him. Walker said it was impossible for him to accept the invitation, because both Stratton and Clowes had had a hand in the action. The Commanding Officer of No. 1 squadron, Squadron Leader P. J. H. Halahan, an old Cranwellian, was a thorough advocate of teamwork. He approved Walker's view, and sent a signal to the Air Officer Commanding-in-Chief; the reply invited the three pilots to dinner. Barratt sent up his personal aircraft, a small civil transport Percival Q.6, to Vassincourt aerodrome for the pilots, and they dined at Maxim's in the Rue Royale. The relative value of Germany's latest fighter and the Hurricane was established; the element of uncertainty was eliminated. The Nazis might have superiority in numbers, but they had not got supremacy in design or pilots; it was this quality in machines and men which became of such supreme importance in all the opening phases of the great battles in the air. It was quality which withheld victory from Germany, and enabled the British, standing alone, to defy the onslaught.

It was strange that it should have been given to No. 1 squadron to demonstrate the inadmissibility of the German 'destroyer' aircraft to fulfil its mission of destruction. No. 1 was originally the Balloon Squadron at Farnborough, on the edge of Salisbury Plain. It did not go to France with the British Expeditionary Force of 1914 for that reason; its foreign service began in 1915; in 1917 its 110-h.p. Le Rhône rotary-engined Nieuport scouts, fitted with one Lewis gun on the top plane, flew from Bailleul aerodrome, carving a proud record of success.

Few pilots who formed its original 1939 team in France were to remain with the squadron to return to England from Nantes aerodrome in June. Some were wounded in action, two were killed, most of the others, under their squadron leader, returned to England after two to three weeks of continual fighting; they passed through Paris on May 26 on their way to form in England a Fighter School to teach other pilots what they had learned, having been awarded ten Distinguished Flying Crosses and three Distinguished Flying Medals, and having destroyed 114 enemy aircraft in ten days.

BOMBING THE
BARGES AT
DUNKIRK

German invasion barges at Dunkirk, dock buildings, unloading cranes, warehouses, wharves, roads, and rail sidings are destroyed or damaged.

Crown copyright reserved

SALVAGING THE
LUFTWAFFE

The wreckage of the Luftwaffe contributed useful scrap metal for British war factories.

Photo Associated Press

RAID ON DOVER HARBOUR

Bombs can be seen exploding in the water, but missing the ships anchored
there, at the height of the raid on July 29, 1940.

[*P.* 173]

Photo Associated Press

This squadron maintained its fine record. It was in September 1942 the top-scoring squadron of the Royal Air Force, with a bag of 230 enemy aircraft shot down. It was then a night-fighting squadron and had gained the highest scores in the infinitely more difficult task of trailing and shooting down the night bombers that used the darkened skies as cover for their operations.

Nos. 1 and 73 squadrons, which had been detached from the Air Component to give fighter protection for the bombers of the Advanced Air Striking Force, fought a novel kind of rearguard action across France, from behind the Maginot Line, through Rheims, to the area of Troyes, then south-west to the Loire district, and finally covered the evacuation of the British Base and Lines of Communication personnel from the neighbourhood of Nantes. But because the enemy forces they had to engage were so numerous, fighting was dictated by the methods of the enemy, and the idea of providing real cover, or of giving regular escorts to the bombers of the Advanced Air Striking Force, were alike impossible of accomplishment. In truth the Hurricanes fought the German aircraft wherever they found them, and that was almost everywhere they flew in the skies of France.

No. 73 squadron was the first to move back, to Rheims aerodrome during the morning of May 10. Presumably it was thought that the aerodrome at Rouvres, the most advanced aerodrome occupied by a British squadron, would soon become untenable; actually Rouvres aerodrome was never bombed by the enemy, and in moving back to Rheims-Champagne aerodrome No. 73 squadron went to one of the first British-occupied aerodromes to be bombed by the Luftwaffe.

The two Fighter squadrons attached to the Advanced Air Striking Force took turn and turn about for the dawn stand-to, and on May 10 when Rouvres aerodrome was visited at dawn by four Dornier bombers the pilots of the Fighter squadron were all in bed. Clearly, the imminence of the German attack was unprepared for on that part of the front. Indeed, there was no direct evidence to the pilots of squadrons that the great attack had begun; there was merely local evidence of unusual activity upon the part of the Luftwaffe, whose aircraft had never penetrated the area so persistently, nor in such numbers. On that morning the German bombers were laden with bombs, which had not been the case before; it was the breaking of the bombing 'truce' by the aircraft of the Luftwaffe which told the fighter pilots of Nos. 1 and 73 squadrons that the 'phoney war' was over and that the real war was on.

One of the most personal fights took place on the opening day of the blitz near Metz, when a pilot officer of No. 1 squadron, separated from his section, was attacked by two Messerschmitt 109's. He shook them off his tail before trailing one himself. He closed in and began to fire. The German pilot dived to ground-level and set course for home. The British pilot followed him across the frontier. They dodged tree-height obstacles as they sped over the land of Hitler's Reich. Some high-tension cables loomed up in front. The German pilot flew under them, no doubt hoping to throw off his pursuer, and with luck to make him crash. But the boy in the Hurricane saw them too, dived underneath them, overtook the Messerschmitt, pressed the fire-button, saw the enemy aircraft catch fire, fall flaming into a wood, and blow up.

Meanwhile in the operations-room at No. 67 Wing Headquarters at Bussy-la-Côte plots of German aircraft appeared in such numbers that it became impossible to arrange for two Fighter squadrons to provide aircraft for interceptions.

During the morning No. 1 squadron was detailed to intercept enemy air activity which might affect the other squadron's move to Rheims. About midday they made their first covering flight over enemy territory, at 15,000 feet above Luxemburg.

Then Wing Headquarters moved back from Bussy-la-Côte. And, last in the day to move, No. 1 squadron retired to Berry-au-Bac aerodrome, where No. 142 bomber squadron had been already bombed and one of its Battles destroyed.

During the fighting of that early period of the blitzkrieg improved Hurricanes became available to the pilots: machines with constant-speed metal airscrews (instead of wooden airscrews), and ejector exhausts, able to take off quicker, climb faster, travel swifter, and reach a higher ceiling. But there were not enough fighters in France to stem the tide of German aircraft that flowed over the land. What were the two hundred or so of fighters and bombers shot down by Nos. 1 and 73 squadrons out of the thousands available to the German hordes? All the valiant flying and fighting which the individual pilots were capable of coaxing out of their stout, well-gunned aircraft were woefully insufficient. So it came about that, although the blitz began on May 10, before that merry month was out the original pilots, worn out by their exertions, required reliefs to be sent from England to take their places, while they went home (except for a few who remained behind to serve as experienced flight commanders) for a much-needed rest from fighting. These young men did not break down under the strain, terrible though it was. They simply could not maintain the physical output needed to continue the task of flying high-speed fighters, often far above oxygen-level, sometimes down to tree-top eight, taking off and landing at mile-a-minute speeds on bomb-torn landing-grounds, leaping from crashing, burning aeroplanes and hurrying back, by whatever means offered, to their aerodromes, to get another aeroplane in which to push off once more into the embattled skies. Some who were wounded lived again, when coming round from the anæsthetic, those frantic moments when life hung by a spun thread in the bullet-riddled air, calling out in their semi-coma the words that drugged personality could no longer restrain, pouring forth in an incoherent torrent a mixture of prayers and curses in response to the impulses of the spirit and the body.

Among that gallant company (although not of the original small company of the first pilots to go to France) must be mentioned Sergeant Geoffrey Allard. He landed on his aerodrome in his Hurricane and taxied in, but did not get out of the cockpit. When the mechanics went to him they found him asleep. He had to be lifted from his machine. Courage was not enough. Flying in peace-time brings deep slumber in its train. Add to it the exhilaration and strain of fighting, the shifting from one aerodrome to another, the makeshift arrangements for food and rest, and it is small wonder that the reserves of vitality were soon exhausted from the physique of these men so that they were incapable of doing more. What they did was a marvel of endurance, pluck, spirit, skill, and training.

Picture Flying Officer Leslie R. Clisby—an Australian pilot in No. 1 squadron who shot down ten enemy aircraft before he himself fell on May 15, in a fight when four Hurricanes attacked thirty Messerschmitts —proud to wear his Royal Australian Air Force royal-blue uniform— alighting beside a Heinkel he had forced to land during a fight in which three Heinkel 111 bombers and two Messerschmitt 110 fighters were brought down, leaping out of his cockpit to give chase to the German pilot who was running for the cover of a wood, bringing him to earth with a low Rugby tackle, seizing the German's revolver, and then handing his prisoner over to the French.

On May 15 forty Dornier bombers with an escort of about a hundred Messerschmitt 110 fighters were attacked by a flight of five Hurricanes of No. 1 squadron. Six or seven of the enemy machines were shot down, two of the Hurricanes were crashed, but all the British pilots returned, one having to bale out.

In addition to the fighting and flying, the fighter and bomber crews had to stand the strain of being targets for the German bombers. No. 73 was bombed at Rheims aerodrome, No. 1 at Berry-au-Bac, No. 12 at Amifontaine, and so on. It was the period when the Germans were attacking aerodromes, railway junctions, and towns, but leaving the road-bridges undamaged for the passage of their oncoming tanks. The damage they actually did to the aerodromes was of slight consequence to the course of the fighting. Ordinary bombing was not a profitable way of knocking out aircraft on the ground. It was more effective to use machine-gun and cannon-gun fire against grounded aircraft, but that method meant flying low over the aerodromes, and that apparently was not one of the tactical methods of the Luftwaffe, which relied on the bomb as the principal weapon of destruction for all targets, and reserved the machine-gun and the cannon-gun for aircraft in the air and refugees on the roadways.

In this provision of cannon-guns in aircraft the Luftwaffe was at that time ahead of the Royal Air Force. Before the war the 20-millimetre Hispano cannon-gun was selected by the Air Ministry to become the standard type for use in R.A.F. aircraft, but aeroplanes were not fitted with it; instead, the machine-gun of rifle calibre was retained in all types of aircraft—in the single-seater fighters, mounted in two batteries of four in each wing, in the Defiants, mounted in one battery of four in a rear-cockpit turret, in the Whitley bomber in a rear turret of four, in other aircraft in various quantities from single to double mountings. This armament was effective against the German aircraft, because the Germans, who had mounted cannon-guns in many of their aircraft, had omitted to carry their process to the logical conclusion and equip their aircraft with adequate armour. Indeed, the British fighter aircraft were better armoured than the German; to that must be ascribed some of the greater measure of success which attended the British fighter pilots in air combat. But when, later, the British pilots were asked to make attacks upon tanks the absence of cannon-guns became serious. Yet in so small a force as the R.A.F. Fighter Command it was impossible to provide aircraft for specialist duties; it was essential to have one standard force designed for air combat duties.

When the decision was taken to move the Advanced Air Striking Force back from its original area,[1] No. 1 squadron moved back on the orders of its Commanding Officer from Berry-au-Bac to Condé Vraux, where No. 114 squadron was stationed with its Blenheim bombers. This aerodrome too had been bombed, and several bombed-up Blenheims had caught fire and been destroyed; but the squadron had not been put out of action. French sappers blew up the bridge over the Marne-Aisne canal just after No. 1 squadron's last transport crossed it with German troops hard on their heels. By May 18 No. 1 squadron was again on the move, from Condé Vraux to Anglure, about fifty miles to the south-south-west. No. 501 (County

[1] See map at p. 145, Vol. I.

of Gloucester) Fighter squadron was already there; by the beginning of June its pilots had shot down more than fifty German aircraft.

The general movement of the aircraft of the Advanced Air Striking Force from the district of Rheims to the area around Troyes was made on May 16. There newly completed aerodromes were taken over. No. 501 (County of Gloucester) squadron, Auxiliary Air Force, equipped with Hurricane fighters, had flown there from England. Headquarters of the force was established in an old château. Pressure on the Advanced Air Striking Force in the neighbourhood of Troyes increased. On May 18 the bulk of the force moved back to the Loire district in Central France. Two Battle squadrons went to Nantes aerodrome on transfer to No. 2 Base Area. Nos. 114 and 139 squadrons (which had been equipped with Blenheim bombers) went back to England; in No. 139 squadron three machines were left to fly home from their aerodrome at Plievaulx on May 18. For another fortnight the Troyes aerodromes were used as advanced refuelling-fields. The complete retirement of all aircraft to the region of the valley of the Loire was made on June 2, and the squadrons were disposed around Blois. On June 10 Air Vice-Marshal P. H. L. Playfair moved his headquarters from Troyes to Muides, near Blois, and Air Marshal A. S. Barratt, Air Officer Commanding-in-Chief, British Air Forces in France, moved his headquarters from Coulommiers to Orléans.

After ten days of continuous action it was obvious that the Battle squadrons could not continue to operate in the face of the tremendous losses they were suffering—amounting to 40 per cent.—and on May 20 they were turned over to night operations. Day-bombing operations were carried out by Blenheims based in England, except for those urgent operations which were essential to give immediate support to the ground forces. The Battles' night sorties were but fractionally lower than their day sorties; the pilots and navigators proved their ability to locate targets accurately at night, although almost all their training had been directed towards the requirements of day bombing and reconnaissance. From the night following May 20 they attacked key communication-points in the enemy system at Dinant, Givet, Fumay, Monthermé, Charleville; ammunition-dumps and fuel-stocks at Florenville and Libramont; motorized and mechanized columns concealed among the woods at Gault, Saint-Gobain, and elsewhere; and the advanced enemy aerodromes which the German Stuka (abbreviation of *Sturzkampfflugzeug*) dive-bombers used at Guise and Saint-Hubert. Night after night the Battles swept into action, and their losses were only 5 per cent. of those they had sustained during the period of day attacks. Advancing German columns between Turnhout and Namur, between Antwerp, Mons, Aulnoye, and Guise, took punishment from their nightly raids.

After the Belgian capitulation the Battles returned to day bombing against enemy mechanized columns, often swooping to two hundred feet to ensure accuracy before releasing their bombs.

On June 3 Paris was heavily bombed by German bombers; there were 906 casualties among soldiers and civilians.

On June 10 the French Government left Paris for Tours.

That evening Italy declared war on Great Britain and France. M. Reynaud appealed to President Roosevelt for material aid of every description except troops. On June 11 Mr Churchill, Mr Eden, and Sir John Dill, the Chief of the Imperial General Staff, went to France and talked with Reynaud, Pétain, and Weygand, returning to London next day. Their conversation was not disclosed.

German bombers bombed Tours military aerodrome, and fighters machine-gunned the railway station, which was crowded with refugees from Northern France. The French Air Force was already almost finished and out of action. Their all-too-few fighters put up a magnificent show during the opening of the blitzkrieg on May 10 and shot down seventy-five German aircraft; but after that effort they faded out. British pilots reported that they seldom saw a French machine in the sky. Occasionally they saw one lone Frenchman attacking with reckless abandon a huge formation of black-crossed swastika-streaked aircraft. So it was not that the French lacked courage. They lacked leadership. They lacked equipment. They were unprepared for the kind of war that broke against them in May–June 1940. The British were almost as ill-prepared; on the ground the British were hopelessly under-mechanized, in the air hopelessly outnumbered; their salvation was not gained through any qualities of leadership that had been displayed in Britain in the years before the war or in the months of quiet that preceded the blitzkrieg; it lay in the geographical situation of the United Kingdom, whose separation from the continent of Europe was the outcome of the glacial pressure of the last European ice-age thirty thousand years before, when the Strait of Dover was carved out of chalk. That situation, and the time it permitted the British people to awake to a sense of the reality of the epoch they lived in, and then to throw themselves into the work of building up the machine of war, and the opportunity it gave to enable the Royal Air Force to fight the first real air battle in history, was the arbiter of their destiny.

But it was unfair of political leaders to blame the people of Britain for the circumstances in which they found themselves. It was cruel. And it was untrue. The leaders said that every one was responsible, because a mandate was given by the people for disarmament before the war. This, of course, is nonsense. The people merely endorsed the policy followed by the leaders of the nation. I know that personally. For when I challenged (as I frequently did) in public, on the platform, the facts of British rearmament, and said that the public was not adequately informed of the true situation, I frequently found that speakers arose among the audiences and said that my statements were not in accord with those of Government speakers in the House of Commons. My statements were true, and I repeatedly challenged any Government spokesman to say otherwise. None did. But the vast mass of the public still continued to believe the half-truths and the barely concealed qualifications with which the true situation was enwrapped. How, then, can a Government spokesman say that the public, the too-readily quiescent public, was responsible? Responsibility must rest upon the shoulders of those who accept the fruits of their offices; not upon the public, between whom and realization of their peril hung that sword of Damocles, the Official Secrets Act, preventing the public from being fully informed, protecting those who would not allow them to know the real position, enabling them to go on in their ways until the truth was disclosed by the force of the enemy's arms. The British public was not to blame, but it is convenient to blame those who are forced to pay the subsequent price of folly.

About June 11 Nos. 17 and 242 and 504 Fighter squadrons were sent to France from England to reinforce the three Fighter squadrons then operating with the A.A.S.F. The main German advance had then reached Chartres, and the French had decided to withdraw to the line Caen, Alençon, Tours, and the Loire valley. The people began to stream out of Paris. German troops were pouring over a military pontoon bridge which they had run across the river Seine. Nos. 12 and 103, two squadrons of Battles, were detailed to destroy this line of advance. Hurricanes were detailed to escort them. The scene of the attack was a strongly defended point, for the bridge was guarded by anti-aircraft gun-batteries, guns on barges, and motor-cycle detachments with machine-guns. While the Hurricanes kept off the German fighters the Battles dived out of the sun to less than a thousand feet before they released their bombs. One Battle fell in flames. Two others failed to return. But the bridge was destroyed.

On June 11 No. 1 squadron was at Châteaudun, still fighting. Near by was 103 squadron, almost all of whose pilots had been lost. No. 12 squadron had lost its complete flying personnel twice over, a total of seventy-two flying men. They were brought up to strength and the squadron carried on. They battled to the last against hopeless odds.

On June 13 Paris was declared an open city and all French forces were evacuated from the capital. Next day the French High Command decided to make a further retreat. But the squadrons of the Royal Air Force had gone back as far as they could. There was no area farther back from which they could operate satisfactorily, for the lines of communication from their home bases of supply would then be hopelessly stretched. For a brief time it was planned to retreat to aerodromes near Rennes and Nantes, but on June 14 the Germans entered Paris and the French Government moved from Tours to Bordeaux. On the following day President Roosevelt cabled that every material help would be sent to France in ever-increasing quantities so long as she continued the struggle.

M. Pierre Viénot, a former Foreign Under-Secretary of State who escaped from France and reached General de Gaulle's headquarters in London in April 1943, said that the French Government contemplated removing to North Africa but were overruled by Laval.

On June 16 Marshal Pétain became Prime Minister and General Weygand Minister of Defence. France was *in extremis*. The British Government made France the offer of an Act of Union. It was rejected. During the succeeding night Pétain opened peace negotiations with Germany, and revealed his action to the French nation in a broadcast speech next morning. Germany refused to make peace unless Italy was also approached. On June 18 the French Government approached Italy through the medium of Spain.

On June 15 the Battle squadrons rose into the air from French airfields and flew back to England after five days of desperate attacks. Nos. 1, 17, 73, 242, and 501 Fighter squadrons moved to Nantes and Dinard aerodromes to cover the final movement and evacuation of the Royal Air Force ground forces, troops, and lines of communication personnel who had been separated from the British Expeditionary Force by the German advance to the coast.

No. 242 (the All-Canadians) squadron was raised in England, at the request of the Government of Canada, from Canadian personnel in the Royal Air Force. Many of its pilots came to Britain a year or two before the war to join the Royal Air Force; several worked their way across, at least two of them in cattle-boats; all had one objective—to fly. The squadron was formed in Yorkshire; its pilots flew together for the first time towards the end of 1939. They shot down twenty-eight enemy aircraft over Dunkirk. After arriving in France the squadron operated from Châteaudun and Le Mans, south-west of Paris, and were in constant contact with the enemy. For three days the pilots operated from one base, but for the remainder of the week they had to split up. They suffered losses, but assisted in destroying a much greater number of German aircraft. Missing pilots turned up after living precariously in German-occupied territory, or even after having been held prisoner for a day or two. Then came the order to move back to cover the evacuation of the Advanced Air Striking Force. In the evacuation of France the records of No. 242 squadron were lost; and although its full fighting score can never be known, during their battles in France, it is certain that its pilots had good reason to claim for the squadron as many German aircraft again as the number accredited to them over Dunkirk. Captain Peter Macdonald (Member of Parliament for the Isle of Wight and a Nova Scotian) was the squadron adjutant. He and the Intelligence Officer got off from Nantes aerodrome in an Ensign air liner carrying aircraftmen of the Royal Air Force and two war correspondents: Ronald Walker, of the *News Chronicle*, and A. H. Narracott, of *The Times*, who were both attached to the Advanced Air Striking Force, and had reached Nantes by train and motor-car on June 16.

Nantes aerodrome was crowded with aircraft—British, French (new and old and American Curtiss fighters), and civil aircraft of many varieties impressed by the R.A.F. for communication purposes. Every one was hurrying, using each available minute before he had to depart, to save equipment from falling into German hands.

Enemy bombers were in the air over the evacuating forces. On June 17 the Cunard-White Star liner *Lancastria* was dive-bombed and sunk at anchor at Saint-Nazaire with about 5300 persons on board, including women and children, some of whom had fled from as far as Brussels. About 2500 were saved. Many were in the water for several hours. No. 1 squadron shot down the bomber that sank the ship, and in its actions from Nantes destroyed fifteen enemy aircraft. The R.A.F. ground staff left France by boat and transport aircraft. After covering Cherbourg Nos. 242 and 17 squadrons left French soil. The fighter pilots were the last to leave, with the enemy vanguard almost within striking distance. The evacuation of Cherbourg was completed and the last two ships were leaving when Air Vice-Marshal K. R. Park flew over the town and harbour. His was the last Hurricane to patrol there. By the evening of June 18 all Fighter squadrons were back in Britain, together with British aircraft based in Southern France after the entry of Italy into the war.

On June 20 the German forces were still advancing south of the line Nantes-Bourges-Lyons. Lyons, the second-largest city in France, was occupied. French plenipotentiaries left Bordeaux to receive the German armistice terms, while Pétain broadcast to the French people his view of the reasons for their defeat. On June 21, while the Germans continued to advance between the estuary of the Loire and the river Rhône, and fought in the Maginot Line, the French delegates met the Germans in the Forest of Compiègne on the exact spot where the 1918 Armistice had been signed and in the railway carriage Foch had used (and which had been kept in a Paris museum, whence the Germans had brought it to the French monument), and were handed their conquerors' terms. These terms were signed next day, before they were made public. Thus did the men of Bordeaux (as they came to be called) betray France, and one great nation fell under the mantle of the twilight which was deepening into night over all Europe.

The German terms were not to enter into force until France concluded an armistice with Italy. Under them Germany was to occupy an area which included the whole Atlantic seaboard and Northern and Central France to the line Geneva-Dôle-Mâcon-Bourges-Tours; French naval, military, and air forces were to be demobilized and disarmed; all armaments and defences were to be handed over; all German prisoners of war in French hands were to be released, while French prisoners of war in German hands were to remain prisoners; no Frenchman was to serve against Germany for other Powers.

But in Britain the newly formed Government was firmly seated. It is a characteristic of the British that they fight best—indeed, are only fully roused—when their backs are against the wall. The British people were shocked, almost incredulous, at the swiftness of events in France, but they set their teeth and grimly rallied to the full support of the Government during some of the blackest hours in British history. Mr Churchill announced that if need be Great Britain would continue the war alone. Instant approval came from all parts of the British Commonwealth. French contracts for American armaments were taken over by Britain. The United States 'froze' French credits and capital in América. From London General de Gaulle broadcast appeals to all Frenchmen who had reached British soil to rally round him; on June 23 he announced the formation of a National Committee to organize French effort outside France to continue the struggle. That was the moment of the birth of the Free French, later—in 1942—to become known as the Fighting French.

On June 24 the armistice between France and Italy was signed in Rome, where the French delegates had proceeded from Compiègne. France was to demilitarize all French frontiers adjoining Libya, and those of the coast of French Somaliland; Italy was to have full rights in the port of Djibouti and on the French section of the Addis Ababa-Djibouti railway; French naval bases in the Mediterranean were to be demilitarized; the other terms were similar to those imposed by Germany. Hostilities in France terminated at 12.35 A.M. (British Summer Time) on June 25, 1940.

On July 3 the last centre of resistance in France, the Fort de l'Écluse, near Bellegarde, in the Alps, surrendered; but already, on June 28, General de Gaulle had been recognized by the British Government as leader of continued French resistance. This recognition was ratified by an agreement concluded on August 7, 1940, between the British Government and General de Gaulle, which settled the status, organization, and conditions of employment of French Volunteer Force air, land, and sea units assembled in Great Britain and elsewhere. On August 27 the Chad Territory of French Equatorial Africa and the Cameroons pledged support to General de Gaulle; two days later the whole of French Equatorial Africa rallied to the Free French Forces. This accession to the Allied cause was most important. It provided territorial continuity across Africa, from the Atlantic seaboard to the Sudan, whereby lines of communication were secured, and over which direct flying routes could be opened for aircraft flying from America, and from the United Kingdom, or for short-range aircraft shipped to the West African coast to save the long journey round the Cape. The men of Bordeaux moved to Vichy, where they formed a sub-capital in the Unoccupied Area of France, leaving the great metropolis of Paris, the city that stood for all that France was, in the hands of German masters. Yet France was not dead. Free France was very much alive.

CHAPTER V

The Air Battle of Britain

§ 1

When France Fell

THE Battle of Britain was the name given to the air engagement between the Royal Air Force and the Luftwaffe above the English Channel and South-eastern England in 1940 after the fall of France.[1] The action was a continuation of the German war plan, following, in logical sequence, the fall of Denmark, Norway, Holland, Belgium, and France. But the German strategists made one primary and one secondary miscalculation. The primary miscalculation was referred to by Field-Marshal Jan Smuts, Prime Minister of the Union of South Africa, in his speech on October 21, 1942, to the members of both Houses of Parliament in Westminster during his visit to the United Kingdom. He said:

> When France fell . . . the enemy looked upon it as also for us the end, and this infatuation of his providentially saved us. Instead of immediately turning on London, he persevered on his planned course to Paris, and gave us the opportunity to recover our breath and prepare for the blitz against London. And what a defence it was! . . . The defeat of the Luftwaffe in that supreme crisis saved not only London and Britain, but, I firmly believe, the whole Allied cause and the future of the world.

That first miscalculation was strategical in origin. It may have sprung from the inordinate love of staging triumphs which the Nazis—in common with all Germans—displayed. The war had to stop in the strategic sense while Hitler had the railway carriage wherein Foch received the German plenipotentiaries in 1918 brought to the identical spot in the Forest of Compiègne, so that the rôle might be reversed; it was a Nazi ritual, and a German funeral. Hitler, the world successor to Napoleon in speed of action, paused too long. He should have poured his legions across the Channel simultaneously with the evacuation of Dunkirk by the British Expeditionary Force. But, blind with

[1] The Battle of Britain is a continuation of the story of Fighter Command, for the earlier part of which see Vol. I, pp. 25–26 and 104–121.

exultation over the impending fall of France, led to believe in his omnipotence by his study of the occult, he challenged fate.

The secondary miscalculation was tactical. The types of aircraft used by the Luftwaffe were designed and built to operate with the advancing hosts upon the ground, to clear the way for them, to smash, but not to occupy. Sheer weight of numbers was to crush resistance. To secure speed the fuselages of the bombers were relatively small in girth; so much so that one, the Dornier 17, was called "the flying pencil." The bomb-load they could carry was not great. Their armament was light, too light to fight effectively against the eight-machine-gun fighter. (The Royal Air Force had proved that, not once, but in every engagement.) The policy of the Luftwaffe was laid down with inexorable logic, the fatal logic of the German military mind. These lightly armed, lightly armoured, fast bombers, when protected by an escort of great numbers of fighter aircraft armed with multiple machine-guns and cannon-guns, were presumed to form an invulnerable air fleet. This logic was carried into the organization of the Luftwaffe formations, which were called Air Fleets, a conception different from that of the British Commands.[1] The British Commands were functional organizations, the German Fleets were rigid tactical organizations. The British system made Air Commands the servants of strategy; the German system made Air Fleets the servants of surface tactics. Between these two outlooks there was a world of difference.

The heavy losses in aircraft suffered by the Luftwaffe from the beginning of the attack upon Poland did not deter the German militarist. French official calculations estimated German losses in aircraft from the beginning of the Western Offensive up to May 17 at 2237, with 1522 pilots killed, wounded, or missing.

The pageantry of Compiègne, set for the afternoon of June 21, saw Hitler, in his hour of triumph, in Foch's chair, accompanied by Raeder, Göring, Keitel, von Brauchitsch, Hess, and Ribbentrop; they sat facing the German-approved French plenipotentiaries—General Bergeret, M. Léon Noël, General Huntziger, and Admiral Le Luc. When the humiliation of France was over it was time enough for the Battle of Britain to begin. The French delegates signed the German armistice terms on the following day, and the coach, which had been brought to Rethondes from the Invalides in Paris, was dispatched to Berlin. . . .

In England, on the east and south-east coasts, ordinary people had noticed the erection of pylons. Some were raised before the war began. Some persons, more curious than their brothers, asked if Britain was preparing a 'death-ray' to prevent the passage of unwanted aircraft.

[1] See Vol. I. pp. 25–26.

These thought that those pylons meant power to destroy. In the end, and indirectly, they were right. But the secret behind those wireless masts was well kept. The pylons were the outward and visible sign of radiolocation, the system of aircraft detection pioneered by Sir Robert A. Watson-Watt, C.B., F.R.S., who before the war was the Director of Communication Development in the Air Ministry. (He was knighted during the war in recognition of his work in radiolocation.) Radiolocation was precisely what the name implied: a method of locating the position of aircraft in space by the employment of waves of radio wave-band length. This method of locating the approach of aircraft helped to overcome the geographical handicap of Britain's island situation, which laid the country open to the danger of surprise attack from the air. Knowledge of the approach of aircraft before they crossed the coastline was of the utmost value. The standing patrol of aircraft, remaining constantly in the air, was a wasteful method of combating enemy aircraft. It used unnecessary fuel and oil, tired the personnel, imposed wear on the machine, and caused a percentage of crashes due to the ordinary risks of flight. Enemy aircraft might be spotted by a standing patrol when the defending aircraft had little fuel left in their tanks and were unable to engage the enemy on that account. Without radiolocation to aid intelligence of enemy aircraft movements, the provision of standing patrols would have been essential, for the Observer Corps, stationed on shore, could not have provided advance information, but information relating to aircraft already so close to the coastline as to give scant warning of impending attack.

Radiolocation spotted all aircraft. There was no distinction between friend and foe. It had a blank spot, for aircraft flying very close to sea-level were difficult to locate, but the Germans did not then know that.

The Observer Corps (it became the Royal Observer Corps on April 9, 1941) began its continuous day and night watch on August 24, 1939. It was manned by 30,000 men volunteers. Most were spare-time watchers. They maintained a network of many hundreds of observer-posts, established on hillsides, in the open country, on high buildings in towns and cities, and at lonely points along the coastline. Each post was connected by permanent telephone-line with an Observer Corps Centre, which, together with the posts under its control, constituted an Observer Group. A Group with an area equivalent to a medium-sized county might have about thirty-six posts. Day and night, the task of the Observer Corps was to detect and keep track of every aeroplane, friendly or hostile, in the air above Great Britain. Each post observing aircraft instantly reported their approximate height, speed, course, and

126

numbers to its Centre; there, seated round a large-scale table-map of their area, plotters moved counters over the map face in accordance with the reports from post crews; each counter represented the track of one or more aircraft. 'Tellers,' overlooking the tables, had direct communication with Royal Air Force Fighter Centres, to whom they passed a minute-to-minute account of the position of every aircraft flying within their area, and almost instantly reported every change of course or height.

Anti-aircraft gun-posts and searchlight sites, observer-posts, aerodromes, operations-rooms, and fighter sectors were all interconnected by telephone on the basis of the General Post Office system, enlarged by additional circuits and field lines and supplemented by dispatch-riders and radio. The telephone system was maintained jointly by the G.P.O. Engineers' Department and the Royal Corps of Signals.

The intelligence obtained from all sources (including ships) was co-ordinated by a central organization, and transmitted to the operations-rooms of the Royal Air Force—at Fighter Command Headquarters, Group Headquarters, Sector Headquarters, and Station Headquarters. Upon table-maps representing the British Isles, the surrounding sea, and part of the continent of Europe (or, to the lesser organizations, the appropriate sectors of the whole map) the plotting of the changing air situation enabled the responsible staff officers to see the position at any given moment. Speed of transmission of intelligence was so rapid that the true situation in the air was but slightly ahead of the situation depicted on the maps, so that, even with the speed of the aircraft of that period, it was possible for the air commanders to think ahead of the actual situation. Moreover, the intelligence channels through which the information was filtered made it possible for the counters to indicate with a high degree of certainty which aircraft were friendly and which were hostile.

It was possible to visualize the lines of approach of enemy attacks while they were in process of development. Royal Air Force commanders in subterranean bomb-proof operations-rooms had the advantage of look-out posts as good as, and perhaps better than, those of the olden-time generals who sat on horseback on a near-by hill and surveyed the enemy troops advancing in the middle distance, and could anticipate the enemy intention, and make the dispositions necessary to engage his air formations, with the object of defeating that intention.

Placing implicit reliance on the accuracy of the picture presented by this intelligence organization, fighters were ordered up and then directed by radio telephony into position to engage the enemy, anti-aircraft gun defences were warned of the approach of raiders, and air-raid warning sirens were sounded in areas towards which enemy aircraft were heading.

The commanders of the Luftwaffe no doubt had counted on the short warning margin which the Royal Air Force would receive from visual observation. On no other assumption is it possible to explain their blunder in failing adequately either to arm or armour their bombers, and to accept speed as the primary consideration in bomber design. (Their own radio detection system, then not fully developed, was faulty.) Had they foreseen the conditions which the Luftwaffe would have to face when making an attack upon the British Isles the aircraft-design department of the Reichsluftfahrtministerium would doubtless have given other considerations urgent priority. But when first the knowledge reached them it was too late. Britain had previously informed her ally, France, of her radiolocation secrets. When France fell Germany had access to them. But Göring's Luftwaffe was already committed. Hitler's intelligence service, with all its fifth-columnists, had failed.

§ 2

The Luftwaffe Feels its Way

The Luftwaffe was organized in five Air Fleets. The First and Fourth Air Fleets were used in the attack upon Poland. The Fifth Air Fleet was employed against Norway. After the fall of France the reinforced Second Air Fleet and the Third Air Fleet faced the British Isles, with their *Geschwadern* grouped in a great crescent from North Holland to Brest. They were commanded respectively by General Field-Marshal Albert Kesselring and General Field-Marshal Hugo Sperrle. Neither was primarily a military airman; they were both professional army officers; but Sperrle, unlike Kesselring, served with the German army air force in the 1914–18 war. Both officers transferred early to the Luftwaffe. These two were the Luftwaffe generals responsible for the air attack which was intended to bring about the defeat of Britain either by itself or by preparing the way for the assault of the surface forces. Both were the same age—fifty-five.

Kesselring believed in the power of the bomber to smash the will of a nation to resist, so that subsequent occupation would be made easy for the ground forces. He had the outlook of the optimist, and may have thought that the power of the Luftwaffe was too great to be countered. Sperrle, it is said, did not subscribe wholly to the bombing of towns by the Luftwaffe because he feared that if things went awry the boomerang might strike back.

Kesselring had commanded the First Air Fleet against Poland; Sperrle, since the outbreak of war, had been in the West. But Sperrle had had practical experience during the Spanish Civil War of 1936–39, in command of the Kondor Legion, the expeditionary force of the Luftwaffe which used the buildings of Spain and sacrificed the lives of Spanish men, women, and children to test in practice German theories of bombing. Spanish towns were more satisfactory bombing ranges than the targets employed for practice in Germany, where buildings, railway stations, and other real-life targets were erected to be blown to pieces by the bombers of the Luftwaffe, then laboriously rebuilt only to be knocked down once more.

In spite of practice in advance, and contrary to theories of the efficacy of bombing, Germany did not turn the weapon of the Luftwaffe against the countries she attacked until the moment her ground troops were ready to make their assault; at least, not in force.

German raids against Britain during the early period of the war were sporadic.[1] The first British civilian was killed by a German bomb at Bridge of Waith, on March 16, 1940, during a raid against Scapa Flow in the Orkney Islands. The first German bombs were dropped on the mainland of Britain near Canterbury on May 9, 1940. Britain's first industrial town to be attacked was Middlesbrough; the date was May 24, 1940. The first British bombs fell on Germany (except for the raid upon Hornum, on the island of Sylt, in the night following March 19, 1940, in answer to the Scapa Flow raid[2]) in the night following May 11, 1940; in that night began the British air offensive against Germany which was destined not to cease until the war ended.

But the German method was not the same as the British. The Luftwaffe was tied to the German Army. It was a part of the Wehrmacht. The independent German air force, which owned and operated all the paraphernalia of ground defence against air attack, in addition to the flying defence, was compelled to align itself with the needs of an army raised specifically for conquest. Therein lay at once the strength and the weakness of the Luftwaffe. All its equipment was designed for the purpose of assisting army conquests. Bombers, predominating over all other types of aircraft, amounted to 65 per cent. of Germany's aircraft numerical strength. The bombers were lightly armed and lightly armoured because they were intended to be used principally against an enemy demoralized by the combined ground and air assault; and by British standards they were almost all day bombers. The Luftwaffe specialized in day bombing because it gave them the accuracy of aim which suited the field requirements of the army

[1] See Vol. I, pp. 108–109.   [2] See Vol. I, pp. 98–100.

commanders. Their dive-bombers were essentially aircraft intended for close tactical work in conjunction with advancing ground forces. The Junkers 87, the standard German dive-bomber, was neither fast nor well armed; it depended for its safety upon the German fighters' command of the air; if that were not gained it became the prey of opposing fighters, and in its downward swoop was a fair target for anti-aircraft gunners. The Royal Air Force had no dive-bombers. The main bombing force of the British air service was a night-bombing force, which was regarded primarily as a defensive force created for the purpose of disorganizing a deploying army or a nation preparing to deploy its military strength.

The Luftwaffe was well organized and well equipped for the purposes of the German attacks upon Poland, Norway, the Low Countries, and France. It fulfilled the mission entrusted to it by breaking the way through in front of the German armies. But when they were confronted with the problem of the British Isles the air force as intended for Continental warfare must have seemed to some of the German air leaders less well suited to its new task than they might have wished. With the types of aircraft they possessed, the leaders of Germany delayed too long their attack upon Britain; the margin was slight, but it was enough to rob them of the victory they had hoped to gain. For this reason the types of air attack made against Britain prior to the launching of the theoretical knock-out blow are worth careful study. It is possible to observe in them a gradual swing-up in the scale of air-power which was turned against Britain as one after another of the Continental countries of Western Europe fell before the swift hammer-strokes of the Third Reich's war machine, and to perceive in them the outline of the coming plan of attack and the manner in which it was at first hampered by the destruction already wrought by German arms and air-power in Western Europe. For several weeks the full strength of the Luftwaffe lay latent, waiting until the railways, roads, bridges, and ports could again be made easily usable to bring up the fuel, oil, bombs, ammunition, food, spares, and other manifold necessities of full-scale modern air war to equip it for the great air assault which was to pull Britain down.

The first large-scale air attack upon Great Britain, which came in the bright moonlight night following June 18, 1940, was a probing attack. About a hundred German aircraft crossed the coast between Kent and Yorkshire. Twelve civilians were killed and thirty injured. A pipeline leading to an oil wharf on the Thames Estuary was struck by a bomb; the resulting fire was soon extinguished. Eight houses in a Cambridgeshire town were demolished. Among the objectives were several Royal Air Force aerodromes, and damage was done in several villages which were close to the air stations.

Royal Air Force night fighters were up searching for the raiders. The pilots' location of the enemy aircraft was aided by searchlights, whose tall fingers served as pointers to the targets, and often as illuminants of them. Shortly before one o'clock in the morning Flight Lieutenant A. G. Malan, flying over Essex in a Spitfire, saw a bomber caught in a searchlight beam at 8000 feet. He climbed towards the enemy, and, from fifty yards, fired a four-seconds burst. The bomber fell spinning to earth. A few minutes later Malan destroyed another bomber in the same way, this time from 12,000 feet. Five more German bombers were destroyed that night by Blenheim night fighters.

Night-fighter defence against the bomber was not much more developed than in the closing era of the Great War, save that it was aided by more accurate ground-crew plotting of the enemy lines of approach and radio-telephonic communication between ground and pilots. Instead of single or twin guns, the Spitfires, Hurricanes, Blenheims, and Defiants that Fighter Command put into the night skies against the German raiders all had machine-gun batteries of rifle-calibre; but none had cannon-guns.

Both German and British night raids were then still made on the principle developed before the war: aircraft flew singly, with wide time-intervals separating aircraft detailed to attack the same targets. A force of a hundred bombers was usually directed against a variety of targets spread over a great area, effecting no more than pin-point destruction which, in the military sense, was slight. But at that time no alternative method had been developed. The difficulties in organization and navigation required by other methods appeared to be insurmountable. Concentrated raids were therefore reserved for daylight. Before long the experience of war was to change this, but here it is important to observe that the leaders of the Luftwaffe, who had built up the largest air force the world had ever seen, had not trained the air crews of that force to make concentrated night attacks. To make precision raids, the crews of the German bombers had to be able to see; in consequence, most of the important raids were made when the sky was lit by the moon and the ground was unobscured by clouds; to hunter's moon and harvest moon was added the expression 'bomber's moon.'

In the night following June 19 more than a hundred German bombers crossed the east coast of Scotland and the east and south coasts of England. Three towns on the north-east English coast were bombed, and more bombs were scattered in Lincolnshire, Southern

England, South Wales, and in a Lancashire town. Three raiders were shot down, and two severely damaged. Eight civilians were killed and about sixty injured.

Two nights later German aircraft again raided England, dropping bombs in the Eastern Counties, but doing little material damage; they killed three civilians and injured three. Two nights passed quietly. In the night following June 24 bombs fell in the Eastern Counties of England, in the Midlands, and in the South-west. The attack upon the South-west was a new development in the war. This area had been regarded as a reception area for those evacuated from danger areas, but the German occupation of Brest on June 20, and their capture of Saint-Malo and Lorient two days later, brought the South-west of England into the Channel front line with but 100 miles of sea separating the British coast and the German-occupied coast in Brittany, fewer than twenty-five minutes' flying distance for the bombers of that period.

In the night following June 25 German aircraft were again over Britain, killing four civilians and injuring about thirteen, but doing little damage. Three bombers were shot down by R.A.F. fighters and two by anti-aircraft gunfire; one was a Heinkel 111 which fell to the guns of a Spitfire flown by Flying Officer A. V. R. Johnstone, of No. 602 (City of Glasgow) squadron, who later became its commanding officer when Squadron Leader A. D. Farquhar was promoted to Wing Commander. Johnstone was on patrol when he saw the Heinkel illuminated by searchlights near the Firth of Forth.

The sporadic raids continued. In the night following June 26 there were sixteen casualties; three German aircraft were shot down, two of which, a Heinkel 111 and a Junkers 88, fell to Spitfires. Next night raiders swept over a wide area, but only three civilians were injured and damage was again slight. Twenty-four hours later five civilians were injured by bombs dropped in South Wales and near the east coast of England; the enemy bomber which fell that night was shot down by a R.A.F. fighter off the coast of Scotland.

In the night following June 28 the Luftwaffe raided the Channel Islands. The islands had been demilitarized and declared undefended, and there was no opposition to the bombers. Twenty-nine civilians were killed in Guernsey and ten in Jersey; many others were injured.

Before the war the islands had had civil airline communication with Great Britain, and there were aerodromes on Guernsey, Jersey, and Alderney. After a brief break when war broke out these communications were reopened. Hundreds of passengers had flown on these routes, finding comfort in the flight compared to the frequent discomfort of the sea passage across the Channel where the water was often rough, too rough for the smooth sailing of ships designed more for the small size of the islands' harbours than for the English Channel's big seas.

The Channel Islands were self-governing. They were not bound by Acts of the British Parliament unless specially named in them. They were free from British income-tax and British conscription for the armed forces, and were perhaps the freest portions of the whole British Commonwealth. Their governing bodies—called States— were based upon the old Norman-French system of government, and remained the most insistent reminder of the Norman conquest of England, which attached the islands to the English Crown under the Dukedom of Normandy. The Bailiff was chief magistrate and president of the States Assembly; during session he sat above and took precedence over the Lieutenant-Governor, appointed by the British Crown, who had a power of veto in certain forms of legislation but might not vote.

In 1937 the islands possessed no form of defence whatever. The Militia had been disbanded. A sergeant, a corporal, and two soldiers comprised the defence force of Jersey. The islanders were firmly attached to a policy of peace, and, like many theorists of the time, did not consider that peace required its military warders to guard its security. Few of the islanders thought that they would ever be involved in war, even if war came to Britain again.

The airline services between England and the islands run by Jersey Airways continued until suspended by Air Ministry order on June 13, 1940. Next day the airline company's evacuation service began to operate. Wives and families of the company's staff were flown to England first, followed by equipment, stores, and spare engines. Maintenance personnel, except for a skeleton staff, were evacuated. The evacuation was aided by two Ensign air liners, formerly owned by British Overseas Airways Corporation, but now operated by No. 24 (Communications) squadron, which brought R.A.F. personnel to the islands. A squadron of fighters occupied the Jersey aerodrome to cover the evacuation. During June 18 and 19 five of the six Jersey Airways De Havilland 86 air liners flew from dawn to dusk and transported 320 passengers to England. From the aircraft French people could be seen leaving Normandy in small boats.

From a cloudy sky appeared one of the oldest types of French monoplanes. It made an unsteady approach. The landing shocked the professional pilots. Its pilot was a Frenchman, aged about fifty. His hands shook uncontrollably, and his face dripped with the sweat of a great ordeal. He was the adjutant of a French air squadron. His unit had heard that the bulk of the French Air Force was going to Morocco. They decided to give in. The adjutant had not piloted since the Great War, but he took up the ancient monoplane and headed west with the idea of coming down on the water beside the first ship he saw, which he assured himself was "bound to be British." The visibility grew worse. He flew helplessly in the clouds. He came lower. The first thing he saw was Jersey airport. The Fighter squadron welcomed him and put him aboard one of the evacuation ships. Two days later the squadron leader again met the adjutant, a happy man, walking in the streets of London.

Alderney aerodrome was mined and obstructed and the island completely evacuated. R.A.F. demolition parties destroyed property, including motor-cars, which might be useful to the enemy. The black smoke of bombing was visible in France as the Germans approached and then took Cherbourg. The R.A.F. left the Channel Islands. Radio communication ceased by order of the Air Ministry. Civilians continued to evacuate themselves by sea. Telephone communication continued until the Germans arrived.

Guernsey was occupied by German troops on June 30, and Jersey next day. One correspondent, who escaped by air shortly before the German occupation, wrote to me: "Hundreds of pals were left behind —due to their own crass stupidity." In the late autumn of 1942 it was announced that Channel Islanders had been conscripted and deported for labour in Germany.

Britain stood alone, without a single outpost, facing the German hordes in control of the Western European coastline from the North Cape to the river Bidassoa (which flows into the Bay of Biscay between France and Spain) a distance of 2000 miles in a straight line. The character of the war changed; for Germany now possessed fjords, ports, harbours, estuaries, canals, locks, docks along that great coast-line; from them her submarines could issue and to them return to find refuge, and rearm, refuel, and revictual. R.A.F. bombers flew under cover of darkness and laid mines in enemy waters.

Along and behind that great coastline the Luftwaffe found many prepared aerodromes, and land to site others, from which a concentration of bombers could be brought to bear upon the British Isles. Liverpool, for example, could be attacked by bombers flying from Holland, Belgium, and Brittany. To Germany, Britain was the only target which mattered. Defeat of the British would establish the Nazi victory and subjugate all Europe, for Britain was the last base wherein forces could be organized to oppose Germany in Western Europe.

But the Luftwaffe was not ready for the new conditions which German arms had created. Göring's 'armed reconnaissances' continued.

During the night following June 29 German aircraft crossed the south and east coasts of Britain and dropped bombs in the Midlands, Southern England, the British Channel area, and Scotland. Two civilians were killed and eight injured. Little damage was reported. During the following night further raids injured a few persons, and reports of bombs came from Eastern and Western England, Wales, and Scotland.

On July 1, 1940, German aircraft made their first daylight raid. They dropped bombs before dark at Hull, in North-east England, and at Wick, in Scotland. Six persons were reported killed and sixteen injured. The same districts were daylight-raided on the following day, when thirteen persons were killed and 120 injured. On July 3, for the third day in succession, these areas were attacked in daylight; six people were killed and seventy-eight injured. Seven enemy aircraft were shot down and six others badly damaged. That night Bomber Command bombed Merville aerodrome. The Luftwaffe made a small-force night raid on the Eastern Counties of England; no casualties were reported.

On July 4 the Germans altered the direction of attack with a day thrust against Portland. A naval auxiliary vessel was hit and fired, a small tug and a lighter sunk; buildings were damaged; eleven civilians were killed; one German bomber was destroyed. But elsewhere over the south coast of England R.A.F. fighters shot down two German aircraft and seriously damaged another. A raid made during the following night caused no casualties; damage was slight.

In the early morning of July 5 British fighters shot down a German bomber off the south-east coast of England. Before darkness came that evening a mixed formation of fighters and bombers was driven off over the south-east coast, and one German fighter was shot down. During the night German bombers crossed the north-east coast of England, but no damage or casualties were reported. On the following day German aircraft crossed the north-east, south-east, and south coasts of England, did damage by bombs, caused casualties, and lost one of their number. A night attack caused damage and casualties on the north-east coast, where Hull and the Humber district were favourite targets. On July 7 enemy aircraft raided South and South-west England in daylight, causing some damage and a few casualties; three bombers and a fighter were shot down. At night they crossed the north-east coast of England, did damage, and left casualties in their wake.

Next day the R.A.F. brought down eight enemy aircraft and lost three fighters while disputing raids directed against the south-east and west coasts of England; after dark, sporadic raids were scattered along the country behind the eastern coastline from the English Channel right up into Scotland; this round-the-clock bombing caused few casualties and did only slight damage.

The policy behind the German air attacks began to be discernible. In France the Luftwaffe, preferring to see where they were going, had concentrated their attacks into the daylight hours; night attacks were fewer and less powerful; this harmonized with army technique. The air bombardment of Britain, unaccompanied by the immediate advance of the army, called for a new decision on air technique. The Luftwaffe was no longer subordinate to army commanders. For the first time, it stood alone. Its commanders were about to offer to the world their demonstration of the employment of air-power as a conquering force. They were the first in this new field of martial endeavour. The low scale of losses in aircraft sent over Britain during the early 'armed reconnaissances' must have raised the hopes of Kesselring and Sperrle, and flattered the heart of the Führer of the Luftwaffe, the gross Reichs-marschall Hermann Göring. And the result of the preliminary probing of the air over Britain was the decision to make the main air assaults in daylight.

Meanwhile, with the richest prize still to conquer, but no doubt with the reassurances of Göring in his ears, Hitler did not hurry. He toured the battlefields in France, and returned to Berlin on July 8 to receive a welcome prepared by Herr Doktor Joseph Göbbels, Reichsminister for Propaganda. Hitler drove through the streets of his capital cheered by crowds; frantically they offered him the Nazi salute.

Mr Winston Churchill's speech on June 4 should have served as a warning to the Führer. The British Prime Minister then said:

> Even though large tracts of Europe and many old and famous states have fallen or may fall into the grip of the Gestapo, and all the odious apparatus of Nazi rule, we shall not flag or fail. We shall go on to the end; we shall fight . . . on the seas and oceans; we shall fight with growing confidence and growing strength in the air; we shall defend our island whatever the cost may be. We shall fight on the beaches; we shall fight on the landing-grounds; we shall fight in the fields and in the streets; we shall fight in the hills. We shall never surrender.

Unlike Paris, London was not declared to be an open town; nor was any other city in the United Kingdom. Instead, there was the promise that Britain would fight wherever the German hordes might

136

try to pass. The Prime Minister's words meant that all Britain was a battlefield. No conditions were asked and none were offered. It was war to the death—the death of Britain or of Nazism and an unrepentant Germany.

On May 14 the Local Defence Volunteers (later renamed Home Guard) force was formed, at first mainly intended to deal with Germans who might be landed in Britain by air. Steadily a programme of preparation was proceeded with. Signposts were removed from all roads. Place-names were removed from towns, railway stations, and the gates of houses and farms which were marked on maps. Defence-posts were built at cross-roads, barbed-wire barricades grew in un-expected (and in expected) places, including Whitehall; beaches were blocked by concrete walls and wire entanglements, and sown with land-mines; roadways leading from the sea were obstructed by anti-tank obstacles; the estuaries were mined and their surfaces covered with floating barrels anchored to the bed, or other objects sufficiently stout to wreck alighting seaplanes were fixed or moored at frequent intervals; commons and open spaces were trenched, obstructed by breastworks, or poles, to prevent the safe landing of landplanes. Those parts of the country nearest to the Germans were dealt with first. The more remote parts were treated later. From an unmilitary, pleasant land, Britain began to assume the aspect of a defended castle protected by a wide moat, the sea.

Mr Churchill spoke again in London on July 14, 1940, and said:

. . . In this strong city of refuge, which enshrines the title-deeds of human progress and is of deep consequence to Christian civilization—here, girt about by the seas and oceans where the Navy reigns, shielded from above by the staunchness and devotion of our airmen, we await undismayed the impending assault. . . . Be the ordeal sharp or long, or both, we shall seek no terms, we shall tolerate no parley. We may show mercy—we shall ask none.

German aircraft losses over Britain were rising. Fighter Command had begun to get the measure of the Luftwaffe generals' technique.

On July 9, when enemy aircraft appeared throughout the day over many parts of England, including the Bristol Channel area and East Anglia, nine were shot down.

Next day the enemy targets were in South Wales, South-west and Southern England, and shipping off the coast. Fourteen enemy aircraft were shot down and twenty-three others seriously crippled. Two British fighters were lost. German raids during the succeeding night were spread lightly over the eastern and south-eastern counties and the Midlands of England, causing some damage and casualties.

There was air fighting over coastal areas at intervals throughout the daylight hours of July 11. The enemy also sought targets in the Midlands. Twenty-three German aircraft were destroyed. Fighter Command lost four aircraft. Some damage was caused on land. A few civilians were killed. H.M. patrol yacht *Warrior II* was sunk in the English Channel. A raid during the following night on the eastern and south-western coasts of England did but slight damage, and caused no fatal casualties.

On July 12 the enemy attacked a convoy off the south-east coast. Their aircraft were engaged by British fighters. Raids upon Scotland caused some damage and a number of civilians were killed or injured. Eleven enemy bombers were destroyed; two British fighters were lost. A night raid over North-east England, Scotland, and Wales damaged houses and injured a number of civilians.

On July 13 the enemy air attacks were directed mainly against shipping, but three persons were killed by bombs on land. The R.A.F. lost three aircraft; twelve German aircraft were destroyed. Enemy aircraft were over South-east and South-west England and Wales during the following night, but no bombs were reported.

From July 7 to July 13 inclusive eighty-one German aircraft were destroyed over and around Britain for the loss of fourteen R.A.F. fighters, a ratio of almost six to one in aircraft, and of about eighteen to one in air-crew personnel. During this period no enemy aircraft was shot down at night. In addition to the aircraft known to be destroyed, many more were seriously damaged. Some probably came down in the sea near the enemy-occupied shore, and others probably crashed on land on the other side of the Channel. Figures for such losses cannot be known during the course of the war. Many, indeed, may never be known.

During the succeeding week (July 14 to 20 inclusive) enemy air activity over Britain was on a smaller scale. Many of the attacks were directed against shipping round the coasts. Forty-five enemy aircraft were shot down, including three by anti-aircraft gunfire from the ground, and one shot down by H.M. minesweeping trawler *Rinovia* in the Channel. On July 14 attacks were made against shipping in the Straits of Dover; R.A.F. fighters shot down seven of the enemy and damaged many more, without loss to themselves. On July 19 twelve German aircraft were shot down while attacking shipping around the southern English coast, districts in Scotland, Wales, and South-east England; there were few casualties and damage was slight; the R.A.F. lost seven fighters. The largest attack against shipping during that period came on July 20 against a South Coast harbour and a convoy in the Channel; a series of air fights felled eighteen machines of the Luftwaffe for the loss of four British fighters; three of the raiders were destroyed by gunfire from the ground. Areas attacked during the week included a South Coast town, South-west England, and South Wales on July 15, when no enemy aircraft were destroyed; Scotland and North-west England on July 16, when three bombers were shot down; Scotland and South-east England on July 17, another casualty-free day for the Luftwaffe; and North-east, South, South-west England, and Wales on July 18, when one enemy aircraft fell into the Channel to British aircraft machine-gun fire. Night attacks were equally spread over the country; from South-east to South-west England, the Midlands, Wales, to North-east and North-west England and Scotland. Damage generally was slight and there were few casualties due to these early night raids. The R.A.F. lost nine fighters during the week.

For the month which began on June 18 air-raid casualties among civilians in Britain were 336 killed and 476 seriously injured.

§ 3
Counter-attack

The declaration of war by Italy against Britain, declaimed from the balcony of the Palazzo Venezia in Rome by Benito Mussolini on June 10, did not ease the strain on the United Kingdom, although it did not at first throw added weight into the direct attack. But it entailed for the British peoples, fighting now by themselves, and aided by the Free French under General de Gaulle, the uncaptured Poles under General Sikorski, and the escaped Czechs under Dr Beneš, together with contingents of Norwegians, Danes, Dutch, and Belgians, a widening of the conflict at the very time when all their energies might be demanded to meet the full concentration of a powerful German assault upon their islands; so that British troops, warships, and aircraft were fighting in the Mediterranean zone, in Malta, and in East Africa, where they were withdrawing under Italian pressure from the Sudanese border with Ethiopia. On August 4, 1940, Italian troops began the invasion of British Somaliland. Without doubt Italian military action against parts of the British Empire was designed to embarrass Britain and render the way easier for the direct assault upon Britain which Germany desired to make. Not for nothing was the principal German marching song (sung at every gathering of German troops) the guttural but swinging "We are sailing against England. . . ." On June 28,

1940, Marshal Italo Balbo died when his aeroplane fell in flames near Tobruk. Rome reported the accident as having occurred "during an enemy bombardment." That was untrue. There was neither a British bombardment nor a British aircraft at Tobruk at the time. But Balbo was a man of proud spirit. It was said that Mussolini was jealous of his popularity with the Italian people, and that that was the reason why he was 'banished' from Italy to become the Governor of Libya after his triumphant flight across the Atlantic with a formation of flying boats to Chicago and back to Rome in 1933. Italo Balbo was friendly to Britain. It was said that he was against Italian intervention in the war. It was learned later that the cause of the crash in which he was killed (he was himself a pilot) was the explosion of a time-bomb which had been placed inside the aircraft.

In addition to the extra burden of Italian military pressure, Britain had to face the diplomatic pressure of Japan, which, aligned with the Axis, seized the opportunity to demand privileges at the moment when she deemed it would be impossible for Britain to refuse her requests. The Japanese demanded that no more military supplies should reach China through French Indo-China, or Hong Kong, or Burma, and at the same time pressed the Netherlands East Indies to permit Japanese commercial penetration. On July 17, 1940, the British Government reached an agreement with Japan that no war material would be imported into China through Burma during the following three months; with Germany at Britain's throat, with Italy gnawing at Britain's house like a desert rat, Japan could not be taken on simultaneously; the 'yellow peril' nation had to be placated for the time if Britain were to survive her life-or-death struggle with the Western Powers.

The inevitable consequences of Italy's extension of the war were to lengthen British lines of communication and multiply the areas which required air cover. But for the first time the German High Command did not possess unity of command over the component parts of the Axis war machine; there were now two dictators in their own right, and there was the cunning third partner, Japan. Britain for the first time had unity of command. For there was in England, in supreme charge under the King, one man, the eldest son of the third son (Lord Randolph Churchill) of the seventh Duke of Marlborough, of whose ancestor, the first Duke of Marlborough, Dean Jonathan Swift, although a political enemy, wrote that he had won every battle to which he had lent his military skill; this man, Winston Churchill, the supreme executive officer of State in Britain, had a remarkable background of experience whereon to build; he was a soldier from 1895 (previously at Sandhurst) until 1916, with experience of war in Cuba, India, Egypt, South Africa, and France; a politician and statesman from 1905 with experience in almost every one of the principal offices of State; a student of war, a writer of note, a speaker of eloquent appeal; the son of an American mother; a thinker of originality and a man of courage. He had been both Liberal and Conservative, and now he entered into the chief office allied with Labour. There were, therefore, as will readily be understood, those who were not in favour of all his policies, but there was none big enough to challenge and defeat him in the political field, nor was there, in the mind of the public, anyone to replace him. He stood head and shoulders above every one, this man of sixty-five, as leader of the British people in their greatest hour of testing, and spoke words of grim defiance to the dictators, within the House of Commons and without. He was the generalissimo of the forces arrayed against Hitler and Mussolini : not in name—for Winston Churchill did not assume military rank higher than that of Hon. Air Commodore, to which he was entitled in the Royal Air Force before the war began—but in character, and, according to some of the generals of that time, in fact. And, indeed, it was his destiny so to be. Moving straight from Admiralty House to No. 10 Downing Street, Mr Churchill brought with him close contacts with naval thought and outlook. For nine months he had striven with the submarine campaign, and now that supreme power was in his hands there was opportunity to deal with the menace from the air. Almost at once Mr Churchill announced Admiralty operational control over the Coastal Command of the R.A.F. This was but a slight change, for Coastal Command had worked in the closest liaison with the Navy. The real change lay in the power which the Prime Minister (as Minister of Defence) possessed of determining from time to time what the strength of the Coastal Command should be; it was possible to draw upon any and all resources of the R.A.F. to increase the strength of Coastal Command; the new arrangement was not so much a change in operational method as a change in the person who had power to say how many shore-based aircraft would be allocated to the requirements of naval anti-submarine air operations. Coastal Command grew in strength, and became a complete air force in itself, replete with fighters and bombers in addition to the flying boats, torpedo-bombers, and general reconnaissance land aircraft which had been its complement when war began. The fighters could come only or be deflected from Fighter Command, the bombers from Bomber Command, or both from overseas Commands.

Mr Churchill himself described the Admiralty during the Great War as a realm within a realm. In the World War he made Coastal Command a realm within the realm of the Air Force. It spread its wings until its operations were undertaken wherever the Navy required. It was no longer, as it had been, a Home command, like Bomber Command or Fighter Command. It was a World Command, as universal as the fleet it served. Its bases spread all round the coasts of the United Kingdom, and were to be found in West Africa, the Mediterranean, in Iceland, America, and elsewhere.

Correspondingly, the growth of Bomber Command was slow. But in time it became a great strategic force and a valuable source of reserve strength, a full quiver wherein the barbed arrows of British air-power were carried. After the fall of France Bomber Command had to play its part in the defence of Britain, dovetailing its offensive operations with the defensive fighting of Fighter Command. From attacks upon those communication points and transport links which the French had believed to offer the best targets during the Battle of France, and the direct attacks upon troop concentrations which were necessary to fulfil the demands of the commanders in the field, the new policy swung Bomber Command towards targets best calculated to undermine the organization of a German attack upon Great Britain.

Targets chosen by the Target Selection Committee for special attention were aircraft factories, oil- and aluminium-producing plants, communications connected with the German industrial war effort—more especially railway marshalling-yards and canals—and, during the period of the Battle of Britain, the Channel ports that faced England, called at the time the 'invasion ports.' This new phase of the Command's activities set in on June 18, 1940, and the targets that night were aerodromes, fuel depots, blast furnaces, marshalling-yards, and trains at Hamburg, Bremen, Rheydt, Cologne, Düsseldorf, Hanover, and Frankfurt. On the night following June 22 the Bremen factory of the Focke-Wulf Flugzeugbau was bombed; a return visit was paid four nights later. Among other aircraft factories attacked were the Junkers (Ju 52 troop-transport aircraft) factory at Deichshausen, the Messerschmitt 110 fighter and fighter-bomber production centre at Gotha where Dornier 17 bombers were also made and, in addition, troop-and-transport-carrying gliders; and the Henschel Flugzeugwerk at Kassel where Dornier 17 and 215 bombers were made.

This phase of Bomber Command's activity ended on December 5, 1940.[1]

German military activity in the Continental harbours from Narvik to Bordeaux, a distance of nearly two thousand miles, was watched continually and vigilantly by the Royal Air Force, and visual and photographic reconnaissance aircraft brought back valuable information.

[1] For the list of targets attacked during this period see Appendix No. 2.

In the early days of September 1940 there were only small concentrations of men and material in these ports, but as the days passed the concentrations became greater, and before long hundreds of barges and other war equipment were assembled at Antwerp, Calais, Dunkirk, Ostend, Nieuport, Le Havre, and elsewhere. There were also submarines in many of the harbours—some of large ocean-going type—large motor vessels, tugs, and merchant ships; on one occasion forty-five large merchantmen were reported at Le Havre.

It was known that Germany had commandeered every available barge of over 500 tons and that armies of workmen were employed in the shipyards, altering the bows of these barges to enable tanks and guns to be more easily transported and disembarked. These alterations required but little time, for the barges were almost ready-made landing-craft for armoured vehicles and were capable of being nosed into any suitable beach, there quickly to unload both vehicles and troops.

It should be remembered that it is possible to sail in a shallow-draught craft right across Europe, from Rotterdam to the Black Sea. It is possible to sail from France to the Baltic, landlocked the whole way. And it is possible for those in possession of the internal communication lines of Europe to collect all the craft capable of such journeys and mobilize them in the Western European ports. This the German High Command proceeded to do as soon as the European coastline from Norway to Spain fell into German hands.

Holland possessed about 18,000 registered barges; Belgium 8000; Germany and France were plentifully endowed with them. Carrying capacity varied between 300 and 3000 tons. More than 3000 were fitted with motor-engines. The self-propelled barges were over 150 feet long; each was able to carry about two train-loads of men or materials.

Daily reconnaissance aircraft reported many of the barges to be moving slowly from one canal to another. Small craft chugged along the coast from port to port. Small warships were moved near the barges. It was noted that the railways were particularly busy, especially between Germany and the Low Countries. Inland, new aircraft shelters were under construction on the numerous aerodromes from which German aircraft could be expected to play their part in an invasion of Britain. It was abundantly evident that the German surface attack upon the British Isles was intended to spring forth from all the ports facing Britain, and that the German Army was to be transported in the small vessels and motored and towed barges which were the carriers of west-central Europe's normal peace-time canal and coastal trade. Nazi Germany had spared herself the cost of building special landing-craft in advance, or perhaps the blitzkrieg had been too speedily successful, and the German High Command was faced with the bugbear of German militarists—improvisation.

With slow-moving craft, such as barges, time was needed to effect the necessary concentration. In the ports the barges were tied up side by side, like great rafts. Their presence could not easily be camouflaged. As the vessels gathered and grew in number, constituting a new threat to Britain, they made an especially suitable target for air attack because they could be fired, damaged, sunk, and their cargo destroyed. Once they were in position they could not readily be moved. They became almost a fixed target.

The several concentrations of vessels and barges swelled until they aggregated some five million tons' capacity. In July the Royal Air Force struck at ports from Rotterdam to Boulogne and against barges found under way on canals leading to the ports. On September 5 a strong bomber offensive was begun and maintained along the coastal crescent from Amsterdam to Le Havre. The naval docks and ship-building yards at Kiel, Hamburg, and Bremen were also bombed, and, in many instances, with the technique of attack then current, the raids lasted for several hours. At Dunkirk the quay between two of the main docks, the large four-bay building, and another building parallel to it were levelled to the ground. Buildings at the south-east end of the Calais dry dock were destroyed by fire, the east side of the docks was damaged, and the lock between the inner basin and the navigation port suffered considerably; there were extensive fires along the Quai de la Louvre, and the electricity works near by were completely destroyed. All the invasion ports were attacked and great damage was done in each. At Lorient, buildings on the jetty were hit and the torpedo-boat station was damaged; hits were scored in barracks, causing many casualties among the troops there; mines laid outside the harbour by aircraft trapped and sank several ships.

These attacks were as much a part of the Battle of Britain as were the defensive combats of Fighter Command. The bombers were the big guns, hitting out at long range; the fighters were the machine-guns, blasting at close range.

The task imposed upon the Luftwaffe was a heavy one. Although its transportation-by-air section was far larger than that of any con-temporaneous air force, it was unequal to the task of carrying by air to Britain a force sufficient to bring about the defeat of the British people on British soil. It had to clear the way for the armada of barges to sail. It had to protect the ports from which they would move forth, guard them on their journey, succour their arrival, and secure the mastery of

A GERMAN RAIDER

CRASHES

A Messerschmitt 109 bursts into flame as it crashes in a field near Folkestone. The victorious British fighter circles overhead.

Photo "Daily Mirror"

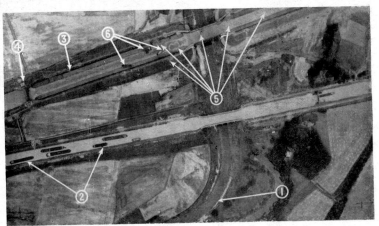

REPAIR WORK ON THE DORTMUND-EMS CANAL

This photograph, taken by the R.A.F. on July 29, 1940, shows the result of several attacks on the new aqueduct. (1) River Ems; (2) barges on old branch of canal; (3) new branch of canal; (4) lock-gates closed, with water on left of gates and damaged section of canal on right of gates dry; (5) craters in canal-bed and hole in aqueduct; (6) repair barges damaged and thrown on canal-bank.

Crown copyright reserved

THE MEN WHO BOMBED BRITAIN

(*From left to right, back row*) Generaloberst Bruno Lörzer (in command of Fliegerkorps II), Staatssekretär Körner, Reichsmarschall Hermann Göring, and General-Feldmarschall Hugo Sperrle look towards England.

Photo Keystone

the air over Britain. It had this duty to perform on top of the grievous losses it had sustained over Poland, Norway, Holland, Belgium, France, and now Britain, where already Fighter Command had successfully barred, and continued with success to bar, the way to Luftwaffe mastery of British skies, while Bomber Command reduced to ashes, splinters, and wrecks the means available to the German High Command to transport its soldiery across the waters that filled the channel which the last glacial period had carved between the continent of Europe and the chalk cliffs of England.

In the night following October 10 there was a combined naval and air bombardment of Cherbourg. The shore defences mistook the naval bombardment for part of the air attack, and their only response to the fire of the British ships was an intensification of all calibres of anti-aircraft gunfire. Not until the British naval force had withdrawn did the enemy heavy coastal batteries open fire, and then ineffectively. The scene was described by the pilot of a bomber operating in the area:

It was like hell let loose. As we went over the English coast the glare and explosions appeared to be so close that I imagined at first we must be off our course; but it was Cherbourg—about one hundred miles away. Clouds drifting across the scene were silhouetted against the white glow of flares which dropped incessantly over the target area from other aircraft illuminating the place. As we neared Cherbourg the enemy ground defences completed the effect with searchlights, flaming onions, and light and heavy anti-aircraft fire.

We were over the target area when, suddenly, the Navy let fly. It was like five hundred thunderstorms rolled into one. One of my pilots said that even the tornadoes he had experienced in the Pacific Islands came nowhere near it. Every cloud flamed bright amber colour, and we could see the bursts of the first terrific salvo plumb in the docks. Until then the ground defences had been blazing away at us, but this sudden blast from the sea foxed them absolutely. They didn't know if it was Christmas or Easter. The searchlights went quite drunk, waving aimlessly about the sky; the guns continued firing, but goodness knows what at! There was complete chaos down below. I said to my crew when we landed, "I've seen a few November 5ths [1] but what about October 11th?"

We were looking round for something left to bomb and observed flashes from a coastal defence battery in action at Henneville, so we dropped our heavy bombs on that, starting a long fire.

In some of the Royal Air Force bombing it appeared that troops were caught aboard some of the barges, probably packed like sardines, either on rehearsal or awaiting their instructions to attack, and in the wild rush to escape from the mass of moored and burning barges many

---

[1] Guy Fawkes Day in England, when the celebrated attempt to burn the British Houses of Parliament is remembered by firework displays.

soldiers were killed, drowned, or horribly burned. Barges laden with petrol and diesel oil added to the horror as their burning contents spread over the water and overlaid the scene with black acrid smoke.

But not only soldiers were needed to attack Britain. Large quantities of munitions of all kinds (and food to feed the troops) were also required. The lines of communication from Germany to the European coast became an important part of the German organization for attack. British bombers sought them out, delivering blows against both railway and inland-water-transport targets. It was the time when the name of Hamm was commonly mentioned in Air Ministry communiqués, for at Hamm was Germany's biggest railway marshalling-yard. (The current grim joke of Bomber Command pilots was to call this target the Hamm and Egg run—the word 'egg' was current R.A.F. and Luftwaffe slang for 'bomb.')

Apart from the actual damage done by the bombs, delays were imposed upon the railways by the dousing of all signal lights during a raid, and by the changed regulations in respect of traffic—for local trains were not allowed to stop in an area where a raid was in progress, schedules were seriously upset, and passengers put to great inconvenience. Goods traffic was held up and became congested. Travel became a trial, for journeys took at least three times as long as in normal times. In an organization so sensitively timed as a railway system, delay throws out the whole scheme of operation; time-loss becomes cumulative and cannot be recovered, particularly when raids are of a repetitive nature.

At that period of the war the most important inland waterway target was the Dortmund-Ems canal, a channel connecting the Ruhr industrial area with North-western Germany, and joining the sea at the naval port of Emden. A stream of industrial barges moved along the canal. The vitiation of its use meant yet another load upon the strained railways. So this canal was high up in the target list. It was attacked sixteen times in the six months beginning in May 1940.

North of Münster the canal was bridged across the river Ems by two aqueducts, the older one borne on four arches, the newer on two. The canal surface was a hundred feet wide upon the aqueducts. The destruction of both aqueducts meant the cutting of the canal; the destruction of one meant a reduction in its traffic capacity. Attacks against such a specific and important target had to be made in the face of severe enemy resistance. They called for courage of a cold and positive kind. There was no fight to rouse the blood, no combat between aircraft and aircraft, no challenge to the spirit and to relative skill. There was only the navigation to a known danger-point, and a resolute driving of one's aircraft up the alley-way of death to the nine skittles of destruction. There was no way out. The job was scheduled. It needed bravery of the highest order to carry out such a task.

Success was not to be easily attained. Nevertheless, by July 29, 1940, photographs showed that the new aqueduct was out of use. The lock-gates on either side of the aqueduct were closed. There was a hole in the aqueduct itself. There were craters in the canal-bed beyond the aqueduct. Barges collected for repair work were high and dry on the banks of the canal. But barges still moved along the old aqueduct, which was still undamaged.

Five Hampdens were briefed to attack the old aqueduct on the night following August 12. They bore a special explosive for the purpose. A half-moon threw enough light upon the surface to make pin-point target identification possible. The bombers were to allow two-minute intervals to elapse between attacks. The first attack was to begin at 1.30 A.M. on August 13.

The target could only be attacked from a particular direction, and anti-aircraft guns were stationed so that attacking aircraft were forced to fly down a lane of bursting projectiles to reach it.

The British pilots flew low to ensure hitting the aqueduct. One after another they flew south to the attack, with the moon shining in their faces. The first Hampden was hit; its wireless operator was wounded. The second Hampden was destroyed. The third caught fire; its pilot climbed while it burned, and he and his crew baled out and were taken prisoner. The fourth was hit in three places, but got home. The last Hampden flew down the shell-bursts at two hundred feet, and attacked the aqueduct from one hundred and fifty feet, while guns of all calibres fired at it at point-blank range. The bomber was repeatedly hit and large parts of its mainplanes were torn away. The pilot, Acting Flight Lieutenant R. A. B. Learoyd, was almost blinded by the glare of many searchlights. He had to keep his head below the level of the cockpit-hood while the navigator directed him on to the target. At last the words from the navigator came through the inter-communication telephone: "Bombs gone!" Learoyd swung his Hampden hard to the right in a steep turn. For five minutes the guns continued to fire at him, but they failed to bring him down.

Back over England, he reached his base. The hydraulic system used to operate the flaps was shot away, nor would the undercarriage indicators work. He flew around in the vicinity of the aerodrome until dawn came and brought light so that he could see to land. Then Learoyd alighted without injury to his crew or further damage to the Hampden. In the citation for the third air Victoria Cross of the war,

147

which was awarded to Learoyd, it was written: "He had attacked this objective on a previous occasion, and was well aware of the risks entailed."

There could be no doubting the success of Learoyd's attack. A photograph taken on September 21, 1940, showed the new aqueduct again in use after repairs, but the old branch of the canal was still out of use, with part of its aqueduct torn away by a bomb-burst and a new wall being built inside the break which would considerably narrow the width of the bridge; water was still seeping away from the canal through the bank broken by bomb explosions, and a new dam was being built to stop the loss of water.

Another form of attack, initiated by Bomber Command while the fighting continued over Britain in the air, was directed against military stores, dumps, and explosives secreted in the wooded hills of the Harz mountains between Bremen and Berlin, in those of the Black Forest, and in the forests of Grünewald and Thüringen. The aircraft dropped leaves which seemed harmless enough when they first fell. But their covering contracted and curled up under the heat of the sun when day came, and exposed the phosphorus contents to the dry air, and they began to burn, setting alight combustible material in the forest undergrowth. These attacks were followed by numerous explosions, an indication that they were achieving their purpose by firing the hidden dumps. The *Neue Frankfurter Zeitung* admonished persons who picked up the leaves as souvenirs and put them in their pockets, where, later, they caught fire!

On the night following September 15 an attack was made upon a concentration of barges located at Antwerp. Flying Officer C. A. Connor, a Canadian, piloted a Hampden of No. 83 squadron. In the nose of the bomber sat the navigator, the most comfortably placed member of the crew, for he could almost stand upright, and had plenty of leg-room. Behind and above the navigator was Connor, perforce seated in one position throughout the flight, for the aircraft possessed only one set of flying-controls. At the rear of the deep-section part of the fuselage were the rear gunner and the wireless operator, occupying the upper and lower gun-positions, from which both could crawl through the aeroplane from one end to the other.

The Hampden left its home base in fine weather, and reached the target area without incident. The pilot here takes up the tale:

We started to make our bombing run, but found that we were not in line to make a good attack, so we turned, circled round, and got into better position. We noticed that the anti-aircraft gunfire was fairly heavy, but during that first run none of it came very close to us. It wasn't long, however, before they got our range, and as we came round for the second attack we met a terrific barrage. We were hit in the wing several times on the way down, and the aircraft shook so much that it was not an easy matter to keep control of it. However, we released our bombs, and it was then that I saw flames reflected in my perspex windscreen, but I was so busy taking violent evasive action against the anti-aircraft guns that I didn't at first give it any serious thought.

While I was avoiding the shells as best I could Sergeant John Hannah, the wireless operator, called me on the inter-communication system and said, very quietly, in his marked Scots accent, "The aircraft is on fire." I asked him, "Is it very bad?" He replied, "Bad, but not too bad."

I gathered from this conversation, and the fact that the reflection of the flames was getting brighter and brighter, that the position was fairly serious. Hannah, cool as he was, did not want to alarm me. I immediately warned the crew to prepare to abandon the aircraft. At the same time I was still throwing the machine all over the place in an effort to dodge the shells, some of which were ripping right through the fuselage while others seemed to be bouncing off. Besides this heavy stuff there was a lot of tracer shooting all round us, and I was not very keen on my crew jumping through that; their chance of landing unharmed would have been small.

In the meantime the fire was getting firmer hold, and I imagine the blazing aircraft must have presented the enemy gunners with a pretty good target. After three or four minutes of more shells whizzing through and past us I was relieved to find that we were out of range. I think it must have been about this time that my navigator and rear gunner jumped for it. There is no doubt that the navigator was quite convinced that there was no chance of the aircraft surviving, while the rear gunner apparently had no option; for he was literally burned out of his bottom cockpit in circumstances which must have made it impossible for him to stay there.

Sergeant Hannah could have followed the rear gunner through the bottom escape-hatch or come forward, closed the bulkhead door, and escaped through the navigator's hatch. He did neither, but remained in the rear cockpit. The large explosive or incendiary projectile which apparently burst inside the bomb compartment of the aircraft set parts of the interior alight and turned the whole of the bomb compartment into a sort of blow-lamp, with the forced draught coming through the large hole caused by the direct hit. The aluminium sheet metal on the floor of Hannah's cockpit was melted away, leaving only a grid formed by the cross bearers. The molten metal was blown backwards and plated in great smears on the rear bulkhead. The electrical leads and all other inflammable equipment inside the cockpit were alight, drums of ammunition blew open, and thousands of rounds exploded in all directions. The outer layer of sheet metal on the door and bulkhead of the rear compartment melted and blistered. Sergeant Hannah could only remain there by using his oxygen-mask and turning on the oxygen to keep himself going. Connor continues:

The fact that the rear gunner jumped gave Hannah more freedom of movement. While he was fighting the flames with his log-book and his hands I could feel the heat getting nearer and nearer to the back of my neck. But when I turned round I noticed that the flames were still some four or five feet away from me. Hannah was wearing his oxygen-mask, but the fumes were evidently too strong, and he found himself beginning to suffocate. Without hesitation, he ripped the mask off and dashed through the fire heedless of the burns which he could not possibly avoid.

After about ten minutes, which seemed like hours, I noticed the reflection in the windscreen had died down and that in place of the heat at the back of my neck there was a welcome and refreshingly cool breeze. I asked the sergeant on the inter-communication system, which miraculously escaped damage, how things were going. He said, in his cheery manner, "The fire is out, sir!" I then asked him how the other members of the crew were getting on. He said, "I'll find out, sir." He then went into the rear gunner's cockpit and said, "Nobody here, sir." He then climbed forward to the navigator's position and reported, "Navigator not present. We are all alone, sir."

He then scrambled into my cockpit and brought me the navigator's maps so that I could steer a course for home. In turning round to take the maps from Sergeant Hannah I realized what he had gone through. His face was badly burned, his flying-suit was scorched all over, and altogether he looked a sorry sight. Through it all he was grinning, and I then knew that although his injuries were severe they were not as bad as they looked. On the way home Hannah sat in the navigator's position, away from the smell of the fire, and when we landed he jumped out of the aeroplane as though what he had done had been an everyday occurrence.

When I looked at the machine I got some idea of what he had gone through. The rear gunner's cockpit and half the interior of the fuselage were charred ruins. There was a hole in the fuselage large enough for a man to crawl through. There were holes in the wings, but far more serious were the holes in the petrol-tanks, and how the petrol did not catch alight and undo all Hannah's good work will remain a mystery. I believe that Hannah was fully conscious of that danger and concentrated on the flames nearest the tanks before he dealt with the other fires which broke out.

The flying-suit which Sergeant Hannah was wearing was to some extent fire-proof, but when exposed to prolonged heat it had been known to burn. Had that occurred Sergeant Hannah (as he must have known well) would have been burnt to death even if he had succeeded in getting out with his parachute. But while he was fighting the fire his parachute was burnt with the rest of the equipment in the cockpit, and there was no doubt that Hannah must have realized that by delaying his escape he deprived himself of the last chance of getting away from the aircraft. His Air Officer Commanding said of him:

> Through his action Sergeant Hannah very probably saved the life of his pilot. He certainly saved the aircraft in conditions when he must have known that his last chance of personal safety was being apparently hopelessly jeopardized. I can only add that no one who has seen the condition of the aircraft can be otherwise than amazed at the extraordinary presence of mind and extreme courage which Sergeant Hannah displayed in remaining in it.

Sergeant Hannah was eighteen. He came from the city of Glasgow, and was born at the not distant town of Paisley, Renfrewshire. Before he joined the Royal Air Force in 1939 as a wireless operator under training he was a salesman for a boot company. He was promoted to sergeant in 1940. For his courage in this action Sergeant John Hannah was awarded the fourth air Victoria Cross of the World War. Pilot Officer C. A. Connor received the immediate award of the Distinguished Flying Cross for piloting the damaged Hampden back to its base; he afterwards said, "If anybody had told me before I started that only half the crew and three-quarters of the aeroplane would return to England I should have been inclined to laugh at them."

§ 4

Britain's Defenders

Before the war began the Metropolitan Fighter Command of the Royal Air Force was organized in three Groups. No. 11 Group was responsible for the defence of the area in the south, including Bristol, Birmingham, and a zone running well to the north of London. No. 12 Group was responsible for the defence force in the north. No. 22 (Army Co-operation) Group — which later became the Army Co-operation Command — administered and directed the Army Co-operation squadrons of the R.A.F. In the spring of 1939 there were forty Fighter squadrons in the two Fighter Groups. (As new squadrons came into being after the war began a third Fighter Group, No. 10, was formed.) On September 3, 1939, the day of the declaration of war by Britain upon Germany in default of an answer to the British Government ultimatum in respect of Poland, the number of Fighter squadrons in the United Kingdom had not expanded to the figure officially estimated as the minimum required for defence. Nor, at that time, did the production of eight-gun monoplane fighters provide an adequate flow of machines. And, as no provision was made prior to the war for Fighter squadrons for an expeditionary force, the dispatch to

France of the fighter units of the Air Component made an immediate reduction of about 20 per cent. in the strength of the Metropolitan Fighter defence. Fighter reinforcements sent to France after the German Army attacked on May 10, 1940, included complete squadrons, replacement aircraft, and pilots. During the fighting on the Continent the strength of the Metropolitan Fighter Command decreased at a slow but constant rate which could not be made good, and before the end of May the British War Cabinet decided to send no more Fighter squadrons to France. In Britain the Fighter defence squadrons were sited along the line of a great inverted question-mark which ran from the area of Merseyside, through Bristol and around London, and passed through the shires of Lincoln, Leicester, Nottingham, and York, on into Scotland. The leaders of the Luftwaffe thought they knew the answer to that mark of interrogation.

When France fell the British aircraft industry faced a crisis, for the greatest proportion of its airframes, airscrews, and engines required light alloys for their construction. Baux, in France, was Britain's nearest and greatest source of high-grade bauxite, the richest of the clay-like alumina ores from which the metal aluminium is obtained; its mines became instead a source of supply for Germany.

Even in 1918, when aircraft were still largely made of wood, the aircraft of the Allies absorbed about 90,000 tons of aluminium. In 1940 the demands of British aircraft factories for the metal were incomparably greater. Bauxite, however, is generously distributed throughout the world, and although the actual world production had passed to the Axis, the potential production was still in favour of the lands outside Axis domination. But time was necessary to readjust Great Britain to the new conditions. The vast supplies of bauxite in Australia, Central and West Africa, British and Dutch Guiana, India, and the United States (not all as good as the French deposits) were much farther away than France, and a time-lag in transportation was unavoidable.

While Bomber Command hammered at aluminium factories in Germany in the effort to level out the unequal position, Lord Beaverbrook, first Minister of Aircraft Production,[1] on July 9, 1940, broadcast an appeal to the women of Britain to give their pots and pans from their pantries and kitchens to fill the gap in supply until new imports were organized; household aluminium was of pure quality, so the refining process was shortened and ingots were made available with the least delay for the rolling of sheets and the forging of blanks. "We want aluminium, and we want it now," said Lord Beaverbrook.

Lord Beaverbrook gave first priority to the construction of fighter

[1] See Vol. I, p. 65.

aircraft. Critics questioned the value of this action, and said that it merely dislocated a large part of the aircraft industry, thus curtailing the production of other types of aircraft without increasing fighter output in time to affect the Battle of Britain, and that when the flow of fighters did substantially increase it produced types which were already due for replacement by more recently developed patterns of the same makes. But Air Chief Marshal Sir Hugh Dowding paid Lord Beaverbrook tribute in recording that he was subjected to anxiety about the shortage of aircraft in Fighter Command until Lord Beaverbrook became Minister of Aircraft Production and that thereafter Fighter Command never had to go short of first-line aircraft.

But during the lull before the breaking of the Nazi storm over Britain the position was not free from anxiety, although every day of delay in the coming of the assault counted in favour of the Fighter Command. Squadrons which had fought in France were back in Britain re-forming and re-equipping. Some new squadrons had been added. Training was proceeding apace. A sound nucleus of battle-tested pilots led the less experienced fighter boys, and showed them how to go about their job. The counter-attacks of Bomber Command upon the aerodromes in France, Belgium, Holland, and Western Germany disturbed the action readiness of the aerodromes and helped to delay the assembling of the Luftwaffe. Meanwhile British fighter aircraft were improved. On June 9, 1940, the De Havilland Aircraft Company was officially requested to convert a Spitfire two-pitch airscrew to constant speed. The first governor unit was ready in four days. The Spitfire, thus modified, had a quicker take-off, faster climb and dive, and a ceiling 7000 feet higher; it outmatched the contemporaneous Messerschmitt 109 at all heights. Forty-four days after the test flight all existing two-speed Spitfires were converted and 400 Hurricane sets were in hand; 1051 fighters were converted by August 16. Output was increased, and before the end of the Battle of Britain some fifteen new squadrons were added to Fighter Command's pre-war total; it was the Command's proud boast that it emerged from the battle stronger than it went into it.

The anti-aircraft artillery defences commanded by Lieutenant-General (later General) Sir Frederick Pile were co-ordinated within the general scheme of air defence under Air Chief Marshal Sir Hugh Dowding. The number of guns available was not commensurate with the duties imposed upon them, but it was far in excess of the number available at the time of Munich. In September 1938, when Britain stood to arms during the first Czechoslovak crisis, there were only about a hundred guns, and not all were either up to date or ready for action.

By 1940 anti-aircraft artillery had reached a stage of efficiency never before attained. The precision of the shooting was so good, by reason of the predictor method of ranging the guns and the efficiency of the guns themselves, as to reduce greatly the number of rounds of shell fired for each aircraft brought down compared to the number of rounds required in the Great War. Nor was the effectiveness of anti-aircraft gunfire peculiar to Britain alone. In 1942 it was the view of competent authorities that British bombers then raiding Germany in force had more to fear from the guns of the ground gunners than from the Nazi fighter pilots who came at them by day and night. The barrage was worse than the Messerschmitt, the Focke-Wulf, and the Junkers 88. The subsequent successes of the high-flying Fortress day bombers of the United States Army Air Force when flying against targets in Occupied Europe and Germany a year later, in suffering but small losses while shooting down many enemy fighters, were indicative of the same factor, for they flew above the level of all anti-aircraft shellfire but that of the largest guns.

Low-flying aircraft were within range of anti-aircraft guns of all calibres—heavy, medium, light, and machine-gun, represented in Britain in 1940 by 4·5-inch, 3·7-inch, 3-inch, and Bofors guns, and Lewis, Bren, and Vickers machine-guns.

In Britain the searchlight companies and the anti-aircraft batteries were Army units, many of those employed for home defence being Territorial units of the Royal Engineers and Royal Artillery.

The Balloon Barrage Command of the R.A.F. completed the ancillary organizations concerned with defence against air attack. Their balloons rode in the sky at a maximum elevation of over 5000 feet, each holding aloft, at an angle varying with the strength of the wind and the lift of the balloon, a single steel cable. The primary purpose of the barrage was to deter low-flying aircraft, for, by keeping the attacker above the lowest stratum of the atmosphere, the larger guns and the fighters were assisted in their work, and if this did not result in the destruction of the attacker, at least it made it more difficult for him to aim accurately when he released his bombs. Although the balloon barrage was supposed to deny attack to the dive-bomber and the low flyer, it did not invariably do so, for there are always to be found men to whom risk is a stimulant, and pilots, both British and German, defied the barrage of wire, came into it, and passed through it, more often than not unscathed. (For the Germans possessed balloon barrages, too.) But from time to time the cables caught and brought aircraft crashing to earth. Occasionally friendly aircraft might be caught, due usually to flight in conditions of bad visibility.

154

§ 5
Phases of the Attack

The German air attacks upon Britain which followed the fall of France were made both by day and by night, but there was a difference in the diurnal plan. The day attacks had the specific purpose of preparing the way for the surface attack of an invading force. This was a short-term policy. The objective target had to be smashed quickly if this policy were to succeed, for the assembled invasion forces could not be held waiting indefinitely under the counter air attack of British bombers, nor could the plan of invasion be delayed until the winter months. The prerequisite for invasion was mastery of the sky, and it was to attain that mastery that the Luftwaffe generals hurled their aircraft against Britain in daylight in 1940. Success was denied to them by Fighter Command (and its ancillary organizations), and the invasion was made impossible because the conditions were never achieved under which it might have been made. For that credit must go to the air-defence organization commanded by Air Chief Marshal Sir Hugh Dowding.

The purpose of the night attacks was at first to prepare the way for the invaders on the ground by disrupting British organization in factories, docks, communications, aerodromes, roads, and cities. When it became clear that the Royal Air Force had denied to the Luftwaffe the mastery of the sky over Britain the German generals employed concentrated large-scale night raids against British cities, hoping, perhaps, to achieve by heavy air bombardment that which their surface invasion forces dared not attempt.

It is therefore desirable, for the sake of clarity, to separate the air action against Britain during 1940 into its component parts, and deal separately with each.

From May 9 until July 9 the Luftwaffe generals probed Britain's air defences in accordance with the German theory of testing enemy lines for weak spots prior to launching the real attack. This period constituted the first, or reconnaissance, phase of the German attack against Britain. The scale of attack increased towards the end of the phase. British fighters shot down seven German aircraft on July 3, two on July 4, one on July 5, two on July 6, seven on July 7, eight on July 8, and nine on July 9; in these actions the Royal Air Force lost three fighters, all on July 8. These were day actions, directed by the German generals in turn against the east coasts of England and Scotland; the south coast; the south-east coast; the north-east coast of Scotland and the south-east and south coasts of England; South and

155

South-west England; the south-east and west coasts of England; the Bristol Channel area and East Anglia and intervening territory. These flights and fights terminated the reconnaissance period.

A new phase began on July 10.

A plan had by then been decided, and drawn up. On that day it was put into operation. Towards the end of this phase the real battle began. Its objective was to defeat Fighter Command.

During this second phase attacks were directed against targets in the Channel (ships and convoys), and on and close to the coast (harbours, air stations, and radiolocation stations). On the opening day of this phase a formation of seventy German aircraft crossed the Dover Strait in a composite pattern of Dornier 17 bombers and Messerschmitt 109 fighters, arranged in tiers from 6000 to 12,000 feet. It was the first big day formation. During that day other enemy aircraft raided South Wales, and South-west and Southern England. Seldom was the air clear of aircraft off the coast of Kent. Fighter Command shot down fourteen German aircraft for the loss of two fighters.

The German bombers were out to wreck whatever they could within the ambit of the targets assigned to them, but the kernel of the plan was to bring the British fighters to action and wear them down by a process of destruction more rapid than our power of replacement. With France trodden down and almost all Europe under the German yoke, the Nazis felt, if they did not voice in the original words, the Hymn of Hate penned by Ernst Lissaur in 1914:

> French and Russian they matter not,
> A blow for a blow and a shot for a shot:
> We love them not, we hate them not. ... .
> We have but one and only hate.
> We love as one, we hate as one,
> We have one foe and one alone—
> ENGLAND!

Now the Luftwaffe was to accomplish what the proud Prussian Army had failed to effect in 1914–18. Hitler was to achieve what Wilhelm II had but essayed. German youth flew in the van of battle—boys, to look at, much like our own. I saw some of them in one *Gruppe* of the Richthofen *Jagdgeschwader* at the close of 1936. They had not long been formed and their aerodrome at Damm was very new. It lay a short distance outside the military town of Jüterbog, some forty flying miles south of Berlin. They were then equipped with Heinkel 51L sesquiplane single-seat fighters, later to be replaced by the Messerschmitt 109. Their manner was stiff by English standards. It conformed to the Prussian military code for officers. They clicked their

156

heels and bowed stiffly from the hips on being introduced. They appeared to lack humour. No doubt they knew what their training meant and where their future lay. Many of them must have fallen like plummets from the battle-skies of Europe. Their Commanding Officer was not a flying man of long standing, but an infantry officer of the Army of the Great War who had been commissioned in the new Luftwaffe, the ranks of which were thin of officers with disciplinary and administrative experience. It is always difficult to understand fully the thoughts of the people of another nation, but I gained the impression from the officers of the Luftwaffe and the Reichsluftfahrtministerium that I met that their appearance of friendliness to Britishers was a military tribute to the acknowledged valour of the men who fought against them in the Great War. But those men were inoculated with the bacillus of hatred of England (they were not bitter against the Scots, whom they regarded as another race held down by the English), and it was in that spirit that they launched their attacks against Britain in the summer of 1940, with arrogance and a belief in the invincibility of their own numerical superiority. But the spirit soars above material things. How the German materialism was to fail!

The second phase of the attack against Britain failed to achieve its purpose of overwhelming in the air the British fighter pilots who guarded the United Kingdom from the Luftwaffe. And on August 25 the strategy of the German air generals changed. The Luftwaffe then tried to knock out Fighter Command in South-east England by attempting to overwhelm the British fighters on the ground. Attacks were directed against aerodromes. This policy continued until September 9, when another switch was made.

From September 10 until September 30 the Luftwaffe was thrown against inland targets, of which London was the principal. Here was an attempt to paralyse the administration of Britain and disorganize the British people.

In October the employment of heavy bombers by day was almost completely discontinued. The formations of bombers escorted by fighters were replaced by a succession of fighter sweeps, also designed to secure the primary objective of overwhelming the defensive power of Fighter Command. Some of the fighters carried bombs. That was the beginning, in this war, of the fighter-bomber. So far as Britain was concerned, the Junkers 87 type of dive-bomber had proved useless. It was too slow and too vulnerable. The fighter-bomber was a different customer. When the bomb was discarded the aircraft became a fighter, with all a fighter's manœuvrability, speed, climb, and fire-power.

This fifth phase ended with the passing of October. By then the issue was all but decided. The Luftwaffe had failed to attain its objective in the autumnal campaigning season. And, according to its wont, the German Army began to take up winter quarters.

A desultory sixth phase brought more attacks against convoys and coastal targets. It slowly died away, and gave place to the swelling night attacks that gathered strength and with increasing ferocity battered at British cities in a series of mass raids which were like the sullen revenge of a bully who has been worsted in fair fight.

Two peak days occurred during the Battle of Britain: August 15 and September 15. On the first of these days the Luftwaffe lost 180 aircraft out of a force of rather more than 1000 all told, of which 600 were bombers; 158 aircraft were destroyed by British fighters, and 22 by the ground defences; the R.A.F. lost 34 fighter aircraft, but 17 of the pilots were saved. On September 15 the Luftwaffe lost 185 aircraft; the fighters destroyed 178 of these aircraft (125 of them bombers) and the guns got 7 more. There is evidence that the German surface forces were ready to move to the attack of Britain on these two days, if the Luftwaffe had succeeded in its part of the programme. The German Wehrmacht, of which the Luftwaffe formed an individual but integral part, depended upon its air forces to open the way. Those air forces tried hard, but Fighter Command fought and outfought them, and sent them, scattering through the sky, back to their flying-fields in Europe, a broken Armada of the air, torn by the storm of the Hurricanes and Spitfires.

§ 6

" This Hour is Thine "

Just before the second phase of the German air attack against England began on July 10, 1940, the step outside the headquarters of a Fighter Command station in the South of England became worn, and it was decided to put a new concrete step in its place. The workmen laid boards over the soft cement to prevent anyone damaging the new step before it set. On the following morning the step was hard. The boards were removed. Cut into the surface of the new step in three-inch letters was the inscription: "This is ONE step that Hitler won't take." The inscription was not removed. The outcome of the battle which followed justified the optimism of the unknown perpetrator.

In their early raids upon Britain (and before that upon France and elsewhere) the Luftwaffe employed noise effects in their bomb attacks, undoubtedly with the intention of creating a feeling of panic among those attacked. Not content with the noises of engine, airscrew, and airframe, which rise to their highest value in decibels during the dive and pull-out from the dive, the Germans attached shrieking sirens to their dive-bombers and screaming whistles to their bombs. The sirens were a development of children's toy trumpets, and were sounded by the violent slipstream of the diving bomber. The screaming bomb was first used by the Germans in the Great War. The sound was created by small hollow tubes or 'organ-pipes' welded to the fins of the bombs. When there was no other noise, as was often the case in country districts, the whine of the screaming bombs could be heard several miles around the place they fell. Probably that was the Germans' intention. It gave the uninitiated the idea that the raiding aircraft was nearer than it actually was, and so increased the area affected by a raid. In well-defended areas the noise of gunfire, and the sounds accompanying the action of Air Raid Precautions personnel, reduced the spread effect of the scream. But the value of these terror-by-noise devices was small against the people of the United Kingdom, however great the panic they may have created among the refugees fleeing along the Continental roads before the advancing German armies. They had, in fact, an advantage in giving earlier warning of the approach-line of the bomb. The Luftwaffe did not long continue to employ them against the United Kingdom.

On July 3, 1940, Air Marshal Sir Philip Joubert de la Ferté, who was then the Assistant Chief of the Air Staff Responsible for Radio [1] and the most senior officer in charge of the development of radio-location, and at that time the broadcaster of the official air war commentary, came to the microphone to inform the public of the system of air-raid warnings. He said:

> The policy under which air-raid warnings are issued is that of His Majesty's Government, in the light of circumstances prevailing at the time. The issuing of air-raid warnings in accordance with the above policy is carried out by the Commander-in-Chief, Fighter Command, Royal Air Force, who decides whether a warning is to be put out. The medium through which these warnings are made available to the public is Home Security, a department of the Home Office.
>
> The general principle which has guided the Government up to the present has been that unless there is a very clear indication, either in the numbers of aircraft detected or from other information received, that an actual bomb attack is developing, no public warning is to be put out. Now, however, the Germans have started seriously to drop bombs in Great Britain. It is immediately obvious that a decision has to be be taken wherein the disturbance to the national life, and in particular to its sleep, by the "take cover" signal is balanced against

---

[1] See Vol. I, p. 63.

the risks to individuals and to industry that is involved in not broadcasting raid warnings. Any decision to hold up the raid warnings, even when there is some indication of impending bomb attack, cannot be taken without putting the people of this country fully into the picture.

This is what the Government are now doing. They are asking you to realize that if from to-day a raid warning was given for every enemy aircraft that crossed our coasts the industrial life of the country would be most gravely interfered with and there would be a severe strain on the patience and on the nervous system of the people as a whole. We therefore ask you to believe that whenever there is good reason to suppose that a serious bomb attack involving real danger to life as well as to property is impending then we shall give you due warning.

On the other hand, there will be many occasions on which the C.-in-C., Fighter Command, in the exercise of his judgment, will withhold the raid warning. Sometimes he may be wrong and in consequence lives may be lost and people suffer injury. We ask you to trust us and to believe that the issue of these warnings is a matter of the most serious concern to highly responsible and well-trained individuals and that we shall not ask you to run risks which are not justified by the general war situation.

To sum up, we are fighting a national war. If it is to be brought to a successful conclusion the wheels of industry must continue to turn so as to provide the fighting men with essential arms. If no risks at all are to be run by the civil population then the fighting men will not get their arms, and we may lose the war. It seems therefore fair to ask you to run some risk so that the greater gain may come to the nation as a whole.[1]

The air attacks came and were heavy. Their fury was greatest from the late summer of 1940 to the early summer of 1941. Nearly 200,000 bombs were dropped up to the end of 1941. By then 20,178 men, 17,262 women, and 5460 children were killed by German raiders, and 50,387 were seriously injured. The civil population accepted the risk of war, and, with the stoicism which is remarkable in the British people, withstood the terrors of the Luftwaffe, and with grim faces survived the ordeal.

The chief terror of the cities came by night. That policy was forced

---

[1] On March 16, 1943, the following question was put to the Plymouth City Council: "Having regard to the public concern when during an air raid bombs were dropped before the sirens sounded, when it was apparent to everybody that enemy planes were overhead, has the Emergency Committee made an inquiry into the matter to ascertain the reason the 'Alert' signal was delayed? If so, were any decisions taken, and can the public be assured that such inactivity will not occur again in similar circumstances?"

The official answer was: "The committee made immediate inquiries, and as a result are satisfied that the late sounding of the sirens was not due to negligence or carelessness on the part of anyone, and regret that no assurance can be given that in similar circumstances this unfortunate experience will not be repeated."

ANTI-AIRCRAFT GUNS DEFENDING LONDON . . .

Photo Fox

. . . FIRE AT NIGHT

Photo Topical Press

ATTACK ON THE CITY OF LONDON

St Paul's Cathedral rears above the flaming city during the great fire raid of December 1940.

Photo Keystone

upon Germany by the failure of the Luftwaffe to break the daylight resistance of Fighter Command. The courage of the people was Britain's second line of defence. The second line stood, and the Luftwaffe cracked under the strain of attacking it. The efficiency of the German Air Force, organized to achieve its purposes by day, was reduced at night, not because the bombs were different, the navigation less efficient, or the defence stronger, but because the machines were designed primarily as day bombers, and when the pilots were forced to fly them at night they crashed in such numbers that the night-raiding casualties in German aircraft were not much fewer in number than those inflicted upon the Luftwaffe by day by Fighter Command. It can almost be said that Night fought on the side of Britain. It was almost as though the sun stood still.

The Battle of Britain, which forced the enemy to attack mainly at night because he could no longer face the day rate of loss, was virtually over by the end of October 1940. Three hundred and seventy-five Royal Air Force pilots were killed and 358 wounded in the action.

And during that time it was as though the thoughts of Tennyson, in the words that he made Love say to Death, took shape:

> This hour is thine:
> Thou art the shadow of life, and as the tree
> Stands in the sun and shadows all beneath,
> So in the light of great eternity
> Life eminent creates the shade of death;
> The shadow passeth when the tree shall fall,
> But I shall reign for ever over all.

§ 7

Convoys and Coastal Targets

Early in the morning of July 10, 1940, Spitfires shot down a Dornier 17 bomber off the east coast of England. Before the day ended fourteen enemy aircraft fell to the guns of Spitfires and Hurricanes of Fighter Command, and twenty-three more were severely damaged. Two British fighters were lost; one of the pilots was saved.

Air fighting continued throughout the day, mostly off the south and east coasts of England, above the waters where the German bombers were endeavouring to sink or damage the vessels sailing in British convoys. Houses were hit and people were killed and injured in two Channel coast towns, a Norfolk coast village, and in the Bristol Channel area.

In the morning Spitfires flying over the south-east coast met a

Dornier bomber escorted by thirty Messerschmitt 109 fighters, flying in three layers between 8000 and 12,000 feet. The Spitfires shot down two of the enemy fighters, and damaged two others. During another fight with twelve Messerschmitt 109 fighters one Messerschmitt dived straight into the sea from 10,000 feet.

Later, Spitfires met several Dorniers protected by a heavy escort of fighters. A Spitfire pilot described the scene as "a cylinder of circling aircraft." He climbed to the top of the cylinder, then spiral-dived down its interior, attacking a Messerschmitt 109 and a Dornier 17 on the way, and put them both out of action.

One pilot stated in his combat report that he "sighted waves of Dornier bombers coming from the French coast." Another "attacked three Messerschmitt 109's and two Dorniers, unable to say if they were damaged. Saw three airmen descending by parachute." In another action a Messerschmitt 109 and a Dornier collided in mid-air. The Dornier crashed into the sea; the Messerschmitt appeared to be disabled.

In the late afternoon Spitfire pilots patrolling off the coast of Kent sighted seventy German aircraft. The enemy formation was stepped up from 6000 feet to 12,000 feet. The Spitfires immediately attacked, set two Messerschmitt 110 twin-engined fighters on fire, shot away the tails of two more, and sent a Messerschmitt 109 spinning down—probably to crash into the sea, but the British pilots had no time to watch the end of its career. They drove the enemy from the sky and cleared it of German aircraft.

Hurricane pilots of No. 111 squadron saw a formation of bombers attacking a convoy under the protection of an inner ring of Messerschmitt 110 and an outer ring of Messerschmitt 109 fighters. The Hurricanes broke through the enveloping fighters and tore into the bombers, and harried them so that their bombs fell wide of the ships and raised splashing fountains of water; they damaged two bombers severely, shot down two fighters, and damaged three more.

Next day twenty-two German aircraft were destroyed around the coasts of Britain—thirteen bombers, eight fighters, and a floatplane. Three were destroyed by anti-aircraft gunfire, eighteen by fighters, and one, the Heinkel floatplane, by a Coastal Command Anson on convoy patrol.

Next day an Anson got a bomber. Heinkel bombers were attempting to attack a convoy when the Anson, with two machine-guns, one firing forward and the other mounted in a dorsal turret, climbed to the attack. At 6000 feet the pilot found that the three Heinkels which he had first sighted had increased to nine. Then Spitfires appeared.

162

The Heinkels, fleeing from the British fighters at top speed, passed the Anson a hundred miles an hour faster than it could travel. But the Anson pilot saw a Heinkel 111 below, and swung on to it.

I did not like the idea of this Heinkel getting away [he said]. I dived to the attack. The Heinkel turned and came at me head-on. I let go with my front gun as we closed. A collision seemed imminent, but at the last moment the German swerved swiftly to starboard. My turret gunner got him on the beam and suddenly the Heinkel pancaked on to the sea. One of the crew baled out at 200 feet. He must have been killed. Three others climbed out on to the water and the bomber sank in a few moments. We guided a British ship to the crew's rescue and continued our watch over the convoy.

Eleven bombers were destroyed that day, July 12; they crashed on land, or in the sea, from Aberdeenshire to Hampshire. The attacking aircraft were Dornier 17, Heinkel 111, and Junkers 88 bombers. Here is a typical combat. Between three and four o'clock in the afternoon Hurricanes sighted a Heinkel 111 flying north at 7000 feet. They attacked. The German jettisoned his bombs into the sea. One Hurricane pilot put a long burst into the Heinkel, and caused an explosion in the German aircraft. "It literally smothered me in oil," said the pilot. "But the Heinkel pilot handled his controls well. Bits and pieces were flying off it all over the place. Smoke was coming from it. The pilot had flattened out and was evidently looking for somewhere to get down. He landed in a flat grass field with only one wheel of his undercarriage down, and that was the end of that."

At this period the Air Ministry issued instructions telling the public how to deal with barrage balloons that might have broken loose. The instructions were serious, but an unintentional air of comedy attached to them, and they are worth recording. Here they are:

Members of the public are requested to co-operate in securing any balloon they find drifting near the earth.

Hanging from a balloon are several guy-ropes. They should be taken one at a time and tied to a tree, post, fence, or anything solid and immovable. The nearest police officer or police station should then be informed of the exact position of the balloon and of the preliminary action taken.

When grounded and damaged a balloon may be dangerous unless properly handled, and the following directions should be strictly observed.

(1) Don't smoke or bring naked lights near the balloon.

(2) Don't touch the cable or other metal parts unless you are sure that they are not electrified by contact with electric wires at any point.

(3) Don't walk on the balloon fabric or remove any part of the accompanying gear.

(4) Don't touch the red rope. Anchor the balloon by the guy-ropes hanging from it.

163

(5) Don't twist the guy-ropes round your wrist. Hold them so that if they are jerked from your grasp they do not hurt you.

(6) Having secured the balloon, inform the police.

The Air Ministry explained that every care was taken by the Royal Air Force to avoid the risk of barrage balloons breaking away from their moorings, but as it was impossible to prevent this entirely, people who carried out these instructions would be helping in Home Defence and earning the gratitude of the Royal Air Force.

On July 13 twelve German aircraft were destroyed in a series of engagements; ten fell during two attempts to raid shipping in the English Channel. Junkers 87 dive-bombers were employed in one attack. Hurricanes met them flying at 4000 feet. Four thousand feet higher were twelve Messerschmitt 109 fighters. The Hurricanes split up and attacked both bombers and fighters, shot down three Junkers and two Messerschmitts, and broke up the attack on the convoy.

On Sunday, July 14, 1940, a convoy passing through the Dover Strait in the early evening became the target for about forty Junkers dive-bombers escorted by Messerschmitt 109 fighters. Guns opened fire immediately the German aircraft came within range and maintained fire for more than half an hour. Within a few minutes a Junkers crashed from a direct hit. The air fighting continued for more than an hour, while the German airmen tried desperately to succeed. A Spitfire patrol shot down four Junkers. Three Hurricanes of No. 3 squadron, led by Flight Lieutenant L. M. Gaunce, shot down two Messerschmitts. Other enemy aircraft were harried and shot about; some were driven down to an unknown fate—a perilous escape or an unseen crash into the sea—and in the end all the remaining German aircraft were driven back whence they came.

At this period a modestly anonymous announcement by the Air Ministry stated that a legless pilot had shot down a Dornier. But Douglas Bader's name was already known in circles that knew about flying. He had played Rugby football for the Harlequins and the Royal Air Force. At Cranwell Royal Air Force College he was captain of cricket. But soon after he was commissioned he stalled over his aerodrome and crashed. He refused to die as most mortals might have died with such severe injuries. After a long period of unconsciousness he awoke to face life with both legs amputated, one completely and the other at the knee. For a time he moved about on crutches. I remember him at that time, sitting in the drawing-room of a country house in Buckinghamshire, listening with a wistful expression on his face to the flying-talk of men who still flew. He sat on a pouffe, pulled up close to the end of the fireguard, and said little, his fine face a little clouded; but his eyes displayed the faith he still had in himself. He was fitted with metal legs, and began to play games again—cricket, tennis, squash. He became more and more skilful in the use of his artificial legs. When war began in 1939 he argued his way before a Royal Air Force Volunteer Reserve Medical Board, whose President, impressed with his enthusiasm, determination, and insistence that he was fit for flying, sent him to the Central Flying School for a flying-test. He was passed for active service with a Fighter squadron. At first he flew Spitfires, and he said that he could get in and out of his aircraft quicker with his artificial legs than other pilots with their own legs. After a few months his engine failed just after taking off, and in the resulting crash both his metal legs were badly bent. But an artificer straightened them and half an hour later he was in the air; a normal pilot would have been in hospital. When the Battle of Britain began Bader, promoted to the rank of squadron leader, was in command of No. 242 squadron, manned by Canadians and equipped with Hurricanes. Before Christmas 1940 he was awarded the Distinguished Service Order and the Distinguished Flying Cross; he had then shot down ten enemy aircraft, and damaged many more.

Not all the German air crews who came down in the sea were rescued, either by their own rescue parties or by the British, but Royal Air Force pilots did all they could to save enemy airmen who were forced down into the water. A Hurricane pilot shot down two Junkers 88 bombers into the Channel on July 16. The first dived from 9000 feet and sank at once without survivors. The second dived to within fifty feet of the sea and then crashed. Two of the crew climbed into a rubber boat. The Hurricane pilot saw a tug a short distance away and flew backward and forward between the tug and the rubber boat until the Germans were picked up. On the same day three Spitfires patrolling off the north-east coast of Scotland forced a Heinkel 111 down into the sea. Two of its crew escaped in their rubber boat and were rescued by a Royal Air Force launch.

German High Command communiqués at this time claimed many more victories than the Luftwaffe actually gained, and admitted fewer losses than were actually suffered. The Germans claimed that seventy-five British aircraft were destroyed between June 23 and July 4; the true figure was thirty. The Germans admitted losing twelve aircraft during the same period; the R.A.F. destroyed forty. From July 4 to 12 the German High Command communiqué 'destroyed' 175 British aircraft, but the British losses were fifty-six. The R.A.F. in that period destroyed seventy-nine German aircraft; the enemy admitted thirty-five. While some of the victories claimed by the German communiqués might have been due to optimism or deceit upon the part of German pilots and air crews, there could be no doubt that the minimizing of German losses by the highest German authority was an official falsification. The Germans of the Third Reich had still to learn that lies which can be exposed are poor propaganda. At that time the Germans had no need to bolster up the feelings of the German people, for they were already exuberant with victories. It appeared, therefore, that the German High Command's endeavour to establish a ratio of victories in favour of the Luftwaffe was intended to maintain the morale of German air crews, for although some *Geschwader* would know the truth because they were engaged against the Royal Air Force and saw the empty places in the messes, yet others which were not so engaged might be fooled into a false sense of superiority. Moreover, some of the units engaged might believe that they alone were the unlucky ones, since they were unaware that their neighbours were also suffering heavy casualties. This German propaganda could scarcely impress neutral countries whose people had access to British news, but might affect the German-occupied countries wherein British news was prohibited under severe penalties.

A Henschel 126 Army Co-operation aircraft was seen for the first time close to the United Kingdom on July 18. This type of aircraft, the German opposite number to the British Lysander, was employed for artillery observation and contact patrol with ground troops. Many were shot down during the fighting in France. The appearance of this aircraft off the south coast of England might indicate the bravado of an inquisitive Henschel pilot, or herald an invasion of Britain. The Henschel was attacked by Hurricanes whose pilots could not claim its destruction. They could say only that it was last seen flying low, partly out of control, with smoke pouring from it.

On July 19 the Luftwaffe continued to attack shipping convoys and harbours. More than 150 German bombers and fighters and British fighters were engaged in two air battles over the Channel off the southeast coast of England. About noon nearly seventy German aircraft attempted to bomb a convoy. Hurricanes on patrol, all too few in number, flew to the attack. Three pilots became separated from their squadron; they attacked a formation of about twenty Messerschmitt 109 fighters, shot down two, and crippled and fired a third. Anti-aircraft guns on shore fired at Dornier bombers attacking ships near the coast; they held their fire until the Dorniers neared the bottom of their dive, and shot three down.

In a second afternoon action more than fifty Luftwaffe bombers and fighters attempted to attack a South Coast harbour. Six patrolling Hurricanes split up to engage them. Three Hurricanes were pounced on by twelve Messerschmitts. The other three Hurricanes counter-attacked. One sergeant pilot dived after a Messerschmitt and found himself in the middle of about ten Junkers 87 dive-bombers; he shot one of them down. Two Spitfires dived to attack a formation of twelve German fighters flying at 13,000 feet. One Spitfire pilot chased his Messerschmitt down to 3000 feet, then had to break off when another 109 got on his tail. He turned about and attacked, firing as the two machines came head-on at each other with a combined speed of over 500 miles an hour. The Messerschmitt caught fire, and as the two machines flashed past each other their wing-tips touched. The British pilot felt his Spitfire shudder. The Messerschmitt crashed into the sea. The Germans lost twelve aircraft that day; the R.A.F. lost five.

Next morning, in the moonlight before dawn, a Blenheim fighter of Fighter Command sighted a Heinkel 115 floatplane off the east coast. The Blenheim pilot climbed several thousand feet, closed range, and caught the Heinkel by surprise. The British pilot fired a burst from his four-gun battery, and saw the Heinkel turn sharply away and escape into cloud. He saw the floatplane again about a mile away, burning with bright yellow flames. Then it crashed, still on fire, into the moonlit sea. Throughout the succeeding day encounters took place over the English Channel and the Dover Strait. The biggest action involved a formation of thirty-five Junkers 87 dive-bombers and Messerschmitt 109 fighters. Four were shot down.

In April 1916, at Stirling, Scotland, No. 43 squadron, Royal Flying Corps, was formed. Deliveries of its war aircraft were delayed by strikes, but it went to France in January 1917 equipped with Sopwith 1½-Strutter two-seaters; later it was equipped with Camels and finally with Snipes, and in the Great War shot down a total of ninety-eight enemy aircraft. On May 3, 1917, while still equipped with the obsolescent 1½-Strutter, No. 43 squadron was used to disperse masses of German troops by machine-gun fire and to attack trenches and transports. These machines had only one Vickers gun firing slowly through the airscrew and one Lewis gun mounted on a manually operated Scarff mounting in the observer's cockpit. But these ground-strafing operations were so successful that they were used extensively in the Battle of Messines a month later.

The squadron was disbanded in 1919 during the demobilization of the Royal Air Force. It was re-formed in 1925. In 1939 it was at Tangmere aerodrome, near Chichester, in Sussex, equipped with

167

Hurricanes and ready for war. In January 1940 it scored its first success in the World War when its pilots shot down a Heinkel 111 off the coast of Northumberland. They continued to shoot down occasional North Sea raiders. In the enemy raid on Scapa Flow on April 8, 1940, they destroyed two Heinkels. During the evacuation from Dunkirk, No. 43 squadron was in action over the beaches; its pilots shot down thirteen enemy aircraft in two days.

In the afternoon of July 21, 1940, a patrol of No. 43 squadron was over the English Channel. It was a Sunday. The six pilots had climbed high over the sea, and were flying in two sections across the bows of a convoy. Squadron Leader J. V. C. Badger, who assumed command of the squadron during that month, led. Flight Lieutenant T. F. D. Morgan, flying as leader of the upper rear section of three Hurricanes, first saw the German aircraft. "Huns ahead!" he called to his leader by radio telephone.

"I looked up into the sun and saw the enemy rising in tiers as far as the eye could see," said Badger afterwards. "Stepped up right into the sun. It was like looking up at the Piccadilly escalator. Dornier 17 bombers came on in waves of eight or ten."

Six Hurricane pilots looked up with amazement at the sight which filled the skies, upward from 13,000 feet, where the lowest Germans flew.

"The situation looked pretty grim," reported Badger. "The best that we could hope for was to upset them a bit. I ordered my formation into line astern."

While Morgan and his two companions climbed from 11,000 feet to engage the Messerschmitts, Badger, with his section, prepared to engage the bombers, which then were just about to dive on the convoy.

They were circling all the time [he said], and I decided to attack from inside their circle. I flew to a point where I judged they would begin their dive. As the Dorniers attacked I singled out one and gave him a short burst. I had to pull away immediately because I was in close line abreast with the following Dornier. I came in again to attack another Dornier and had just opened fire when tracers started whistling past me. I took immediate evasive action. Then my starboard aileron got a terrific crack. It partially jammed, making my Hurricane difficult to control. [A Messerschmitt's cannon-shell had exploded in one wing.] There was nothing for me to do but beat it home. I don't know what happened to the two Dorniers I attacked. There were too many Huns about to wait and see. They were diving one after another on to the convoy. The ships were blazing away at them.

Morgan then told his story.

As my formation flew to engage I saw five enemy fighters trying to form a defensive circle. I closed in and had a crack at the nearest one, giving him a short burst. He staggered, and I saw his port aileron come off. He went into a spin, and I broke away. A few seconds later I saw him crash into the sea. I came in again to engage another Messerschmitt, giving him three bursts. Fragments came from his wings and fuselage. He started to slip to port. Then he turned over on his back and I saw him going down, but I couldn't watch him because out of the corner of my eye I saw two more Messerschmitts diving on my tail. I gave them the slip and dived to engage a Dornier which was trying to get into a defensive circle of ten other Dorniers. As I came in to attack my windscreen suddenly went black with oil. I broke away. I could not see a thing. The Dornier was firing at me. One bullet hit my port headlamp. With oil streaming over my windscreen I was no more use in the fight, so I returned to base.

Five Hurricanes were back on their aerodrome a quarter of an hour after first sighting the enemy formation. One was lost.

"How many did you meet?" asked their Intelligence Officer.

"Oh, about forty Dorniers 17 and the same number of Messerschmitt 109's and 110's—must have been nearly eighty in all," the pilots said.

None of the other Hurricane pilots saw Morgan's Messerschmitt crash, and, under the rules of Fighter Command at that time, its destruction was 'unconfirmed.' Later, during the great battles which were to follow, this rule was changed, for it was obvious that in terrific dog-fights, pilots who were outnumbered by the enemy had no time to spare to watch the fate of aircraft shot down by their comrades, and aircraft which pilots saw crash into the sea were counted as victories.

(In the 105th List of Royal Air Force Awards, dated September 3, 1940, Badger and Morgan were each awarded the Distinguished Flying Cross. The former was cited as "instrumental in destroying six enemy aircraft," while the latter had "destroyed seven.")

In the evening of July 21 the first German fighter-bombers appeared near the English coast. Three Hurricane pilots sighted fifteen Messerschmitt 110's flying in line astern and dive-bombing a convoy. The leading Hurricane dived 4000 feet to attack the Messerschmitt at the end of the line. The bomber crews did not see the Hurricane until it was 500 yards away. Then the enemy formation turned to the right to draw off the Hurricane. But the British pilot opened fire with his eight machine-guns and maintained the fire until he was close up to the Messerschmitt he had singled out; it turned and dived straight into the sea.

During the day some German pilots tried decoy tactics to lure a Hurricane patrol away from its task of protecting a convoy of ships. A Heinkel suddenly dived from the clouds beneath the six Hurricanes, turned, and made off for its base. As the Hurricanes turned to give chase the British pilots kept a look out in other directions and saw a formation of Junkers 87 dive-bombers with an escort of Messerschmitt fighters some distance away, at a greater height. But already the Hurricanes had turned from the lone Heinkel. They flew at once to attack the enemy formation. Below, sitting on the surface of the sea, some distance away, was an enemy floatplane. This too the Hurricanes ignored. And when the Junkers saw that the Hurricanes could not be drawn away from the convoy they withdrew with their escort of Messerschmitts.

During that Sunday of intermittent engagements over the sea three German aircraft were shot down, and two British fighters were lost. Early in the morning a patrol of Hurricanes flying 2000 feet above the water had seen a Dornier 17 at 18,000 feet. They began to climb. The Dornier apparently saw them at the same time, for he at once entered a three and a half-mile dive to sea-level in an attempt to speed up and escape. But the Hurricanes caught him up and brought him down, partly on fire. One of the crew climbed into a rubber boat. A Hurricane pilot circled above on watch, while another went off to find a rescue vessel, and succeeded in directing a motor-torpedo-boat to the German airman. An enemy fighter was intercepted off the coast during the afternoon and destroyed.

The Luftwaffe was well into the second phase of its attack, with its activities now directed towards the task of drawing the fighters of the Royal Air Force into combat with superior numbers to wear down their strength. The attacks on the convoys were possibly incidental to the air part of the plan, but they were not the plan itself.

On July 24 discoveries were made by the pilots of Spitfires, to whom came the biggest battle of the day, in contrast to the former luck of the Hurricanes. In the morning six Spitfires drove off twelve Dornier 215 bombers from a convoy, and six of the Germans jettisoned their bombs a quarter of a mile from the convoy as they fled. Not long after that, a sergeant pilot was attacking a Messerschmitt 109 when he saw three strange aircraft that looked like Blackburn Rocs 2000 feet below him. They had black crosses on the fuselage and wings. They were American Chance Vought 156 dive-bombers which had been captured from the French by the Germans.[1] The British pilot wheeled and dived to the attack. He fired a long burst and saw pieces fall from one of the aircraft, closed to 300 yards, and saw the Chance Vought fall into a spin; with two Messerschmitts for company, it fell into the sea. In a later encounter a flight lieutenant drove another Chance Vought

[1] About a month later a captured American Curtiss Hawk was engaged above the English Channel by a Spitfire.

staggering away with a badly damaged wing, and a Messerschmitt plunged seaward out of control. The killing began early that morning. At three o'clock searchlights caught a Dornier 17 over the north-west coast of England and the gunners opened fire. "Our second burst pushed its tail up," reported the battery. "The enemy then fell into a dive. Its engine cut out. It flattened out, and the engines came on again, but the Dornier at once burst into flames. It crashed eight miles away."

But the biggest fight occurred off the south-east coast of England. Rain falling between two layers of cloud drummed heavily against Spitfires patrolling at 7000 feet. Two thousand feet below, the British pilots saw eighteen German bombers flying like a gaggle of geese in arrow-heads of three. Three Messerschmitt 109's appeared above and behind the bombers; then twelve more of these fighters, higher still; then a formation of Heinkel 113 fighters, rare customers, these. The Spitfires destroyed five Messerschmitt 109's while driving the mixed formation back across the Channel. Rain and cloud prevented them from seeing what happened to nine others, which they had hit with their bullets. One pilot had fired only 120 rounds when his Messerschmitt burst into flames. Before the German pilot could bale out he was shot out into the air from his disintegrating aeroplane. Pieces of the aircraft flew in all directions. A strange object also appeared. The German's parachute opened, and he fell into the sea together with the unusual object; the latter was then seen to be a rubber dinghy, towards which the fallen pilot swam. It was the first intimation the Royal Air Force had that the German single-seater fighter pilot was equipped with a dinghy.

That German pilot was luckier than his comrade who, in the afternoon of July 25, with four other Messerschmitt 109's tried to get on the tail of a lone Spitfire whose pilot had become separated from his squadron. The Spitfire pilot dived for sea-level 5000 feet below and flattened out at a terrific speed. The keenest German, who had followed close behind the Spitfire, could not curve from his dive fast enough, and went straight on into the sea and sank instantly. Not a shot had been fired by any of the six pilots. The Messerschmitt struck the water like a projectile, threw up a cloud of spray, and dived on, like a monster fish, into the depths. His end was like that of gallant Kinkead, the British pilot with the attractive smile, who dived into the waters of the Solent one misty day in a Schneider Trophy seaplane. If an aircraft hits the water flat it will almost certainly break up. Even the slowest stalled landing on to the surface of the water entails great shock to a landplane's structure. But when a fast fighter strikes the sea surface cleanly at a diving angle it will most probably continue its dive without interruption in the new element.

The attacks upon shipping in the Channel and around the British coasts continued with almost monotonous regularity day after day, and with each successive combat between the Royal Air Force fighters and the German bombers and fighters it became increasingly certain that the defending aircraft, despite numerical inferiority, were able to inflict a high rate of loss upon their foes. German High Command communiqués became less extravagant in their claims, and before the end of July their figures of claimed successes fell from a ratio of five to one in their favour to three to one. These reduced German claims were still grossly falsified. From July 13 to July 26 inclusive the Germans claimed to have destroyed 130 British aircraft; the true loss was fifty-five; for this period the Germans admitted the loss of thirty-seven aircraft; the correct figure was 110.

During the week-end of July 27–29 the German generals tried another method of attack, and for the first time employed single-seater fighter-bombers. Messerschmitt 109's carried one bomb, flew high over the Channel, dived fast, came through the clouds, released the bomb, and made off quickly. The altitude of the air fighting rose. On Sunday, July 28, waves of Messerschmitt 109's flew towards the south-east coast of England at a height of 30,000 feet. Spitfires attacked them. One of the Messerschmitts, wreathed in smoke, dived; another Spitfire pilot flying 20,000 feet lower saw the same aircraft still diving towards the sea. Two were seen to crash into the water; a third exploded in the air.

During the preceding period of activity Royal Air Force air crews had observed German seaplanes painted white and marked with a Red Cross, flying over British convoys within a few miles of the British coast. These aircraft carried wireless. They were known to make reconnaissances for the enemy and were used for general salvage purposes. Two of them were forced down early in July, one a few miles from Hartlepool and the other in the English Channel near Walmer. Their crews were made prisoners of war. The log-book of one showed that while flying under the Red Cross emblem it had been used not only as a communication aircraft by General-Major Tittel, the commander of an infantry division, and his adjutant, but also to make bogus war films for the German War News Service. In consequence the British Government transmitted through the proper channels the following communication to the German and Italian Governments:

It has come to the notice of His Majesty's Government in the United Kingdom that enemy aircraft bearing civil markings and marked with

172

the Red Cross have recently flown over British ships at sea and in the vicinity of the British coast, and that they are being employed for purposes which His Majesty's Government cannot regard as being consistent with the privileges generally accorded to the Red Cross.

His Majesty's Government desire to accord to ambulance aircraft reasonable facilities for the transportation of the sick and wounded in accordance with the Red Cross Convention, and aircraft engaged in the direct evacuation of sick and wounded will be respected, provided that they comply with the relevant provisions of the Convention. His Majesty's Government are unable, however, to grant immunity to such aircraft flying over areas in which operations are in progress on land or at sea, or approaching British or Allied territory, or territory in British occupation, or British or Allied ships.

Ambulance aircraft which do not comply with the above requirements will do so at their own risk and peril.

On Sunday, July 28, 1940, two German seaplanes marked with a Red Cross approached the British coast in company with heavy enemy fighter patrols. They were shot down into the sea by British fighters.

On July 29 the Luftwaffe attacked Dover harbour with thirty Junkers 87 dive-bombers protected by fifty Messerschmitt fighters. Formations of Hurricanes and Spitfires rose into the sky to meet the attackers, and within a few minutes the air was filled with battling aircraft.

The bombers flew in two waves, with their escort circling several thousand feet above them. The British pilots attacked both bombers and fighters, and shot down eight Junkers and seven Messerschmitts, for the loss of one of their own aircraft and several others damaged.

A flight lieutenant who took part in this action in a Hurricane was making his first combat after 5000 hours of flying over a period of eleven years in the Royal Air Force and as a civil-airline pilot. During the earlier part of the war he flew Wellington bombers before being transferred to a Fighter squadron. This is his tale.

We were up bright and early, waiting by our Hurricanes, enjoying the fine summer morning and wondering whether we would be sent up before breakfast or not. Suddenly we received the alarm. Enemy bombers were over the Channel. We raced to our aircraft, and, just as the engines were starting up, the air-raid sirens sounded. We took the air to their wail.

I wondered as we took off how I was going to behave if I saw the enemy. When we were at 8000 feet we made a turn and saw thirty or forty Junkers 87's about to dive down and bomb four ships in Dover harbour. As we raced to intercept them I watched the first lot begin their dive. I watched their bombs falling when they got down to 2000 feet, and saw them exploding in the water round the ships. There were ten bombs at one time, and the water all round the ships was heaved up into a number of huge fountains.

As we raced along at 300 miles an hour I saw the bombers waiting their turn to go in and attack. Somewhere above were the escorting Messerschmitts. They were being looked after by a squadron of Spitfires, so we had the bombers pretty well to ourselves. Not all of them got the chance to attack. A number of them did not get their turn. But I shall never forget the sight of them stepped up in the sky.

It was only a matter of seconds before we were diving down to our targets. I first saw a Junkers 87 being chased by six Hurricanes, and I felt like cheering when I saw the bomber go down in flames. Immediately afterwards another Junkers flew right across my bows. I hared after him for all I was worth. I got him in my gun-sights and let him have it. I was overtaking him fast and when I stopped firing he was covering my entire windscreen, only fifty yards away. I stopped firing because he blew up. I had heard about enemy aircraft blowing up in the air, and this was my first experience of it. Both his petrol-tanks exploded at the same moment. Pieces of the aircraft were blown in all directions, and I had to dive away sharply to avoid being hit by the fragments. When I looked again I saw the wrecked bomber tumbling down towards the sea.

Then, below me, I saw three Junkers tearing off for home. They were only about thirty feet above the surface of the water, going away from our shores as fast as they could. I dived and attacked them in turn, and chased them about a dozen miles out to sea. I gave the first one a good burst, and I know I hit him. Then I blazed away at the second and hit him, too, before turning back.

Our squadron came out of the combat untouched except for one bullet through the wing of one aircraft. One bullet-hole for four bombers destroyed and six others damaged. There is no doubt we shook them up a lot. Some of them didn't even get the chance to drop their bombs.

When I first saw the Germans I felt a kind of fascination. I was surprised that I was able to see so much of the battle. After dealing with my first Junkers I was able to notice other members of the squadron shooting down other German bombers. I saw out of the corner of my eyes a short dog-fight which ended in one of our squadron shooting down a Messerschmitt 109. One of the things which stands out in my mind was a sailing boat, with a big red sail, steadily passing down the coast. Aircraft were blazing away at one another in the sky above. Occasionally one would crash into the sea and disappear. But that little boat with the red sail appeared to take no notice. It seemed incongruous.

When the battle was on I was surprised because there was no confusion. Everything was very orderly. Each combat was distinct in itself. Things seemed to happen as in a nicely rehearsed play. I was astonished to find myself able to be a spectator and a fighter at the same time.

From the moment we took off to the moment we landed exactly thirty-six minutes elapsed, though I suppose the fight itself did not last more than five minutes. After that we had breakfast.

Not content with a defensive attitude, the Royal Air Force adopted a pugnacious spirit from the beginning of the air war and whenever opportunity offered. On August 5 nine Spitfire pilots crossed the Channel and engaged five Messerschmitt 109's patrolling in fancied security north of Calais. The squadron leader opened the attack, fired a short burst into a Messerschmitt, and saw it hit the sea. A sergeant pilot crashed another Messerschmitt into the water. Flying with the British squadron was a 27-years-old American who in June had been on the Laredo airfield in Texas, near the Mexican border, instructing young Americans how to fly. After Paris fell this Texan pilot decided to try to join the Royal Air Force. But for him this was not easy. There was no recruiting office in America for any of the belligerents. The United States were neutral. United States citizens had to observe the laws of neutrality. But British agents operating within the law could direct prospective recruits. The pathway from the U.S.A. to the Royal Air Force passed through Canada. So the Texan went to Ottawa, called at the recruiting headquarters of the Royal Canadian Air Force, produced his pilot's log-book with 1500 flying hours entered to his credit, and in fifteen minutes was out in the street again with the promise that he would be in the next boat for England. After a week's wait in the Canadian capital he was aboard.

On arrival in England he was sent immediately to a Royal Air Force Flying Training School, where he thought that after all his flying on big aircraft he might be put on bombers. His own idea was to fly fighters. And fighter pilots were what Britain needed.

"To my delight I was tried out in a Spitfire," he said.

It was beautiful. A little bit difficult at first, of course, but once I got the hang of the machine I knew I could fly it anywhere, anyhow.

After three weeks' hard training, yesterday I was sent to a Spitfire squadron, and here I am, really in a British Fighter squadron at last.

I have never been so tickled in my life when we went across the Channel to look for trouble to-day. It was the Germans who found it. Four miles from Calais at 10,000 feet we saw five Messerschmitt 109's, and somewhere around us was a larger party of Messerschmitts. We sailed into them right away, and our squadron leader set the example immediately by cracking down one Messerschmitt. He and another pilot saw it crash into the sea. Then another pilot chased an enemy aircraft towards France and shot bits off the machine. I had a good crack at one, but suddenly two other Messerschmitts attacked me. Something hit the fuselage, shaking the machine a bit, but we quickly recovered. When I was whirling around the sky another Messerschmitt fired into my windscreen. I had another crack at him before he disappeared. Then we came home.

The fight was great fun. I wouldn't have missed this for all the Japs in China.

The American's Spitfire was temporarily unserviceable. The fuselage was peppered with tiny holes, and one of the control cables inside had been almost severed. In the fight one Spitfire was lost and two Messerschmitts were shot down.

There were other smaller fights throughout this period when Britain's defensive strength was probed by the Luftwaffe generals. There were, too, numerous small-scale night raids and some day raids, that penetrated inland from the area of North-east Scotland, all the way down the east coast of Britain, and along the Channel coast to Cornwall, the Scilly Islands, and up to Wales. But the purpose behind the main engagements of the Luftwaffe hitherto was the study of the fighter defence system and efficiency of the Royal Air Force.

Three men—Göring, Kesselring, and Sperrle—looked hopefully across the North Sea and the English Channel. To them was given the honour of clearing the way for the assault of the German armies which were to overwhelm England. They were conscious of their importance. They were aware of their strength. They were confident of their success. Having made their preliminary study, it was now time, or so it appeared from their subsequent moves, for the Luftwaffe to begin the larger-scale attacks which were to bring about the hoped-for defeat of Britain. The world awaited the outcome of the struggle, and in many places there was doubt against the outcome falling in Britain's favour.

§ 8

Verification

The disparity between Air Ministry communiqués and those of the German High Command announcing the respective claims of aircraft destroyed and admissions of aircraft lost succeeded in creating some scepticism about the tendencies in fight which were early discernible to the British Air Staff. It became necessary for the Secretary of State for Air, Sir Archibald Sinclair, to explain on August 21, 1940, in the House of Commons the Royal Air Force method of checking and verifying enemy losses. He emphasized that an enemy aircraft is reported as "certainly destroyed" only if it has been seen to hit the ground, break up in the air, or fall in flames.

Examples of combat reports from the period immediately preceding the Secretary of State's explanation to the House indicated the method.

. . . Squadron engaged enemy aircraft over Folkestone at 1231 hours. Pilot Officer ——, leader of the first section, attacked a formation of 30 Junkers 87's, fired at one which went down in flames, then attacked over Dover a formation of Junkers 87's and Messerschmitt Jaguars of about 50 at a height of 15,000 feet, fired at one

Junkers 87, which went down in flames. Attacked a third Ju 87 which broke away, smoking heavily.

Two of these aircraft were claimed as destroyed, one as a ' probable.'

Sergeant ——, leader of the second section, at 10,000 feet between Dover and Folkestone fired at a Messerschmitt 109 and saw his bullets going in and clouds of smoke pouring from the enemy aircraft as it disappeared downwards into cloud.

This was a 'probable.'

Sergeant ——, leader of third section, at 8000 feet attacked one of two Me 109's, which were attacking a Spitfire, fired a long burst, and enemy aircraft disappeared into cloud emitting a big cloud of smoke.

This was a 'probable.'

Third pilot of section three got separated from the squadron, fired at a Me 110 in mid-Channel. Saw one of crew bale out. Enemy aircraft turned on its back and went down out of control.

This aircraft was claimed and allowed as destroyed.

Second pilot of section two at 7000 feet fired at a Me 109 as it was climbing. Enemy aircraft went down in flames.

This was 'destroyed.'

Second pilot of section one at 10,000 feet fired at one of 12 Ju 87's, saw it turn over and go down apparently out of control. Broke off the engagement to deal with a Me 109 coming for him. Saw his bullets hit the enemy aircraft, which disappeared into cloud, skidding sideways.

Score: one 'probable,' and one 'damaged.'

Third pilot of section four at 13,000 feet did a steep right-hand turn to avoid three enemy aircraft and found one enemy aircraft in front of him. Fired five short bursts at a Me 109 and saw engine of enemy aircraft in flames, and enemy aircraft go straight down. Engaged a second Me 109 and fired three short bursts which disabled the engine of the enemy aircraft.

Result: one 'destroyed' and one 'damaged.'

Second pilot of third section forced-landed, wounded in the left arm, taken to Ashford hospital. The doctors there report that he claimed one Heinkel 113 shot down in flames.

Counted as one 'destroyed.'

Enemy casualties:
Messerschmitt 109: 2 destroyed, 2 probable, 2 damaged.
Junkers 87: 2 destroyed, 2 probable.
Messerschmitt 110: 1 destroyed.
Heinkel 113: 1 destroyed.

Only those enemy aircraft which were assessed as 'destroyed' were included in Air Ministry figures of enemy losses, although many of the aircraft assessed as 'probables' and 'damaged' could never get home.

To some extent the verity of the pilots' reports must be accepted, because it was not always possible for confirmation to be obtained. But in a Service as closely knit as is the Royal Air Force there is little room for the liar. He would be found out too quickly by his fellow-pilots. He would be denied the comfort of his own Mess. His reputation would follow him wherever he went, and if he were to succeed in gaining early kudos his power to maintain it would soon vanish, and with its going would disappear all hope he might have to establish himself among his fellows, not alone as a fighter but as an accepted individual. In their communal life, flying men in the Royal Air Force insisted on understatement, even to the verge of the farcical. So, when the big scores came in the Battle of Britain the Royal Air Force accepted them without question, although persons outside the Service were at first incredulous. To underline the veracity of the claims was the fact that if the scores were not true, to the point of being meagre in the claims, the pilots of Fighter Command could never have defeated the Luftwaffe and kept Göring's swollen Goliath from breaking through and crushing the David that was the home-defence Fighter force of the last enemy left fighting to defy Germany.

Fighter pilots were careful, too, not to take credit from one another, and their reports proved that they were scrupulous in giving the credit for victories where it was due. This was well illustrated in the story of the action of a Spitfire squadron fighting in a hot engagement over South-eastern England.

A sergeant pilot fired a burst at a Dornier 215 bomber and saw its tail drop off and the aircraft catch fire. But, believing that the Dornier had been fired at by other fighters, he flew off to find a victim of his own and made no claim to victory over this particular bomber. He found a Dornier 17, fired a four seconds' burst at it, and saw it fall away to the left. Two other Spitfires began to follow it down, but gave up when they saw that the sergeant pilot was the rightful 'owner.' Return fire from the rear gunner of the Dornier ceased after the sergeant gave another burst from his guns. The British pilot reported:

I then began a series of quarter attacks and the enemy went down slowly to fifty feet. He went over the coast at Dungeness. I then proceeded to dive steeply on him, and after one dive he seemed to panic and went into the water about three miles out. A trail of oil was left on the sea from the coast to the spot where he went down. Three airmen jumped out, but I could see no dinghy. I flew back to the coast and directed a trawler to the scene.

178

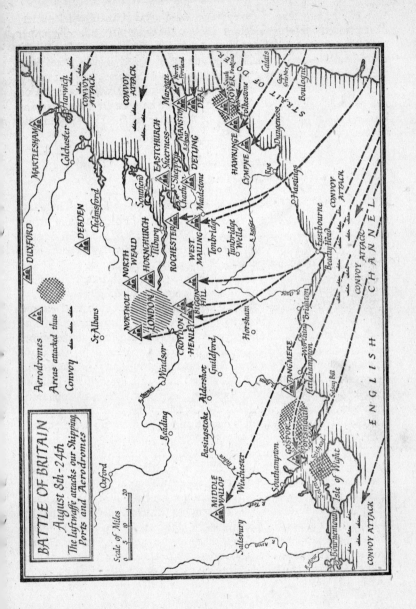

BATTLE OF BRITAIN
August 8th–24th
The luftwaffe attacks our Shipping,
Ports and Aerodromes

Scale of Miles
0 5 10 20

Aerodromes ▲
Areas attacked thus ⬡
Convoy ┅

MARTLESHAM

DUXFORD

DEBDEN

Colchester   Harwich
CONVOY ATTACK
CONVOY ATTACK
Chelmsford

St Albans

NORTH WEALD
NORTHOLT
HORNCHURCH
Tilbury
Southend
EASTCHURCH
Sheerness
R. Sheppey
Chatham R. Stour
MANSTON
Margate North Foreland
DEAL
South Foreland
DOVER
Folkestone Portland
STRAIT OF DOVER
Calais
Gris Nez
Boulogne

LONDON
CROYDON
HENLEY
BIGGIN HILL
ROCHESTER
WEST MALLING
Maidstone
DETLING
HAWKINGE
LYMPNE

Reading
Oxford
Windsor
Aldershot
Guildford
Basingstoke
Horsham
Tunbridge Wells
Tonbridge
R. Medway
R. Ouse
Hastings
R. Rother
Rye
Dungeness
Eastbourne
Beachy Head
CONVOY ATTACK
CHANNEL

Salisbury
Winchester
MIDDLE WALLOP
R. Test
R. Itchen
Southampton
Littlehampton
TANGMERE
Worthing
Defending Britain
Selsey Bill

Portsmouth
GOSPORT
Spithead
Isle of Wight
Bournemouth
R. Avon
R. Stour
CONVOY ATTACK

ENGLISH

CHANNEL

A flight lieutenant of the same squadron was probably the 'owner' of the first bomber the sergeant fired at, for this officer noticed another Spitfire firing at a Dornier 215 at the same time as he was firing. The flight lieutenant reported: "The Dornier exploded about six feet from the rear gunner's position, and the tail unit became separated from the rest of the machine. The crashing of this aircraft was confirmed on the ground." The flight lieutenant claimed half the Dornier. No one seemed to know what happened to the other half. The sergeant did not want it!

§ 9

The Big Offensive Opens

The full weight of the German air attack was first felt on Thursday, August 8, 1940. About 400 German aircraft were counted in action over ships in convoy in the Channel and over parts of the south coast of England. Sixty enemy aircraft were destroyed that day—twenty-four Junkers 87 dive-bombers and thirty-six Messerschmitt single- and twin-engined fighters. Sixteen British fighters were lost, from which three pilots were saved, two of whom were wounded.

The 400 German aircraft did not all come at once, but instead entered into a series of engagements as the convoy moved up Channel. The three main attacks took place at breakfast-time, lunch-time, and tea-time. One squadron of Hurricanes, No. 145, bore the brunt of the day's fighting, fought three times to defend one convoy, shot down a fraction more than one-third of the day's total bag, and by nightfall had the biggest score of enemy aircraft of any home-defence squadron. Squadron Leader J. A. Peel, commanding the squadron, reported that the Messerschmitt 109's met during the morning were painted silver.

The fighting was shared by four other squadrons of Hurricanes—Nos. 43, 238, 257, and 601—and two squadrons—Nos. 41 and 609—of Spitfires. Flying with No. 145 squadron was a Polish pilot who was in action with Fighter Command for the first time; he saw his first large formation of Junkers 87 dive-bombers escorted by Heinkel 113 fighters. "I was attacked," he said, "by three Heinkels who seemed to be working to a plan—one flying alone and the other two as a pair.[1] If you attack the pair the single one tries to get on your tail." He tackled the single Heinkel 113, watched it go down smoking, but was unable to see a final crash. The other two flew off.

[1] See pp. 294–296, describing the combat between Major Helmuth Wieck and Flight Lieutenant John Dundas.

During the last battle of the afternoon this Polish pilot got his first Messerschmitt 109.

Flight Lieutenant A. H. Boyd, D.F.C.,[1] who was transferred from No. 65 squadron to be a flight commander in No. 145 when the latter squadron was formed in October 1939, was shot down on Monday, August 12, 1940, but that did not prevent him from coming to the B.B.C. microphone to broadcast his story of the fight in which No. 145 squadron was engaged on the first big day of the Battle of Britain. He said:

The other flight took off at half-past eight in the morning to patrol the convoy sailing down-Channel south of the Isle of Wight. My flight took off shortly after that. We were lucky to find that the first two formations of dive-bombers, Junkers 87, were left to us. We went straight at them. Some turned back at once, but others went down on the convoy and attacked. We shot up a few of the bombers and then got mixed up with their escorting Messerschmitt 109's. I remember seeing two of them, about a quarter of a mile away, coming straight at me at 16,000 feet.

Suddenly, for no reason at all, one of them did a half-roll and went straight down. I followed, but although I had not fired at him—and so far as I could see no one else did either—he went straight into the sea. It just looked as though he committed suicide. I was so astonished that I could not believe my eyes, and while I was watching for others there was a crash behind my head. A bullet came through my hood, passed through the back of my helmet, tore through the back of my goggles, and before I knew where I was the hood had flown back and my goggles had disappeared. After that all we could see were enemy bombers and fighters going like mad for home.

The squadron got six bombers and three fighters for certain, and six others were damaged that time. I myself got one fighter. After a skirmish with some fighters the squadron leader turned round and saw about twenty of them a quarter of a mile away. He went for the rear Junkers 87, which appeared to be straggling behind, fired at him, and put him into the sea. Then he attacked another, gave him two seconds' burst, and ran out of ammunition. But the squadron leader is sure he hit him, for the Junkers went away to the west, wobbling badly. Then he went back to the convoy. The balloons which the convoy carried had certainly put the dive-bombers off their stroke.

Later the whole squadron was sent up at 15 minutes to 12 to investigate a raid off Beachy Head. We went up to more than 20,000 feet, and saw, at between 30,000 and 35,000 feet, no fewer than thirty-six Messerschmitt 110's. They swung round and returned towards France when they saw us, and as we were unable to reach them we

---

[1] Flight Lieutenant A. H. Boyd was awarded the Distinguished Flying Cross on June 19, 1940, and a Bar on August 13, 1940. He was twenty-seven. In 1926 he had enlisted as a Naval Cadet, R.N. In 1933 he attained the rank of Acting Sub-Lieutenant. He retired from the Royal Navy in 1934, entered the Royal Air Force as a pupil pilot, and was granted a commission in 1936.

turned, and were then told over the radio telephone that a battle was going on south of the Isle of Wight. We had fifty miles to go to the convoy—it took us just about ten minutes—but although we saw the convoy, we saw no German aircraft. I think the Messerschmitt 110's we went to look at were a blind.

I myself led the three machines in my section to a point well south of the Isle of Wight. There we saw two separate squadrons of Messerschmitt 110's. Something went wrong with my radio set. I could hear the squadron leader calling "Where are they?" He knew that I had spotted some, but he could not receive my message. So there were the three of us, circling high above the Messerschmitts, which were now flying in an uncompleted circle at about 4000 feet. We were at 16,000 feet.

I was curious to know why they were circling round like that, and we decided to have a crack. We went down on them. The Messerschmitt which was at the end of the circling line of fighters was shot down into the sea immediately. The lad on my left shot down one Messerschmitt 109 which I think was intended to be a decoy. It was supposed to lead us down to the circle, but our pilot shot him down first before we started on our dive.

Well, we broke up the happy little circle quite effectively. All three of us got at least one, and I think we must have taken them by surprise. We started climbing again, but after about a minute I thought I would like to go back and find out what was happening. I flew over another circle of enemy fighters for about five minutes until they had all cleared off. Then I went down and saw one of their pilots in the water. He was easy to see, for all round him was a big patch of green vapour—a special method used by the Germans when they get into the water. It shows their friends where they are. I have come across it before. You can see the green vapour five miles away.

While I was investigating this I was attacked by a Messerschmitt 110 which I suppose I had overlooked. I skidded round and climbed for him, but he broke away to the left. I was still turning and at about 1000 feet I stalled. He was right in my gun-sights. I just gave him a quick burst, he heeled over, and went straight into the sea and broke up. He really was a sitting bird. Then we went home.

Our day's bag by then was fourteen enemy aircraft, and in the third action of that day we made it up to twenty-one.[1] Our squadron score must now be well over seventy. We shot down our first enemy on May 22—until then we had not had any luck. But by the end of the Dunkirk show our score was about thirty. The squadron was only formed last October, so we haven't done too badly.

On the day described by Flight Lieutenant Boyd, No. 43 squadron, in the third attack, destroyed three Junkers 87's, three fighters, and a fighter-bomber.

On August 10 Mr Churchill sent the following telegram to Sir Archibald Sinclair:

---

[1] Fighter Command's total for the day was sixty.

The War Cabinet would be glad if you would convey to the Fighter Squadrons of the Royal Air Force engaged in Thursday's brilliant action their admiration of the skill and prowess which they displayed, and congratulate them upon the defeat and heavy losses inflicted upon the far more numerous enemy.

In the calendar week which followed this first big engagement the leaders of the Luftwaffe endeavoured to breach the air defence of the British Isles. The German ground forces were almost ready, and August 15 was (evidentially) selected as the zero-hour invasion date. The first blow was launched on August 11. The battle began at about 7.30 A.M. over Dover. Between fifty and sixty German aircraft were in the air. One Spitfire squadron went into action four times that day, and was the first into battle over South-east England. The German aircraft attacked barrage balloons. Messerschmitt 110 Jaguar fighter-bombers bombed Dover harbour. Amid the din of anti-aircraft gunfire, bombs, cannon-shells, and machine guns, the British fighters shot down two German fighters, and the gunners brought down three.

The fighting over the area of Dover continued until about eleven o'clock. While it was in progress the German air generals threw an attack against Portland shortly after ten o'clock. This force comprised over 200 bombers and fighters, of which about 150 reached the coast. The action continued until lunch-time. Spitfire and Hurricane squadrons roared in and out of the enemy formations, breaking them up, zooming and diving to pick off their opponents, in a succession of dog-fights. An Auxiliary squadron shot down ten Messerschmitts; No. 145 squadron shot down five enemy aircraft. Below, in Portland harbour, two naval ships suffered minor damage by splinters. No other ships were damaged. Bombs fell on shore at Portland and Weymouth, damaged houses and communications, set an oil-tank on fire, and did some damage to naval buildings, including a hospital. There were few serious casualties, and only one fatality was reported. During the air engagement nearly forty German aircraft crashed down on land or into the sea.

Before the Portland engagement ended another attacking force came in against the coastline from Dover to the North Foreland. The Spitfire squadron which had opened the day's fighting went into action for the fourth time. An hour before they had been ordered to patrol over a convoy off the East Anglian coast. There the Spitfire pilots found forty Messerschmitt 110 Jaguar fighter-bombers about to attack the ships, took them by surprise, and shot ten down into the sea before they could form their protective circle. Now they met thirty Messerschmitt 109's flying in and out of clouds 4000 feet above the North

183

Foreland. Four Spitfires chased the Messerschmitts through the clouds and brought down two.

That day's actions marked the first attempt upon the part of the Luftwaffe generals to feint and parry, to use part of their force in the attempt to draw off Britain's defence, and then to launch a hard blow against what they hoped would be an uncovered part of the British coast. But those whose resources are not too plentiful are most likely to husband what they have. And so it was with Fighter Command. A force was maintained available at readiness to meet attack. Convoys were protected, and sometimes squadrons so engaged met the enemy and attacked without orders from the ground, as was the case with No. 145 squadron on August 8; sometimes squadrons were ordered up to intercept an enemy force detected by radiolocation and other means. Yet the relatively small strength of Fighter Command was never surprised with all its power either in action or grounded for refuelling so that it could not go into action. These battles in the air were unique. There had never before been battles like them.

The generals of the Luftwaffe made thrust after thrust, and their blows were parried time after time by the British Air Marshals. If the Germans could have made the same attack at the time of Munich it would have succeeded; if they had made it at the outbreak of war it would almost certainly have succeeded; if they had made it as an immediate follow-up to Dunkirk it would have had a chance of success; but in August 1940 the time for success had passed—David had enough stones for his sling, Goliath had not enough strength in his body. Between Dunkirk and Dover some six weeks elapsed, and in that period the gaps in the strength of Fighter Command caused by the fighting on the Continent were substantially filled.

On August 11 the Luftwaffe was beaten back with the loss of sixty aircraft, fifty-five of which fell to the Fighter boys of Britain, of whom twenty-four were missing, with two saved from machines which were lost. Again about 400 German aircraft all told were used by the enemy that day. The rate of destruction—15 per cent.—was greater than that, 10 per cent., which Air Chief Marshal Sir Hugh Dowding, Commander-in-Chief Fighter Command, had forecast as the rate which could not be endured. Thus it became clear to the leaders of Fighter Command that the Luftwaffe could be defeated provided that the losses inflicted on Fighter Command were not so severe that they could not be made good. The saving of pilots from damaged aircraft was almost as important a contribution to victory for Fighter Command as a reduction in the rate of loss of aircraft, for the Empire Air Training Scheme had scarcely begun to supply trained pilots, and it was easier to supply a pilot with a machine than a machine with a pilot. Because Fighter Command could choose its battleground on the English side of the Channel it was possible to save many Royal Air Force pilots, but the personnel of the Luftwaffe who came down alive and uninjured were almost all prisoners of war and so were lost to their Service. In the end, therefore, it was the disparity in the rate of loss of personnel that decided the issue of the day battles and forced the enemy to essay the task by night. On August 11 the Germans lost the following types of aircraft destroyed: 12 bombers, 10 fighter-bombers, 19 single-engined fighters, 18 twin-engined fighters, and one seaplane.

Let us follow the course of that day's fighting through the eyes of Pilot Officer H. M. Stephen, who attacked eight enemy aircraft, shot down five, and damaged three. Soon after four in the morning he flew with the rest of No. 74 squadron to their forward base.

We hadn't very long to wait before we were told to take off and climb up over the Channel. Soon we ran across a squadron of German fighters and in a few seconds the sky was full of both of us. I had a quick bang at one of the enemy, then at another. Then I happened to turn 'up sun' and joined two aircraft that were climbing. I discovered that I was following two Messerschmitt 109 fighters at only a few yards' distance—in fact, I was formating [1] on them. By the time I'd realized my mistake they had turned away from the sun, and I opened fire on them. I came up behind one and gave him a burst, and he dropped down into the Channel. When I gave the leader a burst from twenty yards away he just exploded in mid-air.

When I returned to base I found we hadn't done too badly. The total for that first morning scrap was seven destroyed.

That was between six and seven, and the boys were thinking of breakfast when word came through that things were blowing up again, so coffee and toast were sent out to our hut at the side of the aerodrome. As usual, no sooner had the coffee arrived than we had to take off again on the same old chase. This time I followed my flight commander round and round, but we were out of luck, although on returning we found that the squadron leader had accounted for another, and so had two more of our pilots.

Again we sent for coffee and toast.

The score by 9 A.M. was ten Germans destroyed, our losses being three machines hit and needing repair, and one pilot who had baled out during the first engagement and came down in the sea.

The sky began to cloud over, and we were all very pleased as we thought it would probably give us a rest. But orders came through that we were to stand by. That meant sitting in our cockpits with oxygen-masks, and strapped in, but without our engines running.

Soon after ten-thirty we were told to proceed to a convoy and patrol

---

[1] Present participle of present indicative, 'to formate,' a verb coined in R.A.F. language, meaning 'to fly in formation.'

it. The squadron was just settling down to a dull routine job when all of a sudden there was the most appalling noise on our radio telephones; three people at once had seen about forty Messerschmitt 110 fighter-bombers in groups of three spread over about a mile and flying under cover of cloud to attack the convoy. That cheered us up a lot, and the pilots were telling each other on the radio what they were going to do with this or that particular bomber when they got near it.

One of the flight commanders thought that the enemy had already attacked the convoy and were on the way back. He gave chase, only to discover they were coming towards him, and before he could slow up he had gone right through the centre of them with the other two members of his section, all blazing away. This shook the German pilots so much that they immediately broke formation, which was just what we wanted, as we could deal with them better individually. The mêlée started—what a sight! and what a scrap! The German machines were going round in steep turns. Imagine them. Forty light bombers—very manœuvrable and fast—the famous Messerschmitt 110 Jaguar fighter-bombers. They started chasing us, and we were chasing them in and out of the clouds.

This sort of game went on for a few minutes, then the German fighter-bombers started forming one of their defensive circles. By this time there were several Germans lying in the water, all smashed up, with their crews swimming around. The Spitfires were now diving in and out of the circle and never letting them complete it. I got my sights into one bomber and gave him a long burst, and one of my tracer bullets must have hit his petrol-tank, as in a few seconds he was a mass of flames and down he went into the sea. I climbed up to the cloud base again, when another bomber made a dirty dart at me and went past so close that I was sure neither he nor I could get out of each other's way in time. My guardian angel must have been watching over me, and somehow we missed each other. Then I was able to turn on his tail (he was chasing another Spitfire), and a short burst silenced his rear gunner. Finally, as I closed my range, his machine rolled over and fell upside down into the sea.

After one more attack on another machine I ran out of ammunition. I popped back into cloud again and so back to base. On checking up figures we found that between us we had destroyed another ten, bringing the total up to twenty enemy aircraft destroyed.

After lunch we went up again and had been in the air about fifteen minutes when we saw in the distance about twenty dive-bombers and a fighter escort going in the direction of the convoy. The dive-bombers sheered off, but we were able to close with the fighters, and a small scrap developed. I saw a straggler break away from the main flight and gave chase to him. He turned, and we started a dog-fight; but all the time he was trying to get up into the cloud again, when I got in a lovely burst of machine-gun fire, and he started to lose speed. He dived, and I followed him down, giving him another burst of bullets. The pilot jumped out, but he was now so low that his parachute did not open. His machine crashed into the beach, burst into flames, and sent up a cloud of black smoke.

Back at our aerodrome, we started counting up again and found that the squadron had attacked thirty-eight enemy aircraft and definitely destroyed twenty-one.

On August 12 it was estimated that at one time nearly 500 enemy aircraft were engaged in a triple-pronged attack against Portsmouth and Isle of Wight, the Sussex and Kentish coasts, and the Thames Estuary. The targets were dockyards, harbours, aerodromes, and shipping. Sixty-two enemy aircraft were destroyed; thirteen British fighters were lost, but from one of them the pilot was saved. The enemy aircraft destroyed were twenty-six Dornier and Junkers bombers, twenty-five single-engined Me. 109 and He. 113 fighters, and eleven twin-engined Me. 110 fighters and fighter-bombers; that meant a German loss of more than 100 trained air-crew personnel against the British loss of twelve pilots; the ratio was rising in Britain's favour. Some of the British pilots chased enemy aircraft back to France; one was shot down to crash on the sands of the French coast, another went down smoking towards France. The force which attacked Portsmouth included Junkers, Dorniers, Heinkels, and Messerschmitts; twenty-seven were destroyed, seven by gunfire. Anti-aircraft guns of all calibres played their part. Crews of the heavier guns watched their shells bursting round German bombers no larger than specks in the sky. Some of the specks struggled vainly to keep their height, but a few seconds later were resolved into aircraft crashing to earth. The white parachutes of German airmen were visible among the shell-bursts. One battery got a direct hit on a bomber; it exploded in mid-air; two complete machine-guns from it were seen falling to earth. As the dive-bombers swooped they came into the zone of the lighter anti-aircraft guns, which brought down three Junkers 87's in flames. Still the dive-bombers swooped, until one came within range of the Lewis guns of a searchlight company; the gunners held their fire until it was close above them, saw their bullets hit home, and the dive-bomber continued its dive to destruction. Bombs fell on the outskirts of the dockyard, set fire to a store, and caused minor damage to a jetty; two small harbour craft were damaged and subsequently sank. In Portsmouth town a railway station was hit, a brewery and a number of other buildings were set on fire. In the Isle of Wight a church and some houses were damaged. The casualties were not numerous having regard to the large number of bombs dropped. When fifty bombers appeared off the Kentish coast soon after tea-time they were followed by an escort of about 150 fighters, in formations of thirty, reaching up to about 26,000 feet; seventeen of these aircraft were destroyed. In the other attacks some Royal Air Force aerodromes were slightly damaged; houses and other civil property were hit; casualties were light.

The guns of the Anti-Aircraft Command brought down one-seventh of the aircraft destroyed over Britain during the battle of 1940, and during that year they destroyed 444½ aircraft. The number of guns increased in all the areas of defence month by month, making it continually more difficult for German pilots to attack their targets with true accuracy. Scientific investigation marched hand in hand with practice. By the early spring of 1943 Mr Duncan Sandys, Parliamentary Secretary to the Ministry of Supply, informed Parliament that a new type of mechanical fuse working on the same principle as the mechanism of a clock had been developed and was in mass production; it was twice as accurate as the old type of powder fuse; this enabled accurate fire to be maintained to heights one and a half times as great as before, and gave guns the power to shoot accurately to greater distances. Guns could keep aircraft under fire for a longer time, and more guns could be brought to bear upon aircraft simultaneously. This increased the density of the shell barrage. The greater deadliness of anti-aircraft gunfire effected economy, and in the spring of 1943 anti-aircraft gunners were shooting down on an average eight enemy aircraft for the number of rounds they were required to fire to shoot down one aircraft in the autumn of 1940.

Flight Lieutenant L. M. Gaunce, D.F.C., a Canadian, of No. 3 squadron, engaged on the defence of Britain on that day of August 12, said:

The air was filled with Nazi aircraft. There seemed to be thousands of Messerschmitts, Spitfires, and Hurricanes all mixed up in a series of dog-fights. The three Hurricanes which I was leading concentrated on six Messerschmitts. I saw the South African shoot down his Messerschmitt.

The South African pilot, Flying Officer P. H. Hugo, D.F.C., said:

Dense smoke and liquid poured from the German pilot's machine. Although my engine stopped I dived after him. Fortunately, my engine restarted. The Messerschmitt pilot pulled out of his dive at about 6000 feet and then started to dive again. I was hot on his tail, and at 3000 feet opened fire. The German pilot continued to dive and landed on the water. Within a minute the aircraft had sunk, and I saw the pilot swimming about in the middle of a big patch of air-bubbles which had been caused by the sinking of his machine. I sent back a message on my radio telephone asking for a launch to be sent out to the German airman's rescue and gave his position. I then flew back to my base.

Gaunce continued:

Oil poured from another Messerschmitt which I attacked, covering not only my windscreen but my entire aircraft. I followed him down and saw him crash into the water. I climbed back to 15,000 feet and saw a Messerschmitt chasing a Hurricane. I dived down on its tail to sea-level. He zoomed up to 5000 feet. I followed, and after my first burst of fire he blew up in the air, and I watched pieces of flaming aircraft fall into the sea.

Both these pilots had learned just a few minutes before they took off that day that they had been awarded the Distinguished Flying Cross for work already done.

Soon after dawn on August 13 the Luftwaffe returned to the assault upon Southern England. Altogether, during the day, about 500 enemy aircraft were engaged, and of these 78 were shot down, for a British loss of 13 fighter aircraft and but three pilots; three of the ten pilots saved from the shot-down British aircraft were wounded. The attacks began against points along the Sussex coast and round Kent to the Thames Estuary. In the course of the day bombs fell on seaside towns; in country districts in Hampshire, Berkshire, Wiltshire; in the Isle of Wight; on Southampton; on several Royal Air Force aerodromes. But the harrying by the British fighters and the shelling of the guns disturbed the aim of the German bombers and caused many of their bombs to fall harmlessly; nevertheless, damage was done, lives were lost on aerodromes and in towns, and people were injured. The guns shot down three of the seventy-eight. The assault came in three waves. During one wave enemy bombers and fighters fell out of the sky at the rate of one a minute. One successful fighter pilot was a Pole who had been taken prisoner during the Russian advance into his country; he escaped, reached Rumania and the Mediterranean, then got to Britain to fight with the R.A.F. He said: "I saw three Dornier bombers in front. I attacked one from dead astern. He jettisoned his bombs into the sea, and I got in a very good burst from close range. The Dornier started to dive for the sea and tried to alight. As he was flattening out he burst into flames and went straight in." Another pilot at the end of one action saw several pilots swimming in the water, and watched them being picked up by a launch as he circled above them. As they climbed aboard he recognized three as British and one as a member of his own squadron.

A sergeant pilot told his experiences that day in this way:

It was a beautiful morning, and twelve of us were flying very high over Beachy Head in four sections of three each in line astern. The Commanding Officer led the first two sections, and I led the last. We were told to patrol below the clouds over Dover. Then we had orders to intercept enemy aircraft between us and the North Foreland. We went down to about 3000 feet, just below clouds, turned north, and

189

came over the Thames Estuary. It was very misty, so we went up above the clouds to about 6000 feet.

The sun was coming up from the east—and so were the enemy. We saw two formations of bombers; two lots of twelve aircraft, one behind the other, with about two miles' distance between them. They were 1500 feet lower than we were, so we had an immediate advantage.

Our squadron leader gave his orders quickly, and clearly, over the radio telephone. He would lead his flight of six Hurricanes round the back of the first formation, and the other flight of six would deliver a head-on attack.

As the leader of my flight went down towards the first formation of bombers the enemy darted for the clouds. I led my section after them, and when we came out of the bottom of the clouds I found we were ahead of them, so I swung completely round and led a head-on attack on the second formation of Dorniers, which had then appeared. I'm sure they got an awful shock. They didn't expect an attack from the front like that. You could see the Nazis didn't like it. We came up from below and slightly to one side of the bombers and blazed away for all we were worth. It was impossible to miss them. We simply sprayed them with bullets. . . .

In a battle you don't often have time to see what happens to every enemy aircraft you shoot at, but you usually have a chance to look round and see what is happening near you. I looked around after my head-on attack and saw a grand sight. My flight leader was leading his section up at the bombers head-on. I could see their machine-gun bullets spurting from their wings, and I could see the Germans losing their formation under this terrific fire.

We began to look for odd enemy bombers which were now wheeling about in the sky and trying to form up together. I went above the clouds with another sergeant pilot, and we saw three Dorniers, heading for home. We took one each. The one I fired at shed a lot of pieces from his wings and fuselage. When we landed I asked the other pilot how he got on. "Fine," he said. "I got him nicely. First the rear gunner baled out, and then I saw the Jerry plane go into the sea."

We had quite a good breakfast that morning after a very enjoyable time in a lovely party somewhere off the Isle of Sheppey in the Thames Estuary. Including what we got, the squadron's bag contained four certainties and a number of others probably destroyed or damaged.

In patrols that day No. 43 squadron shot down eight enemy aircraft, No. 601 (County of London) squadron destroyed thirteen, while in the space of a few minutes near Portland No. 609 (West Riding) squadron destroyed nine Junkers 87 dive-bombers and four Messerschmitt 109's without loss to themselves.

Next day the Germans were not so active. Raids were shorter. There was only one mass raid. It took place between midday and one o'clock off the south-east coast of Kent. A few of the enemy aircraft succeeded in crossing the coast to attack aerodromes in Kent. At one aerodrome anti-aircraft gunners opened fire against a formation of bombers and Messerschmitt 109's that flew over them. A light A.A. battery brought two bombers crashing down near them. A heavy battery saw their shells damage one aircraft, while another pilot dived low to escape their fire and ran into the fire of Lewis gunners and was destroyed. Seventeen German aircraft were shot down by fighters. One Spitfire squadron shot down two dive-bombers and four fighters within a few minutes. A pilot officer picked off a Junkers 87 from one formation of thirty and another from a formation of fifty, and sent both down in flames. Seven sergeant pilots of this squadron had a whirlwind dog-fight off Dover and Folkestone.

No. 1 fired two bursts at a Messerschmitt 110, saw one of the crew bale out, and watched the aircraft go down smoking furiously.

No. 2 caught a Messerschmitt 109 as it was climbing and sent it down in flames.

No. 3 attacked one of twelve Junkers 87's at 10,000 feet and saw it drop out of control, then turned to deal with a Messerschmitt 109 which was coming for him. It, said the sergeant, "disappeared into cloud, skidding sideways."

No. 4, flying still higher, made a steep right turn to avoid three enemy fighters, found another in front of him, fired five short bursts and watched it go straight down with its engine on fire, then turned on a second 109 and disabled it.

No. 5, who was wounded, destroyed a Heinkel.

Nos. 6 and 7 attacked Messerschmitt 109's and saw them disappear with smoke pouring from them.

On August 15 the Luftwaffe made a full-scale attack, employing more than a thousand bombers and fighters. The attack was made in nine phases. It was directed mainly against ships, harbours, and aerodromes, but other unintended targets came in for the attention of the German bombers who were deflected from their objectives by guns and fighters. It was the biggest air attack the world had ever seen, and its object was to break through the sky battlements of Britain, batter them down, and force a breach in the defences through which the hordes of armed men drawn up along the western seaboard of Europe could pass to invade the British Isles.

The main objective of the battle was to overpower Fighter Command. Until that was done the mastery of the sky was denied to the German High Command. And in the absence of command of the air and of the surface sea the German Army could not attack the British Islands. Undoubtedly the German leaders believed that if they could obtain control of the skies over Britain they would be able to control the seas from the air. The plan had succeeded in Norway. The Norwegian campaign, from the German point of view, was a full-scale exercise under war conditions for the subsequent invasion of Britain; its complete fulfilment in two months must have been an encouragement to the German leaders, who were doubtless led to expect greater things of the Luftwaffe in the Battle of Britain than the Luftwaffe actually accomplished. They certainly did not expect failure. Yet failure they met, and that not alone because of the valour of the fighter pilots of Fighter Command and the tactical skill of their commanders, but in great measure because by mid-August 1940 the tide of air war had already begun to turn—but its ebb against Germany was then imperceptible. There were none among the Germans who could discern the faint movement of the waters of destiny, and there were few in Britain who could do more than hope that high-water-mark had indeed been reached. America expected the flood to flow over Britain. But instead it was a storm of wind that blew about the island defences and beat itself upon them in vain until its fury was spent. And the flood came not. The cover that Britain raised into the sky was neither great nor strong, but the gaps that were torn in it were made good, and the cover that was there sufficed. It was greater than the power of the Luftwaffe because of the system of intelligence; the technical merit of the eight-machine-gun fighter against the contemporaneous German aircraft; the high standard of training of the British pilots who met the attack, their physical courage and spiritual strength; the choice of battleground which helped to make the British to German ratio of personnel losses as one to twelve; the power of the guns to provide a good measure of protection to the aerodromes; the skill of the leaders of Fighter Command; and the courage of the British people, who scorned the very idea of defeat.

The front upon which the Luftwaffe attacked on August 15 stretched 500 miles from the Tyne to the Tamar. The first punch fell upon Kent, the next upon Sunderland, the third upon Yorkshire; the fourth, and subsequent attacks, which fell upon the south coast, penetrated inland, until at last the storm spent itself in anger against the West Country where it faces south, at the widening mouth of the English Channel.

Anti-aircraft gunners shot down twenty-two German aircraft. Nine fell at Dover, six around the Tyne. Shells from four-point-fives ringed almost invisible Junkers and Dornier bombers with white puffs, and from the sky German airmen floated down towards the gunners by parachute. Bofors quick-firing guns, firing two-pounder shells at two a second, caught Junkers 87 dive-bombers swooping down below

192

6000 feet and made them end their dive in flames. Lewis gunners felled the lowest fliers and others who dived to fancied safety from the shells of bigger guns. Gunners saw their victims crash by the Tees, the Thames, the Medway, and the Humber, by Harwich, Folkestone, Portsmouth, Southampton, and the Isle of Wight.

A hundred dive-bombers swept down out of the sun over Kent. Half attacked Hawkinge aerodrome, and the remainder attacked Manston. Although buildings were hit, neither aerodrome was affected for flying. Fleeing bombers scattered their bombs over Broadstairs and Ramsgate, killing and wounding civilians and damaging non-military property.

In the evening some of the raiders broke through to Croydon aerodrome. One of the first of their bombs fell a few yards from the control tower, but broke only windows. No serious damage was done to the aerodrome, but buildings in the district suffered, fires were caused, and people were killed and injured. This was not a raid on London (as was thought at the time by some), but part of the Luftwaffe plan to destroy Fighter Command's power of resistance by a combination of combat in the air and the bombing of aerodromes. It was significant, however, that not one of the German aircraft which attacked Croydon that day returned—all were shot down.

Bombs fell at Hastings, Rochester, Seaham Harbour, and Portland.

One hundred and fifty-eight enemy aircraft were shot down by the pilots of Fighter Command. No. 602 (City of Glasgow) squadron shot down the first bomber. No. 501 (County of Gloucester) squadron destroyed twelve enemy aircraft during the day, ten of them Junkers 87's of a formation of twenty encountered off the Kentish coast. Thirty-four British fighter aircraft were lost, but seventeen pilots were saved from them. The loss of seventeen British pilots compared strangely with the German loss of personnel from 180 bombers and fighters.

A German High Command communiqué issued on the following day admitted the loss of only thirty-two aircraft. Because most of the fighting took place over the sea, and many of the German aircraft fell into the water, the Germans could falsify their figures, without incontrovertible proof in the shape of wrecked aircraft being brought up against them. But on this occasion they miscalculated the number of German aircraft that fell on land, for the wreckage of forty-nine was strewn upon British soil!

The Germans had need to conceal from the world the true position. On August 15 the British fighters destroyed 127 out of 600 bombers, not counting fighter-bombers in that figure. The Junkers 87 was a two-seater; the Dornier 17 and the Heinkel 111 were four-crew machines; taking an average of only $2\frac{1}{2}$ per machine shot down gives a figure of 317, to which must be added a further 60 or more for the crews of the type 109 and 110 Messerschmitts, and the bombers shot down by the gunners. More than one-fifth of the force of bombers was destroyed, and the ratio of bombers to fighters destroyed was nearly three to one. This proportion was maintained throughout the Battle of Britain. It was the factor which gave the outcome of the battle to Fighter Command, and which defeated the Luftwaffe, for the Luftwaffe generals were unable to continue the attack in the face of these losses against a fighter defence which was not weakened. If the claims of the German High Command had been true the Luftwaffe would have won the Battle of Britain. Because the Air Ministry claims were true the Luftwaffe lost. By no means other than the realization of the claims of the Royal Air Force could this battle have been won for Britain.

On August 15 King George VI sent the following message to the Secretary of State for Air:

Please convey my warmest congratulations to the Fighter Squadrons who, in recent days, have been so heavily engaged in the defence of our country. I, like all their compatriots, have read with ever-increasing admiration the story of their daily victories. I wish them continued success and the best of luck.

During August the Luftwaffe generals ordered attack after attack against the aerodromes of Fighter Command. Biggin Hill, Croydon, Deal, Debden, Detling, Dover, Duxford, Eastchurch, Gosport, Hawkinge, Hornchurch, Kenley, Lympne, Manston, Martlesham, Middle Wallop, Northolt, North Weald, Rochester, Tangmere, West Malling—all these aerodromes were attacked, many of them several times.

The tactics followed by the enemy commanders were the now familiar feint attack against secondary targets followed by the main attack when it was thought that our fighters had been drawn off to another area, or had used up ammunition or fuel and were forced down to refuel and reload. The British commanders had to assess the different attacks and distinguish one type from another, so that the major part of the defence force at their disposal was not ordered up upon the task of beating off the diversionary raids. Fighter aircraft were kept well dispersed at forward aerodromes and satellite landing-grounds. When aircraft had to alight to refuel and rearm at forward landing-grounds patrols were maintained overhead, and this form of protection failed only once. Anti-aircraft guns did much to fend off the raiders from the aerodromes, for, when faced with good gun defences, the German air crews were shy of attacking, and those who were brave enough to

194

come in close against the gunfire were either shot down or had their aim ruined by the necessity to take avoiding action.

Tangmere aerodrome had its greatest day attack on August 16. About 200 Junkers 87 dive-bombers made the assault. Some dived in pairs from 15,000 to just over 1000 feet. No. 43 squadron caught eleven and shot them all down almost simultaneously. Altogether seventeen Stukas fell that day to No. 43 squadron's guns. Around the aerodrome twenty crashed German aircraft lay as evidence of the weight of the attack, but the aerodrome was out of action for only a few hours. Seven R.A.F. personnel and two civilians were killed. The squadrons based on Tangmere did well; between July 1940 and April 1941 inclusive they destroyed more than 500 German aircraft—the measure of their answer to the Luftwaffe's attempt to put their station out of action.

Flight Lieutenant J. B. Nicolson was born at Hampstead in 1917. Nineteen years later he joined the Royal Air Force and in 1937 was posted to No. 72 squadron as a pilot officer. With that squadron at Church Fenton aerodrome, near Tadcaster, in Yorkshire, he flew Spitfires. Next year he married. War came, and after a time he was promoted to flight lieutenant and transferred to command a flight of Hurricanes in No. 249 squadron, and moved south. On August 16, 1940, when Nicolson went on patrol with his new squadron above the Southampton area he knew that his wife was awaiting, up north in Yorkshire, the advent of their first child.

It was a glorious afternoon, with the sun shining from a cloudless sky, and hardly a breath of wind. Three Junkers 88 bombers crossed the path of No. 249 squadron's Hurricanes about four miles away. Nicolson saw and recognized them in the clear air, reported them to his squadron leader, and was detailed to pursue them with his section. The three Hurricanes headed off on the chase. Nicolson got within a mile of the Junkers when he saw them run into a squadron of Spitfires. He guessed that "was curtains for the three Junkers." He was right. He saw the Spitfires shoot them all down. Then he turned and climbed from 15,000 to 18,000 feet to rejoin his squadron over Southampton. He felt disappointed, for he had never fired at a Hun in his life, and he longed to have a crack at them. Suddenly there were four big bangs inside his Hurricane, the loudest bangs he had ever heard.

A Messerschmitt 110 had got on his tail unobserved. One of its cannon-shells had torn through his hood and sent splinters into his left eye, almost severing the eyelid; blood blinded him in that eye. Another struck and exploded his spare petrol-tank, which set the Hurricane on fire. The third crashed into the cockpit and tore away

195

his right trouser-leg. The last hit his left foot and wounded his heel.

Nicolson swerved and dived to the right to avoid further shells, and found that his assailant had overtaken him and was right in the Hurricane's gun-sight, 200 yards ahead, with both aircraft diving at 400 miles an hour. He shouted aloud, "I'll teach you some manners, you Hun!" As the flight lieutenant pressed the fire-button on the circular hand-grip of his control column, and the bullets spurted forth from his eight Browning guns, he saw his right thumb blistering in the heat, and his left hand, holding open the throttle, also blistering in the flames. The instrument-board in front of his eyes was shattered and "dripping like treacle.

"Curiously enough, although the heat inside must have been intense, in the excitement I did not feel much pain. In fact, I remember watching the skin being burnt off my left hand. All I was concerned about was keeping the throttle open to get my first Hun."

The Messerschmitt pilot zigzagged from side to side to avoid the hail of fire from the now blazing Hurricane. In the cockpit the heat was so great that Nicolson put his feet on the seat beneath his parachute while he continued the fight until the Messerschmitt disappeared in a steep dive. (It was later seen by eyewitnesses to crash into the sea a few miles from shore.) Then Nicolson attempted to jump out of his aircraft and struck his head on the framework of the hood—which was all that was left of it. He threw it back and tried to jump again. This time he realized that he had not unpinned the harness-straps holding him into his seat. One broke, doubtless burnt. He undid the other, and at last jumped out.

He turned several somersaults in the air and then dived head-first before he was able, and that only with difficulty, to pull the ripcord with his burnt hands.

It took about twenty minutes to reach the ground. "I must confess that I felt all in as I came down," he said. "I confess, too, that I prayed that I might faint, but I did not lose consciousness at all."

During the descent a Messerschmitt screamed past him, and he closed his eyes and hung limp in his harness, pretending he was dead. It returned once, but he never knew whether it fired at him or not. When it had gone he noticed for the first time that his left heel had been struck. Blood was oozing from the lace-holes of his boot. He could see the bones on his left hand showing through the knuckles. He tried to see what other injuries he had received, and found with relief that he was able to move all his limbs. One trouser-leg was missing, the other was in tatters, and his tunic was badly torn. He looked at his

196

watch and found it still ticking, although the glass had melted and the strap was burnt to a thread. The oxygen-mask was still over his face, for his hands were in too bad a state to take it off. He began to ache all over, and his legs and hands hurt.

When I got lower I saw I was in danger of coming down in the sea. I knew I didn't stand an earthly if I did, because I wouldn't have been able to swim a stroke with my hands like that. So I wriggled about a bit and managed to float inland. Then I saw a high-tension cable below me and thought it would finish me if I hit that. So I wriggled a bit more and aimed at a nice open field. When I was about 100 feet from the ground I saw a cyclist and heard him ring his bell. I was surprised to hear the bicycle-bell and realized that I had been coming down in absolute silence. I bellowed at the cyclist, but I don't suppose he heard me. I touched down in the field and fell over. Fortunately, it was a still day. My parachute just floated down and stayed down without dragging me along as they sometimes do.

When help arrived Nicolson dictated a telegram to his wife to say that he had been shot down but was safe. One of those who came along told him he had watched the combat and had seen the Messerschmitt 110 dive straight into the sea. The doctors came. "Thinking of the shock I know follows severe burning," says Nicolson, "I asked the doctors who examined me to give me a shot of morphia just in case."

On November 13, 1940, he had recovered sufficiently to croon and play a tin whistle as one of the "Harmony Boys" in the hospital concert. He got three weeks' leave and went to join his wife and young baby, afterwards to return to the convalescent hospital for further treatment before he could be pronounced fit. Before going on leave he was awarded the Victoria Cross, the first to be gained by a pilot of Fighter Command, and the fifth award of the Cross to the Royal Air Force in the World War.[1] Looking back upon his experience in his first fight, Nicolson said:

Perhaps pilots who have had more experience of air fighting would have done the wise thing and baled out immediately the aircraft caught fire. I did not think of anything at that time but to shoot him down. All I am anxious about now is to get back to flying and have another crack at the Germans. After all, I feel that four years' training should qualify me for more than one Hun, and I want to have my share.

August 17 was the first quiet day for Fighter Command for some time. In the early hours of the morning the gunners shot down a bomber off Southampton. This was the only aircraft to fall that day

[1] Flight Lieutenant J. B. Nicolson's V.C. was the fourth in order of date of the action for which it was awarded, but fifth in order of the date of the gazetting of the award. The award of the V.C. to Sergeant J. Hannah, of Bomber Command, for bravery in action on September 15, 1940, was gazetted before Nicolson's.

over the fighting area of England. It brought the gunners' score for seven days from the morning of August 11 to fifty-seven bombers and fighters brought down, and for each of the fifty-seven their fire had caused dozens to turn back from their targets.

The quiet day was useful to the Royal Air Force. It gave the pilots who had been through the thick of the fighting the opportunity to look back, think, and plan ahead. One of these pilots was Charles Anthony Woods-Scawen, who had been commissioned as an acting pilot officer in December 1938 and posted to No. 43 squadron. Since the beginning of the assault on France he had lived a life of high adventure. In June he was shot down in France, but escaped from twenty-five miles inside French territory, and got back to his squadron. The citation for the award of the Distinguished Flying Cross on September 3 said:

In spite of the fact that this pilot has been shot down six times, he has continued to fight with unabated courage and enthusiasm, and has shown outstanding qualities as a resourceful and determined leader. He has destroyed a total of six enemy aircraft, and severely damaged several others.

On August 8 he brought down a Messerschmitt 110, and in doing so became separated from the others of his section. While he was flying alone he saw a formation of fifty Junkers 87's flying south, apparently heading for home. He immediately attacked, firing at them as he went through the formation from astern. He reported:

I hoped they would not fire at me, because the danger to each other would be considerable, being bunched together. They fired in spite of this, but with no degree of accuracy. The first one I noticed that was hit poured forth clouds of smoke and broke away from the formation to the left. The next also emitted a little smoke, but dived steeply through the whole formation, narrowly missing one of his colleagues below. My last burst was my longest, and was aimed at the Junkers in front of me from dead astern. The strong slip-stream upset my aim, and as I broke away from the formation I was attacked and hit by Messerschmitt 110's waiting above for me to come out. I took violent evasive action and sighted my last Junkers 87 smoking very strongly and flying very low over the water.

I then returned to the base and saw the medical officer, who said I had "multiple foreign bodies in both legs."

Woods-Scawen's wounds were flesh-wounds. With the elasticity of youth he soon recovered, went back to his aeroplane, and was killed before the Battle of Britain ended. None of the Stukas he had hit when he flew through the formation of fifty was included in the six enemy aircraft which were cited in the *Gazette* as destroyed by him, for his smoking Junkers were neither claimed nor awarded as destroyed.

The Luftwaffe returned to the attack on Sunday, August 18,

deploying at least 600 aircraft—of which 400 were bombers—in three mass raids against aerodromes and harbours in South-east England. Over Kent a squadron of Hurricanes shot down the complete formation of five Messerschmitt 110 fighter-bombers. One Spitfire pilot described the approach of about eighty German bombers flying in line abreast in sections of three supported by many enemy fighters circling above and in front of them. The bombers looked, he said, "like a huge rectangle." Yet his squadron destroyed three Messerschmitt 109 and two Heinkel 113 fighters, five Dornier 17 bombers, and seriously damaged two more 109's.

Eighty-nine of the 400 bombers were certainly destroyed by the British fighter aircraft, again a proportion far higher than the percentage considered by Sir Hugh Dowding to be the essential minimum to produce defeat upon the enemy. During seven days of fighting 73 per cent. of the enemy losses were bombers or fighter-bombers. Here was proof of the inability of the German fighter formations to give protection to their bombers. The tactical control of the British fighter force—using available defence fighters in about equal proportions against enemy fighters and bombers—was answering well.

The Messerschmitt 109 and 110 fighters were vulnerable to attack from the rear because they were not armoured behind the pilot; that omission cost the Luftwaffe dear. The British fighters employed in the opening stages of the Battle of Britain were armoured both in front and behind the pilot.

But everything contributed to the beginning of the British victory. At dawn on August 18 No. 54 squadron had already destroyed or damaged 130 enemy aircraft since the beginning of the war. By nightfall it had destroyed ten more, probably destroyed six, and damaged twelve. Its only casualty for the day was slight damage to two Spitfires by bullets; none of its pilots was hurt. Three Blenheims of Coastal Command saw a formation of twenty Stukas protected by nine Messerschmitt fighters over Portsmouth in the afternoon. The three British pilots at once attacked, shot down two of the Junkers, and severely damaged a third. A Spitfire squadron flew up, finished off the damaged Stuka, and shot down ten Stukas and a Messerschmitt. One of the Spitfire pilots said, "I saw four of the enemy burning on the water near the Isle of Wight. My own victim, a Junkers 87, was probably among them.".

Two of the London defence aerodromes—Biggin Hill and Kenley—were bombed that day. At Biggin Hill the approach of a hundred raiders was plotted. Orders were given for all aircraft to take off and even the non-combatant aircraft got away in time. Spitfires of No. 610

(County of Chester) squadron, stationed at Biggin Hill, destroyed six enemy bombers and five fighters, and the guns destroyed a Dornier 215 bomber. But the raid was a heavy one. Some two hundred bombs were dropped, causing considerable damage. Pilot Officer D. A. R. Elliott was on duty as navigation officer in the operations-room when the roof was demolished. He was the only officer left of the operations-room staff. He was slightly wounded and badly shaken, but he went to assist the wounded, removing the rubble with his hands, and directing the rescue party. Then he organized a party to recover as many maps and documents as possible and set up a skeleton organization in the signals office. Going without food or rest, he acted as controller until he was relieved late at night. For this action twenty-one-years-old Pilot Officer Elliott was awarded the Military Cross.[1]

Kenley was the target for a dual attack by low-flying and high-flying aircraft. Nine Dornier 17 bombers came in at fifty feet, the leading trio machine-gunning the gun-pits before they dropped their bombs on the edge of the aerodrome. The six who followed bombed the buildings. Most of the damage was done by the low-flying squadron. Some of their bombs fell flat and skidded into the building of the officers' Mess. Hangars, hospital, and troop headquarters received direct hits. R.A.F. telephone-lines were broken, but medical aid was called over an Army line that remained intact. The raiders did not go unscathed; twenty-nine were brought down by fighters and anti-aircraft fire from the ground. It was discovered that some of the German bombers were more heavily armoured than before, for some of the machine-gun bullets fired at them—both from the air and the ground—glanced off instead of penetrating. The day of need for cannon-gun fighters in the R.A.F. was drawing near.

There were numerous acts of bravery during raids on aerodromes. Here are three examples. Fifty-years-old Corporal Bruce Jackman, a Buckinghamshire man from Wolverton, ran to a gun-post which he knew was manned by a less experienced crew. He retained one airman and ordered the others to take cover, while he operated the twin Lewis guns with great courage and determination until the gun-post was demolished and he was severely wounded. Twenty-years-old A/C 2 A. D. Rowe, a locksmith from the quiet little cathedral city of Truro in Cornwall, manned one of the two Hispano cannon-guns on an air station with great skill and coolness during a bomb attack

[1] D. A. R. Elliott was born at Hastings and lived at Maidstone. He was educated at St George's School, Knocke, Belgium, and the Collegiate School, Bournemouth. He was commissioned in the R.A.F. in 1938 and was promoted flying officer in September 1940.

and shared in the destruction of at least two enemy aircraft. He remained at his self-appointed post during the whole of the action without any cover and undeterred by the bursting of bombs exploding thirty yards away. He was deliberately machine-gunned from the air, but continued to handle his own gun until the raid was over. When dust and fumes filled a shelter that received a direct hit during an intense raid, and a number of men were killed and two seriously injured, twenty-one-years-old Corporal Josephine M. G. Robins, who had been a riding instructress before joining the Women's Auxiliary Air Force, immediately went to the assistance of the wounded and rendered first aid. "Displaying courage and coolness of a very high order in a position of extreme danger," she fetched a stretcher while the wounded were being removed from the demolished dugout and then stayed with them until they were evacuated. Miss Robins was born at Overstrand, Norfolk, and her home was at Faversham, Kent.

These three, who were awarded the Military Medal, came from Cornwall, Bucks, and Norfolk, but their like were to be found among the men and women of every shire and county of the British Isles and from the lands of the Empire overseas.

Other aerodromes received lesser attacks that day. Then, in the evening, forty Heinkel 111 and thirty Dornier 17 bombers flew up the Thames Estuary in a large rectangular formation, escorted by single-engined and twin-engined Messerschmitt fighters. They met the Thames Estuary anti-aircraft gun barrage. (The Luftwaffe pilots were displaying ever-growing respect for the anti-aircraft guns. They took avoiding action at the first shell-burst. They began to fly at greater heights. They avoided the areas where experience taught them they would find the gunfire heavy. And their great formations provided the guns with excellent targets.) This formation turned about over the estuary and flew from the guns. It was with difficulty that No. 54 squadron's Spitfires caught up with them and shot down four Messerschmitt 110's and a Dornier bomber; Hurricanes, rather more fortunately placed, shot down six 110's, three 109's, and four bombers. It was the first time that Londoners had heard their anti-aircraft guns open fire. That was to become an increasingly familiar sound later.

There followed a five days' lull. The Luftwaffe was no doubt being overhauled and made ready for further action. In Britain, Fighter Command was equally active, if on a smaller scale.

The Gathering of the Allies

In the evening of August 20 No. 302 squadron of the R.A.F. went into action for the first time. The squadron leader was British. The other pilots were Poles. This was the first complete non-British air unit of the air forces of the United Nations, which were destined to exceed the might of the Axis in the air. The squadron was ordered to look for a raider off the north-east coast. Their Hurricanes quickly took off. "We were patrolling at 5000 feet," reported the squadron leader,

> when the Junkers 88 came in sight. We dived and chased him through a cloud. Just as he came out of one cloud and was going into another I gave him a burst. The next thing I knew I was so close I had to break away to avoid crashing into him. Then a Polish pilot blew in and gave him a burst from astern. The rear gunner, I think, must have been killed. The other three members of the German crew baled out and were taken prisoner.

Ten days later the second Polish squadron of the Royal Air Force, No. 303 squadron, shot down its first victim. This squadron traced its history back to 1919, when it was first formed to help Poland in the war against the Bolsheviks. It was called the Kościuszko squadron, after the great Polish patriot. It took part in the defence of Warsaw in September 1939, and on the overrunning of Poland by the German Army the pilots left their country to continue the fight elsewhere. In France the squadron personnel was dispersed, and the pilots fought in various sections of the Armée de l'Air. The pilots reached England in June 1940. Training schools were set up in Britain for the Poles, and on August 5, 1940, the Anglo-Polish Agreement established the Polish Fighter and Bomber squadrons as a separate body within the framework of the Royal Air Force. The Kościuszko squadron, re-formed as No. 303 squadron, R.A.F., on August 1, 1940, at a British fighter station, gave Polish pilots the chance to fight together again. Their experience against the Luftwaffe and their brilliant tactics when fighting together gave them a great advantage in the Battle of Britain. At first they had a British commanding officer, Squadron Leader R. G. Kellett, who had been an Auxiliary Air Force flight lieutenant in No. 600 (City of London) squadron before the war. For his leadership of No. 303 squadron in the Battle of Britain, Kellett received the D.S.O. and the D.F.C. and the Polish Virtuti Militari, that nation's highest award for valour. The two flight commanders were then also R.A.F. officers, and both were awarded the D.F.C. and

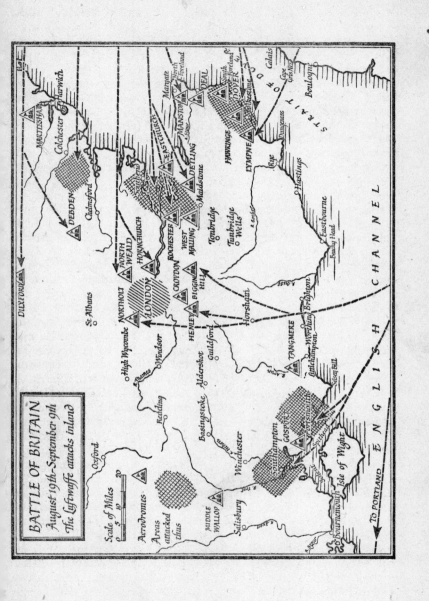

BATTLE OF BRITAIN
August 19th–September 9th
The Luftwaffe attacks inland

Scale of Miles
0 5 10 20

Aerodromes.

Areas attacked thus

the Virtuti Militari. Later the squadron became completely Polish, and was the first foreign squadron to be re-equipped with Spitfires.

On August 30, 1940, No. 303 squadron had not yet gone into action. Six of its Hurricanes were engaged in a training exercise to the north of London with six Blenheim bombers, when they sighted a large enemy force 7000 feet above. A Dornier broke formation and dived below the Blenheims and Hurricanes. One Polish pilot dived after the Dornier while the other five remained as escort to the Blenheims. As the German bomber straightened out from its dive the Polish pilot closed and opened fire. The Dornier burst into flames. One of its crew baled out. The machine plunged earthward, hit the ground, and exploded. The Polish pilot flew back into station with his flight. Next day six pilots of No. 303 squadron, on patrol outside London, shot down six Messerschmitt fighters without loss to themselves. During the entire period of the Battle of Britain the squadron shot down 126 enemy aircraft. By December 31, 1942, Polish pilots—all the Polish pilots—in Fighter Command had shot down 501 enemy aircraft. When they scored their five-hundredth victory they were flying offensively just off the French coast, near the mouth of the Somme, during a sweep from Dunkirk to Le Treport. But before that came about there was much defensive fighting to be fought out over the South of England.

The Poles brought with them their own national customs and traditions. A senior officer, when on parade and about to address his men on formal occasions, called the traditional greeting which goes back to feudal times: "My forehead is towards you." And the squadron called back in unison, "And our foreheads are towards you, chief."

When, after the Battle of Britain, Air Marshal W. Sholto Douglas inspected No. 303 squadron and decorated some of the pilots he gave it the traditional Polish greeting: "*Czołem, Lotnicy*" ("Greetings, airmen"). The squadron replied, "*Czołem, Panie Generale*" ("Greetings, General").

Detachments of the Allied Air Forces in Britain, who were part of the Royal Air Force, ran their own camps under the supervision of R.A.F. Commanding Officers. Some of the customs of the strangers within the Royal Air Force were as curious to the British officers and men as were the British customs to the foreigners, especially in the machinery of their respective national Air Force administration.

At one camp in England the British C.O., a group captain, found it necessary to admonish an airman who had been absent without leave for some days. Through an interpreter he told the airman that he would be court-martialled.

The airman fell flat on his face in a dead faint.

The interpreter blandly explained to the astonished British officer that in his country a court martial usually meant that the offender was shot within four hours!

The machinery for the court martial begun, the airman's own Commanding Officer, a prince of a noble house, was asked to make the necessary arrangements for collecting evidence. With dignity and assurance, he replied, "If *I* say the man is guilty, he *is* guilty."

The requirements of Air Force law were explained to the prince, and he departed with a large number of official forms to be filled in. This task was still in progress two days later when the British group captain made an inspection of the camp. A new notice caught his eye. He had it translated. It read:

IN FUTURE THERE WILL BE NO MORE CRIME IN THIS CAMP.
IT ENTAILS ALTOGETHER TOO MUCH WORK FOR THE OFFICERS.

In addition to Poles there were airmen from Czechoslovakia, France, Holland, Belgium, and Norway flying side by side with the Royal Air Force. After the Germans marched into their country Czechoslovak pilots began to organize mass escapes. Defying the constant threat of the concentration camps and the Gestapo torturers, young Czechs tramped to the frontiers in small groups, inventing a variety of ruses to cross in safety to freedom. Not infrequently their plans were helped by the known inability of Gestapo agents to resist a bribe. One flight lieutenant who escaped to England declared that bribery and corruption were rampant within the ranks of the Gestapo. He showed his 'gratitude' to them by shooting down numerous Nazi aircraft. "Most of the agents were so eager to make money," he said, "that they would supply anyone with half a dozen sets of papers to get across the frontier—provided the reward was generous enough. A fair percentage of our pilots who are now in action against the Nazis are at liberty because the Gestapo men were easily bribed." In some instances goods trains provided the means of escape. The back door of an inn right on the frontier saw many Czechoslovaks walk across the border after Nazi agents had been plentifully supplied with drinks in the beer cellar. Those Czechs who were caught were ruthlessly dealt with; some were shot immediately; others were sentenced to long terms of imprisonment.

Air Vice-Marshal Janousek, later appointed K.C.B., leader of the Czech Air Force in Britain, said:

When it was clear that Hitler meant to destroy Czechoslovakia our airmen were ready to fight regardless of the enemy's overwhelming

205

numbers. They did not get the order to fight. They got an order *not* to fight. That was a blow to them—a worse blow than anything Göring could have given them. They just could not believe the order. Well, there are many things we Czechs could not believe and to which we had to grow accustomed. Göring even tried to secure the services of our airmen for himself. He actually asked our air attaché in Berlin to fly to Prague and offer, in Göring's name, employment in the Luftwaffe to everybody—officers and men—from the Czech Air Force. Our airmen knew better. No flattery could deceive them. One by one they left their homes. . . . Very many had experience of prison life. Hunger was their daily companion. They no longer had smart uniforms. Their cheeks became sunken, their eyes more and more sad. Through Poland, the Balkan States, Asia, and Africa they went to France.

From May 10 to June 20, 1940, Czechoslovak pilots, flying Dewoitine and Curtiss fighters in France with the 'Lafayette' and 'Cigogne' Fighter squadrons, destroyed 140 German aircraft.

". . . Our airmen began to arrive in England at the end of June. Within three weeks the first Czech Fighter squadron was formed, and they had time to get into shape to take part in the Battle of Britain." The first Czech squadron, No. 310 squadron R.A.F., went into action on August 31, 1940, and on its second patrol, in the afternoon, shot down four Dornier bombers and two Messerschmitt 109 fighters; they lost two Hurricanes; from one the pilot baled out and was saved. They shot down thirty-six German aircraft in one month.

Because they were fewer in number, the Free French, Belgian, Dutch, and Norwegian airmen were less conspicuous, but they, too, played an important part in the air defence of Britain at that time. One Belgian pilot shot down three German aircraft and a probable fourth over Plymouth one day. Pilots of the Dutch Naval Air Service flew with Coastal Command. French pilots operated with British Fighter and Coastal Command squadrons; many of these men found their way to Britain after the capitulation of France. A twenty-years-old French corporal stole an aeroplane belonging to the Italian Armistice Commission at Casablanca, and, accompanied by a young sergeant pilot, flew to Gibraltar. The corporal took ship to England, where he was attached to a British squadron.

By air and sea, a number of French pilots arrived at Oran. Two of them, both regular French Air Force pilots before the war, had been instructors in Algiers; they went to Oran with forged papers as fighter pilots. When they heard the news of the French collapse they 'borrowed' an Air France aeroplane, and, with another pilot and three observers, took off for Gibraltar at night. None of them had ever flown at night before. "We hoped for the best," said one. "We had a lot of luggage and it kept shifting about, knocking us all over the machine. Then our petrol gave out, and we steeled ourselves for a landing in the sea, but fortunately we were able to land at Gibraltar." By then it was dawn, and they were on British territory 300 miles from Oran.

§ 11

Ending of the Second Phase

During the five days' lull between August 18 and 24 the Luftwaffe made extensive reconnaissance flights, many by single aircraft, some of which bombed British aerodromes; they lost 39 aircraft, whereas the Royal Air Force lost 10 aircraft and four pilots. On August 24 and 25 the Luftwaffe lost 50 and 55 aircraft—89 to the Royal Air Force and 16 to the guns; Fighter Command losses were 32 aircraft and 17 pilots. On the 24th raids came repeatedly from early morning, one wave following another in swift succession. Until the middle of the afternoon the attacks were directed against aerodromes in east Kent. Then two mass raids were simultaneously thrown, one at the Portsmouth area, and the other against aerodromes almost up to the fringes of London. The sky was cloudless. The first raid, by eighty aircraft, began at 7.45 A.M. and lasted for an hour and a quarter. The second raid began before ten o'clock. Waves of Dornier and Junkers 88 bombers, each thirty to forty strong, flying in herring-bone pattern, passed one after another over Kent, covered by fighters flying at about 25,000-feet. Fighting began anywhere between 3000 and 25,000 feet. British and German pilots fought duels in the sunlight, those at the higher levels breathing oxygen from their masks. At the bottom of the pack a squadron of Defiant two-seater fighters attacked twenty Junkers 88 bombers escorted by Heinkel 113 single-seat fighters. The Junkers at once dived and were followed by the Defiants, whose gunners brought down three Junkers and a Heinkel before the remainder disappeared out to sea.

The Defiant was originally designed as a night fighter; it was employed as a day fighter too. Only one squadron was equipped with this aircraft. Between May 12 and May 31 this squadron destroyed sixty-five enemy aircraft, including its record bag of thirty-seven in one afternoon over the beaches of Dunkirk. In the Battle of Britain —during the period following the incident referred to in the preceding paragraph—the squadron destroyed about thirty enemy aircraft in less than a week. Their losses were heavier now than during Dunkirk; Squadron Leader P. A. Hunter, who had led them so brilliantly then, had been killed, and possibly, after the loss of other pilots and air gunners, the squadron was not so familiar with the peculiar tactics which were necessary to bring out the special qualities of this unusual fighter whose pilot had no guns under his direct control. After this week the squadron was taken off day fighting and applied to night operations, and, until they were finally replaced, the Defiants held the record for enemy aircraft destroyed in one night, and, of all types of night fighters then used, effected the highest percentage of kills per interception. The last of the Defiants had a speed of well over 300 miles an hour.

Shortly after three o'clock 300 German bombers and fighters flew inland to the outer belt of London, and the guns of the capital were in action for the second time. Simultaneously 500 bombers and fighters raided the Portsmouth area; seventy high-explosive bombs fell on the city in five minutes, and 125 persons were killed.

No. 1 Royal Canadian Air Force Fighter squadron, the first to reach Britain, went into action for the first time, flying their Canadian-built Hurricanes, and shot down two Dornier bombers. Defiant pilots, in action for the third time that day, attacked twenty-four Junkers 88 bombers flying in line astern at 8000 feet and destroyed four. Soon afterwards the Defiants destroyed a Heinkel 111 and damaged a Messerschmitt fighter.

The German tactical method was changing under the continued resistance of Fighter Command. Whereas in the earlier attacks the bombers were often much more numerous than the fighters, now the fighters and bombers were nearly equal in numbers. But the manner of the fighting in the air remained substantially the same. Although outnumbered everywhere, the British pilots drove their aircraft into the masses of German machines, broke their formations into smaller groups, and so forced some of them to fight on more even odds; meanwhile, from the mêlée, other German aircraft tried to re-form formation, either to continue their attack or to fly for safety.

The strategy of the Luftwaffe generals was working up to the delivery of their second intended knock-out blow. The results of August 15 had demonstrated that the British defences were stronger than they had calculated them to be. The new peak was to fall one calendar month later, about the time of harvest moon. It had to be planned with military stratagem and subtlety, in concert with the rhythm of their Teutonic minds, to defeat the absurd idiosyncrasies of the English, of whose illogicalities Rupert Brooke wrote in the Café des Westens in Berlin in 1912:

> Here tulips bloom as they are told;
> Unkempt about those hedges blows
> An English unofficial rose;
> And there the unregulated sun
> Slopes down to rest when day is done,
> And wakes a vague unpunctual star. . . .

Meanwhile the increasing pressure of the German air attack carried the battle inland. The days when most of the stricken knights of the air fell into the sea in a fountain of foam were passing. The glory of the fighting was in the air, but the tragedy of the effect of it all lay upon the ground, accumulating, growing, marked ever more frequently as the days passed with the litter and wreckage of broken aircraft. The steel, aluminium, and magnesium alloys of the aircraft of the Luftwaffe that dropped upon the English countryside in twisted airframes, broken engines and airscrews, made a considerable contribution to the scrap that Britain needed to make good her lack of raw materials for war. In the fields of Kent, Surrey, Sussex, and other counties there were great earth craters; there were fires in heath and woodland; in the villages and towns there were wrecked houses and rubble-littered streets; in the country there were broken farms; and on the aerodromes that were the targets of the German bombers there were fires that leaped suddenly and died quickly, and there were others that burnt and smouldered and had to be fought until they were put out while the bombs still fell. But in spite of everything that the Luftwaffe could do, the ground staffs kept the fighter aircraft of the Royal Air Force squadrons serviced for the fray, and, by their efforts and their courage, made possible the air defence of Britain.

On August 24 No. 610 (County of Chester) squadron, flying Spitfires, shot down seven German aircraft, and Sergeant Pilot R. F. Hamlyn shot down five of them. This is his story:

> Saturday was certainly a grand day. It started with the dawn. We were up at a quarter-past four. We were in the air just after five o'clock. Shortly before half-past eight we were in the air again looking for enemy raiders approaching the South Coast from France. We saw three or four waves of Junkers 88's, protected by a bunch of Messerschmitt 109's above. We were at 15,000 feet, between the bombers and the fighters. The fighters did not have much chance to interfere with us before we attacked the bombers.
>
> I attacked one of the waves of bombers from behind and above. I selected the end bomber of the formation, which numbered between fifteen and eighteen. A burst of fire lasting only two seconds was enough. It broke away from the formation, dived down, and I saw it crash into the sea.
>
> I then throttled back so that I would not overtake the whole formation. I was getting quite a lot of cross-fire from the other bombers as

it was, though none of it hit me. If I had broken away after shooting down the first bomber I should have exposed myself to the full force of the enemy formation's cross-fire. I didn't have time to select another bomber as target, for almost immediately a Messerschmitt 109 came diving after me. As I had throttled back he overshot me, and presented me with a beautiful target. He pulled up about 150 yards in front of me. I pressed the gun-button for two seconds. He immediately began to smoke, and dived away. I followed him and saw him go straight into the sea. When the sky was clear of German planes we went home for breakfast.

I didn't get any breakfast. I only had time for a hot drink before we were ordered to stand by again, and by half-past eleven that morning we were patrolling the South-east coast. We were attacked by half a dozen Messerschmitt 109's, and, of course, we broke up to deal with them individually. I had a dog-fight with one, both of us trying to get into position to deliver an attack on the other, but I outmanœuvred him. I got on his tail, and he made off for the French coast as hard as he could go.

The fight started at 10,000 feet. We raced across the Channel like mad. As we were going like that I saw one of our fellows shoot down another Messerschmitt, so I said to myself, "I must keep the squadron's average up and get this one." I didn't fire at him until we were actually over the French coast. Then I let him have it—three nice bursts of fire lasting three seconds each, which, as you may imagine, is an awfully long time!

I started the final burst at 8000 feet, and then he began to go down, and I followed until I saw him crash into a field in France. Then I went back home without seeing any enemy at all. I carefully examined my Spitfire after I landed, certain that I must have been hit somewhere. But, no, not a mark. It was very satisfactory.

Our third show began just before four o'clock in the afternoon. We were flying towards the Thames Estuary at 5000 feet when we saw anti-aircraft shells bursting in the sky to the north-east. We changed course and began to climb for the place where we thought we should meet the enemy. We did. They were flying at 12,000 feet. Twenty Junkers 88's in tight formation accompanied by about twenty Messerschmitt 109's above them. They were flying towards the London area. We could see the balloons shining in the sun. We pulled up towards the fighters. I got under one Messerschmitt and gave him two bursts.

Smoke started to pour out of him, and he went down out of control. Suddenly, tracer bullets started whizzing past my machine. I turned sharply, and saw a Messerschmitt attacking one of our pilots. I turned on the attacker and gave him a quick burst. Immediately he began to slow down and the aircraft began to smoke. I pressed the gun-button a second time, and the Messerschmitt caught fire.

I fired a third time, and the whole machine became enveloped in flames and pieces began to fly off. Finally, as it went down, more pieces came off, all burning. As it tumbled down towards the Thames Estuary it was really a bunch of blazing fragments instead of a whole aircraft. It was an amazing sight. That was my fifth for the day and the squadron's ninety-ninth. The squadron brought the score over the century the next day.

There is a lot of luck about air fighting. I mean it's a matter of luck whether you get into a good scrap or not. I was right through the Dunkirk show and didn't get a thing. But recently I seem to have been lucky. Fights are over so quickly that unless you are right there at the beginning you are liable not to see anything at all. None of the fights to-day lasted more than five minutes each.

But when one pilot is lucky in air fighting the luck of his opponent is out. The first American-born pilot of the Royal Air Force to give his life in the service of Britain was killed in August 1940, fighting in the Battle of Britain. On American Independence Day in the following year Sir Archibald Sinclair, Secretary of State for Air, unveiled in the crypt of St Paul's Cathedral a tablet in memory of Pilot Officer W. M. L. Fiske in the presence of the American Ambassador, Mr J. G. Winant, and leading members of the American colony in Britain. Presented by friends in America and Britain, the tablet was placed next to a bronze bust of George Washington. It bore the inscription: "An American citizen who died that England might live."

In the night following August 24, 1940, German bombers, mostly operating singly, dropped bombs within the London area, in many other parts of England, and in South Wales. It was the first general night attack upon the metropolitan area.

§ 12

Third Phase of the Battle

The main daylight attack on August 25 was directed against Portland. No. 602 (City of Glasgow) squadron took off from their satellite aerodrome near Tangmere at five o'clock. Forty minutes later they saw large numbers of Dornier 17 bombers and Messerschmitt 110's crossing the Dorset coast with a protective screen of Messerschmitt 109's circling round them. Squadron Leader A. V. R. Johnstone (who had succeeded to the command of the squadron on Squadron Leader A. D. Farquhar's promotion to wing commander) afterwards said, "All the pilots could see many more enemy aircraft streaming in from the south." Below lay Dorchester. The Glasgow pilots dived. Each chose his target. The enemy broke up, scattered, and turned back. Three Dornier 17's, six Messerschmitt 110's, and three 109's fell to the twelve Spitfires. Ten Spitfires flew back to base. One pilot jumped by parachute to safety, the other was picked up by a steamer.

Another Spitfire squadron and a Hurricane squadron played valiant parts in this battle of Portland, each shooting down six aircraft. There, too, between half-past five and six o'clock, the gunners felled their total of six for that day. Altogether the Luftwaffe lost forty-three aircraft during that one brief battle.

No. 11 Group of Fighter Command, manning the South-eastern sector of Britain, had borne and was continuing to bear the brunt of the Battle of Britain. It was reinforced by squadrons from Nos. 10 and 12 Groups. The Glasgow squadron, as part of that reinforcement, had flown south from Scotland on August 13. Their hunting partners over the Firth of Forth, the pilots of No. 603 (City of Edinburgh) squadron, came south too.

Shortly before the war the Glasgow squadron was an Army Co-operation squadron. Its conversion to a Fighter squadron was made in the spring of 1939. Its first fighter aircraft were Gladiators. It received the first Spitfire to go to an Auxiliary squadron in May; a Vickers test pilot, clad in a lounge suit, flew it up to them. From Abbotsinch aerodrome, near Paisley, the squadron moved east to its war station, and joined the Edinburgh squadron. These were the first Fighter squadrons in action against the enemy over Britain—when the Luftwaffe attacked the cruisers *Edinburgh* and *Southampton* and the destroyer *Mohawk* near the Forth Bridge in October 1939.[1] Yet when the Glasgow squadron flew south to enter the Battle of Britain the pilots had met the enemy only in small numbers, and their score stood at eight certainties and one probable. When the squadron returned to its home station at Christmas 1940 its pilots had destroyed eight-eight enemy aircraft and had probably destroyed or damaged seventy-seven more.

On August 26, 1940, three waves of German bombers and fighters were thrown against South and South-east England. The first wave came at noon. It split into several parts, apparently with the object of dividing the Royal Air Force fighter force. Some aircraft attacked the balloon barrage at Dover, others dropped bombs on Folkestone, and hit buildings in the centre of the town, while others flew inland over Canterbury.

No. 610 squadron's Spitfires came upon the bombers of Folkestone. One flight climbed to attack the Messerschmitts flying high as escort, while the second flight dived to attack the fighter-bombers. Sergeant Pilot Hamlyn, who had shot down five enemy aircraft two days before, destroyed two. He reported: "I caught one Messerschmitt 109 as it was trying to bomb the town. Then I went after another one farther down and gave him a quick burst. He immediately caught fire, and I saw him crash a mile off Folkestone."

[1] See Vol. I, pp. 105–106.

(Hamlyn shot down another German aircraft on the 27th, and two days later was awarded the Distinguished Flying Medal.)

Most of the raiders came inland, flying high. Spitfires had to climb from 18,000 feet to 30,000 to attack Messerschmitt 109's and Heinkel 113's protecting a formation of thirty Junkers 88 bombers. Defiants met nine Dornier 17 bombers approaching Dover at 13,000 feet, and shot down three, probably four.

The second attack was directed against aerodromes. Raiders were intercepted over the Thames Estuary, Essex, and Sussex. One bomber and fighter formation contained from sixty to eighty aircraft. The Czech squadron, among others, attacked, and its pilots shot down a Dornier 215 and a Messerschmitt 110. No. 1 Royal Canadian Air Force squadron, fighting in this raid, met a formation of Dornier bombers above the clouds, and saw the crew bale out of one and another fall out of control into the clouds.

No. 602 squadron were in action against the third assault, directed against the Portsmouth area about four in the afternoon. They met 150 bombers and fighters flying towards the naval base from the south at 16,000 feet. Squadron Leader Johnstone led the Glasgow pilots into the sun a thousand feet above the enemy bombers, and before the German fighters, flying still higher, saw them, the Spitfires flashed down upon the bombers. Four Heinkel 111's fell into the sea; three more were seriously damaged; a Messerschmitt 109 was destroyed. Then mass panic seized the German air armada. The bomber formation split into two parts, wheeled right and left, jettisoned their bombs in their haste to get away, and fled to the south-east and the south-west. The whole enemy force was scattered. Not a bomb fell on land.

That day (August 26) the enemy dropped bombs in the undefended Isles of Scilly. There were no casualties.

On August 28 the day raids against Kent, the Thames Estuary area, and the East Anglian coast were on a reduced scale. Attacks were renewed about nine o'clock at night. Bombers flying singly or in small groups flew over wide areas of England and South Wales until dawn, attacking a variety of targets which included Chatham dockyard and the aerodromes at Eastchurch and West Malling. Only one of the bombers came as low as 13,000 feet, and it was hit by anti-aircraft gunfire; the damage done by the others, dropping bombs from a great height, was very slight; they flew almost above the range of the guns.

On August 30, with the Luftwaffe still trying desperately to bomb Fighter Command aerodromes in the Home Counties, the scale of the day raids began again to increase. Damage to the aerodromes was not serious, although there were casualties, including both killed and wounded. In the morning raid, made shortly before noon, more than 150 bombers, escorted by about the same number of fighters, crossed the Kent coast, then, dividing into sections of about fifty aircraft, spread fanwise across the sky and attempted to bomb several aerodromes almost simultaneously. But Hurricanes and Spitfires inflicted heavy losses on them, attacking time after time when the odds were ten to one in favour of the German air force. The Royal Air Force pilots broke up enemy formations by charging them head-on, a form of attack which the German pilot has never liked. It is a method of attack which requires consummate confidence, for, once begun, it is fatal to turn off, since to do so exposes one's aircraft to the full fire of the enemy while unable to reply. Time after time the German pilots turned off, unable to withstand the iron will of their British opponents.

A small-scale raid after lunch was followed by a more furious renewal of the onslaught in the afternoon. Action spread over the sky in a number of combats. One flight sergeant said:

> While I was attacking a bomber eight Messerschmitt fighters dived on my tail. I dodged into a cloud. When I came out into clear air a Messerschmitt Jaguar [1] flew across my bows. I opened fire and followed him down. Pieces of fabric were falling from his wings. At one time I saw eight parachutes floating down.

A Hurricane pilot who jumped at 15,000 feet was attacked by three Messerschmitt fighters. Firing at his swaying figure as he floated down, they riddled his body with bullets and killed him.

Although British pilots had joined No. 242 squadron, nevertheless, at the end of August, about 75 per cent. of the pilots were still Canadians. On August 30, 1940, Douglas Bader led them into action over Essex, and brought them back to their aerodrome without a bullet-hole in a single Hurricane fifty-two minutes after taking off. And this is his description of the fight:

> Thirteen of our squadron were on patrol near London looking for the Germans, who we knew were about in large formations. Soon we spotted one large formation, and it was rather an awe-inspiring sight—particularly to anyone who hadn't previously been in action. I counted fourteen blocks of six aircraft—all bombers—with thirty Messerschmitt 110 fighters behind and above, so that altogether there were more than 100 enemy aircraft to deal with.
> Four of the boys had gone off to check up on some unidentified aircraft which had appeared shortly before we sighted the big formation, and they weren't back in time to join in the fun. That left nine of us to tackle the big enemy formation.

---

[1] Messerschmitt 110 fighter-bomber.

I detailed the pilot from Calgary to take his section of three Hurricanes up to keep the thirty Messerschmitts busy. "O.K., O.K.," he said, with obvious relish, and away he streaked to deal with that vastly superior number of enemy fighters. . . .

The remaining six of us tackled the bombers. They were flying at 15,000 feet with the middle of the formation roughly over Enfield, heading east. When we first sighted them they looked just like a vast swarm of bees. With the sun at our backs and the advantage of greater height, conditions were ideal for a surprise attack, and as soon as we were all in position we went straight down on to them. We didn't adopt any set rule in attacking them—we just worked on the axiom that the shortest distance between two points is a straight line.

I led the attack and went for what I think was the third block of six from the back. And *did* those Huns break up? In a few seconds there was utter confusion. They broke up all over the sky. As I went through, the section I aimed at fanned out. I can't give an exact sequence of events, but I know that the Canadian pilot who followed immediately behind took the one that broke away to the left while I took the one that broke away to the right. The third man in our line went straight through and gave the rear gunner of a Hun in one of the middle blocks an awful shock. Then the other boys followed on, and things really began to get moving.

Now, there's one curious thing about this air fighting. One minute you see hundreds of aeroplanes in the sky, and the next minute there's nothing. All you can do is to look through your sights at your particular target—and look in your mirror, too, if you are sensible, for any Messerschmitts which might be trying to get on to your tail.

Well, that particular battle lasted about five or ten minutes, and then, quite suddenly, the sky was clear of aircraft.

One pilot had sent a Hun bomber crashing into a greenhouse. Another bomber had gone headlong into a field filled with derelict motor-cars; it hit one of the cars, turned over, and caught fire. Another of our chaps had seen a twin-engined job of sorts go into a reservoir near Enfield. Yet another pilot saw his victim go down with his engine flat out; the plane dived into a field and disintegrated into little pieces. Incidentally, that particular pilot brought down three Huns that day.

We hadn't shot them all down, of course. They hadn't waited for that, but made off home in all directions at high speed. But, apart from our bag of twelve (eight Messerschmitt 110 fighter-bombers, three Heinkel 111 bombers, and a fourth Heinkel bomber already partly damaged by another squadron), there were a number of others which were badly shot up and probably never got home, like one which went staggering out over Southend with one engine out of action.

As there was nothing else left to shoot at we went home, picking up as we went the infuriated section which had been sent off to investigate the unidentified aircraft and had missed our battle. They hadn't fired a single round between the four of them, and their language when they heard what they'd missed was unprintable.

215

Among the pilots who contributed to the Royal Air Force bag of fifty-nine enemy aircraft destroyed on that day was Flying Officer Wicks, whose escape from behind the German lines in France was recorded earlier in this volume.

On the last day of August German attempts to put the British aerodromes out of action were maintained. Large formations were flung at the desired targets, and damage was done, but at a heavy cost. It was apparent by the changed character of formations that the losses inflicted by the pilots of Fighter Command worried the German leaders. One formation of fifteen bombers had the protection of between 70 and 100 Messerschmitt fighters; Messerschmitt 109's kept guard above while 110's weaved in and out between the sections of bombers; Hurricanes made a head-on attack against the bombers, but had no chance to wait to see the result. Elsewhere a formation of fifty Messerschmitt 110's instantly formed a defensive circle upon sighting a far smaller formation of Hurricanes; this left the initiative to the British pilots, who attacked, broke up the defensive circle, and shot down three of the Messerschmitts; one Hurricane pilot was killed in the fight. On the way home a pilot officer saw about 120 enemy aircraft making for the coast. He was alone, but he attacked, and split off a group of the formation into two sections of five, both of which turned to attack him. After engaging one section he turned to make a head-on attack on the outside aircraft of the other section, and damaged it. "It waffled away," said the pilot officer. With enemy aircraft all round him he fought his way out and returned to his aerodrome with only two hits in his Hurricane.

After another Hurricane pilot had run out of ammunition in shooting down two enemy fighters over Kent he saw a third Messerschmitt 109 dive past him. "I followed him down to ground-level and chased him southward," he said.

> He did not rise above a hundred feet until well south of Maidstone, and then he throttled back. I overtook him and flew alongside him, pointing downward to the ground. He turned away, so I carried out a dummy quarter attack, breaking away very close to him. After this he landed his Messerschmitt in a field at about 140 miles an hour. I saw the pilot get out apparently unhurt, and as I circled round him he put his hands above his head, so I waved to him and he waved back. Then I circled low over him and threw him a packet of twenty cigarettes which I had with me. I saw him pick them up, and again he waved. Then I saw what I believed to be members of the Home Guard go in to the field and take him prisoner. After that I returned to my base.

In three patrols that day No. 603 (City of Edinburgh) squadron, led by Squadron Leader G. L. Denholm, destroyed fourteen German aircraft and probably three more; ten were Messerschmitt 109's. Flying Officer B. J. G. Carbury, who came from Wellington, New Zealand,[1] shot down five of the squadron's bag that day.

The anti-aircraft gunners continued to play their part in beating back the day raids on aerodromes, and during the first nine days of September, while the German air generals maintained their offensive against the inland aerodromes of Fighter Command, the Luftwaffe lost 434 aircraft, including 78 shot down by gunfire; during this period the Royal Air Force home defences lost 144 aircraft, from which 78 pilots were saved.

On September 1 Spitfire pilots were sent up to intercept a raid thought to be approaching an Essex aerodrome. "This attack," reported the squadron leader, "seemed to have been diverted by intense A.A. fire in the Kent area." As the baffled German bombers flew south a pilot officer in a Spitfire pounced on a formation and sent a Heinkel 111 crashing down from 15,000 feet. Another Spitfire squadron saw enemy aircraft laying a ring of smoke over an Essex aerodrome in advance of the bombers' approach—an example of daylight pathfinding tactics, and an attempt to blind the gunners. The Spitfires waited. The Heinkels arrived, flying in line astern, with two tiers of Messerschmitt 109's above them. The Spitfires shot down three Messerschmitts; a Hurricane squadron shot down four more; a Hurricane pilot who chased a German Fighter squadron saw one of their aircraft plunge into the sea ten miles from the French coast. Over Maidstone, Croydon, and the southern outskirts of London, British fighters fought and forced back the enemy attempting successive raids.

The loudspeaker systems on the British fighter stations, installed for making announcements or giving orders, broadcast a running commentary during fights. Here is a typical example, taken from a Fighter Command station in South-east England.

Hours
15.05: Hello! Hello! Attention. Enemy aircraft entering mouth of the Thames, flying towards London. Our aircraft are taking off to intercept.
15.08: Enemy near Gravesend.
15.10: Our aircraft have sighted the enemy.
15.12: Our aircraft are now attacking. The enemy are very numerous and showing fight.
15.15: The fight appears to be going well—for us.
15.17: The enemy fighters have deserted the bombers they were escorting. They are employing defensive tactics against our

[1] The Auxiliary Air Force squadrons had already lost their local territorial character.

217

aircraft. Another squadron is beating up the bombers, who are turning east.

15.20: Two of the enemy fighters have been shot down. Our aircraft have broken up their defensive formation.

15.26: Another enemy aircraft is down—in the sea. The pilot is swimming for shore.

15.30: The enemy is scattered over the sea, and beating it for France.

15.40: Our aircraft are back and are coming in to land. Yes, they are all here. Closing down.

The operation occupied barely thirty-five minutes. The fighters had flown more than 135 miles, checked, fought, and driven back a horde of enemy fighters, and landed safely at their base. Ten minutes later some of the pilots, having tea in the Mess, were discussing football.

September 2 was another day of many raids, with the main attack directed against Fighter Command aerodromes on the north and south sides of the Thames Estuary. The bombers again flew in smaller formations, heavily escorted by fighters, in the ratio of about one to five. Thames-side gunners and the guns of ships opened a heavy barrage which prevented most of the bombers from getting near their targets. No. 46 squadron, in company with three other squadrons, routed a mixed formation of bombers and fighters over the estuary. In the one year of war that had ended by that nightfall Fighter Command pilots had shot down 1776 enemy aircraft; anti-aircraft gunners had destroyed 204. During the twelve months pilots of the Command had flown more than 17,000,000 miles, in flights mainly of less than an hour's duration. Their mileage had risen month by month. In September 1939 it was 200,000, and not an enemy was shot down. In December 1939 the figure had not reached the half-million mark. In March 1940, when pilots flew to protect shipping and fishing fleets, it rose to 1,700,000 miles. In August 1940, in the Battle of Britain, the pilots flew 4,500,000 miles. Ground crews had worked hard to aid the pilots to achieve the rising mileage. They worked harder still during the Battle of Britain, when bombs fell about them on the aerodromes, and life sometimes became a hell of work, noise, dirt, death, scanty meals, and scantier sleep.

On September 4 the Luftwaffe changed its route and came in on its main attack, not from the east over the Thames Estuary, but from the south, crossing the coastline all the way from the North Foreland to Selsey Bill. But Fighter Command was still ready for them. There was fighting at all heights from sea-level up to 30,000 feet. No matter how often they changed their tactical method of approach, the Luftwaffe could not reach their targets and get away again unscathed. And bombers who hit what they wanted to hit were in the minority.

218

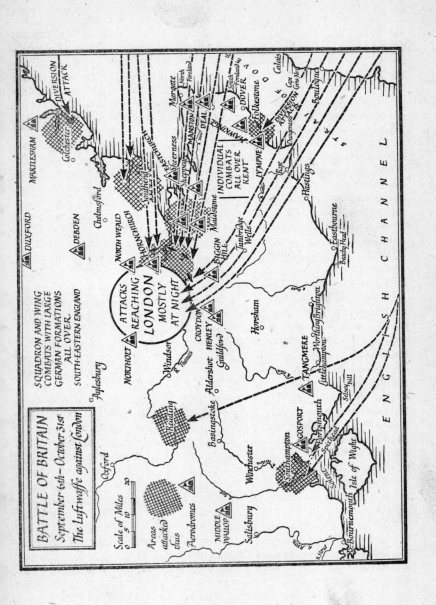

BATTLE OF BRITAIN
September 6th – October 31st
The Luftwaffe against London

Scale of Miles
0 5 10   20

Areas
attacked
thus

Aerodromes

SQUADRON AND WING
COMBATS WITH LARGE
GERMAN FORMATIONS
ALL OVER
SOUTH-EASTERN ENGLAND

ATTACKS
REACHING
LONDON
MOSTLY
AT NIGHT

INDIVIDUAL
COMBATS
ALL OVER
KENT

DIVERSION ATTACK

DIVERSION ATTACK

MARTLESHAM

DUXFORD

Aylesbury

Oxford

DEBDEN

Colchester

Chelmsford

NORTH WEALD

HORNCHURCH

Southend

Sheerness

Eastchurch

Sheppey

Margate

North Foreland?

MANSTON

DEAL

DOVER

Folkestone

Calais

Boulogne

South Foreland?

Dungeness

Cap Gris Nez

LYMPNE

Rye

Hastings

Eastbourne

Beachy Head

R. Ouse

Tunbridge Wells

BIGGIN HILL

Maidstone

R. Medway

NORTHOLT

Windsor

R. Thames

CROYDON

HENLEY

Aldershot

Guildford

Horsham

Worthing

Brighton

Littlehampton

TANGMERE

Selsey Bill

Basingstoke

Reading

Winchester

Southampton

GOSPORT

Portsmouth

Spithead

Solent

Isle of Wight

Bournemouth

R. Avon

R. Stour

Salisbury

MIDDLE
WALLOP

ENGLISH CHANNEL

Saturday, September 7, 1940, was a perfect autumn day. The morning was quiet, and the people of South-east England, soldiers and civilians alike, basked in the sunshine, grateful for the peace of nature, almost undisturbed by man. But in the afternoon the diapason of the bombers' approach came again from the blue sky. The formations crossed the coast from Dover to Dungeness a little after four o'clock; 375 bombers and fighters, advancing in waves. Some of them attacked aerodromes in Kent, Essex, and Surrey; the others made for London. At 4.56 P.M. the sirens of the capital announced the attack.

The target was the East End Docks. It was broad daylight. The Germans could see what they were bombing, and many bombs hit their objectives. Those that fell wide dropped among the rows of dockland houses and the streets of tenements. The havoc in the neighbourhood was grimly unpleasant. The docks blazed, mile after mile, along both banks of the river. The attack lasted ninety minutes. Soon after six o'clock the raiders were gone. But the fires still burned, and the regular and auxiliary firemen toiled and sweated at their task.

There was bitter fighting in the air that afternoon above the roofs and docks of East London, and the German wireless admitted that their first (and only mass) daylight raid on London was "paid for with great sacrificing." A quarter of the raiding force was destroyed. One hundred and three German aircraft fell that day; twenty-two British aircraft were lost, from which nine pilots were saved.

While Londoners listened to the thud of bombs the pilots who flew overhead in defence of the world's largest city were impressed by two aspects of the attack—first, the endless variety of the targets that lay spread below the Luftwaffe, over East London, the docks, and beyond, north, south, and west; and, second, the number of targets available to themselves in the air. "It was impossible to miss the aircraft we aimed at," said one squadron leader. "There seemed to be oceans of them. At one time when we were immediately below one formation we pulled our noses up and sprayed them for all we were worth as they flew across the path of our fire." A flying officer spoke of attacking three formations of bombers coming up the Thames "about three miles above the rooftops of London. I could see bombs falling off different points up the Thames and a huge column of flame leaping up from one point where a bomb fell on the south bank of the river."

No. 603 (City of Edinburgh) squadron shot down in flames a Heinkel 111 bomber and two Messerschmitt fighters. No. 242 squadron chased a large formation from East London to the coast and shot down four Dornier 215 bombers, six Messerschmitt 110 fighter-bombers, and two 109's. The Polish 303 squadron had the biggest bag of the day—

they sent ten Dornier 215 bombers and three Messerschmitts crashing down; two of the Polish pilots were wounded, and a third baled out. Three of the Poles got two bombers each; a fourth got one bomber and a fighter. Flight Lieutenant A. S. Forbes, one of the squadron's flight commanders, who led the Poles into action that day, said of them, "When they go tearing into the enemy bombers and fighters they go so close you would think they were going to collide." That was the secret of their success—close-range attack.

Forty Dornier 215 bombers flew over East London, with a small formation of Messerschmitt 110's a short distance behind and above, and at about 30,000 feet a larger formation of Messerschmitt 109's. A squadron of Spitfires attacked the 109's. A squadron of Hurricanes attacked the rear of the Dorniers. The German formation began to turn, and as the Dorniers wheeled to the right No. 303 squadron approached, flying in sections of three, in line astern, 4000 feet above. Forbes said:

> We were roughly over Enfield when we turned towards the Thames Estuary and climbed from 15,000 to 24,000 feet. We saw anti-aircraft shells bursting some distance away and below. Then we attacked forty Dorniers flying north. The Hurricanes attacking their rear made them turn east. We swung round, and I led the squadron in close formation down on them from out of the sun. We caught them broadside on as they were still turning. Each pilot chose his own target. We just gave them all we'd got, opening fire at nearly 150 yards' range and only breaking away when we could see the enemy cockpit filling our gun-sights, and finishing the attack at point-blank range. We went in practically in one straight line, all blazing away. I saw the Dornier I destroyed being hit in the engine, and all along the starboard wing all shapes and sizes of pieces flew off. Its engine burst into flames, and the pilot turned away in a long dive towards the sea. The fight must have gone on well down the river, for when we dived away we were doing at least 400 miles an hour. I was hit in the starboard wing by a cannon-shell. Splinters peppered the fuselage, and fragments no bigger than pin-heads peppered my leg. My hydraulic system was hit also, and with oil and glycol beginning to leak into the cockpit, I decided that the best policy was to try to save my aircraft; so I came home and landed safely.

It was the start of the Battle of London. The fires which raged in the docks were a beacon to the night bombers. At ten past eight they appeared. They continued to come until 4.30 A.M. The night-attack force numbered some 250 aircraft, all bombers. Night defence was in its infancy. There were not many guns for the defence of Britain, and they were spread over the kingdom to provide cover to the greatest possible area. No artillery barrage was possible, and German bombers continued to fly over the capital and unload their bombs into the inferno that lit up East London until it was possible to drive a motor-car through the city streets at speed without headlights. There were nine big fires—seven in the docks, one at Bishopsgate Goods Yard, another at Woolwich Arsenal; and there were many lesser fires. Wood blocks in the roadway were set on fire by the heat. Altogether 306 people were killed and 1337 seriously injured. Dawn came about five o'clock and brought relief from the bombing.

That was the testing night of the war-organized fire services. They fought through the new and foul experience, and triumphed, and from their unprecedented task came forth knowledge, high courage, and the organization to cope with its recurrences during the whole month of September, when they were tried to their utmost; by their fortitude these men—and the women who worked with them—contributed their full quota to the victory of the Battle of Britain.

After that attack the dispersed anti-aircraft guns were brought to London from all over the country, and two nights later the gun defences of the capital were doubled. But the gunners still employed pre-war methods of gunfire, using sound-locators to attempt precision shooting, and this seriously curtailed the volume of fire, which at night was the most important factor. Acting on fresh instructions, on the third night each gun-site did its utmost to fire with the maximum rapidity just in advance of the incoming aircraft. It was the first real barrage. It worked. The fierceness of the shelling forced the bombers up from just above a thousand feet to over 20,000 feet, while some turned and fled, and nine, at least, were destroyed. It was the beginning of the system of gunfire defence which was subsequently scientifically developed, and was later everywhere employed against night-bomber aircraft.

It was apparent to the British commanders that the German attack upon Britain was proceeding in accordance with an intended programme, and that the methodical Teuton was working to a time-schedule which had to be kept if it were not to fall to pieces—for the German is a poor improvisator. So, although Fighter Command had not been defeated (and that should have warned the Luftwaffe generals that their assault upon British aerodromes had not achieved its purpose), the succeeding part of the plan was engaged upon, presumably in the hope, if not the belief, that the first part of the programme—namely, the annihilation of the British fighter aircraft—was close at hand, and that it would be fulfilled. The immediate part of the plan was clear. London was the target. A knock-out blow at the capital was intended. London was to go the way of Warsaw, where 85 per cent. of the buildings had been damaged before the German occupation.

One young Hurricane pilot who destroyed six enemy aircraft, severely damaged a number of others, received the Distinguished Flying Cross for his gallantry, and then died in action, left a diary which is an eloquent pilot's-eye view of part of the Battle of Britain. This is what this young man who flew and fought for his fellow-men wrote.

September 2, 1940. First day at our new station. Leapt from our virgin couches at 0650. This shook me a bit. Was still slightly dopey when at 15,000 feet we sighted a large lump of blitz. Solid block of twenty Dornier 215's with a large fighter escort. Attacked *en masse*, then dived away as fighters came down. Joined "Butch" again after a frantic tail-watching breakaway, and started after bombers again. Suddenly we see a Dornier coming towards us—running for home. We jump on it—"Butch" sits on its tail, pumping lead at it. I do quarter attacks. He doesn't like this, lumps fall off and smoke pours out. I am awake now and feeling hungry. "Butch" says, "Don't waste any more ammunition on him; this guy's finished." I say, "O.K., Bud!" and formate on the Do. as he heads for Rochford. He is a wreck—rudders in ribbons and pieces falling off all the time. One guy comes out at 100 feet. Parachute streams as he hits the ground—bounces. "Butch" and I are very cocky, go home and shoot a horrid line.

Two more quick sorties seeing nothing, and then more *Blitzkrieg* on the fourth do. We run into a whole pile of Messerschmitt 110's and Dorniers. Too far to attack the bombers, so we start mixing it with the 110's. They circle and a lot come down vertically behind us. I lose "Butch" and everybody else as I turn round and round, watching my tail. Then a 110 rears up in front of me, plan view, as he does a steep turn. Range is almost point-blank as I turn inside and plug him. He disappears under my nose, and when I see him again he is diving vertically, starboard engine and wing blazing. I feel very cocky again, look for the fight, and find it is out of sight. I go home and find that I've only fired 300 rounds.

We sleep very soundly.

September 3. Unsuccessful day—made no contact.

September 4. Two patrols—0920 and 1230, but no contact made, and no fun at all. Just roaming around looking for the "Hun in the Sun." Watched night bombers in the dark, parachute flares and A.A. bursts all over the sky. Slept well.

September 5. Another big day. Over Thameshaven we meet twenty-five bombers and scores of Messerschmitt 109's. Fired at a Dornier 215, but had to break away when fighters came down *en masse*. Chased bombers for ten minutes but couldn't catch up. Came home and found "Butch" had baled out and landed in a garden where a terrified woman looked at him and then ran into the house. No more action to-day.

September 6. Up in the morning over the Thames Estuary to meet another raid. We nip in before the Hun fighters can get at us and do a quick flank attack. Fighters follow at once. I follow behind the bombers, watching two Me 109's coming up behind me. Before they get into range I turn sharp left and whip under them. Unfortunately C——, who is following me, gets plugged by one of these guys and has to crash-land. I get into a circle with two 109's, and shoot at the second. He starts to dive, so I pull the plug and chase him. Third burst sets him on fire, whole of starboard wing and fuselage.

We are down to fifty feet, so I leave him to burn and climb to 10,000 at full bore. Fighting is still going on, and two more 109's come for me. They work in pairs, and it seems fairly easy to get Number 2. Again I pick him out, and we tear down to 0 feet. We race along the Pilgrims' Way, and I fire the rest of my ammunition into him. Both radiators stream glycol, and I can smell him burning. I formate on him when I finish my rounds, and he has his oxygen-mask off, looking out at me. I leave him to go home and see him crash-land a few miles on. Going home I see a parachute and circle it—a British one. Later it turns out that it was the C.O., who got shot down by 109's.

In the evening a party, then on to a dance with the boys of another squadron. Slept at —— and stayed in bed till 9.

September 7. I have the rest of the day off, and a very good thing too. Squadron gets into the big London raids and loses quite a few— F—— died in hospital, W—— missing, several more shot down and baled out. S—— and I drove down to Maidstone Hospital to pick up the C.O. Coming back, we get to the Blackwall Tunnel when the trouble starts raining down all round us—no time to get to a shelter. We stand under an arch and watch the bombers approaching in waves, hear the bombs whistle down and then the explosions. Molotov breadbasket showers incendiaries round us, several in gasworks, which fortunately does not go up. Watch Cockneys put out one incendiary, discover a gloomy type leaning against a lamp-post, who discloses he is waiting for the pub. to open!

The C.O. feels a bit hard-done by as he's been shot down and wounded yesterday, then gets bombed to-day. S—— drives like a demon along a street and skids to a stop. Bus-driver pulls up beside us and says, "Come on, nah, turn it up, mate—you're on the blinkin' floor this time." Laughter mingles with bomb-crashes! We all have stiff whiskies in the Russell. Go back in the dark via Hampstead Heath, fires light up London, and fire-engines are coming from all suburbs into docks. Stop at a pub just outside Edmonton and get a riotous reception and lots of beer from excited public bar. I shake hands with everybody and get quite merry.

September 8. One short sortie in the evening but saw nothing at all.

September 9. Again no engagement. On patrol with another squadron we see 109's high above us, but they won't come and play. Wrote some letters.

September 10. Cloudy day. Blessed relief and lots of sleeping during the day. Went up and did cloud-flying.

September 11. First sortie in the morning brought us head-on into a bunch of He 111's. I do such a violent breakaway that I do an inverted spin. I lose 5000 to 6000 feet before I can get out of it. Can't find the fight at all after that, so I go home fed up. All set to get my own back at the second do, but all we see are one or two 109's miles away. No fun.

AN R.A.F. OPERATIONS CONTROL-ROOM IN ACTION

Control officers sit in the gallery above the sector table-map whereon W.A.A.F. operators control the counters representing aircraft.

Crown copyright reserved

224

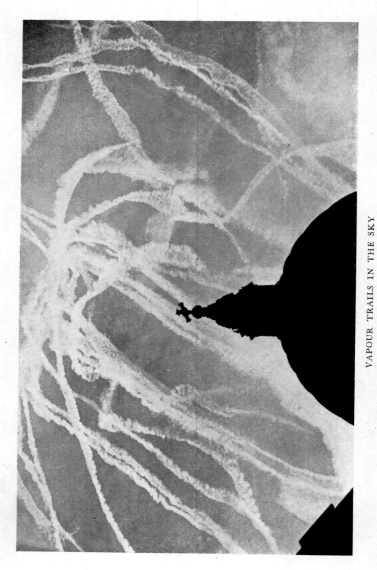

VAPOUR TRAILS IN THE SKY

R.A.F. planes weave strange patterns in the sky above St Paul's Cathedral.

Photo Associated Press

225

September 12. Another cloudy day and patrolling in ones and twos to try cloud interceptions.

September 13. Thirteenth, and a Friday! More cloud-flying expeditions, and everybody very testy about it. Went to B——'s house about 2200. Drank champagne and some beer. Bombing and A.A. fire all the time as it was a beautiful night.

September 14. A trip down into Sussex with another squadron, and saw more of our fighters than I've ever seen before. I got attacked twice, and everybody split up and came home singly or in pairs. Those attacking me must have been 113's, but every time I went to attack what I thought were these guys they were Spitfires! Most foxing!

September 15. The best day we've had. We go off at lunch-time with another squadron and meet sixteen Dorniers and lots of 109's. We go into the bombers, but "Butch" breaks early as he gets hit. I break with him, lose him, then go for the bombers again. Meet them coming home, and no Messerschmitts in sight. So I attack one on the edge of the formation. Get him straight away, and he leaves the rest of his boys. Follow him, plugging all the time. A quarter attack comes off beautifully, see bullets going in, in a line from the nose back to the tail, at intervals of a foot all the way down. See that rear gunner is lying back in his seat, probably dead. Dornier is smoking like a chimney, can smell it from behind him, oil comes back on to my aircraft, and pieces fly past me.

Then three blasted Spitfires horn in and drive me away from my own private and personal Dornier. One guy bales out from the Jerry. He has his arms folded and seems quite resigned. His ship crashes in flames, and Spitfires shoot a line all round it, probably dropping visiting cards: "I did this myself, see you in the Brasserie 8.30 Saturday" kind of thing. They're getting quite a reputation for pinching a bomber when a Hurricane has got it on the run. So I go home first and claim it before they can!

Afternoon brings even better pickings. Again we attack Dornier formation, and break it wide open. They scatter all over the sky and go for the clouds. I get one straight away with a long burst. He catches fire and goes straight in. Chase another one in and out of clouds, port engine catches fire and "Butch" and I claim him as a probable; damned sure he was finished. Then I see two Messerschmitt 109's behind me and whip round in a left-hand climbing turn. Horrid moment as I see his cannon winking at me, but he misses. Turn and start circling with the two of them. Gradually tighten the turn till I get a shot at No. 2 from above. See my bullet hit his left wing, and he is so shaken he dives into a cloud. Chase these two again and lose them. Then see two fighters coming straight for me. I think they're Spitfires, so I don't fire. Dodge under them and find they are the same two yellow-nosed Messerschmitts! Annoying, because they make off, and I can't catch them.

Most successful day for the squadron, a bag of ten destroyed, thirteen probable, and others damaged. Our losses—nil. My bag— two destroyed, one probable, and one damaged. Beginning to shoot a bit of a line. Celebration in the evening.

September 16. Scrambled out of bed in absolute confusion. Cloud up to 20,000 and mighty cold. We see dozens of vortices but no enemy aircraft.

Some pilots had extraordinary escapes. A pilot of No. 601 squadron had his Hurricane hit by what "felt like a tornado. I felt a pain in my right thigh, felt the engine stop, heard hissing noises and smelt fumes," he said. He continued:

My first reaction was to pull back the stick, but there was no response. That was at 19,000 feet where the combat ended. The next thing I remember is falling through air at high speed and feeling my helmet, flying-boots, and socks torn off. Lack of oxygen must have dulled my senses. My Hurricane had disappeared. My parachute opened at 7000 feet. About 2000 feet lower a Messerschmitt 110 fired at me while being closely pursued by Hurricanes. I landed on the water, just after seeing a motor-boat pass about a mile away. My C.O. told me later that they did not see me coming down, although they saw a German parachutist about 200 yards away from me. After about twenty minutes I saw a Hurricane search the bay, and I soon recognized it as belonging to my flight commander. He waved to me and spent some considerable time trying to inform a motor-torpedo-boat of my whereabouts, flying backward and forward between the boat and me. I was eventually picked up and taken to hospital, where my shrapnel wounds were X-rayed and dressed.

Flying Officer Ralph Hope, nephew of Mr Neville Chamberlain, was among those who escaped during that autumn. He flew with No. 605 (County of Warwick) auxiliary squadron, formerly commanded by Squadron Leader Lord Willoughby de Broke, M.C., A.F.C. Hope wrote of his escape in a letter, which read:

. . . at about 21,000 feet we got involved with a squadron of Me 109's. They got me even before I saw them, which was very annoying.

I first felt a curious sort of bump, and as I turned to see what was up my controls felt funny, a lot of red sparks and black smoke appeared round my feet, and a cloud of white smoke—probably glycol—began streaming back from the engine. The aircraft began going downhill fast. I slid back the hood and began to get out; my goggles were whipped off and my helmet began to lift up in the slip-stream.

I realized I had not undone my straps, so I pulled out the retaining-pin and stood up, standing on anything which came handy (the seat, the instrument-panel, or the stick, I don't really know). The air seized hold of me and there was a wrench as my oxygen-tube snapped off (I had forgotten to undo it), and I shot out into the sky.

The aeroplane disappeared. It was nice and cool falling. I was head down, of course, but found the position quite comfortable. There was no sense of speed, or any feeling of falling. I had a look at the clouds below me (they were at about 4000 to 5000 feet) and then collected the odd bits of my helmet and had a look round. My parachute was still in my seat, both my boots were on, and I didn't seem to have lost anything except my goggles and a handkerchief and map. They must have fallen out of my pockets in my knees when I first went upside-down.

After a while I thought about pulling the ripcord. I seemed to have fallen a goodish way, so I pulled. The canopy streamed out, there was a hard jerk, and there I was right side up, quite comfortable, and floating slowly—oh, so slowly—earthwards. I was at about nine to ten thousand feet then, so I had fallen for about eight to nine thousand feet and might have fallen further with advantage.

When I looked up I could see the shining white canopy, and little silver specks having no end of a dog-fight in the clear blue above me. A Spitfire dived down past me with a high-pitched whine, but that was the only disturbance. The parachute began to swing me about, and it was not long before I felt sick—very sick, in fact, by the time I landed.

It was fun going into the clouds as the sun played a sort of "Spectre of the Brocken" effect on my shadow as I approached them. When I emerged the countryside looked pleasantly open, and after drifting quite a way I thought I saw where I should land. Two farm-hands had the same idea. We were all wrong, as, in spite of attempts on my part to avoid it, I came down in a spinney of young oak-trees, pulling up short about twenty feet from the ground, hanging in my harness.

I managed to get hold of a trunk, pull myself over to it, get out of the parachute harness, and climb to the ground, where I remained quite still until I was found. The Army soon took charge of me, gave me a drink and some lunch, and drove me back to my base.

The only damage I sustained was a hefty bruise on my right shoulder from hitting the tail as I jumped, and a bruise on my leg and a torn trouser from the somewhat unceremonious descent through the upper branches of the oak-tree.

Now I go about with my arm in a sling, feeling particularly good as I have been given a week's sick leave.

His leave was extended to a fortnight. Then he and another pilot went up on patrol over South-east London. What happened in the upper sky will never be known. People in the streets saw a falling Hurricane, and realized that the pilot was attempting to direct it towards an open space which had been dug up for allotments, for in all other directions round about were the unbroken rows of houses. At the last moment, when he was sure that his crippled aircraft would miss the rooftops, the pilot jumped. But it was too late for the parachute to open. And Ralph Hope died. His letter is among the records of the County of Warwick squadron.

Another pilot sat up in a hospital bed to tell this story:

We were on patrol over Kent at a height of about 30,000 feet when we spotted about fifty Junkers 87 dive-bombers escorted by ten Messerschmitt 109 fighters. The whole squadron at once dived to the attack, and while the others were engaged with the Messerschmitts I dived straight down to 6000 feet to attack the bombers.

I singled one out and fired for about two seconds while still diving. The Junkers went straight into the sea. No one baled out. I saw nothing but a small patch of oil on the water.

I was having some difficulty in seeing out of my cockpit. My windscreen was covered with a thick layer of ice which was very difficult to rub off. I made several criss-crosses on the ice, to get some sort of view, while I continued to dive. When I pulled away I turned back towards another Junkers 87. I gave him a short burst and saw the bullets disappear into the fuselage and pieces fly off. The Junkers shivered a little, but continued to fly.

A moment later, while manœuvring for another attack on the Junkers, the pilot, to use his own word, was "distracted" by a cannon-shell which entered the left wing-tip of his Spitfire and blew the end off.

Several more shells entered my left wing near the outer gun [he said], and one near the gun beside the cockpit. I felt a sharp pain in my left leg and right arm, but I could not see anything wrong at the moment.

I turned my aircraft right round and headed straight for my attacker. I gave him a five seconds' burst, and black smoke started to pour out as he turned away. I put several more short bursts into him as he went away from me, but I did not see him come down.

By now the fight was well out over the Thames Estuary, and I had only about eight gallons of petrol left. I was feeling very faint and found blood pouring from my wrist and leg. I pushed my arm hard against my leg to stop the flow of blood and turned my oxygen full on to counteract the dizziness. Flying with one hand, I headed for the coast and an aerodrome just inland. I could not make it, and had to do a belly landing in a field with my wheels up.

Flight Lieutenant J. A. Kent, A.F.C., was twenty-six in 1940. He had already lived an adventurous life before he became a flight commander in the Polish R.A.F. 303 squadron and fought during the Battle of Britain. A Canadian, born and schooled in Winnipeg, he made his first flight when he was fourteen, learned to fly two years later, and was the youngest licensed flyer in the Dominion at the age of seventeen. When he got his commercial pilot's licence two years later he was the youngest commercial pilot. He sailed for Britain in 1935 to join the R.A.F., and was commissioned that year. In 1937 he was a flying officer, in 1939 a flight lieutenant. He was awarded the Air Force Cross before the war started, in the 1939 New Year's Honours List, for a particularly dangerous flying job. He said of one fight:

We saw between sixty and eighty Messerschmitt 109's, and though there were only five of us Spitfires at the time, we had a height advantage of some 6000 feet. We just nipped down on them.

The one I got first began to belch black smoke and went streaking down, leaving a tremendous trail of smoke that stayed in the sky for at least ten minutes. Then I had a terrific dog-fight with another Messerschmitt which attacked me immediately afterwards. He could fly, too, could that Hun. He kept swinging up and round into the sun, and several times I had to guess where he was as he disappeared with the sun right behind him. I squirted at him several times like that, and finally saw him come out of his protecting sunshine with his tail nearly off.

The fin and rudder were in tatters. As we rushed towards one another I could plainly see the pilot looking straight at me. We missed each other by feet. As he turned to the left he made a target of himself, so I squirted him for a few seconds. He flicked over on his back and with grey smoke simply pouring out went straight down towards the Kentish soil. He went into the ground with an awful smack. There was a flash of flame, a cloud of black smoke, and when I looked again there was nothing but a gaping hole with a few tiny pieces of scattered wreckage round the edges. I saw some British Tommies run across to the crater he had made and look down. Then they waved up at me and gave me the 'thumbs up' sign.

Kent was then a squadron leader. Not long before he had been awarded the Distinguished Flying Cross. The citation read:

Early in October 1940 this officer, when entirely alone, attacked forty Messerschmitt 109's and shot down two of them. He has personally destroyed at least four enemy aircraft. Flight Lieutenant Kent has been responsible in a large measure for the fighting efficiency of his squadron and has materially contributed to its successes.

Kent was proud of the Poles with whom he had fought. This is what he said of No. 303 squadron.

I want to tell you that it was a grand experience fighting with the Poles. When the squadron was first formed at the end of July the nucleus consisted of an English squadron leader and two flight commanders, of whom I was one. The Poles who came along had plenty of fighting experience. They had fought in Poland, and later in France, and when we got together in the early days of August we were all flat out to have a crack at the Huns. By the end of the month we had taken our place in the front line.

The first morning in the front line we were sent to escort a formation of our bombers. We ran into a raid and we got a Dornier first crack. The next day we got six Messerschmitt 109 fighters, and from then on we slapped 'em down as they'd never been slapped before. In their first four weeks that Polish squadron shot down more than 100 enemy aircraft, and in five weeks we had shot down more than 120.

You can take it from me that those Poles were magnificent fighters. They introduced their own technique into air fighting. They sailed right into the enemy, holding their fire until the very last moment. That was how they saved ammunition and how they got so many enemies down on each sortie.

No. 303 squadron flew and fought with remarkable success during that fateful month of September 1940. Its bag was 108 German aircraft shot down—77 by Polish pilots, 17 by the one Czech pilot in the squadron, and 14 by the three British pilots.[1]

During the Battle of Britain No. 302 squadron destroyed $26\frac{1}{2}$ enemy aircraft, although most of the time they were stationed outside the main fighting zone. Eleven of these victories were scored on one day, September 15, when they were brought in to fight in the main battle.

More Polish pilots, flying in R.A.F. squadrons other than the Polish squadrons, destroyed eighty-nine enemy aircraft during the Battle of Britain.

The Polish successes throughout the period of the battle were one-seventh of the whole, a remarkable achievement indeed, which will be written in the history of Poland, and become immortal.

In the Polish 303 squadron was a Czech—Sergeant Josef Frantisek, one of the greatest of sergeant pilots. When the Nazis invaded Czechoslovakia he was one of the pilots who took off and attacked them. He machine-gunned advancing columns until he had no more ammunition left. Then he flew on to Poland and offered his services to the Polish Air Force. He was accepted, and subsequently fought in the thick of the air fighting over Poland. When the end came [2] he and other members of the Polish Air Force flew their damaged aeroplanes to Rumania. There they were interned. After a week they escaped together and made their way to Syria, where they offered to fight for France. Their offer was accepted, and they went by boat through the Mediterranean to Marseilles. In France they were attached to the Polish squadrons fighting with the French Air Force.

Josef shot down eleven German aircraft over France. When France fell, in the company of Poles and Britishers he got to England. Some of those who escaped made a circuitous journey, fleeing first by boat or aircraft to Oran, thence travelling by motor-car to Casablanca, whence they contrived to get to Gibraltar, and from there the Royal Navy got them to Great Britain. When the Battle of Britain rose to its greatest height Josef shot down seventeen German aircraft over England and the English Channel. His squadron commander said of Frantisek: "I would regard him as the first big air ace of this war. He was so kind, unassuming, and gentle on the ground, but in battle he

---

[1] See p. 204 for the squadron's complete score in this battle.

[2] Poland faced the whole might of the Luftwaffe with only 370 first-line aircraft—the strength of the Polish Air Force in September 1939. The German Army attacked with ten armoured and six mechanized divisions, against which Poland, then in the process of modernizing her Army, could place only one armoured brigade and one mechanized brigade.

was a deadly killer." In France he was awarded the Croix de Guerre, from General Sikorski he received the Virtuti Militari (the Polish Victoria Cross), from Britain he received the Distinguished Flying Medal, and from the hands of Dr Eduard Beneš the Czech Military Cross. He died on October 8, 1940, on his own aerodrome, when his wing-tip struck a hummock as he was landing after patrol. His aircraft cart-wheeled and crashed. The earth claimed another of the men of the air who had never met his match in flight. He was twenty-eight.

In the fights over Britain, officer pilots and sergeant pilots worked side by side. They occupied different Messes, but they used the same duty huts. There was something to be said against the system of differentiation into commissioned and non-commissioned ranks of men who undertook the same work. It appeared unfair that men who ran the same risks should not share the same luxuries and privileges on the ground. But, in fact, the upward avenue was always open to the sergeant pilot who was suitable for commissioned rank. Many rose to positions of high responsibility. Others remained in the non-commissioned ranks. Not every man is suitable for commissioned rank. Some have not the gift of holding authority over their fellow-men. Some prefer to do the work in the air without accepting the responsibility of the officer upon the ground. Some are more at home in the sergeants' Mess than in the officers' Mess. To commission all pilots might put a ban upon the air activity of many men who probably would not pass the tests for officers at a first attempt. But after a period in the Service, rubbing shoulders with their fellow-pilots, many a sergeant pilot has found himself ready to assume the responsibility of commissioned rank, which formerly he would have feared to undertake.

The record of sergeant pilots in the Battle of Britain is a proud one. Here are just a few of those who flew then, and their records by the end of the year of 1940. There were many more like them.

Twenty-seven-years-old Sergeant Andrew McDowall, of No 602 (City of Glasgow) squadron, Auxiliary Air Force, shot down eighteen enemy aircraft, won the Distinguished Flying Medal and bar, and gained a commission. On one occasion he attacked five Messerschmitt fighters single-handed, and when he pressed the fire-button got no response from his guns. A German bullet had punctured the compressed-air bottle, and the guns were out of action. He began "to take evasive action." Swerving and dodging about the sky, he worked his way back across the Channel towards the English coast with enemy bullets and cannon-shells crashing into his Spitfire. One tore through the armour-plate behind his head and cut open his jaw, another shoved his seat forward until he was jammed against the instrument-board. His fuselage became a colander. His tailplane was smashed. Grimly he hung on, and as he neared the coast those five Huns left him, and he crash-landed in a field, because he could not reach the lever to let his undercarriage down.

Sergeant J. H. Lacey, D.F.M. and bar, was born in Wetherby, Yorkshire, a little market town on the Great North Road. Before the war he worked in Southampton as "an unqualified chemist's dispenser." He joined the R.A.F.V.R. in 1937 and in the war flew with No. 501 (County of Gloucester) squadron. He felled twenty-three enemy aircraft—one for each year of his life—and gained his commission. Another Yorkshireman, twenty-seven-years-old Flight Sergeant G. C. Unwin, D.F.M. and bar, from Bolton-on Dearne, and of No. 19 squadron, shot down thirteen. Sergeant D. E. Kingaby, of No. 92 squadron, a former insurance official from Cambridge, and born at Holloway, destroyed at least nine of the enemy, four of them in one day. Twenty-three-years-old Horatio Chandler, of Bexhill, Sussex, joined the Auxiliary Air Force in January 1939 and was promoted sergeant in March 1940; he fought over the beaches of Dunkirk and over South-east England in defence of London, flew on guard and battled in the sky for the safety of the northern cities of the assailed island of Britain, and by the autumn of 1940 had at least six victories to his credit.

Many of those sergeant pilots who flew and fought at that time led sections of fighters with flying officers and pilot officers under their leadership. In the air they could command, and did command, with skill and gallantry. If the men who flew were graded and distinguished one from another by their different ranks, their orders, crosses, and medals, the aircraft were the same, one identical with another (except for modifications due to technical improvements), differing solely by the skill and courage of the individual man who sat within the cockpit, who handled the controls, thumbed the fire-button, and drove the aircraft at the speed of Schneider-Trophy racers right into the heart of the enemy formations.

More they could not give. In this, whatever rank they had the honour to hold, they were alike. And, if the system sometimes seemed unfair, and brought criticism upon itself, it must be remembered that many problems were involved—authority upon the ground, the selection of ultimately higher-ranking officers, the matter of eventual demobilization and the restoration to civil life of thousands of pilots, for many of whom experience of commissioned life in the Service might prove a handicap rather than an advantage.

But it was no hard-and-fast system. Geoffrey Allard was a flight lieutenant when he was killed on active service in March 1941. He joined the Royal Air Force in 1929 as an aircraft apprentice, and was commissioned in 1940. He destroyed seventeen enemy aircraft, seven in three days. Sergeant J. H. Lacey was a flight lieutenant before the end of 1941. In February 1943 Wing Commander A. E. Lowe, M.B.E., was appointed to command a bomber squadron in which he once served as corporal, and in addition was appointed to command the air station from which the squadron operated. He joined the Royal Air Force at the age of sixteen in 1930, and was first trained as an electrician. . . .

The end of the second phase of the German air attack on Britain merged fully into the third phase. The attempted knock-out blows on Fighter Command's aerodromes ended with simultaneous attacks against London. In the night following September 8 the casualties were again heavy—286 dead and about 1400 seriously injured. Three enemy aircraft were shot down by gunfire during the night, following the destruction of eight (five by fighters) during the day.

On September 9 the Luftwaffe returned to the attack against the capital. Large formations attempted to penetrate the defences in the evening. They were again met in the skies, and suffered heavy losses. Fighters shot down forty-nine, and the guns destroyed three. Thirteen British fighter aircraft were lost, but six of the pilots were saved.

No. 242 squadron's pilots fought over the streets of London. They met the enemy approaching the south side of the Thames, chased them up river from London Bridge, over the Houses of Parliament and Westminster Abbey, to Hammersmith, and destroyed six bombers. A pilot officer, once a salmon fisherman in British Columbia, shot down one bomber, a pilot from Saskatchewan another, and a lad from Ontario a third.

That day the commanding officer of No. 1 Royal Canadian Air Force squadron, Squadron Leader E. A. McNab, took off alone when raiders were approaching South London. One flight of his squadron, already ordered up, had disappeared from sight before he took off. He patrolled high above his aerodrome, looking for trouble. Sighting some Messerschmitts many miles away, he flew to attack them. The rear one, at which he fired, climbed violently, fell over, and then went straight down, as McNab said afterwards, "with white smoke pouring from its belly."

Squadron Leader McNab had been in the Royal Canadian Air Force since 1926 and had flown 2000 hours before the war. Apart from normal Service flying, he had carried mails to Ottawa and made a photographic survey of part of the Hudson Bay area. He helped to form in Montreal the Auxiliary squadron from which about half of the pilots of this No. 1 R.C.A.F. squadron that was fighting over England were drawn. At the start of the war he was in England, on exchange with a Royal Air Force officer attached to the Royal Canadian Air Force.

At about six in the evening of September 9 No. 303 squadron encountered near Beachy Head forty German bombers and numerous fighters speeding homeward after a raid and being harassed by many Spitfires and Hurricanes. Sergeant Josef Frantisek wrote of the occasion:

When we arrived in sight of the Germans swarms of Messerschmitt 109's dived from a great height to attack us. I saw one going in to attack a Hurricane in front of me. I attacked it, starboard beam, and the Messerschmitt began to burn. The pilot tried to escape by climbing, and I saw him open the cockpit preparatory to jumping. Then the aircraft fell in flames.

I then saw a Hurricane in flames, and the pilot jumped. A Spitfire came and circled him to protect him.

Then I went for a Heinkel 111, and two Messerschmitt 109's attacked me. I played hide-and-seek with them in the clouds for a few minutes. During a right turn I came out of cloud and saw, ten yards away, a Heinkel 111 coming out of the clouds in front of me.

I very nearly collided with it, and fired at the front of the fuselage from above and behind. The front of the enemy aircraft fell to pieces with the cockpit and both engines in flames. I do not know if this aircraft fell to the ground or into the sea, because of the clouds. As I broke away one Messerschmitt 109 attacked me from above and another from below. I hid in the clouds and flew towards France to keep under cover.

Over the Channel I came out of the clouds and was hit by four shells, one in the port wing, one in a petrol-tank, and one through the radiator. Two Spitfires came to my rescue and shot down the Messerschmitt 109, which was apparently the one which I had hit earlier. I was then obliged to find a landing-place, for my engine temperature was mounting dangerously.

On a little hill north-east of Brighton I found a field of cabbages and made an excellent landing. The police came immediately. Not only did they not make any difficulty, but they were very kind to me. I anchored the Hurricane, shut off the petrol and oxygen, and left the machine guarded by policemen. They took me by car to Brighton, and I returned to my base by train.

On the morning of September 10 the Air Ministry and Ministry of Home Security communiqué, issued through the Ministry of Information, stated:

Following the heavy losses inflicted on him by our fighters and the repulse of his attacks yesterday evening, the enemy has now thrown off all pretence of confining himself to military targets.

Reports received during the night show that bombs were scattered at random over London without any distinction of objective. They fell in the City and caused fires in the immediate vicinity of St Paul's Cathedral and Guildhall; they fell on a large maternity hospital which was twice attacked, a number of casualties being caused; they fell on a Poor Law Institution for the aged, on a London County Council housing estate, and on a large number of workmen's cottages, especially in the East End of London, which were heavily and repeatedly attacked; and they were also scattered in the residential districts of West and North London.

The total casualties were, in round figures, 400 killed and 1400 injured. Most of the fatalities occurred when an elementary school in the East End of London, wherein families whose homes had been destroyed were temporarily sheltering, was hit and collapsed.

§ 13

The Crucial Hour

At various times during the afternoon of September 10 a few German aircraft made use of cloud cover to fly over the London area, reconnoitring the effect of their comrades' night raids, and no doubt taking photographs for the Luftwaffe generals. They dropped no bombs on London. A few bombs fell in Kent and Sussex. The fourth phase of the battle had begun.

The Royal Air Force Command had forced the Luftwaffe into making their major attack under cover of night. The problem of the night bomber was added to that of the day bomber. It was a problem which had engaged the staff of the Royal Air Force in the years before the war; experiments in night interception had been made during pre-war exercises. But the speeds of bombers had risen much since then, and the difficulty of interception was enhanced. Although there had been many night combats, and a considerable number of successes, always there was the difficulty of seeing the enemy aircraft. It was exceedingly difficult to judge distance, and the risk of collision in the air was very real. Often the enemy bomber flashed into the pilot's vision at uncomfortably close range. And there were lonely, discouraging patrols when nothing was seen; these tried the spirit. At that time Blenheims, Defiants, Hurricanes, and Spitfires were used for night patrols. And while night defence against bombers was still in its infancy, success depended more upon the skill of individual pilots in a specialized job than upon a scientific method of operation. Some pilots appeared to have greater success than others, and seemed to possess a special quality of finding and a natural technique in attacking

235

enemy aircraft at night. Names began to emerge with their successful encounters—A. G. Malan, the Hon. Max Aitken (Lord Beaverbrook's son), Stanford Tuck, John Cunningham, and later the one-armed J. A. F. Maclachlan. Searchlights were a great help to pilots in picking up the bombers; moonlight was still more valuable. To accustom their eyes to the conditions of night visibility, night-fighter pilots wore dark glasses while they were at readiness, awaiting the orders of the controller, before taking off.

London was the principal target for the German night bombers during their first period of mass activity. From September 7 until November 2 there was a nightly attack. Only on one night was the attack light, that following October 6, when but one bomb fell. On other nights the bomber force varied between 50 and 400 aircraft. They flew on radio bearings. With the great stretch of the Continental European seaboard at their disposal, the German air experts devised the beam system of night navigation, with the marker beam to denote arrival over target area. When pilots flying down the directional beam encountered the interjection of the cross-beam they could begin to unload their cargo of dynamic death. The method was simple in conception, and in practice required the minimum of training; it took longer to train British air crews to become efficient in individual navigation, to find their way to their targets, often blindfold through cloud or fog, rain, snow, or moonless night, without outside aid by wireless beam, or even directional bearings. But for emergency the Royal Air Force developed the homing service, whose personnel was ever on the watch for crippled aircraft, air crews who were lost, or, later, during the concentrated raids, for aircraft crowding the air-lanes dangerously after a sudden change from good to bad weather, to guide them safely to a landing at the nearest, safest, or most convenient aerodrome.

But, if the German method were the quicker in output of pilots and navigators, the British method was the better in the long run. With the German beam method of night navigation, aircraft had to follow one another down certain pre-selected beam-paths. There was a limit to the number of beams which could be projected towards a particular target. There was thus no possibility of carrying out concentrated mass raids by this method. The German attacks continued in relays of aircraft hour after hour, giving the fire-fighters more time to deal with conflagrations, giving the anti-aircraft defences more time to concentrate upon individual aircraft, and so enabling the work upon the ground to proceed, in spite of casualties. But the concentrated night attacks subsequently developed by Bomber Command were so powerfully delivered that the surface defences were driven underground until the raid was over, when they had to come out and attempt to quell fires which had secured firm hold within the target area.

Fire was the great destroyer. The high-explosive bombs blasted buildings, killed people on the ground, buried them under debris, crushed them under beams and blocks of masonry. But fire ravaged the buildings and spread from one to another, devouring their contents, leaving them empty shells. The area scorched by fire was greater than the area demolished by high explosive. Incendiaries fell in thousands; high explosives fell in hundreds. Civil defence workers could do little about the high explosives except search among the wreckage of buildings for the trapped victims, and demolish dangerously damaged structures. But the regular and auxiliary firemen had hard work to fight the flames that licked up from the incendiaries, and from the high explosives too. The call was ever for more and more hands to fight the fires, and in Britain a corps of fire-guards was raised compulsorily among all civilians to beat the flames. But in the beginning, while civil defence, at first called 'air-raid precautions,' felt its way among new conditions, the enemy was given opportunity to strike at night with all he possessed, facing no other nation as foe, opposed only by the British people led by indomitable Winston Churchill, first Minister of the King, who in speech hurled defiance at the enemy, and in act went out among the people who were bombed and spoke to them words that gave them the courage he himself possessed. Nor was he isolated from danger. One large bomb, weighing almost two tons, fell about forty feet from the Cabinet War Room during a session of the Cabinet. The buildings in the neighbourhood rocked with the force of its explosion, and, as one officer sleeping in his office in a near-by Government building said, "It shook me, and I leapt out of bed." The Cabinet War Room was deepened a further forty feet underground.

September 1940 was the month of crisis for London; 5730 people were killed, nearly 10,000 seriously injured. The tonnage of bombs that did this cannot be accurately assessed, but it is thought to have considerably exceeded 1000 tons. Roads were blocked by shattered buildings; water, gas, and electricity mains were cut, telephone exchanges put out of action; railway lines and railway stations were hit, businesses interrupted, hospitals damaged. The German air crews dropped their cargoes of bombs by aim when they could, by chance when harried by night fighters, and in fear when faced with the increasing barrage of gunfire that ringed London and bellowed defiance from the parks and open spaces within and without the metropolis.

That was the month when Hitler hoped (it is thought) to achieve spectacular victory over the British people. And to achieve his aim the Luftwaffe directed a round-the-clock offensive against London.

On September 11, after a quiet morning, large formations of Heinkel 111 bombers, Junkers 88 bombers, Dornier 215 bombers, Messerschmitt 109 and 110 and Heinkel 113 fighters, attempted to break through to the London area shortly after three in the afternoon. While small formations came in near Dover and began to attack fighter aerodromes in Kent and Surrey, and about fifty aircraft approached the Southampton area, the main formations, of about 225 aircraft, crossed the coast between North Foreland and Dungeness and made for London. They were met, mainly by squadrons of Hurricanes, and thrown back in disorder. Two squadrons of Hurricanes—Nos. 229 and 303—whose pilots were British, Canadian, New Zealand, Polish, and Belgian, attacked one formation of nearly 150 aircraft whose bombers were flying at 18,000 feet, with fighters above them. Many unloaded their bombs over the woods of Surrey and Sussex, and fled towards the coast, hotly pursued and chased out to sea by the Hurricane pilots. No. 303 squadron destroyed four Heinkel bombers, three Dorniers, three Messerschmitt 110's, and four 109's, while No. 229 squadron shot down five Heinkels and probably destroyed two more. By routing this spearhead of the Luftwaffe attack, the Hurricane pilots gave other squadrons a chance to deal with a few thin groups which vainly tried to reach London.

No. 1 R.C.A.F. squadron shot down three bombers over Kent. A fourth Hurricane squadron intercepted about fifty Heinkels attempting to raid the London docks. The Hurricanes attacked head-on when south-east of London and broke up the formation. They destroyed two bombers and damaged four others. With the squadron was Wing Commander F. V. Beamish, A.F.C., officer commanding the squadron's air station. He had become an R.A.F. Cadet at Cranwell in 1921 and obtained a permanent commission as pilot officer in 1923, rising to wing commander in January 1940. He was now thirty-seven, but he flew regularly to inspect his patrols in the air. He too probably shot down a Heinkel, but had to break off his attack when five Messerschmitts swooped on his tail. He dodged them and escaped unhurt. (Earlier in the month Beamish had shot down in flames two Junkers 87 dive-bombers who were in a covey of eight attacking a convoy.)

On that day—September 11—a total of 93 enemy aircraft was destroyed, nine by anti-aircraft gunfire. Among them were 56 heavy bombers and 22 fighter-bombers. Twenty-four British aircraft were lost, but seven of their pilots were saved.

238

During the night that followed the raiders came over the London area in waves. They began to arrive shortly after the fall of darkness and continued throughout the night. They met the first big experimental barrage. Guns drawn from many parts of the country were in position in and around London. The bombers were driven up from 1200 feet to 22,000 feet. At least nine were shot down. Aimless and random bombing increased. Precision bombing was almost impossible. Thereafter some of the bombers turned their attention to the gun-sites, on the age-old principle of war that force must be met by force. There was a marked change in the casualty lists. During the afternoon attack on September 11 there were 110 fatal casualties and about 260 persons were injured. In the succeeding night about 40 were killed and about 170 injured. On the following day attacks were light, and in the night the enemy formations were small; in many instances the attacks were made by single aircraft, which dropped bombs through heavy clouds.

British pilots strove hard to get their fight-damaged aircraft back from battle. Every machine was precious, and baling out was a last resource, for the repair service was giving good results.

A Spitfire pilot who destroyed a Messerschmitt 109 had his own aircraft damaged by shells from another Messerschmitt. He said, "My fuselage and one wing were hit, the rudder controls severed completely. The elevator cables and wireless were also hit. I managed, however, to return to my base and forced-landed with very little additional damage to my wing-tips."

After shooting down a Junkers 88 a squadron leader had to break away from the fight because his Hurricane cockpit was filled with smoke and fumes from a smashed cooling-mixture pipe. He had also been hit in the sole of his shoe, in the hood behind his head, in the airscrew, and in each mainplane, while three ignition leads to one block of cylinders were shattered. He reported, "I had difficulty in getting back to my base."

A flight sergeant who made a Messerschmitt 109 dive towards the sea pouring out clouds of black smoke said:

> There was a shattering noise in my cockpit, and my aircraft was enveloped in clouds of steam. Owing to the steam I could not see out of my cockpit, so I undid my straps, raised myself, and flew the aircraft by looking over the top of my windscreen. I lowered the undercarriage and made a normal landing at my aerodrome.

Another squadron leader found his cockpit filling with smoke during a battle over the Channel. He dived sharply away from the fight, found it difficult to see, but knew by the sun that he was flying north. Then he found he was being pursued. But the pursuer fortunately turned out to be a flying officer of his own squadron, who at considerable risk to himself had followed the squadron leader to protect him and watch where he fell. The squadron leader said:

> I found it impossible to sit in the cockpit and prepared to bale out. Half out of the cockpit, however, my head was clear of fumes. There was no fire, and the engine was running, so I decided to make for land. When I reached the coast the Hurricane was still going splendidly, so I followed a Spitfire back to an aerodrome. By holding my breath, I managed to lower the undercarriage and flaps [1] and make a landing.

On September 13 a small number of German aircraft penetrated to the London area and deliberately bombed conspicuous buildings. They dive-bombed their targets that day. One attacker was caught in a cable of the balloon barrage and crashed. Another was shot down by a fighter. One attack was made against Buckingham Palace, where the King and Queen were in residence. Several bombs fell within the precincts, and one damaged the Palace Chapel. Three members of the staff were injured. Incendiary bombs fell in Downing Street, but did no damage. Elsewhere, in Essex and Kent, Sussex and Surrey, bombs were dropped.

Enemy attacks during the night, mainly directed against the eastern, southern, and south-western districts of London, were kept out of the central districts by the gun barrage. One Heinkel 111 bomber was caught in the beams of several searchlights. A fighter pilot flying several miles to the south saw the searchlight beams converge. For twenty minutes he chased the bomber. Some of the searchlights lost the enemy, but three or four continued to hold him. The fighter opened fire. The bomber dropped his bombs to lighten his load. Bullets from the rear gun hit the windscreen and wing of the fighter. But the fighter's bullets had struck home, and the Heinkel fell flaming through the night sky. The fighter followed it down and saw the explosion when it crashed.

In the afternoon of September 14 the Luftwaffe tried new tactics against London. They sent over two mass attacks in quick succession. Most of the bombers crossed the coast at nearly 25,000 feet, protected by hordes of Messerschmitt fighters. The first attack started about 3.30 P.M., when 150 bombers and fighters came in between Dover and Dungeness. They were immediately harassed by Spitfires and Hurricanes, and the enemy formations were forced to split up. As they flew over Kent, Sussex, and Surrey their path to London was often cut by British fighters. Some of the bombers tried to reach London by the Thames Estuary, but the anti-aircraft gunners drove them off. Here

[1] This could be done only by getting inside the cockpit again.

a Spitfire Auxiliary squadron caught a formation of Messerschmitt fighters flying in line abreast at a greater height. When they saw Spitfires the Messerschmitts went into line astern, but made no atte to attack. The Spitfires climbed after them and sent two Messerschmitts crashing on land near Maidstone, while a third dived into the sea.

The first attack had hardly been driven off when a second wave of 150 bombers and fighters approached the south-east coast. By this stratagem the Luftwaffe generals may have hoped to catch the Royal Air Force at a disadvantage. They probably thought that the fighters engaged against the first wave would have had to land to refuel and reload and thus be out of action; they probably under-estimated the number of British fighters available, or else their pilots and air crews exaggerated the number of fighters they usually encountered, and so made their leaders believe that Britain's full sector strength was up to meet every attack. The new German formations passed over Dover and began to fan out above the lovely Kent countryside, with its rolling downs, green fields, woods, hedges, towns, villages, and stately homes in trim parks and pleasant gardens. A formation of their escorting Messerschmitt fighters, stepped up from 15,000 to 25,000 feet, and about sixty strong, flying north over Surrey, was engaged by Hurricanes. After a dog-fight in which only one enemy aircraft was shot down the Messerschmitts turned and made for the coast.

Bombs fell in South-west London, in Brighton, Eastbourne, Ipswich, and some other towns that day, for low clouds made it difficult for Fighter Command aircraft to intercept every raider; but despite the difficult conditions which faced them, British pilots shot down fifteen enemy aircraft for the loss of nine of their own fighters, from which six pilots escaped; and before dawn the guns had already destroyed two German aircraft and the fighters one.

Fighter pilots who leapt to safety from their aircraft never knew how or where they were going to finish their descent. Some were killed by scurrilous German fighter pilots as they swung in their harness below their billowing canopies; many were shot at and missed.

One Royal Australian Air Force flight lieutenant had to get out quickly when his oxygen apparatus blew up and his cockpit caught fire. Before he could jump he had to dive away from his flight, so that, when he left, his aircraft would not endanger the pilots following. This made exit from his burning aircraft a difficult feat. "I was upside-down when the parachute began to open, and somehow it didn't go according to the book," he said.

My feet became enveloped in the thing. I wriggled and kicked, and to my intense relief saw the brolly float up and open out. I was then only 500 feet from the ground.   But one complete panel was torn out, and flapping, and the chute hung at an alarming angle.   I came down rather too quickly, and landed heavily in a potato-field, somewhat winded.   I had hurt my legs and back, but not seriously.

Before I could get up half a dozen Land Girls came running up with sticks, a spade, a hoe, and a pitchfork.   I called out, "Hello, girls, help me out of my brolly, will you?"

Realizing I was British, they dropped their weapons, and asked if they could get a car or an ambulance.   Suddenly they dived for their sticks again, yelling, "Hold off!"   I looked round and saw them running at a Home Guard who, 200 yards away, was stalking me, with his rifle to his shoulder.   The girls kept between me and the Home Guard's rifle until they persuaded him that I was harmless.

When the ambulance came I thought my adventures were over, but I was wrong.   Within a mile of the start the ambulance took a bend too fast, and turned over.   I scrambled out with a few bruises and was picked up by a fire-engine dashing to the spot where my Spitfire was blazing furiously.   The fire-engine ended up a minute later in the ditch.   After that I decided to walk.

Another pilot whose damaged Hurricane was falling out of control baled out at a great height over the outskirts of London.   His parachute drifted over the roofs of London, and he touched down right in the heart of the West End.   Bystanders fetched a taxi for him, and he was driven to the nearest Mayfair hotel.   He walked in, dressed in flying-suit, wool-lined boots, and Mae West, reported to the Air Ministry by telephone and asked for a Service car to take him back to his base, then washed the grime of battle off his hands and face, and went in to lunch.   But few pilots were so fortunate. . . .

It was Sunday, September 15, 1940.   The morning was veiled by mist, the light mist that is characteristic of an English September morn.   About eight o'clock the mist lifted.   There were light clouds half a mile above the ground.   A gentle wind kept the sky bright and brought showers to some places.   Across the Channel, in all the coastal ports from Germany to France, the invasion ships and barges were gathered.   They were Bomber Command's principal targets on the nights of September 13, 14, 15, 17, 18, 19, 20, 21, and 22—on the 16th the weather was unfit for operations—and by day on September 13, 16, 17, and 21.   The woefully undersized Bomber Command, already strained by its effort during the Battle of France, and affected by the priority necessarily given to fighter aircraft, did not concentrate thus upon targets unworthy of its immediate attention when there was so much to do everywhere.   When Mr Winston Churchill and Field Marshal Jan Smuts spoke to three thousand mine-owners and mineworkers' leaders in Central Hall, Westminster, on Saturday, October 31, 1942, asking the men to go back to the pits and produce to the maximum in the common cause, the Prime Minister said:

> I have often asked myself what would have happened if Hitler had . . . put three-quarters of a million men on board all the barges and boats and let them stream across and take the chance of losing three-quarters of them. There would have been a terrible shambles in Great Britain, because we had hardly a weapon. We had not, at that time, fifty tanks. We had a couple of hundred field-guns, some of them brought out of the museums. We had lost all our equipment at Dunkirk and in France.

The Third Reich theory of war demanded the way to be cleared for the surface forces. Having built air-power to smash the way in, they feared to face the consequences of unbroken air-power arrayed against them. August 15 had been *der Tag*. But the Luftwaffe failed to smash its way through. *Der Erste Tag* was postponed—Hitler's first military postponement. *Der Zweite Tag*—oh! fatal delay—was fixed for September 15. R.A.F. reconnaissance aircraft had reported the barges.

German reconnaissance aircraft appeared off the English coast—off Harwich, in the Thames Estuary and the Dover Strait, off Lympne and the long flat snout of Dungeness—about an hour after the mist cleared on the mid-month Sunday of September.

The attack began about 11.30 in the morning. Aircraft crossed the coast near Ramsgate, Dover, Folkestone, and Dungeness, in one wave of about 100, closely followed by a second wave about 150 strong. None flew much below 15,000 feet, and many were as high as 26,000 feet. They flew above clouds, in clear sunshine, towards London, a combined force of Dornier 17 and 215, Junkers 88 and Heinkel 111 bombers, escorted by Messerschmitt 109 and 110 fighters. Some bombers flew in small vee- or diamond-formations, others in fives in line abreast; the fighters flew in arrowheads of three aircraft, so that each squadron of nine aircraft [1] looked like a sergeant's chevrons. Most of the fighters flew above the bombers, but some were below.

Twenty-one squadrons of Hurricanes and Spitfires were ordered up to meet the attack, sixteen from No. 11 Group, and five from Nos. 10 and 12 Groups—a Fighter force approximately the numerical equal of the whole German force. (A considerable force of fighters, held in reserve, did not go into action in the morning.)

The air battle fought that day was the greatest the world had ever seen, yet it was currently comprehended only by those pilots and air

---

[1] Luftwaffe fighters were organized in *Geschwader* (regiments) of eighty-one aircraft, comprising three *Gruppen* (wings) of twenty-seven, composed of three *Staffeln* (squadrons) of nine containing three *Ketten* (flights) of three aircraft.

crews who fought it out over an area which covered the whole South-eastern sector of England and the Channel, from West and North London to the coast of France, and those in the operations-rooms concerned with the battle. In one operations-room of No. 11 Group was Mr Churchill, cigar in mouth, watching the reported progress of the fight that was going on above the clouds. His cigar remained cold and unlighted. But when he left, as the first battle of the day was ending, his face wore a smile of grim satisfaction. So much hinged upon the outcome of that day. And soon after noon the issue was indeed decided. It left no cause for doubt. The modern archers of England, whose Hurricane and Spitfire wings flashed like arrows across the blue heaven, had not lost the skill of their ancestors. The means were different, but the method was the same—manœuvrability and hitting power to break the spirit of the stronger foe.

The groundsman, continuing with his normal work, his normal relaxation, or dealing with his duties in civil defence on that Sunday of September, saw little of the fight. Through an occasional hole in the clouds he might have caught a fleeting view of a twisting vapour-trail in the upper air, or seen tiny dots wheeling far above, heard the whine of an occasional bomb and the crash of its explosion, and stopped to listen to the dull boom of a crashing aircraft, or perhaps have seen the wreck spout into flame that poured forth a column of black petrol-smoke; but that was all. With his whole future being decided in the sky beyond the clouds by a few of his fellow-Britishers and some of their allies, there was nothing he could do about it. It was not war. It was war in the air. Two hundred and fifty men flew between him and a life of slavery.

Two small enemy formations penetrated to the London area. Their bombs hit, among other buildings, Buckingham Palace again, and the Queen's private apartments were damaged by a bomb which did not explode; elsewhere in the London area houses were hit, some fires broke out, and damage was done to gas- and water-mains.

Douglas Bader, commanding No. 242 squadron, led a wing of four or five squadrons of Hurricanes and Spitfires which met the enemy at 12.15 P.M. near Hammersmith just south of the River Thames. Bader said:

We were at 20,000 feet, and ran into a large block of Junkers 88 and Dornier 17—about forty in all and without a single fighter to escort them. This time, for a change, we outnumbered the Hun, and believe me, no more than eight got home from that party. At one time you could see planes all over the place, and the sky seemed full of parachutes. It was sudden death that morning, for our fighters shot them to blazes. One unfortunate German rear gunner baled out of the Dornier 17 I attacked, but his parachute caught on the tail. There he was, swinging helplessly, with the aircraft swooping and diving and staggering all over the sky, being pulled about by the man hanging by his parachute from the tail. That bomber went crashing into the Thames Estuary, with the swinging gunner still there. About the same time one of my boys saw a similar thing in another Dornier, though this time the gunner who tried to bale out had his parachute caught in the hood before it opened. Our pilot saw the other two members of the crew crawl up and struggle to set him free. He was swinging from his packed parachute until they pushed him clear. Then they jumped off after him, and their plane went into the water with a terrific smack.

Bader could admire his enemy. He said, "I've always thought it was a pretty stout effort on the part of those two Huns who refused to leave their pal fastened to the doomed aircraft."

No. 242 squadron fought twice that day. In the morning they chased the enemy from Hammersmith to Beachy Head, shooting down five Dornier bombers and sharing a Messerschmitt 109. In the afternoon they fought above the merchant ships which still, in spite of all air-raid alarms, passed unhindered up the Thames Estuary to London's docks, and added three more Dorniers, a Heinkel 111, and three Messerschmitt 109's to their collection.

No. 1 R.C.A.F. squadron sighted fifteen to twenty enemy bombers approaching South-east London. Squadron Leader E. A. McNab, making the first attack, saw a Heinkel 111 at which he fired drop its bombs, turn out of formation, and dive for cloud. He was then himself attacked by Messerschmitt 109 fighters and could not wait to see what happened.

A few minutes later he joined forces with two other Hurricane pilots and with them sent a second Heinkel diving down to crash on the mudflats on the north side of the Thames Estuary. The youngest pilot in the squadron also destroyed a Heinkel; he had been intended for a business career and was working his way through the warehouse of a steel firm in Montreal when he decided he would rather fly. So, he said, "I packed up my job, and here I am."

No. 46 squadron also helped to smash the first of the two attacks on the London area. They handled the enemy very roughly, and the whole formation turned to the south and away from the docks as the Hurricanes went in to attack. In the afternoon the squadron fought again; their day's bag was at least five enemy bombers, with others badly damaged.

The Burma squadron was confronted with a big bunch of different bombers in a formation of anything from thirty to sixty—there was no time to count them—with escorting fighters above. As Squadron

Leader R. R. Stanford Tuck, D.F.C., led the squadron in to the attack he saw three of the formations nearing London. He picked off a Messerschmitt 110 and shot it down over Barking, and at the same moment a bullet came through his own windscreen and passed a few inches from his head.[1]

The Edinburgh squadron fought the approaching German aircraft from Dover to the Thames Estuary and destroyed four Messerschmitts and a Dornier 17.

Bader's combined wing of Hurricanes and Spitfires destroyed fifty-two enemy aircraft during its two sorties, one in the morning and the other in the afternoon.

Fighter pilots, meeting the waves of enemy aircraft coming in from the south and east, breaking their formations and sending the scattered survivors fleeing homeward whence they came, had scant time to look below towards the groundscape over which they flew, and which was, perhaps mercifully, well covered with a white counterpane of cloud. Their minds were intent upon their job. But . . .

John Sample was an estate agent in Northumberland before the war. He joined No. 607 (County of Durham) Auxiliary squadron in 1934. In November 1939 he went to France with his squadron when it joined the Air Component, British Expeditionary Force. Flying Officer Sample, as he then was, led his section on a dawn patrol over France in May 1940, intercepting three Heinkel 111 bombers, and the section shot down all three. Immediately afterwards Sample's Hurricane burst into flames, but he escaped by parachute. He was awarded the Distinguished Flying Cross. By the middle of May, when the

---

[1] Stanford Tuck had developed into a fine Fighter pilot. Born at Catford, London, in 1916, he was educated at St Dunstan's College, Catford, and entered the Royal Air Force when he was nineteen. Now, at twenty-four, he was just at the age when he could give of his very best as a fighter in the air. He had been promoted to flying officer in 1938 and became flight lieutenant and squadron leader in 1940. By June 11 he had shot down eleven enemy aircraft and won the Distinguished Flying Cross as a pilot of No. 65 squadron. On September 11, 1940, he was posted to command the Burma squadron, and led it into action for the first time on the 15th. By October his score had mounted to fourteen certainties, with many more 'probables' and 'damaged,' and he was awarded a bar to the D.F.C. By the end of the year, when he had shot down eighteen enemy aircraft, he received the Distinguished Service Order, and on April 7, 1941, he received a second bar to his D.F.C. His personal score was then twenty-two. He was later promoted to wing commander, and during a relief spell from operational flying he, with other Royal Air Force pilots, visited the United States to advise the United States aircraft industry on R.A.F. requirements. After his return he led a Fighter wing, and was last seen by a fellow Spitfire pilot who was patrolling with him on January 28, 1942, going down near Boulogne after his Spitfire appeared to have been hit by gunfire. On February 1 he was posted a prisoner of war.

squadron returned to England, it had shot down seventy-eight enemy aircraft.

On September 15 Sample was a squadron leader leading No. 504 (County of Nottingham) squadron of Hurricanes into battle somewhere south of the Thames Estuary. Flying at 17,000 feet behind several other squadrons of Hurricanes and Spitfires, these British pilots first saw the German bombers three or four miles away at about 19,000 feet. The German fighter escort "was scattered around." This is the story that Sample had to tell.

The bombers were coming in towards London from the south-east, and at first we could not tell how many there were. We opened our throttles and started to climb up towards them, aiming for a point well ahead where we expected to contact them at their own height. As we converged I saw that there were about twenty of them, and it looked as though it was going to be a nice party, for the other squadrons of Hurricanes and Spitfires also turned to join in. By the time we reached a position near the bombers we were over London—central London, I should say. We had gained a little height on them, too, so when I gave the order to attack we were able to dive on them from their right.

Each of us selected his own target. Our first attack broke them up pretty nicely. The Dornier I attacked with a burst lasting several seconds began to turn to the left away from his friends. I gave him five seconds, and he went away with white smoke streaming behind him. As I broke away and started to make a steep climbing turn I looked over the side. I recognized the river immediately below me through a hole in the clouds. I saw the bends and the bridges and idly wondered where I was. Then I saw Kennington Oval, and I thought to myself, "That is where they play cricket."

I found myself soon below another Dornier which had white smoke coming from it. It was being attacked by two Hurricanes and a Spitfire, and was travelling north and turning slightly to the right. As I could not see anything else to attack at that moment I climbed above him and did a diving attack. Coming in to the attack, I noticed what appeared to be a red light shining in the rear-gunner's cockpit, but when I got closer I realized I was looking right through the gunner's cockpit into the pilot and observer's cockpit beyond. The red light was fire. I gave it a quick burst and as I passed him on the right I looked in through the big glass nose of the Dornier. It was like a furnace inside. He began to go down, and we watched. In a few seconds the tail came off, and the bomber did a forward somersault and then went into a spin. After he had done two turns in his spin his wings broke off outboard of the engines, so that all that was left, as the blazing aircraft fell, was half a fuselage and the wing roots with the engines on their ends. This dived straight down, just past the edge of a cloud, and then the cloud got in the way, and I could see no more of him.

The battle was over by then. I couldn't see anything else to shoot at, so I flew home. Our squadron's score was five certainties—

including one by a sergeant pilot, who landed by parachute in a Chelsea garden.

To the sergeant pilot, fighting his first engagement with 504 squadron, the attack was a confused picture. Like many pilots before him, he was unable to keep check of all that happened during his first fight. He fired three times at Dorniers, which might have been the same machine or three different aircraft. Black oil fouled his windscreen from what seemed to him the first Dornier, and pieces flew off it; flames leaped out from the second; a German parachute came from the third, and his wing almost touched the chute. He saw the third Dornier spiralling down. Then one of his wings hit something, and his own aircraft went spinning towards the ground, no longer controllable. He struggled to get out, while the Hurricane spun faster and faster, holding him into his cockpit by centrifugal force. He entered the clouds. When at last he got away the speed was so great that the wind hit him like a solid thing.

He was just in time. A few seconds later he was lying on his back in a Chelsea garden, after catching his feet in the guttering of a house and then sliding off its roof. Two girls ran into the garden from the house and helped him to his feet. He kissed them both. The Dornier bomber crashed just outside Victoria railway station. Some of its crew landed by parachute on Kennington Oval.

No. 504 squadron was one of the second line of defending Fighter squadrons—the inner ring, as it were, of the defences, organized to meet those raiders who succeeded by sheer weight of numbers in penetrating the outer defences over the Channel, the coastline, the Thames Estuary, the Sussex and the Kentish wold and weald. Fourteen squadrons of Hurricanes and three squadrons of Spitfires were concerned with the inner defences, and Londoners saw some of these units in action over their heads through cloud-gaps, amid feathering streamers of vapour-trails that curled across the blue sky.

The British fighters attacked in formations of one or two squadrons, or wings comprising three or more squadrons. Theirs was the aerial counterpart of the cavalry charge. They charged into the array of bombers and fighters advancing between the dome of blue and floor of cloud, and broke them into 'rags and tatters' by the fury of their onslaught. They selected the bombers as their main target, and made their assault so decisive that bombers were knocked down and bomber formations split up before the nearest Messerschmitt 110 fighters could close to the firing range of their cannon-guns (a maximum of 1000 yards, with aim uncertain at that range), while the more distant Messerschmitt 109's, flying far above, where they should have had the advantage of the dive to give them speed, were frequently quite unable to intervene on behalf of the bomber crews. British fighter pilots made many broadside or quarter attacks, keeping their forward-firing guns aligned upon the bombers as they passed, and then swung round to fall into position behind the bombers and continue to rake them with fire from the rear. This form of attack had been developed with success in Norway; it exposed the British fighters to the minimum fire-power of their opponents, whose bombers were, in any case, under-gunned for defensive fighting, and exposed the enemy to the maximum fire-power of the Hurricanes' and Spitfires' eight Browning machine-guns.

After the first onrush, during which the British pilots each selected their individual targets, the fighters became separated, dealing singly, or in little groups, with enemies who were then scattered about the sky. The German foray became a battle, the battle a pursuit, for it is one condition of air fighting that there can seldom be a stand-up struggle; it mostly consists in a running fight between pursuer and pursued, because air fighting is dynamic—rather like a motion picture which, through a succession of fixed scenes, changes so swiftly the sequence of each as to produce upon the senses the effect of continuous movement.

In their initial attacks upon the German forces the leaders of the squadrons and wings of the Royal Air Force sometimes provided their own fighter cover. One section of the formation kept guard against the fighters above while another section fell upon the bombers. If the German fighters hesitated to attack, the upper formation of British fighters could reinforce the attack upon the bombers or cut off any who tried to escape. This method was developed during the Fighter formation battles of 1917.

The escort for the bomber is often in a quandary, for he is faced with the alternatives of staying with the bomber, which means he cannot join in the fight, or of engaging the opposing fighters, in which case he may lose touch with his charge. On the whole the German fighter pilots chose the first alternative, and this may well have been in accordance with their instructions. It seems, therefore, that the Luftwaffe generals were primarily at fault, for they should have sent over fighters to engage the British Fighter Command in order to win the tactical air engagement before commencing the day-offensive bombing programme. In the attempt to do both at once they failed in both. Later they tried the fighter offensive, using fighter bombers as an incentive to bring the British fighters up to battle. But then it was too late. The British fighter boys had gained immense confidence in their prowess and in their machines. The Luftwaffe had been severely mauled and was less strong than at first. The British squadrons were on top and they could not be pulled down.

On no occasion was the tactical superiority of the British Fighter squadrons better displayed than on September 15, 1940, when out of a total of 185 German aircraft destroyed—seven by the guns—no fewer than 131 were bombers, and of these 125 were shot down by Fighter Command. The additional destruction of fifty-three German fighters by British squadrons that day, compared with a total British loss of twenty-five aircraft and only eleven pilots (for fourteen were saved from destroyed machines), was eloquent testimony to the comparative value of the two Fighter forces.

The British Prime Minister sent a message to the Secretary of State for Air (Sir Archibald Sinclair) the following day:

Yesterday eclipsed all previous records of the Fighter Command. Aided by squadrons of their Czech and Polish comrades, using only a small proportion of their total strength, and under cloud conditions of some difficulty, they cut to rags and tatters three separate waves of murderous assault upon the civil population of their native land, inflicting a certain loss of 125 bombers and 53 fighters upon the enemy, to say nothing of 'probables' and 'damaged,' while themselves sustaining only a loss of 12 [1] pilots and 25 machines. These results exceed all expectations, and give just and sober confidence in the approaching struggle.

W.S.C.

But it would be a mistake to say that the German fighters did not fight well. Some of them did, notably the yellow-nosed Messerschmitt 109 squadrons, whose machines were flown by the best personnel of the fighter *Geschwader* of the Luftwaffe. The Polish No. 303 squadron, whose members in the morning engagement were scattered across the sky through following a German Fighter squadron, had many fierce fights with small numbers of German fighters. But the indisputable fact remained that Fighter Command that day destroyed about one-half of the bomber force sent against London in spite of its powerful escort of German fighters. And that explains why the Battle of Britain was a victory for the Royal Air Force.

The morning battle was over by 12.30 P.M. The London sirens sounded the 'Raiders Passed' at 12.56. At 2.15 P.M. the banshees wailed again their warbling note of approaching death. Twice more the 'Alert' sirens were to be heard that day—at 7.15 in the twilight, and at 8.11 in the dark.

The afternoon attack came again in two waves of about 150 and 100 aircraft. They crossed the coast near Dover and approached London over Kent. Twenty-one squadrons were again ordered up to intercept the enemy.

[1] One more pilot was rescued after the Prime Minister had sent his message.
250

All made contact. The sky over the whole of Kent was swiftly filled with battling aircraft. As in the morning, most of the bombers were Dorniers 17 and 215. Some of the British squadrons were fighting their second great action that day, others were engaging the enemy for the first time for four days, for the three days preceding the big attack of September 15 were comparatively quiet.

Not all twenty-one defence squadrons were dispatched simultaneously. They were ordered up in accordance with the pre-determined scheme of defence which had proved so successful in the morning. The height, position, and speed of the enemy were reported by intelligence, and at the estimated correct moments squadrons were ordered off from suitably situated bases, so that by climbing on a given course they could reach a point in the sky from which they would be advantageously placed to commence their attack. That was the tactical generalship of the action. The short duration of high-speed fighter aircraft flying at full throttle made it impossible to keep squadrons in the air. They had to arise when the enemy were definitely known to be approaching a given area. The battle had to be fought out over England, for in no other way was it possible for the Commander-in-Chief and his Group Commanders to receive intelligence of the enemy The enemy bombers had to be allowed to come over England to give the intelligence system time to operate and place its analysis on the plotting tables of the operations-rooms. Then the Commanders' decisions had to be swiftly made. On the air stations the alarm called the crews into action. Their orders crackled through the ether into their radio telephones. A complete system of control existed over the aircraft until the actual moment when the squadrons reported that they were about to engage the enemy. And the victory was shared by the precision of the staff-work and the courage and skill of the pilots. Each was complementary to the other, and neither could have operated effectually independently. The enemy's most furious and maintained onslaughts broke neither the machine in the air nor the machine on the ground. Both were too strong and too flexible for him, although both appeared to be slender threads upon which to suspend the safety of the British Commonwealth of Nations.

Group Captain S. F. Vincent, A.F.C., was forty-three. In the Great War he flew and fought over France in No. 60 squadron. Now he commanded an air station in No. 11 Group, Royal Air Force, whence squadrons of Hurricanes and Spitfires daily rose to meet the Luftwaffe. He too flew to inspect the work of his squadrons at close quarters, just as Lieutenant-Colonel Jack Scott, Major H. P. van Ryneveld, and other officers had flown alone over the German lines in

France twenty-three years before to see how their pilots fared; it was traditional in the Royal Air Force. On September 15 Vincent saw a formation of eighteen Dornier 215 bombers approaching from the south at 12,000 feet, escorted by twenty Messerschmitt 109's. "There were no British fighters in sight," he reported, "so I made a head-on attack on the first section of bombers." When he broke away all but five of the bombers were flying south in retreat. He attacked again, and saw the last of his bullets strike a Dornier, and the bomber drop out of the formation.

That afternoon none of the raiders flew much below 15,000 feet. Between each group of nine bombers were nine Messerschmitt 110 fighter-bombers; little arrowhead flights of Messerschmitt 109's circled above, sometimes as high as 35,000 feet.

Some squadrons were ordered to deal with the enemy's high-flying fighter screen midway between the coast and London; others were ordered to attack the bombers before they reached London's perimeter fighter aerodromes.

Pilots of a Hurricane squadron racing to the attack met the big formation of raiders "stretching several miles" over the Greater London area.

As they opened fire they saw another Fighter squadron attacking part of the same enemy air fleet five miles away. Squadrons climbing to the attack from the same aerodrome found themselves fighting perhaps twenty, perhaps fifty, miles apart. The Polish 303 squadron entered the clouds at 8000 feet. They struck a particularly thick patch, and during the dangerous blind climb became separated. Five emerged close together at 22,000 feet, and saw below them a vast sierra of white cloud. They saw and attacked a formation of sixty bombers flying in groups of five. The escort fighters were more than a mile above the bombers. The Polish pilots came on the bombers out of the sun (which made their attack a three-quarters head attack), spraying as many machines as possible to do the utmost damage, instead of selecting individual target aircraft. They passed along the flank of the formation, raking its entire length. The violence of the attack demoralized the German pilots; two of the Dornier 215 bombers collided. The Messerschmitt escort struck too late. The bomber formation, attacked thus on the left flank, and simultaneously, miles away, on the right flank, began to crumple. Their formation was split up. It could not re-form. The fight became again a series of individual duels between single machines and aircraft flying in little groups. One of the five Poles was killed; two had to bale out.

The battle with the Messerschmitts was fought in crystal-clear air at least 4000 feet above the clouds. There were Messerschmitts with snouts of many hues, the dexterously handled yellow-nosed squadrons, and others with white noses, red noses, and orange noses. Soon they were too busy guarding themselves to be able to guard their charges, the bombers. The pilots breathed oxygen as they flew and fought, their aircraft forming long plumes behind them, weaving the dizzy design of a senseless pattern of vapour-trails against the upper blue. The fight went on from London to the south coast. Three sergeant pilots of No. 46 squadron ordered to intercept bombers approaching the London docks sent one down over a Surrey aerodrome, one just north of Dungeness, and a third over the south coast farther to the west.

About seventy German aircraft of the formation of 250 got through the outer defences and reached the outskirts of the capital, where they were met by Hurricane squadrons from all three Groups of Fighter Command.

Squadron Leader John Sample led his squadron into the air again after an hour on the ground, and in the afternoon No. 504 squadron added three more to the score of five which they had gained in the morning.

". . . Meeting more bombers and fighters coming in," said Sample,

I started to chase one Dornier which was flying through the tops of the clouds. Did you ever see that film *Hell's Angels*? You remember how the Zeppelin came so slowly out of the cloud. Well, this Dornier reminded me of that. I attacked him four times altogether. When he first appeared through the cloud—you know how clouds go up and down like foam on water—I fired at him from the left, swung over to the right, turned in towards another hollow in the cloud, where I expected him to reappear, and fired at him again. After my fourth attack he dived down headlong into a clump of trees in front of an Essex house, and I saw one or two cars parked in the gravel drive in front. I wondered whether there was anyone in the doorway watching the bomber crash. As it hit the ground a tremendous sheet of flame went up.

Then I climbed up again to look for some more trouble and found it in the shape of a Heinkel 111 which was being attacked by three Hurricanes and a couple of Spitfires. I had a few cracks at the thing before it made a perfect landing on an R.A.F. aerodrome. Then the Heinkel's undercarriage collapsed, and the pilot pulled up, after skidding fifty yards in a cloud of dust. All of us dived low, and I saw a tall man get out of the right-hand side of the aircraft, and when I turned back he was helping a small man across the aerodrome towards a hangar."

Curiosity led to the death of a number of civilians who rushed across to a Dornier 17 bomber which, damaged by a Hurricane, was brought down from 400 feet by gunfire. One of its bombs went off, and several of the civilians were either killed or wounded.

The Axis partners were working in concert. While German air pressure against England built up steadily during the first half of September, Marshal Graziani's army began its advance into Egypt at the end of the first week of the month. It reached and occupied Sidi Barrani in the evening of September 16. And there it stayed, until the counter-tide of General Sir Archibald Wavell's offensive swept it back. If the Luftwaffe had forced a passage for the German invasion forces to attack Britain Graziani and his men might have had more resolution for their attack upon Egypt. But September 15 marked the peak of the Luftwaffe's daylight assault upon Britain.

Even the weather was on the side of Britain in that climacteric. The period of harvest moon is usually calm, and harvest moon came on the night following September 16. But, after the fine day of September 15, the succeeding day was cold and wet, and in the following night there was high wind and heavy rain; the weather was unfit for Bomber Command's operations.[1] The gale blew for nearly forty hours. It rose to hurricane force in the English Channel and drove up big seas which would certainly have swamped barges. This was the first recorded instance in forty-six years of such weather at the time of harvest moon. It was a reversal of the conditions at Dunkirk. If the weather had not favoured the evacuation then the British Expeditionary Force might well have been captured by the German Army, as was part of the less fortunate 51st Division at Saint-Valéry when the fog shut down upon the beaches in the night.

In the next strong daylight attack the German tactics were changed. There was need. The heavy (for that period) bombers were absent. They had suffered grievous losses. In the afternoon of Tuesday, September 17, more than 200 Messerschmitt and Heinkel fighters crossed the Channel, whose waters were lashed to foam by the gale. High above, the wind blew at 100 miles an hour. The first enemy formation approached the British coast at three o'clock, and for half an hour they continued to come across in waves of twenty and thirty. They flew in the direction of London. Fighter Command dispatched large forces of fighters to intercept them, and contact was made over Kent. No major battles occurred. The enemy did not penetrate further than Maidstone, where twelve Auxiliary Air Force Spitfires routed a formation of Messerschmitt fighters and damaged several, but did not claim to have destroyed even one. But five of the enemy were destroyed by fighters (two Messerschmitts collided in the air

[1] See p. 242.

when a solitary Spitfire attacked seven) and two by anti-aircraft guns. After dark, enemy bombers attacked South-east England; the gunners destroyed four, and a fighter shot down another. The bag was twelve for the day, for the loss of three British fighters and only one pilot. The new German tactics did not look so good.

Next day the Luftwaffe lost forty-eight aircraft, one by anti-aircraft gunfire, over England. The Royal Air Force lost twelve fighters and three pilots. The Luftwaffe generals were using their wits in an effort to break through the Fighter screen and knock it down. The daylight attacks came in five distinct waves, each following the same course from between the North Foreland and Dungeness towards London. The first wave, containing about 100 fighters, broke at 9.30 A.M. Noon had just passed when the second wave of five groups of bombers and fighters broke over Kent; one formation reached the London area, the rest were turned back. The third came soon after four in the afternoon, when about 100 aircraft struck over Kent towards the Thames Estuary, and before it subsided the fourth wave, of 250 bombers and fighters, were on their way in, a hundred of them by Dungeness. In the evening came the fifth wave. Hurricanes and Spitfires met them. One bunch of fifteen bombers, surrounded by "a sphere of Messerschmitt 109 fighters," was dispersed by Spitfires so quickly near the coast of Kent that only three British pilots got the opportunity to fire. A Hurricane patrol attacked a formation of bombers heavily protected by Messerschmitts stepped up in tiers above them over the Thames Estuary. "They jettisoned their bombs even before we attacked," said one of the pilots, "and went straight out over Folkestone." The third and fourth attacks were the most roughly handled by the British fighters. One squadron of Spitfires met a group of bombers and fighters over Kent and shot down five Heinkel bombers and one Messerschmitt 110 fighter-bomber, and shared in the destruction of another Heinkel bomber. No. 242 squadron shot down eight Dornier and three Junkers 88 bombers and shared in the destruction of three more Junkers 88's near the Thames Estuary; in the same fight two other patrols of Hurricanes accounted for nine more bombers. The enemy were in two large formations at 17,000 feet when the Canadians dived and split up the leading group of about twenty bombers which were flying in close formation. "The sky," said Bader, "seemed to be full of Spitfires and Hurricanes queueing up to attack enemy aircraft. It was the finest shambles I have ever been in. We had position, height, and numbers. The enemy were a dirty-looking collection."

In its last six fights No. 242 squadron had shot down about a half-century of German aircraft for the loss of only two of its own pilots.

After the continued failure of the day attacks by small groups of bombers and large groups of fighters, the Luftwaffe generals threw bombers flying singly and in small formations against London and other cities and towns. Many fairly heavy-calibre bombs were dropped, indiscriminate damage was done, and many civilians were killed and injured. The largest bombs dropped by the Luftwaffe weighed about one ton and three-quarters. The widespread nature of these attacks was well indicated on the night of September 18, when, in addition to London, bombs fell on Merseyside, Lancashire towns, and towns in Berkshire, Essex, Hertfordshire, Kent, the Midlands, the North-east and the South-west, and Sussex.

In the air fighting at that time incidents were as numerous as before. On at least three occasions British and German pilots were simultaneous victors. One Hurricane squadron, ordered to intercept a formation of enemy fighters between Dover and Folkestone, met the enemy at 20,000 feet. Among the British fighters was a sergeant pilot who succeeded in getting on to the tails of two Messerschmitt 109's whose pilots had dived at him. He fired several long bursts at them. "As I was breaking away," he said, "a cannon-shell, or a large-bore bullet, passed through the hood over my head, through the windscreen and the armour-plating cowling over the gravity tank, and into the petrol-tank itself. I was immediately drenched with petrol and became semi-conscious. I baled out and landed safely." The sergeant made his way to a near-by aerodrome to be told that the pilot of the Messerschmitt he had attacked had baled out too, and had landed near the aerodrome. The British pilot had only a few scratches and a slightly cut face from the windscreen, and was fit to fly again another day, but the German pilot was a prisoner of war and would not fly again until after the war, if then.

A pilot officer flying in a Hurricane squadron which attacked a formation of fifty German aircraft fell behind his section. Two Messerschmitt 110's flew straight at him at full throttle in line astern. "Realizing that I would present an easy target if I broke away," said the pilot officer,

I flew straight at them and started firing at 300 yards. I kept up the fire for five seconds and then gave another burst of five seconds. Both enemy planes turned away at point-blank range and passed straight through my sights. The first one must have shot at my sights before it broke away, as my instruments were shattered. A moment or two later, as the second Messerschmitt appeared, there was a great explosion in my aircraft as my petrol-tank was hit, presumably by

256

cannon. My cockpit immediately became a mass of flames. I baled out, falling in the sea three to four miles from Brightlingsea. I noticed at the same time two other parachutes coming down. One fell not far from me. A German sub-lieutenant was using that parachute. He and I were picked up by the same motor-boat.

No. 85 squadron was engaged with thirty Dornier 215 bombers and about 100 Messerschmitts when Pilot Officer W. H. Hodgson's Hurricane was hit by an explosive shell from the cannon-gun of a Messerschmitt 109. Gliding away from the enemy with his engine on fire, the pilot undid his straps and prepared to bale out. Then he saw that he was over a thickly populated district of London. Rather than take the risk of his pilotless machine crashing into houses, he decided to stay in it and try to steer it to open country. Oil sprayed in a thick sheet from the engine. He switched off his engine and by a succession of violent side-slips got the flames under control, and managed to prevent the fire from spreading. People on the ground looked up, watching the erratic flight of the Hurricane until the smoking aircraft passed out of view. The squadron leader of a Spitfire squadron circled above the crippled Hurricane, guarding it from possible attack by three Messerschmitt 109's flying overhead. Eventually the pilot landed his Hurricane, with the wheels up, in an empty field. It was not beyond repair, more than a fair exchange for the Messerschmitt 109 which its pilot had sent crashing to earth in flames, and a damaged Dornier 215 which he could not follow down.

During the period from September 17 to 25 the night attacks against London continued, but the day-bomber attacks were made on a reduced scale. Occasionally a single aircraft or a small group got through to the London area by day, but the greatest activity was on the part of fighters. On the 23rd large formations of German aircraft, mainly composed of fighters, crossed the Kent and South Essex coasts. They dropped no bombs, and their formations were broken up, and a series of engagements between British fighters and the dispersed German fighters occurred over the Kent and Essex coasts. In the evening another large German fighter force crossed the Kent coast, but did not penetrate far inland; they recrossed the coast when our fighters approached. Seaside towns on the Sussex coast, particularly Eastbourne, were attacked that day.

On September 23 eleven enemy aircraft were destroyed and eleven British fighters were lost, although eight of the British pilots were saved. Three days before, seven British fighters were lost (the pilots of three being saved) for the destruction of four enemy aircraft. On September 24 eight enemy aircraft were destroyed for the loss of four

British fighters and three pilots. On the 25th twenty-six enemy aircraft were destroyed for the loss of four British fighters and only one pilot. Next day thirty-three enemy aircraft were destroyed for the loss of eight British fighters and three pilots. On September 27 133 enemy aircraft were destroyed; 34 British fighters and 17 pilots were lost. On September 28 six enemy aircraft were destroyed, and seven British fighters were missing. Next day ten enemy aircraft were destroyed between midnight and midnight; one fouled a balloon cable and crashed into the sea off the south coast during the morning darkness; another bomber was shot down by fighters in the Thames Valley in the morning; anti-aircraft guns shot another into the sea off the south-east coast; four bombers were shot down in South-east England by the guns, one before dawn; a bomber and a fighter were shot down by British fighters during the evening, and a night bomber attacking London was shot down by guns at ten at night; altogether nine bombers and one fighter were destroyed that day, three by fighters; four British fighters and two pilots were lost. On the last day of September forty-seven enemy aircraft were destroyed during attacks on Britain, one by guns; twenty-two British fighters were lost, but twelve pilots were saved. Between September 20 and September 30 278 enemy aircraft were destroyed during attacks upon Britain.[1] Two hundred and sixty-six were destroyed by fighters for the loss of 101 British aircraft—a ratio of 2·64 to 1, a figure which was lower than earlier results. The reason for the rise in the ratio of British fighter loss was not so much that our pilots who fought in the later stages of the Battle of Britain were less experienced, due to casualties among the original R.A.F. pilots; it was due mainly to the losses in aircraft (including those made unserviceable until repaired), so that reserves had to be called upon; among the reserve aircraft were the earlier types of fighters, unarmoured behind the pilot, and thus more vulnerable when engaged in fighter-versus-fighter combats. This was a legacy from the pre-war theory that the fighter need be armoured only in front to protect it from the rearward fire of bombers—a theory that was quashed by the earliest actions on the Western Front prior to the Battle of France. The Royal Air Force had supplies of fighters sufficient to win the Battle of Britain, but it was necessary to fall back upon the incompletely armoured fighters before the battle ended. Here was another proof of miscalculation by the German air staff, who applied their fighter-attack tactics too late in the battle to influence its course.

The changing course of the war in the air was evidenced in the Air Ministry Bulletin (No. 1808), which referred to the attacks of September

[1] See table opposite.

COMPARATIVE TABLE OF AIRCRAFT LOSSES BETWEEN SEPTEMBER 20 AND 30 INCLUSIVE

DATE	ENEMY LOSSES		R.A.F. LOSSES		REMARKS
	DAY	NIGHT	FIGHTERS	PILOTS	
Sept. 20	4	1 (g)	7	4	Locality S.E. England.
21	2	:	: :	: :	
22	1	: :	11	3	Locality S.E. England, fighter combats.
23	11	:	4	3	
24	8	2 (g)	4	1	
25	26 (4g)	:			Twenty enemy aircraft destroyed between Bristol and the English Channel, including at least 15 heavy bombers and 3 fighter-bombers.
26	33 (1g)	1 (g)	8	3	Southampton and Isle of Wight area; 15 enemy bombers destroyed, at least.
27	133 (2g)	:	34	17	Locality S.E. England and Bristol areas.
28	6	: :	7	7	Mostly fighter combats.
29	7 (4g)	2 (g) / 1 (BB)	4	2	
30	47 (1g)	: :	22	10	Localities S.E. England and Bristol.
TOTAL	278 (12g)	7 (6g) (1BB)	101	50	

g = anti-aircraft guns.

BB = Balloon Barrage.

24 as "tip-and-run raiding." A hundred and eighty aircraft formed the second wave of the morning, following an earlier raid by 120 aircraft just before 8.30 A.M. Both raids were directed against the Thames Estuary-London area from the coast near Dungeness. In the afternoon two groups of twenty and fifty aircraft attacked the Southampton area. If the official attitude was almost contemptuous, the attitude of the R.A.F. fighter pilots was precise. One pilot said, " We lost no time in attacking them head-on. They at once jettisoned their bombs and broke up. Only four of our men got a chance to fire."

The scale of the German air attack rose again on the following day. Between 100 and 200 enemy bombers and fighters flew north-west across the Dorset coast just before noon and attacked Bristol. Bombs were dropped near the coast and in the outskirts of Bristol. Fighter pilots saw two wedges of Junkers 88 bombers in tight arrowheads of three with about forty aircraft in each wedge. Messerschmitt 109 fighters flew higher in their favourite stepped-up formations. Dornier 17 and 215 and Heinkel 111 bombers flew in the same close arrowhead formation. When attacked by the British fighters the bombers kept to their tight formations, and as the British pilots dived out of the sun they came under heavy cross-fire from the German air gunners. The Messerschmitt fighters formed defensive circles when they were attacked. Spitfires and Hurricanes did equal damage among the German machines. One Spitfire squadron shot down five, and probably destroyed several more. The Nizam of Hyderabad Spitfire squadron destroyed five of an enemy formation of eighty bombers and fighters. One Hurricane squadron chased a big formation of Heinkel 111 bombers from the mouth of the Severn well out into the English Channel, and, with its pilots diving in line astern from 22,000 feet, picked off one Heinkel after another until they had destroyed six and seriously damaged others. But the bombers were not prevented from reaching Bristol, their objective. Most of the fighting occurred after the attack, during the return of the raiders to their bases in France. Bristol was an 'arms' town, the headquarters of the Bristol Aeroplane Company, Ltd., whose aircraft and engines were a direct challenge to the Luftwaffe. Before the fall of France it was listed as a reception area. It was one of the British Broadcasting Corporation's war-time studio centres and the headquarters of the Air Ministry Department of Civil Aviation.

Next day, September 26, Southampton was the main target, with feint attacks against towns eastward to Hastings. The air battle lasted half an hour. Hurricane and Spitfire squadrons met the German aircraft over the Isle of Wight soon after four in the afternoon; some they fought over the island (as was the case when nine Spitfires of the Nazim of Hyderabad squadron attacked thirty Junkers 88 bombers at 14,000 feet; although the Messerschmitt escort attacked the Spitfires, the British pilots shot down three bombers and chased the others out to sea); others they harried as they flew up Southampton Water; more Spitfires destroyed a Heinkel bomber and two Messerschmitt fighters, while Hurricane squadrons destroyed five Messerschmitt 110 fighter-bombers.

A pilot of No. 607 (County of Durham) squadron brought down, without firing a shot, two German bombers from a formation that was heading for Southampton. Probably his experience is unique. This is what happened. His squadron attacked in close formation, too close to give him room to manoeuvre.

"Owing to the position of my Hurricane and that of another machine of my squadron the usual break-away was impossible," he said. "And before other avoiding action could be taken I crashed into a Dornier 215 with my right wing. The wings of both planes broke up." The British pilot then crashed into another Dornier 215 with his left wing. "I then went into a rocket [wingless] dive."

With both its wings shorn off, the Hurricane fuselage fell like a spent arrow straight to the earth, and while it rushed down the pilot climbed out of his cockpit and leaped into the air. He sprained his ankle, but suffered no other injury. His squadron leader saw both Dorniers crash.

Part of the big enemy formation still pressed on its way. Bombers reached Southampton and caused damage, despite erratic bomb-aiming due to shell-bursts from the anti-aircraft guns and bullets from the British fighters.

The bombers, having unloaded their cargo, turned for home. Into the air arena, reinforcing the fighters already there, raced the Polish 303 and the British 229 squadrons, who together had played a valiant part in the defence of London on September 11. The pilots of these two squadrons sighted a wedge of fifty Heinkel 111 bombers flying in arrowheads of three at 16,000 feet, with a fighter escort flying at a slightly greater height, and immediately attacked. The two squadrons destroyed nine Heinkel bombers and four Messerschmitt 109 fighters The Poles chased some of the enemy to the French coast. Sergeant Josef Frantisek got two Heinkels. He reported:

I attacked one Heinkel 111, and after a short while he burst into flames. I then attacked another Heinkel 111, and did not notice that I was already over France. I shot the enemy aircraft down, and he fell to earth in France. It was then that I noticed that I was over France and turned and flew back to my base.

In the whole action Fighter Command lost eight fighters, but five of the pilots were saved. Thirty-three enemy aircraft were destroyed, one by the guns; approximately half were bombers, and half fighters and fighter-bombers; before midnight a bomber night raider was destroyed by the guns.

On September 27 four waves of aircraft came over England in the biggest attack since the 15th. Escort strength was increased to four fighters to one bomber. At 8.45 A.M. about 180 German aircraft crossed the coast near Dungeness. About thirty Messerschmitt 110's got through to London; a few carried bombs, which fell in Central London and south and south-west districts. The Messerschmitts circled over London awaiting the heavy Dornier and Heinkel bombers. They waited in vain. The heavy bombers had been driven back over Kent, where Spitfires and Hurricanes competed with one another to deal with them. "We split up to attack two formations of bombers," said one pilot. "My lot tried to take on a group of fourteen Heinkel 111's with twenty-four escorting Messerschmitts above them. When we arrived we found they were already being attacked by other Hurricanes. We sighted another formation of enemy bombers and went off to attack them." Polish Squadron 303 and No. 1 Royal Canadian Air Force attacked together; the Canadians shot down six and the Poles ten. Flight Lieutenant J. A. Kent described the scene and the fight, thus:

A terrific anti-aircraft barrage was being put up round London, and from where we were we could see the capital gradually become encircled by a ring of smoke puffs from the bursting shells. Then we saw the hordes of German bombers and escorting fighters coming in over Kent. As R.A.F. fighters got stuck into them we could see them falling away, plunging down with smoke pouring from them. It almost seemed that there was an invisible barrier over a certain part of Kent and that as soon as the bombers reached it large numbers of them suddenly began pouring out smoke and going down. It was an amazing sight, and if I hadn't seen it all happen I would never have believed it. All this was happening in the few minutes before we arrived. Our squadron was accompanied by the Canadians, so I felt quite at home as we went into the battle. I got behind one bomber and went straight in at him. When I was about 75 yards from his tail his rear gunner suddenly realized that I was there and opened fire. I fixed him with my first burst. Then I pressed the gun-button again and kept my thumb on it for several seconds, and shortly afterwards he began to go down in flames. I watched him and saw him go into the sea with an almighty splash. Another German bomber which crossed my sights got a quick burst from another pilot, and as he went gliding down I saw a red glow appear under his belly, and as the glow got bigger, so his dive got steeper. He exploded before he hit the water, and it began raining little pieces of aeroplane from the spot where he had blown up.

"There were about thirty Heinkel bombers," said another of the pilots,

protected by fifty to sixty Messerschmitt 109's. We attacked the bombers from astern and were ourselves attacked by the Messerschmitt fighters. We turned, they broke up in disorder, and we got four of them. Meantime, the bombers had wheeled south and were heading back to France. We again went in to attack from astern. Just afterwards we saw another formation of forty Dorniers approaching head-on. They formed a defensive circle. So did some Messerschmitt fighters above them. Two more Hurricane patrols came in to attack them. We had no more petrol and had to go home.

(Full-throttle flying for the climb and the ensuing fight soon exhausted the contents of short-range fighters' petrol-tanks. Under these conditions duration of flight might fall to less than an hour, and in the earliest Spitfires to about forty-five minutes. Thus the exactitude of the intelligence and of the ground control was of the highest importance, for any failure to issue the correct orders to the Fighter squadrons might readily entail the dispatch of a patrol which failed to find and engage the enemy, or one which found the enemy too late to be able to wait to fight, and either might let the bombers through. But the story of the Battle of Britain is a tale of meticulous care in preparation and the almost faultless execution of the intelligence system and of the rectitude of the staff decisions which were taken thereupon. To these, no less than to the valour of the pilots, was due the victory.) The Messerschmitts waiting over London fared badly. One Hurricane patrol shot down four and damaged others. One crashed in flames. The crew of another baled out. Three survivors, all that the Hurricane pilots could find of the original formation, were chased ten miles out over the English Channel, fleeing towards France.

Hoping by a double punch to get through the fighter defence, the Luftwaffe commanders sent the next two waves over simultaneously at 11.30 A.M., one thrusting towards Bristol, the other repeating the attack upon London. Seventy-five aircraft flew over Poole, crossed Frome, and flew on above the rolling hills of Somerset. Many were turned back before they reached Bristol. Those who got through were attacked by more fighters. The survivors were fought all the way back to their southward crossing of the Dorset coast. The Nazim of Hyderabad squadron shot down four German aircraft and shared a fifth. Bristol did not suffer as on the 25th. The second London attack was made by about 300 aircraft. It failed. The attackers were driven back before they reached the capital; indeed, few penetrated much farther than the centre of Kent, whence some were deflected northward towards the Medway and the Thames; No. 46 squadron shot down four Messerschmitt 110 fighter-bombers over Essex.

The dragooned and disciplined German air crews, who had flown steadily over England week after week in the effort to effect there what they had been led to believe was possible—nay, certain—were at length beginning to doubt the validity of their optimism. They were more readily turned. They were more chary of accepting fight. More and more their crews could be heard calling the warning, "Achtung! Achtung! Schpitfeuer!" over their radio telephones whenever they sighted the British fighters. In the end the best-disciplined troops, in the air as on the ground, must bow to the inevitable fate of the force insufficiently well equipped, or insufficiently numerous, to complete the task assigned to them. There is reason to believe that the date of the intended German assault upon Britain was to have been 1942. If this was so, the actual attack was antedated by two years. Even the tremendous pressure upon German industry during the quiescent winter of 1939–40 failed to build the Luftwaffe up to a force great enough to maintain its pressure upon the island kingdom and simultaneously to withstand the losses inflicted upon it by Fighter Command during the Battle of Britain, following, so swiftly as they did, upon the losses suffered in Norway, Holland, Belgium, and France. Indeed, is it too much to say that the beginning of the success of Fighter Command in the Battle of Britain was to be found in the resistance offered by Norway, Holland, and Belgium? For the successive toll taken of the Luftwaffe by these three small and heroic States was a factor contributory to the victory subsequently won by the Royal Air Force over England's wolds and meadows, villages and towns.

Even aircraft officially 'unfit for action' joined in the combats over the English countryside. One sergeant pilot, flying a damaged Spitfire from his aerodrome to a repair base, came out of the clouds to find his own squadron engaging an enemy formation, and saw a Messerschmitt 109 in the act of attacking one of his fellow-pilots of the squadron. He immediately swung on to the Messerschmitt's tail and fired a long shot from about 600 yards. The Messerschmitt dived towards the sea. The damaged Spitfire followed, and closed to ten-yards range. The Messerschmitt hit the water with a mighty splash. "I saw two or three black dots coming towards me, which I imagined to be enemy aircraft, so I went full out and hedge-hopped away," said the sergeant.

Stanford Tuck had a similar experience. He was taking his bullet-holed Spitfire to be patched up when he struck one of the big daylight attacks. He attacked two Junkers 88's and chased one about thirty-five miles out to sea and shot it down. As he climbed in a turn the other

264

Junkers opened fire at him with cannon-shells and shot away his oil and glycol-coolant tanks and part of his airscrew. Tuck climbed as hard as he could with the engine turning as fast as it would. It soon caught fire, but bore him sixty miles before it packed up. Blinded by smoke and smothered in oil, Tuck jumped. His parachute opened with a jerk a second or two before his feet hit the ground. Royal Observer Corps men who saw the jump told him he was not more than 500 feet up when he leapt for life.

On September 27 coast watchers near Beachy Head saw a Spitfire pilot ram a Junkers 88. They said the ramming was deliberate. The Spitfire tore the tail off the enemy aircraft, the Junkers dived to a headlong crash, and two of the crew were killed and one taken prisoner. The Spitfire pilot was also killed. Why he rammed the enemy we shall never know.

The fourth wave of September 27 approached London at about three o'clock, when some 160 aircraft flew up from the south. Their formations were attacked and scattered over Surrey and Kent; twenty or so reached the London area, there to do little damage by bombs dropped chiefly in South London.

That day's attempts brought the Luftwaffe only more discouragement. Their losses were 133 aircraft, of which 91 were fighters. Six were destroyed on September 27 by one man, Pilot Officer A. G. Lewis, who by that feat raised his personal score to eighteen. This officer, who was born in Kimberley, South Africa, in 1918, was awarded a bar to his D.F.C. There were a few casualties in the London area; more in Maidstone. Fighter Command lost thirty-four aircraft, from which seventeen pilots were saved. For the second month in succession more than a thousand enemy aircraft had been destroyed during attacks upon Great Britain.

On September 28 the Secretary of State for Air, Sir Archibald Sinclair, sent the following signal to Air Chief Marshal Sir Hugh Dowding, Commander-in-Chief, Fighter Command:

I have received the following message from Prime Minister: "Pray congratulate the Fighter Command on the results of yesterday. The scale and intensity of the fighting and the heavy losses of the enemy, especially in relation to our own, make September 27 rank with September 15 and August 15, as the third great and victorious day of the Fighter Command during the course of the Battle of Britain."

The day that message was sent the flow of the turning tide of battle was beginning to be discernible. In three main operations—one in the early morning, one soon after midday, and one during the afternoon—the German generals employed forces consisting very largely of fighter aircraft. The first two attacks were directed against London; in the early attack a few aircraft penetrated to East London and dropped a small number of bombs, doing little damage and causing but few casualties; the second attack did not reach London. The third attack, directed against Portsmouth, also failed; no bombs were reported, and the force was driven off by fighters. The combats were almost all between fighter and fighter. Six enemy aircraft were destroyed. Seven British fighters were lost.

But the Luftwaffe generals had learned their lesson too late—the lesson that the opposing air force must be shot out of the skies before the full weight of air-power can be applied, and that the mastery of the air must be decided by fighter aircraft before the struggle upon the ground or sea can be vitally affected. The employment of the German bomber formations in the contested air over Britain conformed to the German theory of total war wherein the air forces were auxiliaries to the surface forces. The theory did not fit the case when, as in the case of the assault upon Britain, the surface forces could not move because they feared to make the sea-crossing without the mastery of the skies having been first secured. And it is probably true that in the barges and small boats the German soldiers, crowded together in a mass of sweaty humanity, when tried out in exercises, as they were, along the French coastline, found that they came not from seafaring stock, but were landsmen, unused to the tossing of the waters, and were sick. In such sorry plight it was more than ever necessary to secure the air above them, else all were surely lost. And Reichsmarschall Hermann Göring had assured Germany that his Luftwaffe would not fail, just as he had assured Germany that bombs would not fall on the Reich. And finally the German intelligence service must have been at fault, or it would have known how woefully unarmed Britain was at that time upon the ground when the Local Defence Volunteers were armed with staves, shotguns, and whatever weapons came most readily to hand from private house and farmhouse—for there were few available in arsenals, and the Regular Army needed everything that the factories could produce.

On September 29 there were raids by single aircraft on Edinburgh, the Midlands, and South-east England. Emphasis began to be laid by Germany upon the night-bombing policy, a policy contrary to the Wehrmacht theory, whereby daylight was desired to enable swift results to be obtained. In France night bombing had been seldom resorted to, and daylight attacks were the planned method of operation with the German ground forces. For the first time necessity, in the guise of Fighter Command, forced the hand of the German air commanders, and made them turn almost exclusively to night bombing as their main principle of bombing operation over Britain. The denial of tactical day success to the air arm of Germany marked the victory of Fighter Command in the Battle of Britain. That denial forced the Luftwaffe to undertake strategical night bombing, for which it was less adequately well trained. Night bombing was, of course, employed from the first against Britain; but the series of air attacks that began in the night following June 18 slowly gave place to round-the-clock bombing, for it was by daylight bombing that the Luftwaffe intended to breach the defence of Britain and open the way for the Germany Army. On September 7 Göring said, "This is the historic hour when our air force for the first time delivered its stroke right into the enemy's heart." And the Luftwaffe sent 375 bombers and fighters against London in daylight, to begin the attempt to browbeat the capital into submission. It was the only successful day attack upon London. The bomb-aimers could see their targets, and many found their aim was good. The bombing by night did not have the same military value. The denial of Britain's daylight air to the Luftwaffe foiled the plans of the German High Command. . . .

But there were yet some days to go before the Luftwaffe finally acknowledged its defeat by day. On September 29 nine Heinkel 111 bombers, unescorted, flew fast and high, bearing north-east towards Liverpool from a Brittany aerodrome. At about 6.30 P.M. they were sighted by nine Hurricanes on patrol over the Irish Channel, midway between St David's Head, in Wales, and Rosslare, in Ireland. No doubt they had hoped to sneak through to the Mersey unobserved. The Hurricanes at once attacked. The Heinkels turned to the west with the Hurricanes after them. One bomber crashed into the sea near Wexford. The Heinkels wheeled and flew to the south, jettisoning their bombs as they fled to help them to escape. Try where they would, the German air commanders could not find a blank spot in Britain's air defence. Nine bombers and a fighter were shot down that day—six by the gunners—between midnight and midnight; the R.A.F. lost four fighters and two pilots.

On September 30 the Luftwaffe made six large-scale attacks against the south areas of England. At 9 A.M., and again at 10.15 A.M., enemy aircraft crossed the coast near Dover and penetrated about forty miles inland, but none reached London. Bombs were dropped at Bexhill and Hastings. Soon after 11 A.M. about seventy bombers and fighters crossed the coast between St Alban's Head and Portland, and spread fanwise across Dorset and Somerset. Few penetrated any distance inland. The fourth attack began soon after 1 P.M., when about 180 aircraft flew over Dungeness, only to be broken up over the North Downs and scattered before reaching the outskirts of London, so that a mere few succeeded in dropping bombs in the western suburbs of the capital. At tea-time between 200 and 300 aircraft set the same course for London; again, they failed to break through to London as a formation; only a few reached the metropolis. Half an hour later a left-hook formation shot out to cross the Dorset coast. A patrol of Spitfires drove off a formation of Junkers 88 bombers before they reached the shore, and sent them scurrying back to France, with four of their number down in the sea.

The most intense fighting of the day occurred during the midday attack on South-east England, when two squadrons of Spitfires attacked a formation of twenty Dornier 215 bombers with fifty to sixty Messerschmitt 109's flying behind, on either flank, and above the bombers. The leader of one squadron of Spitfires went right through the enemy fighter screen and "shot up the leading group of bombers." One of his pilot officers dived on a Messerschmitt 109 and sent it down, smoking, in a vertical dive to hit the ground in full view of the victor. The second formation of Spitfires attacked the fighters, sent one down in flames, and crashed four on land, while a sixth blew up in flight. Others were badly damaged. The Polish 303 squadron chased thirty more Dornier 215's from Beachy Head to the French coast, and shot down a Messerschmitt of the escort near Beachy Head, two more as they approached the French coast, and one of the Dorniers in France. The squadron had by then destroyed more than 100 enemy aircraft.

During the attack towards London at tea-time, Group Captain S. F. Vincent, one of the R.A.F.'s 'station masters,' was again flying to inspect the work of his patrols in the air. Once more Vincent saw eighteen Heinkel 111 bombers coming north over Surrey towards London with an escort of Messerschmitt 109's above them. He turned upon the bombers, and attacked them head-on, until they fled southward from this persistent Hurricane. Then he flew to attack the Messerschmitts, three of whom, flying in line astern, were attacking another lone Hurricane whose pilot was attempting to dive away. As Vincent closed in the pilot of the second Messerschmitt opened fire and shot down his own leader. A moment later Vincent's guns shot down in flames the Messerschmitt pilot who had made the mistake. Or was it a mistake?

A New Zealand Hurricane pilot on leave was driving his car near Windsor Great Park, the Royal lands of Windsor Castle. "Hearing the noise of aircraft above the clouds," he said, "I pulled up at the side of the road. Two Ansons [1] were flying together fairly low. Suddenly a Messerschmitt came screaming down. The Ansons took no notice. They just carried on." The Messerschmitt pilot made a steep turn at about 1800 feet. His engine spluttered. His aircraft high-speed-stalled, fell, and hit the ground.

I immediately started the car [said the British pilot], and, driving into the Park, went across the grass to where the aircraft was. The pilot put his hands up, and I immediately took him prisoner. I drove him in my car to an R.A.F. station. On my way I stopped a Special Constable to tell him what had happened. He came to the R.A.F. station with me. When I arrived all I had to do was to hand over my prisoner.

There was some damage in Dorset, the Thames Valley, and Suffolk. Elsewhere the great German formations left little mark of their passage that day over the southern fringes of England. They had not reached their allotted targets, despite the loss of forty-seven aircraft, one by gunfire. The R.A.F. lost twenty-two fighters; but twelve of their pilots were safe.

That day it was announced that the King had appointed Air Chief Marshal Sir Hugh Dowding, G.C.V.O., K.C.B., C.M.G., to be a Knight Grand Cross of the Military Division of the Most Honourable Order of the Bath.

§ 14

The Luftwaffe Admits Defeat

The honour conferred upon the Commander-in-Chief of Fighter Command by the King might have been recognition that Sir Hugh Dowding had won the Battle of Britain. The award, made upon September 30, might be taken to mark the end of the battle. But it was the peculiarity of this air assault upon the United Kingdom that just as the beginning was not clearly defined, so the end was equally rough-cut. Indeed, the end of the night assault upon Britain could scarcely be said to have arrived until the moment when the legions of Germany were about to march eastward into Russia in June 1941; the ebb of the day attacks did not come until November 1940, the month when the Luftwaffe returned to their attacks upon shipping convoys off the British coasts. The day Battle of Britain was, as it were, an unfinished symphony ending in the third *adagio* movement. The night Battle of Britain continued to its allotted *allegro* movement in May 1941, when the music of the German night bomber switched from its symphony over Britain to its fantastic Russian concerto.

[1] Lightly powered, lightly armed training and reconnaissance aircraft.

On October 1, 1940, a small number of aircraft reached London and dropped bombs; elsewhere enemy attention was directed to near-coastal targets in the South of England. On the following day, from about 9 A.M., attacks against London by forces of from forty to eighty bombers and fighters continued until four in the afternoon; all were intercepted and broken up by British fighters, and few aircraft penetrated to the London area. One of the nine raiders destroyed during the morning and afternoon attacks was shot down by Hurricanes of the Fighter Command a few minutes after it had machine-gunned the streets of an Essex town. The Hurricane pilots found the Dornier 17 by accident while on their way home from a patrol over the North Sea. By the time they reached it the German pilot had climbed to 4000 feet and begun to dodge in and out of the clouds. But several of the Hurricanes got in bursts of fire, and the Dornier crashed twenty miles away, close to a searchlight post, whose crew took four of the German airmen prisoner. One of the Hurricanes landed near the post, and when the pilot got out of his cockpit the searchlight men stared in amazement, for the air fighter was just over 4 feet 3 inches in height, the smallest pilot in Fighter Command. Vernon Charles Keogh, "Shorty" to his pals, a native of Brooklyn, New York, was one of the best-known professional stunt parachutists in the United States, and his extensive pre-war flying experience included several hundred hours of stunt flying with air circuses. After joining the Royal Air Force he put in some sixty hours of operational flying with No. 609 Auxiliary Fighter squadron before transferring to the first Eagle squadron of all-American fighter pilots in the Royal Air Force. Propped up on his own special cushions, he was repeatedly in action during the hectic days of the Battle of Britain, full of offensive spirit and a fighter pilot of outstanding ability. While flying with the Eagle squadron he was lost during a patrol off the east coast of England on February 15, 1941.

During the night following October 2, 1940, a tremendous explosion was heard all over South-east London. The gunners thought they had hit a German bomber, but the noise was altogether exceptional. In the morning they found that one of their shells had exploded the bombs in the bomber's racks and blown the aircraft to pieces in mid-air. The fragments were found scattered over several miles of South-east London.

On October 3 attacks by single aircraft were directed over a wide area which included London boroughs, the Thames Valley, Essex, Kent, the Midlands, and Cornwall. Enemy aircraft machine-gunned streets, and a few persons were slightly injured when a train was machine-gunned. That day the Air Ministry announced:

During air battles over Britain our fighter pilots often have to land by parachute after baling out of damaged aircraft. This is happening every day.

While the necessity for public vigilance in regard to parachute landings continues, it is emphasized that force should not be used unless parachutists adopt a threatening attitude or attempt hostile acts. Not only is it likely that the isolated parachutist may be a British fighter pilot, but he may well be one of our Polish, Czechoslovak, French, Belgian, or Dutch allies who cannot speak English. Also the pilot may be wounded, injured by a bad landing, or exhausted and unable to answer questions quickly or clearly.

The greatest care and discretion should be shown before assuming that a parachutist is an enemy. If he is identified as an enemy or if his identity cannot be established at once, for example by production of his R.A.F. identity card, he should be made prisoner and handed over to the police or military authorities.

On October 4 a number of single German aircraft flew in cloud and scattered small numbers of bombs haphazardly, mainly over South-eastern England. Some of these bombs fell in built-up areas. In spite of the difficult conditions there were many air fights, and at least five Junkers 88, Heinkel 111, and Dornier 17 bombers were hit by the bullets of British fighters; two were seen to crash, but it was impossible to see the fate of the other damaged, crippled, and burning bombers as they disappeared in the thick banks of cloud that filled the sky between 1000 and 7000 feet. The German communiqué admitted the loss of two of the 'probables.'

Next day saw almost the last sorties of the German heavy bombers in the daylight air over Britain. Small knots of bombers, protected by Messerschmitt fighters in fifties and hundreds, flew over South-eastern England for many hours. These manœuvres began about ten in the morning. By midday four waves of fighters, some with small formations of bombers, had flown over the Kent coast to varying distances inland. Some reached the Thames Estuary, some turned back soon after crossing the coast. One raid, between eleven and twelve o'clock, reached Central London, it cost the Luftwaffe eighteen aircraft, against three R.A.F. fighters. In the afternoon the Luftwaffe continued the same programme, and added two waves of sixty or more aircraft which crossed the Hampshire and Dorset coasts and flew a short distance inland, only to be driven south again.

The leader of a Hurricane squadron described the noonday battle as "most enjoyable." He said:

We were a pretty good height when the Germans came out of the clouds. We were roughly evenly matched, and by the time the battle really started there were about 100 aircraft whirling about in the sky. It was rather like a tornado, moving back and forward across the country, because we started to attack near Rochester, and the fight moved across Kent out to sea, and then half the battle came back again.

Twenty-three German aircraft were destroyed, one of them a German Army Reconnaissance Henschel 126 which was shot into the sea off the south coast of England. The R.A.F. lost nine fighters, but only two pilots.

A flight commander, who had shot down five German aircraft, and whose squadron had destroyed more than sixty and damaged some forty probables, described his feelings after four months of fighting in the air since Dunkirk. He said:

At Dunkirk we brought down Junkers, Dorniers, and Messerschmitts in our very first fight. Our 'bag' has risen since, but we have not got away unscathed. I wouldn't say that we still have that first elation, for we know now, with absent faces in the Mess, something of the tragedy of war. But we are still full of fight . . . far happier fighting than ruminating over it. I, personally, always find the period of waiting rather trying . . . something of the natural apprehension the infantryman feels, waiting to 'go over the top.' One begins to imagine all kinds of things not quite right with the aircraft, the armament, or oneself, and to be afraid of bungling something.

Once I am up, I find the machine and myself O.K., and I have too much to do to be apprehensive of anything. If a pilot comes out of an action with a kill or two to his credit he feels an insatiable desire to go on shooting down Germans. If he foozles an opportunity for a kill, and comes home with nothing to show for it, he usually looks a bit depressed. You can always tell, in the Mess, who has had a successful day, and who hasn't.

I always tell my pilots that they can't expect to 'bag' a German every time they go up. But actually I like to see them peeved if they've been unsuccessful. I know then they are still full of fight. They always will be. More so now, perhaps, than when we first went into action. For we've been at grips with the Luftwaffe in so many circumstances that we've come to know their measure. It's the measure of a bully, and every one likes to paste a bully.

When the Germans are overwhelmingly stronger in numbers they will attack, but when their challenge is accepted, and the British Brownings begin to take toll, they go into a tight ring of mutual protection—like a boxer going into a huddle behind his fists.

On one occasion I got separated from the squadron and found myself running into a layer of Messerschmitt fighters, who were protecting a convoy of German bombers below them. It was my job to attack, and I flew straight towards them. I put in a long burst at the nearest Messerschmitts and then shot upward to make another attack. Immediately, the fighters—and there must have been quite seventy of them—went into a protective circle, looking like a cat chasing its own tail, and they remained like that, all on account of one Spitfire. Meanwhile, they were deserting the bombers they had

272

been sent to escort, and a British squadron met the bombers, who paid the price for their fighters' timidity.

But I must not give the impression that all German pilots are chicken-hearted. We have all met exceptions to the rule who were both spoiling for a fair fight and quite capable of giving as good as they got. But speaking of the Luftwaffe at large, they will never succeed in effectively damaging this country's war effort . . . while British pilots retain their present morale and fighting spirit.

The Luftwaffe had not benefited by the Nazi incubus. Its ways were still those of the German Air Force of the Great War, which possessed outstanding pilots (of whom, perhaps, Leutnant Werner Voss was the most sporting and courageous), but whose average pilot was not the equal of the average British pilot. In war it is the quality of the average man that brings victory, not the exceptional performances of a few stars. And because Britain raises the highest average quality in fighters in all Europe, the United Kingdom has for centuries overthrown all Continental dictators.

The Luftwaffe generals now turned almost all their heavy bombers over to night attacks, and employed mainly fighters and fighter-bombers for the remaining daylight assault against England. The first big fighter attack was launched on October 7. About 450 aircraft attempted to attack London. Among them were a few heavy bombers. But most of the aircraft were single-seater Messerschmitt 109's, some carrying bombs. The attack on London was made in five waves, beginning at 9.30 A.M. and ending in the late afternoon. The weather was clear, and the speed of these attacks was faster than any previously made. The Messerschmitts came in at 20,000, 25,000, and 30,000 feet. One Hurricane squadron encountered fifteen Messerschmitt 109's carrying bombs, with an escort of forty or fifty bombless Messerschmitts behind and above them. The Hurricanes destroyed seven Messerschmitts. Hurricanes, Spitfires, and Messerschmitts circled and fought, and wove strange patterns of vapour-trails in the higher sky. Two waves of the attack brought some of the raiders to the London area, and in the early afternoon a dog-fight between Hurricanes and fifty Messerschmitt 109 and four Heinkel 113 fighters, fought at 30,000 feet over London, was invisible from the ground. The faster speed of these bomberless combats entailed long chases and running fights. The Hurricanes ended this combat far over the Channel, sending two Messerschmitts splashing into the sea and crashing a third on land. That afternoon a raiding force of heavy bombers, Messerschmitt 110 fighter-bombers, and Messerschmitt 109 fighters flew over Dorset and Somerset; Spitfires and Hurricanes based in the West of England destroyed at least five heavy bombers, six Messerschmitt

Jaguar fighter-bombers, and one Messerschmitt 109. Fifteen enemy aircraft were destroyed in the attacks against London; only one was a heavy bomber. The R.A.F. lost sixteen fighters; ten of the pilots were saved.

Next day there was almost continuous raiding against the London area from 9 A.M. to 1 P.M. by forces of Messerschmitt fighters, accompanied by small numbers of bombers (mostly Junkers 88), which crossed the Kent coast very high and flying due north. As each force turned back after either reaching London or being driven back by British fighters, another of similar composition crossed the coast on the way in. Mostly they flew between 20,000 and 30,000 feet. Defending pilots described one force of Messerschmitts as spread out over two square miles of sky, in three layers, one at 16,000 feet, another at 20,000 feet, and the highest at 25,000. Spitfires attacked the middle layer. The flight lieutenant who led the Spitfires damaged a Messerschmitt and followed him down. "I drew alongside," he said, "and pointed to the ground. The German pilot waved back. He threw back his hood and made signs that he was going to land. I watched him crash-land in a field and flew around until I saw that he had been taken prisoner."

Another Messerschmitt caught by the first round fired by a heavy gun at Dover crashed in shallow water and its pilot waded ashore.

Some bombs were dropped upon London from a great height, but, despite the fact that traffic was at its busiest, casualties were not numerous. A train was hit by debris; two omnibuses were seriously damaged. The results were small compared to the expenditure of effort. Aircraft unable to penetrate to London dropped bombs at random on coastal towns in Kent and Sussex. Two British fighters were lost. Eight German aircraft were destroyed. Spitfire pilots who saw fifty Messerschmitts diving in different directions over a Kentish aerodrome sent one of the enemy vertically through the cloud with black and white smoke pouring from it. A Hurricane pilot dived 800 feet through a blinding rainstorm to destroy a Junkers 88. Aircraft of Coastal Command shot down two Heinkel 60 floatplanes into the Channel without survivors. The newly formed No. 311 Czechoslovak Hurricane squadron destroyed a Junkers 88 in its first engagement. Three of the pilots were ordered up to intercept the German bomber, which was plotted making for Liverpool. They were back on their aerodrome again in eleven minutes, and the enemy was shot down. This squadron was trained alongside the first Czechoslovak squadron, which had then shot down about forty enemy aircraft.

The German High Command communiqué issued on October 9

stated that three of their aircraft did not return from operations on October 8. The British Air Ministry issued a communiqué in the evening of October 9 (No. 1953) stating the facts. It read as follows:

The German High Command communiqué almost always contains an untrue statement of enemy air losses.

To-day's High Command communiqué, for example, only admits that three of their aircraft did not return from yesterday's operations.

In fact, as already announced, eight German aircraft were destroyed yesterday. Of these, two were Heinkel 60 floatplanes which were shot down in the sea without survivors. Details of the remaining six are as follows:

AIRCRAFT AND MARKS	PLACE	CREW	NAMES
Heinkel (burnt out)	Stansted Park, Stoughton, near Chichester	All killed. One only identifiable	Feldwebel Ernst Ens.
Ju 88 Black eagle in a red circle	Bromborough Docks, Wirral	One dead Two injured One uninjured	Leutnant Hubert Schlegel. Unteroffizier Helmut Weth. Sonderführer Horst Lehmann. Oberleutnant Helmut Bruckmann.
Ju 88 (blown up)	Toovies Farm, Copthorne, Worth, Sussex	Four dead	1 disc, No. 65119, found.
Dornier (in sea)	5 miles S.E. Fraserburgh	Three uninjured	Oberleutnant Egon von Eickstedt. Oberfeldwebel Hubert Freund. Hauptman Konrad Hardt.
Me 109 Figure 2 (in black) Red cat with arched back in circle	Hazeleigh, 5½ miles east of Chelmsford	One wounded	Feldwebel Paul Boche.
Me 109 (wrecked)	East Cliff Pavilion, Folkestone	One uninjured	Oberleutnant Werner Voight.

Note: It will be appreciated that information of this nature may be of great value to the enemy and cannot be published as a general rule.

Nearly every day during October 1940 the Messerschmitt fighters flew over South-east England. Many penetrated to London, for they were fast, flew high, and ever higher, and were difficult to catch, more difficult than the slower and lower-flying heavy bombers, which had been diverted to raids at night, or when used by day flew mostly as single aircraft employing the cover of bad weather to get them through Britain's fighter screen. But heavy loads of bombs were dropped on London during thirty nights of October (on the 6th only one bomb fell); the worst attack came on the 15th, the night of full moon, when more than 400 bombers dropped more than a thousand bombs, killing 430 civilians and wounding about 900. Until November 2 the night attacks upon London continued without intermission—a period of fifty-seven nights of bombing since Göring "delivered his stroke right into the heart." London was not the only target, either by night or day, but throughout the Battle of Britain it remained the main target. With the change in bombing tactics the aircraft losses of the Luftwaffe fell, and those of the R.A.F. rose relatively. But nothing could stem the flow of the current in favour of Fighter Command. The losses which the Luftwaffe could inflict were insufficient to break Fighter Command, and instead of failing its strength grew. It became increasingly difficult for British pilots to witness the destruction of their victims, for the height at which fighting occurred tended constantly to increase; crashes could not always be confirmed when enemy aircraft fell into the sea; yet in the three weeks and a half to the end of October No. 11 Group of Fighter Command, upon which the brunt of the fighting fell, certainly destroyed 167 enemy aircraft for a loss of 45 pilots.

During this phase the fighting passed almost out of the hearing of the public; visual indication that it was in progress was provided by the white trails of the ribbon clouds that formed behind high-flying aircraft manœuvring at so high a level that their noise was almost inaudible to people on the ground. Few among the millions of people in South-east England understood the strain upon the pilots "grappling in the central blue" and breathing oxygen through their face-masks to support life while they fought above London, sometimes at a height greater than the summit of Everest.

But not always was the fighting in the upper strata of the flying air. Sometimes it came down to the level of the sea that separated England from the Continent. Early in October Pilot Officer K. W. McKenzie sighted a formation of eight Messerschmitt 109's. He attacked and damaged one which dived to sea-level. After expending all his ammunition McKenzie flew alongside the Messerschmitt and tried without success to force it into the sea. Then, because of the obstinacy of the German pilot (understandable enough), he deliberately flew into the Messerschmitt and severed its tailplane with his wing-tip. The German fighter crashed into the sea. McKenzie was at once attacked by a number of Messerschmitts, but in spite of its damaged condition he succeeded in flying his Hurricane back to land and made a crash-landing. In one week he destroyed five enemy aircraft, and was awarded the Distinguished Flying Cross.

On October 12 the Messerschmitts came over Kent in large formations; and again they came in considerable numbers on October 15. It was at this period that Archibald McKellar (who began the war as a flying officer of the City of Glasgow squadron, rising to squadron leader and the command of the County of Warwick squadron) shot down five enemy aircraft in one day, four of them in a single flight. He it was who, with a companion in another Spitfire, shot down the first raider to fall during the German attack on the British warships in the Firth of Forth.[1] He brought down the first German aircraft on British soil, forcing it to alight near Dalkeith, on October 28, 1939.[2] He was one of those small-statured Scots who are born fighters. On October 2, 1940, he was awarded a bar to the Distinguished Flying Cross; the citation read: "During a period of eight days in the defence of London, Flight Lieutenant McKellar destroyed eight hostile aircraft, bringing his total to twelve. . . ."

In mid-October McKellar (now Squadron Leader) led the Hurricanes of No. 605 squadron over Kent. He saw fifteen Messerschmitt 109's at 18,000 feet. Fifty more followed them at different heights. Having the advantage of height, McKellar at once led his squadron in a dive attack upon the fifteen enemy aircraft, which were flying very fast, and, as it proved, were carrying bombs. There followed ten minutes of fierce, fast fighting. McKellar reported:

Messerschmitt No. 1. I saw a bomb being dropped from this machine. Pieces flew off from his wing, dense white smoke or vapour poured from him, and he went into a most violent outside spin.

Another Hurricane pilot saw this Messerschmitt crash in a field just as McKellar turned to deal with

Messerschmitt No. 2. In my mirror I could see another Messerschmitt 109 coming up to attack me. I therefore turned sharply and opened fire, and could see my bullets hitting the machine. It burst into flames almost at once, and went diving down.

One more Messerschmitt was on his tail, so McKellar spiralled down to 15,000 feet, outmanœuvred his assailant, and chased

---

[1] See Vol. I, pp. 105–106 and 108.   [2] See Vol. I, p. 108.

Messerschmitt No. 3. I gave him a burst, and at once he appeared to be hit, as dense white vapour came back on me, fogging up my windscreen. This speedily cleared and I gave him another burst. The machine burst into flames and fell into a wood.

Looking up, he saw

Messerschmitt No. 4. This machine was nipping in and out of the clouds, which were very broken and scattered. I followed, attacked, and saw the Messerschmitt catch fire and the pilot bale out.

Three hours later McKellar went up again and shot down a fifth Messerschmitt 109. That brought his personal record to seventeen German aircraft destroyed.

He had been awarded the Distinguished Flying Cross on September 5 for his "great sense of leadership and tactics in launching his flight against ninety " enemy aircraft during "his first large-scale encounter." It was his first fight with No. 605 squadron since his transfer from the City of Glasgow squadron. Leading the Hurricanes at 15,000 feet over Maidstone, Kent, he saw seventeen Heinkel bombers, flying west towards London, at about 18,000 feet. Twelve Messerschmitt 110 fighters flew close behind and just above the bombers; higher still, in tiers, were five formations, comprising about sixty Messerschmitt 109's. The Messerschmitts dived on the Hurricanes (now climbing on a course parallel to that of the bombers) to force the British fighters to keep away from their charges. McKellar led two Hurricanes against the Messerschmitts and three fell in flames, to crash near Croydon. The Hurricane formation re-formed. Now they were level with the bombers. Suddenly, unaccountably, the Heinkels turned south, into the sun, into the Hurricanes, which, perhaps, were invisible to the German pilots on account of the glare of the sun. The two formations approached head-on, at a combined speed of about 1000 feet a second. By radio telephone McKellar ordered each Hurricane pilot to pick his own target. He selected the leader of the Heinkels, now only two seconds' flight away. It was a desperate death-charge, breath-taking in its cold fury. His Browning guns spat out eight streams of bullets at the Heinkel. Formidable though they were, those twin batteries of machine-guns could vomit forth no more than 320 rounds before the two aircraft must crash, one into another. But the bomber's nose splintered, the wing petrol-tanks caught fire, the Heinkel exploded. There was a sheet of flame, a cloud of black petrol-smoke. McKellar flew through the cloud. There was no collision. The Heinkel had blown itself to fragments.

McKellar turned left, sighted on another Heinkel, fired, saw one of its wings break off, and the wreckage fall like a plummet, swung right, squirted the last of his ammunition into the third bomber in the leading vee, saw it turn on its back, catch fire in each wing, and then dive, doomed, to earth. The three bombers fell like skittles in a bowling-alley, for the explosion of the first Heinkel, as much as McKellar's bullets, had destroyed the other two. The German fighters were still there, and with no pause for reflection McKellar found himself aerobating for his life to escape the Messerschmitts that dived upon him. The fight ended over Farnborough, Hampshire.

During the eight succeeding days the Scots fighter destroyed one German aircraft daily. McKellar added three more German aircraft to his score, bringing it to twenty destroyed. He was awarded the Distinguished Service Order while Squadron Leader of the County of Warwick squadron; his collateral mention in dispatches was made on October 31; and he was killed in battle on November 1, at the age of twenty-eight.

The losses suffered by the Luftwaffe were not calculated to inspire the morale of its personnel, nor were they likely to be popular with the German people. German High Command communiqués continued to minimize losses. Four bombers were shot down on the night following October 16, but the Germans admitted the loss of only two. The Air Ministry stated that the four destroyed aircraft were to be found near Harwich, Bishop's Stortford, Denbigh, and Frome.

Bombs in small numbers fell on the London area by day on October 9, 10, 12, 13, 15, 17, 20, 21, 23, and 24. The Messerschmitts that dropped these bombs were hard to intercept among the clouds, and often they could hit back. It was a period of strenuous endeavour for the pilots of Fighter Command, accompanied by less spectacular results, and losses more evenly distributed on both sides. But it was an admission of the failure of the bombing programme of the Luftwaffe against Britain. Often a British pilot, attacking a Messerschmitt, scarcely knew that he was being attacked by another German fighter until his aircraft was hit by a cannon-shell or a burst of bullets. The three following cases illustrate the conditions under which the British pilots strove.

A Hurricane pilot, homeward-bound after a patrol, sighted a formation of Hurricanes, and, to the east, a larger formation of Messerschmitt fighters. "I chose what I thought to be the last of a series, and attacked the nearest machine," he said.

After two short bursts from the starboard quarter the enemy aircraft caught fire and the pilot opened his hood. Just then I was struck by cannon-fire in the cockpit. Everything faded out completely, and I vaguely remember pulling the aircraft out of a steep dive. I undid the strap and cleared my right eye with my glove and remember seeing the hood shattered. I slid back the sliding portion and climbed out, and after a short interval pulled the ripcord. I lost consciousness several times on the way down and eventually landed in a field. I tried to stand up after a few minutes, but could not, and eventually some one came along and attended to me.

A Spitfire pilot, separated from his squadron during a fight with Messerschmitts, encountered a Dornier 17 bomber and shot it down in flames. At that moment he felt a bang behind him, and found his hood and mirror shattered. "I decided to jump as I thought I was on fire," he said.

Having undone my strap and raised myself out of my seat, I saw a Messerschmitt 109 attacking me. Realizing that I would be at a disadvantage landing from a parachute, and still having ammunition left, I turned into the enemy, which, evidently not thinking I was damaged, made off at high speed. I had lost a lot of height by this time, so I decided to forced-land as my engine was still running. I endeavoured to do up my harness again, but failed, so I put down the undercarriage in the hope that I could make a normal landing.

And, in spite of smoke and fumes, the pilot brought his Spitfire down safely.

A Hurricane pilot led his squadron against an enemy formation which they turned back from an important target, and the enemy flew back towards France. "I was just about to break away," said the pilot,

when a tremendous explosion took place. Smoke poured from under my instrument-panel, and I was covered with petrol. Without waiting to see the effect of my fire, I succeeded in getting my aircraft under control. I then saw two other Hurricanes of the squadron. They had not noticed my condition, so I headed for the coast on my own. I had to turn off the ignition and petrol because of the strong smell of burning. I glided as far as I could, keeping a look-out for any ship which might be near by. When I was down to 5000 feet I saw a tramp steamer, and, manœuvring the aircraft to windward of the ship, I baled out at 4000 feet. The wind took me about a mile to the leeward of the ship. About five seconds after abandoning the aircraft I saw it blow up in the air and heard a tremendous report. After being in the sea for about twenty minutes a boat from the ship picked me up.

British fighter pilots did not then carry rubber dinghies, and were equipped solely with 'Mae West' life-saving waistcoats.[1] Long immersion in the sea produced numbness due to cold. This pilot was among the fortunate ones to be picked up quickly.

With the increasing number of forced landings in aircraft, the Air

[1] See Vol. I, p. 117.

Ministry issued instructions to the public on the rescue of pilots from crashed aircraft. These were:

When a British pilot is trapped in his crashed aircraft members of the general public who are on the scene should observe the following rules in attempting a rescue.

Approach the aircraft from the rear—away from the airscrew. If the aircraft is upside-down and one wing is higher than the other approach on that side from the rear.

Fire extinguishers, if fitted, are automatic and cannot be operated from outside the aircraft.

To open the cock-pit hood look for the release catch at the front end and draw the hood backwards. If the hood cannot be opened break the transparent material with anything hard.

To remove the pilot look on his chest for the locking pin which attaches his harness to the aircraft. Pull the cord fastened to the locking pin; then lift the harness attachments from the central pillar, and remove the pilot with his parachute attached to him.

Practical, experienced aid should be obtained if opportunity and time allow. It is important that a wounded man should be disturbed as little as possible, and every care must be taken to avoid harmful movement.

In the case of fire or danger of it, speed of removal is the primary consideration.

After the pilot has been removed his parachute may be released by means of a round aluminium disk attached to the front of the pilot. Turn the disk as far as possible in the direction of an arrow marked "Turn to unlock," and then press in to the pilot.

Splints, stretchers, or lifting tackle may help in the removal of casualties if there are sufficient openings in the aircraft.

But the defensive fighting that brought British pilots down on British soil or in British coastal waters was passing. In the second half of October British squadrons were beginning again to fight over the beaches of France and Belgium, chasing German raiders on the run. The day of British fighter sweeps over the Continent had not yet arrived, but it was not far distant. Three times in one October week Spitfire pilots shot down German aircraft within range of their own anti-aircraft guns. "We chased fifty Messerschmitt 109's from over London," said one pilot of No. 74 squadron, "and came into range halfway between Dover and Cap Gris-Nez. As we approached the French coast we continued to attack, weaving in line astern. The enemy were in a ragged-looking formation. One of our chaps got the first one. I got the second." Before returning the same pilot spotted a Heinkel 111 lying in the water just off the French coast; a second Heinkel and eight Messerschmitt 109's circled round it. He attacked the circling Heinkel and sent it into the sea to join the first.

No. 602 squadron sighted fifteen Messerschmitt 109's skimming the highest cloud at 30,000 feet heading towards France, over Ramsgate. The Scots gave chase. The Messerschmitt rearguard turned to a head-on attack. A dog-fight began. Two Messerschmitts were shot into the sea. A third crashed on the beaches of Dunkirk, where the men of the British Expeditionary Force had awaited embarkation. It was the first time the City of Glasgow squadron had visited Dunkirk beaches, for the squadron was in the north when the evacuation took place.

On October 25 Luftwaffe activity increased. About 400 aircraft crossed Kent and the Thames Estuary, their formations varying in number from 20 to 100 aircraft. They came in four main waves. A few aircraft reached the London area. Fighting took place above clouds and at heights up to 34,000 feet. Messerschmitts were shot down near Maidstone, Hastings, Rye, Tonbridge, Gravesend, Sevenoaks, Dover, and Canterbury; others fell in the sea; ten British fighters were lost, but seven pilots were saved; fifteen German aircraft were certainly destroyed, but the Luftwaffe's losses may have been greater, for it was usually impossible for the British pilots to follow their victims down through the clouds to observe their fate.

On the following day six small formations, each of about twenty to thirty Messerschmitts, attempted to attack London. They flew in and out of clouds, at heights varying from 15,000 to 25,000 feet. Only one or two, during the morning, got through to Central London. Spitfires routed thirty yellow-nosed Messerschmitts over Tunbridge Wells; one crashed into the sea six miles off Dover, a second crashed in flames in Sussex, a third was last seen streaming petrol and thick smoke from the fuselage, a fourth dived into cloud smoking heavily, a fifth limped home hit by machine-gun bullets. One 'probable' was later confirmed destroyed. Hurricanes shot down two certainties. For the Luftwaffe's five destroyed, the R.A.F. lost two fighters.

On October 27 Hurricanes and Spitfires doubled their score of the previous day. The British official communiqué said that the German Air Force continued "to fidget" about over the South of England. Some of the Messerschmitts were almost playful in their behaviour. One Hurricane squadron found twenty Messerschmitts 'milling about' at 20,000 feet above Surrey. When the German pilots sighted the Hurricanes they formed into two sections and made dummy dive attacks on each other. Then two Messerschmitts broke away and dived steeply down in front of the Hurricanes. But the British pilots were not lured below the main Messerschmitt formation by these tactics, which were as old as formation air fighting. Other formations of Messerschmitts were sighted in clutches of fifty. A station commander, flying with a Hurricane squadron, was just about to attack a Messerschmitt in one of these formations of fifty to the south of London, when, he said, "a Spitfire pilot sprang in and crashed it down in grand style, the Messerschmitt 109 pilot baling out" in the Canterbury area. A single Dornier 215 bomber was seen and chased more than forty miles by a Hurricane pilot who followed it into the clouds and fired whenever the Dornier came out into clear sky. The bomber finally disappeared in a steep spiral dive, smoking heavily, but the British pilot did not see it crash. The bombs it dropped did no damage. Eight British fighters were lost that day, with four of their pilots saved. Some bombs were dropped in the London area, at places in South-east England, and in Hampshire.

This is one pilot's account of a Spitfire-versus-Messerschmitt fight at that period. The pilot was weaving above his squadron over South-east London when he was sent off to identify an enemy formation. When he returned to direct his pals to the attack he joined up by mistake with six Messerschmitts, and began to weave above them "When I realized what I was doing I got a pretty fair shock," he said.

I went in to attack double quick. One Messerschmitt did a barrel roll to the left. I fired at him as he did so, and he dropped back. I was then engaged from astern, and lost a bit of ground. By the time we got to Hastings I had caught up the rest of them again, and knocked bits off one. Another was half a mile or more below and behind the others as they crossed the coast. He was dropping back rapidly, and I was hoping to finish him off when six more Messerschmitt 109's came down at me from over the Channel in line abreast. They went into line astern and circled round me at about 30-yards intervals. But number six was about 100 yards behind number five, so I went for him. He climbed steeply in a close turn. I had about 300 miles an hour on the clock, so I pulled up almost vertically and gave him a burst flat into his feet from beneath. He rolled over and went straight down. By this time number one was on my tail, so I went down behind number six, who was still going straight down in a slow aileron turn at 10,000 feet. But number one was still worrying me, so I went into a steep left-hand turn—and blacked out. On recovering from my black-out there were no more enemy in sight, so I climbed up again and went home.

The last big day of October month came on the 29th, when the Luftwaffe lost thirty aircraft against the loss of seven Royal Air Force fighters from which five pilots were saved. Attacks were directed against London and Portsmouth. Few bombs were dropped on London, mostly on the outskirts, for few of the enemy reached the capital. No. 603 (City of Edinburgh) squadron of the Auxiliary Air Force destroyed eight out of about fifty Messerschmitt 109's that tried to reach London shortly after midday. The shell-bursts of anti-aircraft guns indicated the Messerschmitts to the Scottish squadron, whose pilots were flying at about 30,000 feet. The Spitfires gave chase and the Messerschmitts turned for home. The Spitfires shot down four before the Germans reached the coast, drove them out to sea, and shot down four more in the Channel. The squadron had already accounted for more than seventy enemy aircraft.

It was the end of the Messerschmitt attempt to break down the resistance of Fighter Command. The Battle of Britain was won. It did not end as surface battles end. It simply died away, leaving behind it only the wreckage of the broken and bullet-riddled enemy aircraft that had fallen in England. At one period of the battle more than two thousand infantry soldiers were required to guard the fallen aircraft of the enemy.

It was a period of tense adventure for the pilots. You could see the strain engraven on their faces. They took off and rose into the air, never knowing what to expect, conscious that "the last enemy" flew near them, but almost unaware how gallant was their every action above the English fields and towns. One pilot became a local hero after crashing his damaged Hurricane into an enemy bomber. But he did not mean to ram the bomber. A bullet struck his aircraft and made his aileron control useless just when he had begun to attack a bomber formation. "My Hurricane hit an enemy bomber—a Dornier 17—tearing one of its wings off," he said.

The Hurricane was wrenched clear of the enemy aircraft, minus its port wing and most of the engine. The cockpit was full of fumes and the machine was falling out of control in an inverted spin, so I left hurriedly. I pulled my ripcord a couple of seconds later, because I was too scared to do a delayed drop. I saw the enemy aircraft explode after three people had baled out. I then saw another Dornier 17 spinning into the clouds minus part of its wing. I landed in a ploughed field, and just afterwards another Dornier 17 spun out of the clouds and crashed about two miles away.

A German pilot, who was taken prisoner in Kent, had an extraordinary experience. While flying at 25,000 feet his rubber dinghy accidentally became inflated, attacked him in the rear, and began to force him out of the cockpit. In an effort to master the dinghy he lost control of his aircraft and went into a spiral dive. When he pulled out the engine stalled, and through loss of height he was forced to land.

One British pilot's report read:

I fired a fairly long burst into a Dornier 17. I fired at a Messerschmitt 109; fired at another Messerschmitt 109. I climbed to 25,000 feet and dived into an enemy formation. I fired at a Messerschmitt 109, obviously hitting it hard. I fired another short burst on passing. I was then told to make a nuisance of myself.

A Messerschmitt 109 crashed at Plummers Plain, by Horsham, in Sussex, on October 29 and caught fire. The pilot was trapped within his aircraft. Frank Burgess, a cowman, ran from a neighbouring field. T. G. Child and Charles Gardener, two labourers (and members of the Home Guard) who were engaged on building work, dropped everything and ran to the aircraft, which was burning with increasing fierceness. In the crash one of the wings of the Messerschmitt had been wrenched off and the cockpit was tilted at an angle which made it difficult to remove the pilot. Two of the men held up the wing while the third pulled the pilot from the burning aircraft. By this time the pilot's outer clothing was all on fire. Before the rescuers had carried the pilot more than five yards from the aircraft a shower of machine-gun bullets from the blazing wreck compelled them to leave him for a few seconds. Then they went back despite the danger of further bullets and the risk of an explosion, dragged the pilot to a safer distance, and then stripped off his clothing. Had they been a minute later in arriving on the scene the German pilot must have been burned to death. Gardener was burned on the wrist. All three men were later awarded commendations.

Mr James Ingledew, a farmer, saw a Spitfire spiralling towards the ground at high speed one day in November. Realizing that a crash was certain, he called out to his sister to telephone the nearest aerodrome while he rushed to the aircraft, hoping to save the pilot, now lying with his head in the wreckage and his body enveloped in flames. With ammunition exploding in every direction Mr Ingledew pulled the pilot clear and removed him to a safe distance. Unfortunately, the pilot was already dead. For his bravery the farmer was awarded the British Empire Medal.

In November the Luftwaffe returned to their attacks upon shipping. It was their admission of failure. They had fared badly since they began their major attack against Britain on August 8. In twelve weeks of tremendous effort upon the part of the staff and air crews of the Luftwaffe the German Air Force had lost 2433 bombers and fighters to the fighter pilots of the Royal Air Force, the gunners of the anti-aircraft batteries, the cables of the balloon barrage, and other causes. Bombers and fighters had been destroyed in almost equal numbers. Allowing the usual average numbers in pilots and other members of air crews for the machines destroyed, the Luftwaffe had lost over 6000 airmen killed and taken prisoner. Fighter Command had lost 375 pilots killed and 358 wounded. These were the numerical measurements of defeat.

The defeat could be measured in other ways. The strength of Fighter Command had increased despite its losses. The strength of the Luftwaffe had decreased. Before the middle of October was reached the aerodromes of South-east England had recovered from the damage done to them by the Luftwaffe a month and more before. The Luftwaffe had failed to gain the mastery of the skies over England, and by that failure had lost all hope of victory over its last belligerent and uncomprehending foe. Within the square-cut Teuton craniums befuddled German brains must have wondered how it came about that England did not know she was defeated in August 1940, but instead drove back the German air-power baffled and dismayed so that it recoiled within itself, repentant of its day extravagances, and looking for the victory to come by night attack instead.

§ 15

Ebb of Battle

On the first day of November the gunners of Dover scored a direct hit on a Messerschmitt 109 flying at 24,000 feet, and saw it spiralling down into the sea in flames. The most important attack of the day was made upon a convoy off the Thames Estuary. The German pilots' aim was spoiled by gunfire and fighter bullets, and their bombs fell into the water. J. A. Kent, who had left his flight in 303 squadron on promotion to squadron leader, celebrated his first day in action leading his new squadron of Spitfires by destroying a Messerschmitt 109. His squadron was at 21,000 feet when vapour-trails disclosed ten yellow-nosed Messerschmitts 9000 feet below. Some of the Spitfires attacked the Messerschmitts, while others went for the bombers they were escorting. Kent picked out a Messerschmitt whose pilot wheeled round so quickly that the two machines almost collided as they passed. "I saw the German's face quite clearly," said Kent.

He looked rather grim. We were so close that neither of us could fire. But I whipped round again and got on his tail. The Nazi went screaming down towards the shelter of cloud. I dived after him, firing several short bursts. He was hit before entering the cloud. I followed. When I came out into clear sky again I saw the Messerschmitt crash into the sea.

The squadron destroyed five. Next day Kent destroyed two of the squadron's four, when he led fifteen Spitfires against sixty Messerschmitts over the Thames Estuary.

On November 2 two strong formations of fighters and fighter-bombers again attacked London, the second and stronger one consisting of about 100 aircraft. Neither dropped bombs on London, although a few of the enemy flew over the capital at a great height dnring the second raid.

On November 3 the gunners scored the half-aircraft mentioned at p. 188. It was a Dornier 215 bomber. Two Hurricane pilots saw it above the clouds, and both fired two bursts at it. One Hurricane pilot dived within ten yards of the Dornier before it disappeared into cloud, and the German air gunner fired back. The British pilots last saw it with one engine stopped, and smoke pouring out. The gunners spotted the Dornier when it came below the clouds. They saw it was not quite out of action, and decided to finish the pilots' work for them. A few rounds brought it crashing down near the Essex coast.

On November 7 three formations of German aircraft approached the Thames Estuary and the Portsmouth area. (On the previous afternoon the Southampton area was the scene of attack.) One Messerschmitt 110, flying alone over London, was shot down by two Hurricane pilots 31,000 feet over Chiswick, to fall on the outskirts of the city. In the following afternoon No. 17 squadron was ordered to patrol over a convoy off the East Anglian coast. They found twenty-five Junkers 87 dive-bombers attacking two destroyers. The bombers were diving from 7000 feet to 500 feet when the Hurricanes arrived on the scene. Too high above to be able to intervene were 'masses' of Messerschmitt 109's. The Hurricanes waded in at a low height, shot down fifteen Junkers, probably destroyed six more, and damaged two others, leaving only two out of twenty-five untouched.

On November 10 a force of enemy aircraft which crossed the Dorset coast was turned back and dispersed by strong British fighter forces, and no bombs were dropped.

Garibaldi, the Italian liberator, who received aid from Britain, said on April 12, 1854: "If ever England should be so circumstanced as to require the help of an ally cursed be the Italian who would not step forward with me in her defence." Mussolini, the Italian dictator, who swung Italy into an alliance with Germany, stated that in 1940 he had asked his friend Adolf Hitler for the privilege of participating in the air war against Britain and had received his consent for some squadrons of the Regia Aeronautica to operate side by side with the Luftwaffe from French bases against England.

Royal Air Force pilots occasionally thought they saw Italian aircraft over England during the period of the large-scale German daylight attacks, but none were brought down to confirm the possibility. The first definite action of the Regia Aeronautica against the United Kingdom fell upon Armistice Day, 1940, the day held sacred by the Allies of the Great War in remembrance of the dead who had died then. Action by the Luftwaffe that day was understandable, and several formations of German aircraft attempted to reach the metropolitan area during the morning; a very few got through to London and dropped a small number of bombs. It was, however, a strange day for the Italian Air Force to choose to become embroiled in battle in the English air. Perhaps the stimulus was a German joke—that were consistent with the Teutonic idea of humour! In passing, let it be said that twelve German aircraft were destroyed that day for the loss of two British aircraft and their pilots.

It was afternoon when nine Italian Caproni Ca 135 bombers, escorted by Fiat C.R. 42 fighters, attempted to attack shipping off the Thames Estuary, while German aircraft attacked towns on the south-east coast. Here is the story, told by Flight Lieutenant H. P. Blatchford, who led the Hurricanes of No. 257 squadron that day because the squadron leader, to his subsequent annoyance, was having the day off. Blatchford said:

We started with the usual afternoon blitz, just like any other day during the past three months, and were ordered up on patrol out to sea. Our job was to join up with No. 46 Hurricane squadron as their bodyguard.

When we were about 12,000 feet up I saw nine planes of a type I had never seen before, coming along in tight 'vic' formation. I didn't like to rush in bald-headed until I knew what they were, so the squadron went up above them to have a good look. Then I realized they were not British, and that was good enough for me.

We went in to attack, starting with the rear starboard bomber and crossing over to attack the port wing of the formation. The Italians (as they turned out to be) stood up to it very well. They kept their tight formation and were making for the thick cloud cover at 20,000 feet. But our tactics were to break them up before they could do that, and we succeeded.

I singled out one of the enemy and gave him a burst. Immediately he went straight up in a loop. I thought he was foxing me, as I had never seen a bomber do that sort of thing before. So I followed him, when he suddenly went down in a vertical dive. I still followed, waiting for him to pull out. Then I saw a black dot move away from him and a puff like a white mushroom—some one baling out. The next second the bomber seemed to start crumpling up and it suddenly burst into hundreds of small pieces. They fell down to the sea like a snowstorm.

I must have killed the pilot. I think he fell back, pulling the stick with him. That's what caused the loop. Then he probably slumped forward, putting the plane into an uncontrollable dive. But what usually happens then is that the wing or tail falls off, and it was a surprising sight to see the plane just burst into small pieces.

I started to climb again, and I saw another two of the bombers in

288

the sky. They were mixed up in a fight and were both streaming smoke. At that moment another one shot past me flaming like a torch and plunged into the sea.

After seeing that I thought the battle was over and I could go home, but, just as I turned to do so, I saw a dog-fight going on up above with another type of aeroplane I had never seen before. They were Fiat fighter biplanes. There must have been about twenty of them milling round with the Hurricanes. I went up to join in the party, but the fighter I singled out saw me coming and went into a quick turn with me on his tail. His plane was very manœuvrable, but so was the Hurricane, and we stuck closely enough together while I got in two or three bursts.

It was a long dog-fight, as dog-fights go. We did tight turns, climbing turns, and half-rolls, until it seemed we would never stop. Neither of us were getting anywhere until one of my bursts seemed to hit him, and he started waffling. For a moment he looked completely out of control, and then he came in at me, and we started all this merry-go-round business over again. I got in two or three more bursts and then ran out of ammunition. That put me in a bit of a fix, and I didn't know what to do next. I was afraid if I left his tail he would get on to mine. Then he straightened up. He was just thirty yards ahead, and I was a few feet above. At that moment I decided that as I could not shoot him down I would try and knock him out of the sky with my aeroplane.

I went kind of hay-wire.

It suddenly occurred to me what a good idea it would be to scare the living daylight out of him. I aimed for the centre of his top main-plane, did a quick dive, and pulled out just before crashing into him. I felt a very slight bump, but I never saw him again, and somehow I don't think he got back.

By now the scene had changed a bit. No. 46 squadron was chasing the Italians all over the sky. I did not know at the time, but I found when I got down that their squadron leader [L. M. Gaunce, D.F.C.] was a great friend of mine from my home-town of Edmonton, Alberta. He bagged a couple in that fight.

And now, I thought, it's home for me. But the day wasn't over yet. As I was flying back, keeping a good look-out behind, I saw a Hurricane below me, having the same kind of affair with a Fiat as I had just had. I went down and did a dummy head-on attack on the Italian. At 200 yards he turned away and headed out to sea. I thought, "Good, I really can get home this time." But just before I got to the coast, still keeping a good look-out behind, I saw another Hurricane, with three Fiats close together worrying him. Down I went again, feinting another head-on attack, and again when I was about 200 yards away the Italians broke off and headed for home. That really was the end of the battle.

I was a bit worried because my plane had started to vibrate badly, but I managed to land all right. I had got out of my Hurricane and was walking away when my fitter and rigger ran after me, saying that I had six inches missing from one of my propeller blades and nine inches from another.

All the same, it certainly was a grand day for the squadron.

But it was a bad day for the Italians. No. 257 squadron had destroyed five of the bombers and two Fiat fighters, while No. 46, wading in later to the fray, had shot down three bombers and three fighters. Most of the Italian aircraft shot down fell into the sea. All the Hurricanes returned.

The motto of No. 46 squadron—"We rise to conquer"—was maintained. The squadron was formed in April 1916 at Wyton, in Huntingdonshire, and went to France in 1916 flying Sopwith "Pup" Scouts armed with one Vickers machine-gun firing through the airscrew. In 1917, after being recalled for a period of six weeks for service in England in defence of London against the Gotha raiders, the squadron returned to France, and in November of that year was re-equipped with Sopwith Camels with two machine-guns firing through the airscrew. No. 46 pilots shot down sixty-six enemy aircraft in the Great War. In December 1919 the squadron was disbanded under the disarmament programme, not to be re-formed until September 1936 under the pressure of Hitler's rearmament of Germany. In Norway the Hurricane-equipped No. 46 squadron scored eleven confirmed victories [1]; over and around Britain forty more enemy aircraft fell to the eight-gun fighters of No. 46 squadron, from the time it was refurnished with aircraft and remanned with pilots at an Essex aerodrome after the sinking of H.M.S. Glorious, until the end of 1940.

By November 10, 1940, the anti-aircraft gunners in the United Kingdom had shot down 400 German aircraft. In thirteen weeks from August 8 they had destroyed 357, one-seventh of the total destroyed by all weapons; 196 of the gunners' victims were bombers, 112 were fighters, and 49 were unascertained types. During one week in August the gunners shot down 50 bombers and 14 fighters, an average of nine a day.

The daily losses of the Luftwaffe continued to mount. On November 14 nineteen German aircraft were destroyed in daylight. Fifteen were Junkers 87's which came with a formation of more than forty dive-bombers to attack Dover harbour. Two of their Messerschmitt escort were also destroyed. Two British fighters were lost, but both their pilots were saved. Seventeen Messerschmitt fighters, or fighter-bombers, and one Dornier bomber were destroyed on November 15 for the loss of two fighter aircraft and one pilot. The main attack was made against London by about thirty Messerschmitts flying in pairs; they flew up the Thames, but turned away when they saw Spitfires on patrol. Two days later Fighter Command drove back medium forces of raiders from the Kent coast, the Thames Estuary, and Suffolk, destroying

[1] See Vol. I, p. 223.

twelve for the loss of five fighters and only one pilot; anti-aircraft guns destroyed another.

A strange incident occurred on November 21. Few enemy aircraft approached England, but three Spitfire pilots sighted a Heinkel 111 bomber over Kent and gave chase. The Heinkel pilot turned and made for cloud to take cover. The three Spitfires opened fire as he fled. The last to attack was overtaking the Heinkel fast. His fellow-pilots saw this Spitfire fly straight on into the bomber, and both aircraft crashed in flames. The British pilot and the crew of the Heinkel were killed. Each of the other Spitfire pilots received return fire, and it was presumed that the pilot of the colliding fighter was either killed or wounded just before he normally would have broken away. Next day another lone bomber, this time a Dornier 215, was shot down by two Hurricanes over Guildford. The daylight tactics of the Luftwaffe bombers were now remarkably like those of the days before the Battle of France—mainly a matter of reconnaissance. All the weight of the bomber attacks was now falling by night, and spreading over a wider area, taking in cities in many parts of the provinces, for the Luftwaffe had given up the continuous pounding of the capital. The daylight activity of the Luftwaffe fighters had changed from escort duty to fighter sweeps; on November 23 one sweep over the Kent coast at about 9.30 A.M. cost them a Messerschmitt 109; another sweep in the afternoon cost them three Messerschmitts. Four Messerschmitts destroyed that day without loss to the Royal Air Force! The German tactics were accomplishing nothing.

Squadron Leader G. L. Denholm, D.F.C., led No. 603 (City of Edinburgh) squadron off its aerodrome at about 11.40 that morning. It was a sunny day, with a slight ground haze which grew into mist from 18,000 up to 26,000 feet. The Edinburgh boys were on a routine patrol with another squadron, and after patrolling for some forty to fifty minutes they were ordered to go here and there to investigate various raids which were reported over land and near the coast. Denholm said:

I was leading the squadron when my engine began to misfire and splutter, so I called up one of my flight commanders and told him to lead while I broke away and tried to clear my engine. By diving and roaring the engine I managed to make it run smoothly again, and then took up position at the rear of my squadron.

While we were climbing through some cloud we lost touch with the other squadron. We carried on alone and were on a southerly course, approaching Dover, when we were warned to look out for a formation of Italian aircraft. Every man was immediately on the alert. From the back of the squadron I heard the formation leader suddenly report aircraft dead ahead of us. At the same time some one else reported unidentified aircraft to the east, but the leader wisely held our course to fly towards the aircraft he had already seen. After a couple of minutes we saw the enemy aircraft flying south-west down the Channel. They were still some distance away, and were 1000 feet below us.

They were Italian fighters, Fiat C.R. 42's, and were well over the sea, flying at about 20,000 feet. When I first had a good look at them they gave me the impression of a party out on a quiet little jaunt. There were about twenty of them, flying along quite happily in good formation.

When our leader gave the order to attack and told us to sweep round and down on their tails we were in a very advantageous position. Our Spitfires must have been about 100 miles an hour faster than the Italian fighters, and it was dead easy to overtake them and blaze away. They were flying in a sort of wide fan-like formation, and when we went to attack each of our pilots selected his particular target. You can imagine how effective the first few dives were when I tell you that one of our pilots at one time saw six Italian fighters either on fire or spinning down towards the sea.

The Italians looked quite toy-like in their brightly coloured camouflage, and I remember thinking that it seemed almost a shame to shoot down such pretty machines. I must have been wrong, for the pilot who saw six going down at the same time said afterwards that it was a glorious sight.

But I must say this about the Eye-ties: they showed fight in a way the Germans have never done with our squadron. It is true, though, that they seemed amateurish in their reactions. By that I mean they were slow to realize that we were anywhere near them until it was too late. They kept their formation well, but it didn't save them.

After a short while the Italians were dodging this way and that to escape our aircraft as best they could. One of them broke formation and turned towards France. I chased him and fired at him several times. I believe I hit him, and would have finished him off if my engine hadn't begun to splutter again when I was half-way across the Channel. So I left him to limp home while I turned towards the English coast to find the rest of the battle. It had vanished by this time, for the whole fight lasted only ten or fifteen minutes, so I came home.

In that last appearance of the Regia Aeronautica off the coasts of Britain No. 603 squadron shot down seven Fiat fighters, and brought the squadron score to over 100. By the end of the first week in December the Edinburgh boys had added ninety-one victims to the bag of seventeen collected by them in Scotland.

A wing commander, while instructing two Polish pilots during a practice flight on November 23, noticed a vapour-trail in the sky. He opened out and climbed to 25,000 feet. The lone aircraft turned south and began a shallow dive, silhouetted against the sun. The wing commander closed to identify the aircraft. "It was a Junkers 88," said the wing commander.

The Polish pilot began the attack. I fired three bursts from long range and the Junkers turned sharply beneath me. I dived to get on his tail, and after the Pole had made another attack smoke appeared. I easily closed the range to fifty yards, firing long bursts. One of the Junkers engines caught fire, then the whole fuselage burst into flame, the German turned on his back, dived to the ground in a sheet of flame, and crashed near Cirencester.

On November 27 a Canadian flight lieutenant sighted a Messerschmitt 109 over the Thames Estuary, and after a chase over Kent damaged the German fighter's coolant system. The German pilot, then over the North Foreland, realized that he would be unable to reach his base and searched for a place to land. He chose a Royal Air Force aerodrome. The Spitfire pilot landed alongside. When the German pilot was arrested the flight lieutenant flew back to his own base.

Royal Air Force fighter pilots were now carrying the fight across the Channel at every opportunity. A Spitfire squadron that day chased a few Messerschmitts to the French coast and shot one down and damaged another, coming down to 3000 feet in the fight. The pilots decided to climb back over the English Channel until they were all together again at 26,000 feet above the Thames Estuary. And that was when the adventures of one of the British pilots began.

Suddenly I was jumped on from out of the sun by a few Messerschmitts [he said]. First they hit my tail, and my controls went all sloppy. I immediately tried to get away, but a moment later incendiary bullets hit my engine. Then a hail of machine-gun bullets came through my hood and shattered my instrument-panel, and a second after the compass was shattered by further bullets. The only instruments left O.K. were my altimeter and my airspeed indicator. All this happened in the space of a few seconds while I was in the act of escaping.

The British pilot was now back over North-east Kent, and below lay a small village.

I rolled over on my back [he continued], headed my machine for the marshes, and went into a steep inverted dive. I saw my airspeed indicator leaping up, until it got between 650 and 700 m.p.h. with the throttle wide open. At about 6000 feet the aircraft caught fire, and then she straightened out on her side and went into a slight dive, almost horizontal, in a sort of fluttering way. This gave me a chance to free myself from the machine, and at about 4000 feet I baled out.

It was pleasant when I got out, but it wasn't pleasant watching my Spitfire going down. Just as I pulled the ripcord she hit the mud.

293

There was a blinding flash, and a cloud of black smoke hung like a pall over the spot. The Spitfire had disappeared.

Soon I had to think about myself, for I was right over the mud of the Thames. I came down, and the parachute dragged me, face downward, through the mud, until it finally collapsed. While it was dragging me along I must have looked like a porpoise going up and down through the mud.

A man who is a Home Guard in his spare time came in gumboots to my rescue. He helped me out. Then there arose the problem of how to get me clean. It was decided that the best thing in the absence of a shower-bath was for me to be washed as I stood. I went into a yard and they threw buckets of water over me—warm water, luckily. They also got a stirrup-pump and squirted me with that. Then I took off all my clothes and was washed a bit more, and afterwards put on a suit of clothes lent to me by the Home Guard. I had my leg patched up, and after a few hours was driven back to my home station. I arrived there at 10.30 at night, and all the boys got a good laugh seeing me in a suit which was too small for me. The trousers were half-way up my calves.

The Air Ministry communiqué for that day of November 27 was laconic. It read: "Eleven enemy fighters in all were destoyed by Fighter Command pilots. Two of our fighters were lost, but both pilots are safe."

The pilot who arrived safely in the mud of the Thames was in hospital for a few days after a piece of bullet was extracted from his leg. During his absence a letter from the village in North-east Kent was received by the commanding officer of his station. It read:

. . . the people of a very small village in North-east Kent would very much like to thank the pilot of a fighter plane who baled out over some marshes for staying at his controls and steering his damaged plane away from the village and a factory which is in the vicinity before baling out.

Hearty congratulations and good luck always!

Helmuth Wieck fought with the Luftwaffe over Europe, first in Spain, then in Poland, later in France and the Low Countries, and then over England. He was Germany's first great air ace of the Second World War, credited in November 1940 with fifty-six victories in air combat, and he had risen to the command of the Richthofen Jagdgeschwader. Hitler had decorated him with the Knight's Cross of the Iron Cross with Oak Leaves. Helmuth Wieck was a killer, the pride of Göring.

During the afternoon of November 28, 1940, Major Wieck and his squadron were flying at 25,000 feet over the south coast of the Isle of Wight. Approaching the same area at exactly the same height was No. 609 (West Riding of Yorkshire) squadron, led by Squadron Leader M. L. Robinson, D.F.C., who had at least six enemy aircraft to his

294

credit, and who had twice destroyed two in the same day. At the head of one of the sections was Flight Lieutenant J. C. Dundas, D.F.C. and bar, who had destroyed at least twelve German aircraft. Here was a good sound British squadron, of the Auxiliary Air Force, mounted in Spitfires, and there was the crack Messerschmitt circus of the Luftwaffe, led by the current German Air Force ace. The planes of the German circus were flying north, into the wind, with the sun on their tails; all the conditions were favourable to them, for the sun shone full in the eyes of the British pilots, and the strong wind would have carried them quickly out over the sea as soon as they began to circle in a dog-fight. Yet, instead of engaging the Spitfires, the Messerschmitts retired out of sight. But there was cunning in this manœuvre. Ten minutes later the Messerschmitts reappeared, having climbed to a much greater height. They were above the Spitfires, and their main formation came in over the top of No. 609's machines. Robinson turned his squadron to fly directly underneath the Messerschmitts, and the British pilots waited.

The Germans detached a section of three Messerschmitts. They wheeled away into the sun with the evident purpose of engaging at once. Presumably their object was to split up the Spitfires so that their comrades could come down upon single, unguarded opponents. The three Messerschmitts dived out of the sun in close formation—a sure indication of more than ordinary stuff, for the usual German Fighter squadron seldom flew in really tight formation. Everything betrayed the marshalling of experience in combat to take full advantage of the situation for the benefit of the German circus.

No. 609 squadron broke up into ordered sections to defeat the purpose of the arrowheaded Messerschmitt divers, and as the three 109's flashed past and down Robinson gave orders to his pilots to re-form. Then in his earphones he heard the voice of Flight Lieutenant Dundas say, "Whoopee—I've got a 109."

"Good show, John," said the squadron leader; "re-form as quickly as possible."

No answer came.

Again Robinson called Dundas. Still there was no answer. One of No. 609's section leaders saw a parachute with a tear in it going down about ten miles west of the white fingers of the Needles. The squadron searched the sea for over an hour, until petrol began to fail, and the Spitfires were forced to return, having seen no sign of a surviving pilot in the water.

Major Helmuth Wieck had led the trio of diving Messerschmitts. Flight Lieutenant John Dundas had got him as he flashed down and past. But Wieck's pair, the two who followed him like aerial leeches, had caught the British pilot an instant later, and Dundas fell with the triumphant "Whoopee" on his lips. The last fight of this Doncaster pilot of twenty-five, who had been an Auxiliary Air Force officer for two years, and whose name will be remembered in Stowe School, where he was a scholar, was symbolic of the whole Battle of Britain, an epic of the upper sky.

At 5.40 A.M. on November 29 a British destroyer flotilla, commanded by Captain Lord Louis Mountbatten, made contact with at least three German destroyers, which fled through the darkness towards Brest, firing torpedoes. H.M.S. *Javelin*, the flotilla leader, was hit. Several hits were made on the enemy ships, but the damage done to them could not be ascertained. As the *Javelin* limped home she was assailed off The Lizard by bombers of the Luftwaffe. But by then she was under the cover of British fighter aircraft. Shortly after 11 A.M. one of the escorting Spitfire pilots saw a Dornier 17 bomber approaching the destroyer. "I first saw a Dornier climbing hard in an effort to reach cloud cover," said the squadron leader who flew this Spitfire.

When the German pilot saw me he turned, but I came in on his near side and fired a burst which stopped his port engine. He fell a few hundred feet and made for a low cloud-bank. I got in two more bursts from close astern and then followed him into thin cloud for five or six minutes, getting in three more bursts. His one remaining engine stopped, and he flicked to the right and crashed in flames.

Emerging from the cloud a few moments later, the squadron leader suddenly sighted a Junkers 88. He got in a short burst before he had to break away to avoid a collision with the bomber.

Spitfires relieved one another to guard the destroyer. One pilot saw another Junkers 88 dive out of the clouds and release four bombs from about 3000 feet. "I chased after him and got in several good bursts from my machine-guns before he disappeared into cloud with smoke coming from both engines. I followed him through the cloud, caught him again in the open, and smashed the rear-gunner's cockpit with a burst of fire from close range." When it was last seen this Junkers was on fire, with bits breaking off in mid-air.

Another pilot saw another Dornier fly directly over his head at 3000 feet. After a chase in and out of cloud this flying officer saw the German aircraft "start falling to pieces and go spinning down through the clouds. I followed him down and saw him hit the water."

A pilot officer drove off and damaged another Junkers 88 as it attempted to dive-bomb the *Javelin*. "While I was firing we both entered cloud," he said, "so I couldn't see the result of my attack. But

296

I did see one of my bursts, fired at point-blank range, go into the belly of the enemy aircraft."

And under the umbrella of the Spitfires the torpedo-damaged destroyer *Javelin* reached port safely.

Major Edward ("Micky") Mannock died in action in the Great War. The manner of his death was never fully established. He went out and he did not return. But already his career as an air fighter had earned for him the Military Cross and bar, and the Distinguished Service Order and two bars; the posthumous award of the Victoria Cross was richly gained. When he died in July 1918 he had already destroyed fifty enemy aircraft, and those who flew with him said many more, for he was apt to give to other pilots the profits of his greater skill so that the less experienced would be encouraged, and he scorned to claim anything but absolute certainties. But he did more than that. He created a tradition which lived on in No. 74 squadron, a tradition of utter fearlessness. Mannock was the commander of A Flight in "The Tigers," as No. 74 squadron was called. He was promoted to major, and led No. 35 squadron when he was killed. But his name is ever associated with his original squadron. Their crest, granted by the King years after the Great War, is a tiger's head, and their motto is "I fear no man." In the Great War they shot down 140 enemy aircraft and sent another ninety crashing out of control; their own losses were fifteen pilots killed and five taken prisoner.

Two who followed in Mannock's tradition in No. 74 squadron were A. G. Malan and H. M. Stephen. Malan was twenty-nine in 1940. He was born at Wellington, South Africa, and educated at Wellington School and in the South African training ship *General Botha*. He served for two years in the Royal Naval Reserve as sub-lieutenant, and in 1936 joined the Royal Air Force as a pupil pilot. In June 1940 he was awarded the Distinguished Flying Cross when he had led his flight of No. 74 squadron, and sometimes the squadron, on ten offensive patrols in Northern France, personally shooting down two enemy aircraft and possibly three others. He was awarded a bar to the Distinguished Flying Cross in August, when he had shot down three more enemy aircraft and assisted in destroying another three during the Dunkirk operations. He was awarded the Distinguished Service Order in December 1940, when he had been promoted to squadron leader and the command of No. 74 squadron. Malan had then destroyed at least eighteen enemy aircraft and possibly another six, while the squadron had destroyed at least eighty-four since early in August. Malan later became the Royal Air Force top-scoring fighter pilot in the Second World War, with a personal bag of thirty-two aircraft destroyed, and, on promotion to wing commander, assumed command of the station from which he had flown with No. 74.

Stephen received the Distinguished Service Order as a Field award on the immediate recommendation to the King of Air Marshal William Sholto Douglas, C.B., M.C., D.F.C., who succeeded Air Chief Marshal Sir Hugh Dowding in November 1940 as Air Officer Commanding-in-Chief, Fighter Command, and was promoted from Air Vice-Marshal on appointment.[1]

Pilot Officer H. M. Stephen's Distinguished Service Order was the first ever to be awarded in the Field to a member of Britain's Home Defence Forces. It was also a high award to an officer who held the lowest commissioned officer rank in the Royal Air Force. Stephen was a sergeant pilot in the Royal Air Force Volunteer Reserve flying with an Auxiliary squadron before being commissioned in April 1940. He received the Distinguished Flying Cross in August 1940 and a bar to the Cross in November. He was twenty-six, came from Ballater, Aberdeenshire, and before the war was employed on a London evening newspaper. On the morning of November 30 his own personal score stood at nineteen enemy aircraft destroyed. The Royal Air Force station from which No. 74 squadron operated had shot down a total of 599 aircraft since the beginning of the war. That day the weather was bad. Mist shrouded the aerodrome, and the visibility was little more than 300 to 400 feet. But there was that 600th enemy aircraft to be got. The squadrons and ground staffs had already subscribed to a prize for the fortunate pilot.

Twenty-two-years-old Flight Lieutenant J. C. Mungo-Park, D.F.C., was Stephen's flight commander. They had fought side by side in offensive patrols over France during the Battle of France, over the beaches of Dunkirk, and throughout the Battle of Britain. The flight lieutenant had already shot down eleven enemy aircraft. Together they took off on a voluntary patrol.

[1] At the special request of the Minister of Aircraft Production—Lord Beaverbrook—Sir Hugh Dowding was seconded to the Ministry of Aircraft Production for special duty in the United States of America, to advise on aircraft types. Dowding returned to Britain in the autumn of 1941 and retired from the Royal Air Force on October 1, 1941. Six weeks later he accepted the invitation of the Secretary of State for Air to undertake a review of R.A.F. establishments to see if the numbers of men and women employed could be reduced without prejudice to operational efficiency, and whether the best use was being made of personnel, and was reinstated on the active list and restored to full pay on November 10, 1941; having completed his review, Sir Hugh Dowding was again placed on the retired list at his own request on July 15, 1942. In the King's Birthday Honours List in June 1943 Air Chief Marshal Sir Hugh Caswall Tremenheere Dowding, G.C.B., G.C.V.O., C.M.G., was elevated to the Peerage and selected the title of Baron Dowding. He was the second R.A.F. officer to be ennobled by the King.

They climbed through the clouds and flew above the Thames Estuary. Quite suddenly they saw separate small formations of German fighters coming at a great height from France. They climbed again, gave chase, and closed with them over Dover, Sheppey, Southend, and Burnham-on-Crouch, then out to sea and back to Ramsgate, where they passed through one lot of smoke-trails to seek two Messerschmitts flying at about 34,000 feet. They noticed with surprise that other fighters paid no attention to them.

"The flight commander made for one of the two higher aircraft with me close behind," said Stephen.

The German turned to the right when he eventually spotted us. As he swung to the right I went straight across and gave him a deflection shot. My flight commander, by now dead astern of the enemy, gave him a three-seconds burst. Our first shot caused him trouble. We saw him try to climb but fail in the attempt. Then in turn we each gave him some more bursts. Smoke began to pour from his aircraft, and he dived away.

"It was simply marvellous when we began to play about with the 109," said Mungo-Park. "It was bitterly cold—so cold, in fact, that my colleague had to press the gun-button with his left hand, because his right hand holding the control column was practically numb."

"At terrific speed we followed him down," said Stephen.

I was doing more than 500 miles per hour, and when I was down to 6000 feet I straightened out. Meanwhile the German pilot had baled out; his machine crashed near Dungeness and he was taken prisoner.

We then both returned to the aerodrome, where pilots from other squadrons were disappointed that they had not got the 600th victim, for naturally we were desperately keen to claim him. Yet they will join in the party we are giving to celebrate the victory.

With the party held on the first Royal Air Force station to celebrate its six-hundredth victory over the Luftwaffe, this account of the day Battle of Britain may fittingly close. The ordeal of the United Kingdom was not yet over, but the heavy losses the enemy had suffered in his vain daylight attempt to destroy Fighter Command in preparation for the invasion of Britain forced him to substitute large-scale night bombing attacks in a last resort to break Britain's will and power to wage the war. In doing this the Luftwaffe departed from its designed rôle as tactical spearhead for the German Army and became instead an independent strategic force.

The high concentration of attacks upon the capital that had marked the battle of London ended in November 1940, and the provincial towns then began to suffer heavier blows than the comparatively light attacks they had known in October.

The strategic conception of the main German air attacks upon Britain from November 1940 to May 1941 can be observed in the table of raids below. These were not like the mass raids developed later by Bomber Command. The Luftwaffe never attained to such

LUFTWAFFE'S MAIN NIGHT RAIDS ON BRITAIN FROM NOVEMBER 1940 TO MAY 1941

NIGHTS FOLLOWING: 1940		NIGHTS FOLLOWING: 1941	
Nov. 1	Birmingham	Mar. 13	Clydeside
14	Coventry	14	Clydeside
15	London	16	Bristol and Avonmouth
19	Birmingham	18	Hull
22	Birmingham	19	London
23	Southampton	20	Plymouth
24	Bristol and Avonmouth	 21	Plymouth
28	Liverpool and Merseyside	21	Liverpool and Merseyside
30	Southampton	Apr. 3	Bristol and Avonmouth
Dec. 1	Southampton	4	Bristol and Avonmouth
2	Bristol and Avonmouth	8	Coventry
3	Birmingham	9	Birmingham
6	Bristol and Avonmouth	10	Birmingham
8	London	10	Coventry
11	Birmingham	11	Bristol and Avonmouth
12	Sheffield	12	Birmingham
15	Sheffield	15	Belfast
20	Liverpool and Merseyside	16	London
21	Liverpool and Merseyside	19	London
22	Liverpool and Merseyside	21	Plymouth
22	Manchester	22	Plymouth
23	Manchester	23	Plymouth
29	London	27	Plymouth
		27	Portsmouth
		28	Plymouth
1941		29	Plymouth
Jan. 2	Cardiff	May 1	Liverpool and Merseyside
3	Bristol and Avonmouth	2	Liverpool and Merseyside
4	Bristol and Avonmouth	3	Liverpool and Merseyside
10	Portsmouth	4	Liverpool and Merseyside
11	London	4	Belfast
12	London	5	Belfast
14	Plymouth	5	Liverpool and Merseyside
17	Bristol and Avonmouth	5	Clydeside
Feb. 17	London	6	Liverpool and Merseyside
19	Swansea	6	Clydeside
20	Swansea	7	Liverpool and Merseyside
21	Swansea	7	Hull
Mar. 10	Portsmouth	8	Hull
13	Liverpool and Merseyside	10	London

a perfected technique. The number of German bombers engaged in any one of these raids varied from fifty to four hundred. The attack on Coventry on November 14 (which caused severe damage and thus introduced the temporary use of a new verb, 'to coventrate') was made by about 400 bombers in full moonlight during a period of eleven hours. In December the great fire attacks began; loads of incendiary bombs were dropped to set city centres alight. This was the month of the great London fire. Southampton, Sheffield, and Manchester blazed. These were week-end attacks, when the Luftwaffe generals probably hoped to catch the city centres denuded of thousands of urban workers who might quickly have put out the burning bombs. Yet this plan failed too. The buildings were blasted and burned out of the centres of cities, people made homeless, added strain thrown on the workers during and immediately after the raids, and subsequently by the additional duties of Civil Defence (the name which, in September 1941, replaced the former Air Raid Precautions designation and also embraced the Fire Service). But the German bombers were not designed for their task. Their loads of bombs, heavy though they were, were not heavy enough. The aircraft employed, numerous though they were, were not numerous enough. The day bombers, turned into night bombers, crashed in great numbers on their own airfields. And by May 1941 the plan was abandoned.

Kesselring's air fleet went south; the air attack upon Crete began on May 20, 1941. But the main bomber fleet of the Reich went east, where German armies were massed along the frontiers of Europe in preparation for the assault against Russia that began on June 22, 1941, from the Baltic to the Black Sea. No more than a token force of heavy bombers now faced Britain from the airfields of the Low Countries and France. Never again was the Luftwaffe to possess such power to make heavy blows on Britain. Instead, it became again the tool of the German Army, doomed to bleed copiously and to begin to break to pieces in Russia and the Mediterranean zone of war. By sacrifice of life, limb, and sight, and the courage and endurance of those who lived unharmed, the pilots of Fighter Command—aided by their comrades of Bomber and Coastal Commands and the Fleet Air Arm —and the masses of the British people, bore their "scepter'd isle" through twelve months' ordeal by bomb and fire; and kept their freedom so, to prove in time to German hearts and hearths the error that the German Führer made when he turned eastward, leaving Britain undefeated.

APPENDIX I

GERMAN RAIDS AGAINST THE UNITED KINGDOM
APRIL 10–JULY 7/8, 1940

Date	Place	Number of Aircraft Attacking	Number of Aircraft Destroyed	Damage
April				
10	Scapa Flow	?	4 and 3	None. Two more raiders damaged.
30	Clacton-on-Sea	Mine-laying aircraft	1	One Heinkel 111 bomber crashed with its mine. Crew of four killed. Two civilians killed, and 156 injured. Nearly 30 houses destroyed, and 50 others made unusable.
May				
9	N.E. coast of Scotland	?	2	First bombs on mainland.
	East coast of England	?	1	Ju 88 destroyed by Hurricane.
	Bombs fell near Canterbury			
24/25	North Riding of York, Norfolk, Essex	?	...	8 civilians injured in Yorkshire.
June				
4/5	R.A.F. aerodromes in Yorkshire, Lincolnshire, Norfolk, Essex	?	...	Bombs fell in rural districts. Damage slight; six persons injured.
5/6	Aerodromes in 12 counties from Hampshire to Durham. H.E. and incendiary bombs dropped	?	...	Material damage slight; one aircraftman killed, six men injured.
7/8	Aerodromes in 10 English counties	?	1	Material damage slight; no casualties reported.
18/19	About 100 German aircraft crossed English coast from Yorkshire to Kent, attacking several R.A.F. aerodromes	100	7	Oil pipeline on Thames Estuary wharf set on fire. Bombs fell on Cambridge town and several villages. Casualties: 12 killed, 30 injured.
19/20	More than 100 aircraft from South Coast of England to Scotland	100 plus	3	Bombs fell on three towns in N.E. England, and one town in Lancashire, in Lincolnshire, S. England, and S. Wales. 8 killed, about 60 injured
21/22	Eastern counties of England; aerodromes	?	...	Damage slight; 3 civilians killed and 3 injured.
24/25	English Eastern counties, the Midlands, and the South-west	?	...	5 civilians killed and about 20 wounded.
25/26	...	?	3 and 2	Damage slight; 4 killed, about 13 injured.
26/27	...	...	3	Damage slight; 16 casualties.
27/28	...	?	...	Little damage; 3 civilians injured.
28/29	Eastern England and South Wales	?	1	5 persons injured.
29/30	Southern England, the Midlands, Bristol Channel area, Scotland	?	...	Little damage; 2 killed, 8 injured.

Date	Place	Number of Aircraft Attacking	Number of Aircraft Destroyed	Damage
June 30/ July 1	Eastern and Western England, Wales, East Scotland	?	...	A few persons injured.
July 1	Wick and Hull—first daylight raids, made just before dark	?	...	Six persons killed and 16 injured. R.A.F. shot down German floatplane off N.E. coast of England.
2	N.E. English coast	?	...	Damage to houses; 13 killed and 120 injured.
3	East coasts of England and Scotland	?	7	Six killed, and 78 injured. No damage to military objectives. Six other German aircraft badly hit.
3/4	Eastern counties of England	Few	...	No casualties reported.
4	Portland	?	1	One naval auxiliary vessel set on fire; lighter and a small tug sunk; 11 civilian casualties.
	Over South Coast of England	?	2	Shot down by R.A.F. fighters.
4/5	England	?	...	Slight damage; no casualties.
5	Off S.E. coast of England	?	1	German bomber shot down by fighters in early morning.
	Over South-east coast of England	?	1	One German fighter shot down from a formation of fighters and bombers before dark.
5/6	N.E. coast of England	?	...	No damage or casualties reported.
6	N.E. Scotland, S.E. and S. England	?	1	Some damage and casualties.
6/7	N.E. coast of England	?	...	Some damage and casualties.
7	S. and S.W. England	?	4	Some damage and a few casualties. Three bombers and one fighter shot down.
7/8	N.E. England	?	...	Some damage and casualties.

The earliest raids upon Britain by the Luftwaffe were in the nature of reconnaissances for what was to follow. The targets were varied—laying sea-mines, bombing aerodromes, ports, coastal and industrial towns. The bombers crossed the British coast at many points from the North of Scotland to the South of England. They penetrated to Wales, Merseyside, and the Bristol Channel.

APPENDIX II

ACTIVITIES OF BOMBER COMMAND
JUNE 18–DECEMBER 5, 1940

DATE	TARGET	AIR-CRAFT LOST
June 17: Night	Military objectives in Gelsenkirchen, Homburg, Wanne-Eickel, Essen, Dollbergen, Hamburg, Aachen, Duisburg, Rheydt, Cologne, Coblenz, Schiphol-Amsterdam airport	
18: Night	Aerodromes, fuel depots, blast-furnaces, marshalling yards, and trains at Hamburg, Bremen, Rheydt, Cologne, Düsseldorf, Hanover, and Frankfurt.	
19: Night	Military objectives at or near Lünen, Hamm, Bielefeld, Münster, Düren, Schwerte, Euskirchen, München-Gladbach, Hamborn, Emmerich, Hamburg, Brunsbüttel, and Norderney	
20: Day	Two attacks upon Rouen aerodrome, and one upon Schiphol-Amsterdam. Great damage to enemy aircraft	
20: Night	Military objectives at Essen-Frintrop, Osterfeld, Hamm, and Ludwigshafen-Oppau	
21: Day	Two aerodromes and an oil refinery in North-west Germany; two ships sunk and an oil-storage depot set on fire in Willemsoord, Netherlands coast	
21: Night	Aircraft factories and storage buildings at Bremen, Kassel, Rothenburg, and Göttingen	
22: Day	Merville aerodrome	
23: Day	Aerodromes and railway junctions in Holland and Germany	
23: Night	Munition factories and railway centres in Mecklenburg, the Ruhr, and the Rhineland	2
24: Day	Aerodromes at Eindhoven, Amsterdam, and Rotterdam	
24: Night	Aerodromes at Amsterdam, De Kooy, Mülheim-Kassel, and the naval base at Den Helder; aircraft factories and other objectives at Dortmund, Kassel, and Bremen; communications on the Dortmund-Ems canal and rail centres between the Ruhr and the frontier of Holland	
25: Night	Military objectives at Arnhem, Borkum, Lingen, Hamm, Dorsten, Osterfeld, Mannheim, Bremen, Cologne, and Heligoland	
26: Day	Oil plant at Gelsenkirchen; rail sidings at Soest. A new German aerodrome at Bomoen, near Bergen, left in flames	
26: Night	German aerodromes at Dortmund, Bonn, Hangorf, and Langenhagen; oil refinery at Cologne; explosives factory at Ludwigshafen; rail centres at Osnabrück, Rheydt, Hamm, and Soest; Dutch seaplane bases, aerodromes, docks, lock-gates, and bridges	
27: Day	Ammunition store at Willemsoord; oil refineries at Hanover and Bremen; seaplane bases at Den Helder and Texel	
27: Night	Ruhr; Dortmund-Ems canal; Nyborg island, west of Copenhagen	
28: Night	Aerodromes in France, Germany, and Holland; chemical factories in the Rhineland; Ruhr	
29: Day	Abbeville aerodrome; Willemsoord harbour	

Date	Target	Aircraft Lost
June 29: Night	Aerodromes, railways, and a chemical factory situated in Northern and Western Germany, Holland, Belgium, and France	
30: Day	Aerodromes at Merville and Vignacourt.	
30: Night	Hamburg, Darmstadt, Osnabrück, Hamm, Wesel; aerodromes near Bremen, Dortmund, and on the island of Norderney	
July 1: Night	Military objectives, including aerodromes, in Northern and Western Germany. The battleship *Scharnhorst* under repair in a floating dock at Kiel received many direct hits; extensive fires were started at the naval base in Kiel	
2: Night	Docks, railways, and aerodromes in Germany, Denmark, and Belgium	
3: Day	Aerodromes, oil plants, and communications in Holland and Belgium	
3: Night	Aerodromes at Aachen, de Kooy, and Merville	
4: Day	Aerodromes and oil refineries in Germany, Holland, and Belgium	
4: Night	Naval bases at Wilhelmshaven, Emden, and Kiel; two aircraft factories; Brussels aerodrome	
5: Day	Deichshausen aircraft factory; two Dutch aerodromes	
5: Night	Naval bases at Kiel and Wilhelmshaven; Cuxhaven and Hamburg docks; railways at Cologne; two Dutch aerodromes	
6: Day	Aerodromes in France, Belgium, and Holland, and other objectives in Holland	
6: Night	Shipyards at Bremen and Kiel; armament depot at Emden; Brunsbüttel; seaplane bases at Norderney and Hornum	
7: Day	Aerodrome at Eschwege (near Kassel)	
7: Night	German railways; naval barracks and bases; aerodromes in the area Ludwigshaven—Osnabrück—North Frisian Islands; aerodromes at Rotterdam and Brussels; Ostend harbour	
8: Day	Dutch canals; Aalborg harbour; aerodromes at Douai and Soissons; patrol vessels off Danish coast	
8: Night	Naval bases at Kiel and Wilhelmshaven, setting two German destroyers or light cruisers on fire; aerodromes in Holland, oil refineries at Homburg, marshalling yards at Hamm	
9: Day	Objectives at Bergen—ammunition dump set on fire, ship and seaplane slipway damaged. Stavanger aerodrome against fierce opposition	9
9: Night	Wilhelmshaven and Bremen shipyards; Ruhr railways; aerodromes; oil refinery in Germany and Holland	
10: Day	Saint-Omer and Amiens aerodromes	5
11: Day	Concentration of barges, flying boats, and lock-gates at Boulogne in dawn attack; military objectives in France and Low Countries during daylight	
11: Night	Aerodromes in Holland; munition factories, blast furnaces, and other objectives in Germany	
12: Night	Naval bases at Emden and Kiel, damaging petroleum sheds, factory buildings, and docks	
13: Day	Brussels aerodrome; concentrations of barges on Bruges-Ostend canal; objectives at Monheim in the Rhineland	
13: Night	Hamburg; Bremen; Wilhelmshaven; Emden; the Ruhr; objectives in Holland and Belgium	

DATE	TARGET	AIR-CRAFT LOST
July 14: Day	Barge concentrations at Bruges and Saint-Pierre (north of Bruges) destroyed	
14: Night	Aircraft factories, stores, oil refineries, railway yards in Germany; aerodromes in Germany and Holland; oil-storage depot in Ghent	
15: Day	Aerodromes at Lisieux and Evreux (Normandy)	
15: Night	Aerodromes, oil refineries, railway yards, blast furnaces, harbours in North and Western Germany and Holland	
16: Day	Aerodromes in France; barges on river Lys near Armentières	
16: Night	Bad weather prevented raids	
17: Day	Barge concentrations in Holland and Belgium	
17: Night	Merville and S'Hertogenbosch aerodromes; oil installations at Ghent and Gelsenkirchen. Bad weather	
18: Day	Barges near Rotterdam; Boulogne harbour; Le Havre warehouses; Saint-Omer aerodrome	3
18: Night	Aircraft factories and depots at Bremen, Diepholz, Paderborn, Rotenburg (Thuringia); oil depots at Bremen and Hanover; aerodrome at Eschwege (near Kassel); railway marshalling yards at Hamm; ammunition trains near Soltau, east of Bremen; munition factories at Essen; naval base at Emden; Harlingen and Willemsoord harbours; supply depot at Ghent	
19: Night	Naval base at Emden; Harlingen harbour (Holland); aircraft factories at Wismar (Baltic coast), Wenzendorf (near Hamburg), and Bremen; aerodromes and seaplane bases on North-west German coast and North Holland; oil plants at Bremen and Gelsenkirchen; railways in the Ruhr	1
20: Day	Wireless station at Utsire Island, near Stavanger; aerodrome at Flushing	3
20: Night	Naval base at Wilhelmshaven; aircraft factories, aerodromes, and oil depots in Central Germany, the Ruhr, Holland, and Belgium; oil refineries at Hamburg and Bremen	
21: Day	Supply ship of 14,000 tons off Danish coast	5
21: Night	Oil depots; aircraft factories and aerodromes; docks, goods yards, barges in France, Belgium, Holland, and Germany. French airmen from General de Gaulle's Free French Force took part in these operations, flying in British aircraft with R.A.F. crews	
22: Night	Similar targets to night of July 21	3
23: Day	Patrol boats in Dunkirk harbour	
23: Night	Military objectives in Germany and Holland, including 12 aerodromes, harbours, docks, railways, oil tanks, anti-aircraft batteries, searchlights	1
24: Day	Leaflets dropped over France explaining terms of French Armistice with Germany and British action against the French fleet	
24: Night	Docks at Emden, Wilhelmshaven, Hamburg; aircraft factories at Wismar and Wenzendorf; seaplane bases at Borkum and Texel. Bad weather	
25: Night	Oil plants and depots at Bremen, Sterkrade, Bottrop, Kastrop-Rauxel, Dortmund, Kamen; aircraft factories and stores at Gotha, Kassel, Eschwege; 14 aerodromes in Germany and Holland; blast furnaces and goods yards in the Ruhr; railways in the Essen-Dortmund area; the Dortmund-Ems canal; docks and wharves at Hamburg. Weather conditions were unfavourable and opposition fierce	5

DATE	TARGET	AIR-CRAFT LOST
July 26: Day	Dortmund power-station; Amsterdam-Schiphol and Rotterdam Waalhaven aerodromes	
26: Night	Oil stores at Cherbourg, Saint-Nazaire, and Nantes. Weather bad	
27: Day	Supply ship in Norwegian waters and another off Dutch coast. Day and—	
27: Night	night attacks against oil depots at Amsterdam and Hamburg; eight aerodromes in Holland and Germany; docks and wharves at Wilhelmshaven and Bremen; barges at Stavoren (Friesland); the Nordsee Canal (Holland)	
28: Day	One bomber attacked Leeuwarden aerodrome, Holland, and drove down an enemy fighter during its return	
28: Night	Oil depots, docks, and railway yards in Northern and Western Germany; 17 aerodromes in Germany, Northern France, Belgium, Holland; oil tanks at Cherbourg	3
29: Day	Barges and vessels at Emden, Hamburg, and off Terschelling; oil refinery in the Ruhr; aerodromes in Germany and Holland; large supply ship damaged near Flushing	1
29: Night	Oil refineries, aerodromes, shipping, docks, rail and road communications in the Ruhr, North-west Germany, and the Low Countries. Visibility was so low that 24 bombers returned without dropping their bombs as they were unable to locate their targets	
30: Day	Railway sidings at Ostend; aircraft on Querqueville aerodrome (Cherbourg); hangars and aircraft on Saint-Inglevert aerodrome (Boulogne); gun emplacements on Norwegian coast; supply ship off Haugesund; Emden naval base	1
30: Night	Aerodromes at Duisburg, Antwerp, Courtrai; goods yard at Soest; oil refineries at Homburg and Monheim. Raids curtailed by bad weather	
31: Day	Military objectives in Germany; shipping off German and Dutch coasts; two fighters shot down by bombers	1
31: Night	Aerodromes in Germany and Holland; supply depots at Osnabrück; oil refineries at Misburg and Emmerich; shipping on Zuyder Zee	2
August 1: Day	Leeuwarden, Haamstede (Holland), Cherbourg aerodromes	3
1: Night	Krupp works, Essen; oil plants at Gelsenkirchen, Kamen, Homburg, Düsseldorf-Reisholz; supply depots at Hamm, Krefeld, Mannheim; aerodromes in North-west Germany	
2: Day	Hangars and grounded aircraft on aerodromes in France, Belgium, Holland	1
2: Night	Oil depots at Emden, Hamburg, Misburg, Salzbergen, Emmerich; aerodromes in Germany; one bomber forced down in sea	1
3: Day	Aerodromes in France and Holland — Abbeville, Schiphol, Haamstede	
3: Night	Naval base at Kiel; oil plants at Bottrop, Monheim, Gelsenkirchen; oil tanks at Rotterdam; aerodromes in Western Germany and Holland; railways in Westphalia, the Ruhr, the Rhineland	3
4: Night	Oil plant at Sterkrade (Ruhr); Krefeld aerodrome	

DATE	TARGET	AIRCRAFT LOST
August		
5: Night	Military objectives at Wismar, Kiel, Hamburg; Hamm railway marshalling yard; Schiphol and Borkum aerodromes	
6: Day	Le Bourget aerodrome, Paris raided by one bomber	
6: Night	Oil plant at Hamburg; supply depot at Schwerte; A.A. battery at Hamborn; factory at Mörs; aerodromes in Northern Germany and Holland. Weather bad	1
7: Day	Cherbourg and Haamstede aerodromes	
7: Night	Kiel dockyards; oil plant at Homburg; Hamm store depots; aerodromes in North-western Germany. Bad weather	
8: Day	Schiphol and Walkenburg (Holland) aerodromes	1
8: Night	Hamburg docks; supply depots at Hamm, Soest, Cologne; aerodromes in Germany	1
9: Day	Guernsey aerodrome (twice); seaplane base at Poulmic (near Brest)	
9: Night	Oil tanks at Flushing; munition factories at Ludwigshafen and Cologne; railways in the Ruhr; aerodromes in Germany, Belgium, Holland	
10: Day	Schiphol, Waalhaven, Flushing, Querqueville, Dinard, Caen, and Guernsey aerodromes	
10: Night	Hamburg docks; Wilhelmshaven naval base; Duisburg wharves; oil supplies at Frankfurt and Homburg; supply depots at Hamm and Soest; a power station and explosives factory at Cologne; a chemical works and blast furnace at Frankfurt; aerodromes in Germany and Holland	1
11: Day	Dinard, Caen, Guernsey aerodromes; seaplane slipway at Brest	
11: Night	Oil plants at Dortmund, Kastrop-Rauxel, Gelsenkirchen, Wanne-Eickel; oil depots at Cherbourg; other military objectives in the Ruhr	3
12: Night	Gotha airframe factory; 17 aerodromes; Borkum seaplane base; objectives in North-west Germany, Holland, France; Den Helder harbour (in co-operation with Fleet Air Arm). Aircraft encountered ice and cloud	4
13: Day	Waalhaven, Hingene, Cherbourg, Caen, Morlaix aerodromes; seaplane base at Brest; and other objectives	12
13: Night	Italian aircraft factories at Milan and Turin; Junkers aircraft factories at Dessau and Bernburg (north of Leipzig); munition factories at Lünen and Grevenbroich; military objectives in the Ruhr; 14 aerodromes in Germany, Holland, Belgium, France. One bomber returning from Italy came down in sea, but crew were saved	2
14: Day	Aerodromes in Northern France	
14: Night	Oil-refining plants at Blaye, Paulliac, Ambes (on Gironde estuary, France) set on fire; railway sidings and a power station at Cologne; aerodromes in Northern France, follow-up attacks	4
15: Night	Italian aircraft factories at Milan and Turin; blast furnace at Genoa; oil plants at Gelsenkirchen, Reisholz; supply depots at Hamm and Soest; wharves at Emmerich; munition factories at Lünen, Essen, Gladbach, Düsseldorf; Den Helder dock basin; aerodromes in Germany, France, Holland. No aircraft lost raiding Italy	3

DATE	TARGET	AIR-CRAFT LOST
August		
16: Night	Hydrogenation plant at Leuna; benzine refinery at Bohlen; Zeiss works at Jena; Messerschmitt aeroplane works at Augsburg, Junkers assembly plant at Bernburg, airframe factory at Frankfurt, aircraft stores at Kolleda; Ruhr railways; aerodromes inside and outside Germany	3
	One aircraft of Coastal Command damaged an anti-aircraft ship in Stavanger Fjord	
17: Night	Seaplanes and shipping at Boulogne (attack described at time as heavy, three tons of bombs having been dropped); German oil plants, munition factories, aircraft stores, and railways; 26 aerodromes in North-west France, Holland, Belgium	
18: Night	Italian aircraft factories in Milan and Turin; aluminium works at Bad Rheinfelden; chemical works at Waldshut (near German-Swiss frontier); Freiburg and Habsheim aerodromes; Boulogne harbour	
19: Day	Flushing aerodrome; anti-aircraft position near Amsterdam	1
19: Night	Kiel naval base; oil refinery at Hanover; power stations at Zschornewitz (north of Leipzig); communication points in Ruhr and North-west Germany; oil tanks at Ambes; 30 aerodromes inside and outside Germany	2
20: Day	Aerodromes in Western Europe; two German destroyers in North Sea, one damaged	
20: Night	No raids owing to bad weather	
21: Day	Aerodromes in Western Europe	
21: Night	Oil refineries and installations near Hanover and Magdeburg; rail centres north-west of Hanover, in the Ruhr and Rhineland; Hanover, Caen, Abbeville, Texel aerodromes. Weather adverse, opposition strong	1
22: Night	Synthetic-oil plant at Bottrop; power station near Cologne; high-explosive factory near Frankfurt; aircraft factory at Frankfurt; docks at Duisburg; rail communications in Ruhr and Rhineland; 22 aerodromes in Western Europe. One bomber forced-landed, crew killed	1
23: Day	Aerodromes and other military objectives in North-west Germany, Belgium, Holland, and North-west France, including coastal batteries on French coast	
23: Night	Aerodromes in France in South Brittany, Normandy, Flanders, Orléans, Paris; Eindhoven aerodrome (Holland); benzine refinery and storage plant at Sterkrade (Ruhr); Mannheim railway yard; gun positions on French coast	3
24: Night	Italian aircraft factories at Milan and Sesto Calende; military objectives in Frankfurt, Ludwigshafen, Stuttgart, and other towns; docks and aerodromes at Flushing; aerodrome buildings at Le Crotoy (Somme); gun positions near Cap Gris-Nez; aerodromes in Germany, Holland, Belgium, France	2
25: Day	Aerodromes in Holland and Belgium	
25: Night	Aerodromes in Northern France; military objectives in Berlin area; supply depots at Cologne, Hamm, and Schwerte; docks at Bremen; oil tanks at Cherbourg and Flushing; seaplanes and motor-torpedo-boats in Boulogne harbour	5
26: Day	Aerodromes	1

Date	Target	Aircraft Lost
August 26: Night	27 aerodromes in France, Belgium, Holland, and Germany. Main attack against Leuna synthetic-oil plant, near Leipzig; oil depot and aircraft factory at Frankfurt; military objectives at Cologne, Hamm, Griesheim, Hoechst, and Schwerte	1
	Factories and works at Turin and Sesto San Giovanni; six tons of bombs dropped on these targets	
27: Night	Kiel and Wilhelmshaven docks; transformer station near Frankfurt; Messerschmitt aircraft factory at Augsburg; oil tanks and supply depots at Mannheim; several German aerodromes; oil tanks near Cherbourg, Brest, and Bordeaux	1
	Fiat works at Turin; Marelli magneto factory at Sesto San Giovanni, Italy	
28: Night	Targets in Berlin area; airframe factory at Leipzig; Junkers works, Dessau; oil plants at Reisholz, Dortmund, Nordenheim; several aerodromes in Germany, Holland, and France. (Direct hit exploded large vessel lying in the canal at Rathenow, west of Berlin)	
29: Day	Aerodromes in Holland; shipping off Dutch coast	
29: Night	Krupp works, Essen; oil refineries and plants at Gelsenkirchen, Bottrop, Saint-Nazaire; power stations at Duisburg and Reisholz; goods yards at Hamm and Soest; military objectives in Ruhr; aerodromes in France, Belgium, Holland, and Germany	3
30: Night	Military objectives in Berlin area; oil-supply depots at Gelsenkirchen, Magdeburg, Cherbourg; goods yards at Hamm and Soest; gun emplacements at Cap Gris-Nez; shipping at Emden; aerodromes in Holland and Germany	2
	Fleet Air Arm bombed quays and rail sidings at Boulogne	
31: Night	Aero-engine factories and night-lighting installations at Berlin; oil tanks near Rotterdam; oil plants at Cologne, Magdeburg; goods yards, Hamm, Hanover, Osnabrück, Soest; shipping at Emden; industrial targets and aerodromes	2
	Fleet Air Arm bombed oil-storage tanks at Rotterdam	
September 1: Day	Aerodromes in Holland	
1: Night	Aircraft factories at Munich, Stuttgart; oil plants at Hanover, Ludwigshafen, Nordenheim; munition factories at Bitterfeld, Leipzig; power station at Kassel; goods yards Mannheim, Soest; shipping at Emden; submarine and motor-torpedo-boat base at Lorient; enemy aerodromes. One aircraft crashed when landing.	
	Fiat works at Turin, and Marelli magneto works at Sesto San Giovanni, Italy	
2: Day	Oil tanks, Flushing; Ostend Harbour; supply ships off Dutch and Norwegian coasts	1
2: Night	Dynamite works, Schlebusch (N.E. of Cologne); Bayer explosive works near Cologne; Bosch ignition factory, Stuttgart; oil installations at Ludwigshafen, Frankfurt; Dortmund-Ems canal; Lorient port; gun emplacements at Cap Gris-Nez	2
	Power-station, Genoa; and railway junction near Genoa	

DATE	TARGET	AIR-CRAFT LOST
September		
3: Night	Power stations, lighting installations, armament factory in Berlin area; oil tanks, Magdeburg; blast furnace, Merzig; goods yards, Hamm, Soest; military objectives in the forests of the Harz Mountains west of Berlin and the Grunewald forests north of Berlin; German, Dutch, and Pas de Calais aerodromes; barges concentrated in the Beveland canal and at Terneuzen in Scheldt estuary; Ostend docks. Fleet Air Arm co-operated in Dutch coastal operations	
4: Night	Power station and aircraft factory in Berlin; synthetic-oil plant, Stettin; oil tanks, Magdeburg; goods yard south of Bremen; oil tanks, Cherbourg; Terneuzen docks; military objectives in the Harz Mountains, the Thuringian forests, and the Black Forest; aerodromes in France and Belgium. One of our aircraft crashed when landing on its return	2
5: Night	Stettin oil plant; oil tanks, Kiel; oil refineries at Hamburg and Regensburg; objectives in Harz Mountains and Black Forest; Emden docks; goods yards at Hamm and Soest; aerodromes in Holland and Germany; Calais harbour; gun positions at Cap Griz-Nez; Boulogne harbour (in conjunction with Fleet Air Arm) Fiat aero-engine works, Turin	3
6: Night	Power station, oil installations, railway yards in Berlin area; targets in forests of South-west Germany; Ruhr and Rhineland aerodromes, rail communications, and other military objectives; aerodromes at Venlo, Calais, Dunkirk Boulogne harbour (in conjunction with Fleet Air Arm)	2
7: Night	Krupp works, Essen; war factories at Emden and Zweibrücken; oil plant Gelsenkirchen; rail depots at Mannheim, Ehrang, Hamm; war stores in Black Forest fired; shipping in Boulogne, Calais, Dunkirk; gun emplacements and searchlight near Cap Gris-Nez; Brussels, Eindhoven, Colmar, Gilze-Rijen, Krefeld, Querqueville, Soesterburg, Wesel aerodromes	
8: Day	Shipping in Boulogne, Dunkirk, and North Sea	5
8: Night	Ship and barge concentrations, Hamburg, Boulogne, Bremen, Calais, Emden, Ostend; oil tanks; ammunition dumps. Weather bad	8
9: Night	Lighting installations, Berlin area; shipyards at Bremen and Hamburg; Kiel, Wilhelmshaven, and Wismar docks; goods yards Brussels, Krefeld; rail communications; factories Barnsdorf, Essen; aerodromes; gun emplacements at Cap Gris-Nez; ship and barge concentrations Boulogne, Calais, Ostend	3 [1]
10: Night	Potsdam railway station, Berlin; Bremen docks and Focke-Wulf airframe factory; Wilhelmshaven naval barracks; rail targets Brussels, Duisburg; gun emplacements Cap Gris-Nez; docks, harbours, and barge concentrations on French, Belgian, and Dutch coasts; aerodromes in Europe. Weather bad	4
11: Day	Supply ship sunk off Dunkirk; supply ship fired, and another damaged off Cap Gris-Nez; German motor-torpedo-boats machine-gunned; engagement with force of German fighters and bombers, three destroyed, others damaged. (In conjunction with Fleet Air Arm)	3

[1] One crew rescued next day.

DATE	TARGET	AIRCRAFT LOST
September 11: Night	Rail stations, goods yards, and an aerodrome, at Berlin; Bremen, Hamburg, Wilhelmshaven docks and shipyards; Coblenz, Cologne, Ehrang, Hamm, Mannheim goods yards; Namur rail junction; Mannheim oil plant; explosives factory, Frankfurt; barge concentrations, shipping and docks Boulogne, Calais, Flushing, Ostend; aerodromes in Germany and Holland	
12: Day	Shipping off Le Havre, a tanker and a supply ship hit	3
12: Night	Emden oil stores, shipping, docks; Brussels, Ehrang, Hamm, Osnabrück, Schwerte rail centres; Norderney seaplane base; aerodromes	
13: Day	Barges near Rotterdam; tanker convoy off Zeebrugge, one ship exploded, after a direct hit	
13: Night	Barge concentrations and dock installations at Antwerp, Boulogne, Calais, Dunkirk, Ostend. Heavy destruction by fire and explosion	} 2
14: Night	Antwerp, Boulogne, Calais, Dunkirk, Flushing, Ostend docks, barges, ships; supply depots at Aachen, Brussels, Hamm, Krefeld, Mannheim, Osnabrück; rail communications at Ahaus, Husten, Rheine, Sundern, Westhofen; gun emplacements at Cap Gris-Nez; aerodromes. Bad weather	
15: Night	Military objectives in Berlin; Antwerp, Boulogne, Calais, Dunkirk, Flushing, Hamburg, Ostend, Wilhelmshaven docks, ports, ships, barges, war supplies; Hamm, Krefeld, Osnabrück, Soest rail centres; Hamburg goods yard; Rheine rail junction; Le Havre ships and docks; German cruiser hit off Terschelling; a tanker and a supply ship in the Elbe estuary damaged; a supply ship sunk off Ijmuiden; two supply ships in convoy off Dutch coast sunk and others damaged	
16: Day	Calais, Dunkirk, Veere (Walcheren) harbours, ships, barges; convoys of barges off Zeebrugge and Ostend; Haamstede aerodrome (Schouven island)	
16: Night	Operations suspended because weather made accurate bombing impossible	
17: Day	Ostend port; shipping at Zeebrugge; convoy and barges off Dutch coast; Ijmuiden aerodrome	
17: Night	Antwerp, Boulogne, Calais, Dunkirk, Flushing, Hamburg, Terneuzen, Zeebrugge; rail centres Brussels, Ehrang, Hamm, Krefeld, Osnabrück, Soest; Stockum (near Cologne) goods yard; gun emplacements, Cap Gris-Nez; Cherbourg—two supply ships sunk and fires started	
18: Night	Invasion bases at Antwerp, Boulogne, Calais, Dieppe, Dunkirk, Le Havre, Ostend, Zeebrugge; rail targets at Brussels, Ehrang, Hamm, Mannheim, Osnabrück; Cherbourg; shipping off Dutch coast; De Kooy (Holland) aerodrome; convoy off Borkum (direct hit on destroyer)	2
19: Night	Dortmund-Ems canal aqueduct north of Münster; Dunkirk harbour; Flushing harbour and Verbreed canal; Ostend docks and warehouses; canal between Veere and Middelburg (Holland); Moselle bridge near Trier; rail and goods yards, Coblenz, Ehrang, Mannheim, Neckarau; Münster-Hansdorf and Bergen-op-Zoom aerodromes. Through heavy rainstorms	7

DATE	TARGET	AIR-CRAFT LOST
September 20: Night	Antwerp, Boulogne, Calais, Dunkirk, Flushing, Ostend, Zeebrugge harbours and docks; rail targets at Brussels, Ehrang, Hamm, Krefeld, Mannheim, Osnabrück, Soest; Dortmund-Ems canal rail communications near Duisburg; a supply train; munition factory near Maastricht; two supply ships hit; aerodromes	2
21: Day	Shallow-draught shipping at Antwerp, Calais-Saint-Omer canal, Flushing, Ostend, Rotterdam, Terneuzen; convoy of 12 merchant vessels near Boulogne; a large supply ship south of Borkum struck by incendiaries; small ship hit off Ameland island (Holland)	
21: Night	Ships, barges, docks at Boulogne, Calais, Dunkirk, Ostend	
22: Night	Antwerp, Brest, Calais, Dunkirk, Flushing, Le Havre, Ostend, Zeebrugge; aluminium works at Lauta, north-east of Dresden, and railways in same area, one supply train hit near Dresden	
23: Night	Berlin area—including Rangsdorf rail station, several goods yards, including Grunewald, west tower of Wilmersdorf power station, Danzigerstrasse and Neukölln gasworks, Brandenburg motor works and other factories in Charlottenburg and Spandau; air-craft factory, Wismar; shipyards and docks, Bremen, Cuxhaven, Hamburg, Wismar; Hanover and Münster goods yards; rail communications in North Germany; Kiel canal lock-gates; the Channel ports; several aerodromes	
24: Day	Minesweepers in Channel, two hit, a third damaged, and one enemy aircraft destroyed	1
24: Night	Berlin area—military objectives; Finkenheerd power station (near Frankfurt-on-Oder); Brussels and Hamm goods yards; Magdeburg rail communications; gun emplacements, Cap Gris-Nez; Boulogne, Calais, Cherbourg, Le Havre, Ostend; convoy off Terschelling, one vessel left sinking	2
25: Night	Antwerp, Boulogne, Calais, Dunkirk, Flushing, Ostend; Brest oil tanks; Berlin power stations, rail communications, Tempelhof aerodrome; Ehrang, Hamm, Hanover, Mannheim, Osnabrück goods yards; Kiel docks	
26: Night	Boulogne, Calais, Le Havre, Ostend; Kiel; military objectives in North-west Germany	1
27: Night	Boulogne, Calais, Dunkirk, Le Havre, Lorient; rail yards at Hamm and Mannheim; munition factory at Düsseldorf	
28: Night	Berlin area—power stations and A.A. gun positions; Wilhelmshaven naval base; munition works, Hanau (near Frankfurt-on-Main); rail centres and aerodromes in North Germany; Boulogne, Calais, Dunkirk, Fécamp, Lorient ports; Cap Gris-Nez gun emplacements	
29: Night	Oil refineries at Hanover and Magdeburg; aluminium works, Bitterfeld; gasworks, Stuttgart; Cologne and Osnabrück goods yards; aerodromes in Belgium, Holland, Germany; mine-laying harbours and estuaries	

Date	Target	Aircraft Lost.
September 30: Night	Berlin area—military objectives; oil refineries at Leuna and Hanover; munition factory near Magdeburg; aircraft factory at Rotenburg; rail communications and goods yards at Bremen, Brussels, Ehrang, Mannheim, Osnabrück; Amsterdam, Boulogne, Calais, Cuxhaven, Dunkirk, Le Havre, and Ostend docks; several aerodromes; in conjunction with Fleet Air Arm, docks and petrol stores at Rotterdam and Vlaadringen, and oil dump at Haamstede aerodrome (Holland)	5
October 1: Night	Berlin—munition factory; Duisburg and Cologne—power station; oil plants at Cologne, Gelsenkirchen, Holten, Sterkrade; goods yards, Coblenz, Gremberg, Hamm, Soest, Westerholt; Holten and Sterkrade rail junctions; aircraft factory, Amsterdam; several aerodromes; gun emplacements, Cap Gris-Nez; Boulogne, Calais, Dunkirk, Flushing, Le Havre, Rotterdam	3
2: Night	Hamburg and Wilhelmshaven docks; Amsterdam, Antwerp, Calais, Cherbourg, Flushing, Ostend, Rotterdam, Ushant ports and shipping; oil plants, Bottrop, Hamburg, Stettin; Krupp works, Essen; goods yards, Cologne; rail junction near Hamm; several aerodromes. Thick cloud, poor visibility	2
3: Day	Shipping off Dunkirk; Rotterdam; barge concentrations, Heusden, river Maas; industrial plant near Wesel; rail communications and oil-storage depots near Cherbourg. Weather unfavourable	
3: Night	Operations cancelled on account of weather	
4	Operations cancelled on account of weather	
5: Night	Oil plant, Gelsenkirchen; Krupps works, Essen; goods yards, Cologne, Hamm, Osnabrück; shipping at Rotterdam; shipping and warehouses, Brest; barge and motor-transport concentrations Gravelines; mine-laying	3
6: Day	Boulogne, Calais, Ostend ports; ship and barge concentrations, Den Helder, Dordrecht, Enkhuizen, Harlingen, Stavoren; Diepholz aerodrome (West Germany); one enemy fighter shot down; two armed merchant vessels off Dutch coast, when one aircraft lost	1
6: Night	Operations cancelled on account unfavourable weather	
7: Day	Concentrations of shipping on Dutch coast and at Le Havre; an enemy fighter shot down into Channel	
7: Night	Berlin military objectives—three main power stations, Tempelhof goods yard, several industrial plants; Fokker aircraft works, Amsterdam; Wilhelmshaven naval docks; Gremberg, Hamm, Mannheim, Soest goods yards; Boulogne, Cherbourg, Dieppe, Dunkirk, Gravelines, Lorient, Ostend, Rotterdam, Zeebrugge ports and shipping; gun emplacements, Cap Gris-Nez; several aerodromes	1
8: Day	Boulogne and Lorient ports	
8: Night	Bremen and Wilhelmshaven naval bases; oil refineries, Gelsenkirchen, Hamburg; power station, Kiel, Krupps works, Essen; metal works, Hanau; Fokker aircraft works, Amsterdam; goods yards, Mannheim, Nuremberg; Channel ports; several aerodromes	

Date	Target	Aircraft Lost
October 9: Day	Oil plant, Hamburg; barges and bridges at canal junction south of Helder (Holland); rail sidings near Hamburg and Warendorf; Texel aerodrome; shipping, Le Havre	1
9: Night	Oil plant and munitions factory, Cologne; aluminium works, Grevenbroich; Krupps works, Essen; power station, Reisholz; railways and goods yards, Brussels, Cologne, Düsseldorf, Gremberg, Königshofen, Wesel; Channel ports from Amsterdam to Le Havre; several aerodromes; Brest, where German destroyers were hit (in conjunction with Fleet Air Arm).	1
10: Night	Oil supplies at Cologne, Gelsenkirchen, Hamburg, Hanover, Leuna, Magdeburg, Reisholz; warships at Wilhelmshaven; Krupps shipyards, Kiel; shipping in Amsterdam, Boulogne, Brest, Calais, Flushing, Le Havre; Den Helder docks; Cherbourg coastal batteries; Fokker aircraft works, Amsterdam; factories at Bottrop; blast furnace, Oberhausen; railways, Gelsenkirchen, Hamm, Soest; De Kooy, Kloppenburg (south-west of Bremen), and Osthein (Bavaria) aerodromes; Norderney seaplane base; two German aircraft destroyed; co-operation in naval bombardment of shipping and port of Cherbourg	
11: Night	Oil plants, factories, docks at Bremerhaven, Hamburg, Kiel, Wesermünde, Wilhelmshaven; Channel ports from Rotterdam to Cherbourg; several aerodromes; gun emplacements, Cap Gris-Nez. Very unfavourable weather	
12: Day	Convoy off Norway, one supply ship bombed, others machine-gunned	
12: Night	Berlin—a power station, a gasworks, an important goods yard; aluminium works, Heringen; Krupps works, Essen; metal works, Bitterfeld; power station, Waldeck; blast furnace, Torgau; oil plants, Cologne and Hanover; goods yards, Cologne, Hamm; Dortmund-Ems canal aqueduct; Fokker aircraft works, Amsterdam; Channel ports; power station, Lorient; gun emplacements, Cap Griz-Nez; several aerodromes	
13: Night	Kiel and Wilhelmshaven naval bases; Krupps works, Essen; oil plants, Duisburg and Gelsenkirchen; Channel ports from Ostend to Le Havre; several aerodromes, A.A. batteries, searchlight positions. Bad weather	1
14: Night	Berlin—military objectives; oil plants at Bohlem, Magdeburg, Misburg, Rotha, Stettin; Emden, Den Helder, Hamburg, and Le Havre docks; rail communications at Göttingen, Hanover, Lingen; several factories; several aerodromes. Bad weather prevented location of some primary targets	4
15: Night	Hamburg and Kiel; oil plants at Gelsenkirchen, Magdeburg, Salzbergen; goods yards at Hamm, Krefeld, Schwerte, Soest; rail junctions at Halle and Nordhausen; Channel port; gun emplacements, Cap Gris-Nez (bad weather); munition factories, aircraft factories, and power stations were bombed as alternative targets by some aircraft	
16: Night	Bremen, Cuxhaven, Hamburg, Kiel docks; synthetic-oil plant at Leuna; munition factories and a power station in Saxony. Weather bad	5

DATE	TARGET	AIRCRAFT LOST
October		
17: Day	Power station, Brest. German destroyers off Brest, result unknown	
17: Night	Operations cancelled on account of weather	
18: Night	Hamburg and Kiel shipyards; aluminium works at Lünen; a factory at Dortmund; wharves at Duisburg; rail and goods yards at Dortmund, Osnabrück, Schwerte. Operations curtailed on account of bad weather	
19: Night	Rail yards at Osnabrück; aerodrome in North Holland. Operations curtailed on account of bad weather	
20: Day	A Hudson of Coastal Command shot down one German aircraft in North Sea	
20: Night	Berlin—military objectives; Hamburg and Wilhelmshaven naval docks, where a large warship was hit; oil refineries, Cologne and Gelsenkirchen; aluminium works, Cologne and Grevenbroich; Krupps works, Essen; objectives in Ruhr; Antwerp, Flushing, and Rotterdam ports; several aerodromes	
	Italy—industrial plants, Milan, Turin; steel works at Aosta	1
21: Day	Boulogne, Gravelines, merchant ship hit; convoy off French coast bombed	
21: Night	Hamburg docks; synthetic-oil plant, Reisholz; goods yard, Düsseldorf; Stade aerodrome. Weather bad	1
22: Day	Direct bomb-hit on (nearly) 2000-ton German cargo ship three miles off Hook of Holland	
22: Night	Operations cancelled on account of weather	
23: Day	Two supply ships torpedoed in North Sea and another machine-gunned	
23: Night	Berlin—military objectives; Emden—railways, wharves, warehouses; oil plants, Hanover and Magdeburg; goods yards east of Berlin, near Hanover, and at Frankfort; industrial plants and rail junctions in Northern and Western Germany; docks at Hook of Holland; several aerodromes	1
24: Night	Berlin area—military objectives; oil plants, Gelsenkirchen, Hamburg, Hanover; docks and shipping at Bremerhaven, Cuxhaven, Hamburg, Le Havre, Lorient, Rotterdam, Wilhelmshaven; power station, Hamburg; rail communications and goods yards, Bottrop, Duisburg, Emmerich, Hamm, Münster; Dunkirk, Flushing, Ostend ports; several aerodromes	1
25: Night	Naval dockyard at Baltic entrance to Kiel canal; oil refineries and storage plant at Hamburg and Hanover; docks and shipping at Bremen, Den Helder, Hamburg; Ostend; industrial plants near Kassel and Osnabrück; Schiphol–Amsterdam, Brussels–Evere, Cuxhaven, and Haamstede aerodromes; batteries near Cap Gris-Nez. (Weather conditions difficult.) Power-station, Brest	1
26: Day	R.A.F. torpedo attack on shipping off Norway coast sank one supply vessel; one German fighter shot down. One German floatplane shot down in North Sea by R.A.F. bomber	
26: Night	Berlin—aircraft works, power station, goods yard; oil plants, Cologne, Leuna, Stettin; railways, Bremen, Brussels, Dortmund; naval docks, Bremen, Cuxhaven, Hamburg, Antwerp and Flushing ports; several aerodromes. Weather bad	2
27: Day	Shipping and convoys off French and Dutch coasts	1

DATE	TARGET	AIR-CRAFT LOST
October 27: Night	Oil refineries and plants at Gelsenkirchen, Hamburg, Hanover, Magdeburg, Ostermoor; goods yards, Hamm, Krefeld, Mannheim; Hamburg and Wilhelmshaven docks; Antwerp, Flushing, Lorient, Ostend ports; 14 aerodromes	1
	Czechoslovakia—Skoda armament works, Pilsen	
28: Night	Bremen, Cuxhaven, Emden, Hamburg, Kiel, Wilhelmshaven; shipping in Boulogne; oil plants at Cologne, Hamburg, Homburg; rail centres, Coblenz, Cologne, Krefeld, Mannheim; 19 aerodromes; numerous A.A. batteries	1
29: Night	Berlin (attacked in snowstorm); oil plants at Homburg, Magdeburg, Sterkrade; shipyards, docks, and ports at Den Helder, Flushing, Bremen, Ijmuiden, Ostend, Wilhelmshaven; rail communications, aerodromes, searchlights, A.A. batteries. Weather forced some bombers to attack alternative targets	2
30: Day	Cherbourg harbour; shipping off French coast	
30: Night	Emden naval base; Antwerp and Flushing ports. Operations restricted by rough weather	
31: Day	Merchant ship bombed off Norway coast; one Coastal Command aircraft lost	1
31: Night	Operations against Germany cancelled on account of weather	
	Italy—oil tanks and military objectives at Naples	
November 1: Night	Berlin—several main railway stations and goods yards damaged in heaviest raid on Berlin yet made; oil plants at Gelsenkirchen, Magdeburg; factory near Gelsenkirchen; blast furnace in Krupps works, Essen; Osnabrück rail junction; gun emplacements, Cap Gris-Nez; 15 aerodromes where aircraft about to take off to attack Britain were seen to be damaged.	2
2: Night	Operations cancelled on account of weather	
3: Day	Flushing port; Soesterberg aerodrome	2
3: Night	Germany—Kiel } (Weather bad) Italy—Naples }	
4: Night	Docks and shipping, Boulogne, Le Havre, Ostend. Operations hampered by bad weather	
	Italy—Naples, military objectives	
5: Day	One Coastal Command aircraft, attacked by two fighters, shot one down into the sea	
5: Night	Shipbuilding yards at Bremen and Bremerhaven; petroleum sheds at Emden; power station, Hamburg; submarine-building yards, Vegesack, near Bremen; Antwerp, Boulogne, Calais, Dunkirk, Flushing ports; several aerodromes	
6: Day	Oil refineries at Salzbergen; shipping in Cuxhaven; Haamstede aerodrome; motor vessels in convoy off Den Helder	
6: Night	Berlin area—factory at Spandau and rail junction northwest of city; synthetic-oil plants, Homburg, Leuna; Duisburg docks; Düsseldorf—factories; rail yards and junctions near Cologne, at Halle, near Pretsche (on the Elbe); gun emplacements, Cap Gris-Nez	
7: Night	Krupps works, Essen (heavy attack); synthetic oil plant, Cologne; blast furnaces at Düsseldorf and Oberhausen; docks on Dortmund-Ems canal; Duisburg docks; shipping in Dunkirk; Lorient submarine base; many aerodromes	

Date	Target	Aircraft Lost
November 8: Night	Munich—railway stations and goods yards: oil refineries, Gelsenkirchen, Frankfurt; aircraft factories, Amsterdam, Nuremberg; goods yards, Duisburg-Ruhrort, Hamm, Hook of Holland, Osnabrück, Soest; rail communications, Le Havre, Mainz, Mors, Saarbrücken, Stuttgart; submarine base, Lorient; 18 aerodromes	
	Italy—aircraft factory, Turin; Pirelli magneto works, Milan	
9: Night	Boulogne and Calais docks; aerodromes used in raiding Britain; in conjunction with Fleet Air Arm, submarine base at Lorient	
10: Day	Shipping in Boulogne and Calais harbours	
10: Night	Oil plants, Gelsenkirchen, Bremen, Ruhrland; Krupps works, Essen; Fokker works, Amsterdam; factories at Dresden and Mannheim; docks and shipping, Cherbourg, Duisburg, Dunkirk, Flushing, Kiel, Le Havre, Lorient; rail junctions Danzig, Dresden, Dessau, Mannheim, Münster; 14 aerodromes	} 5
11: Day	Lorient; Brest, Saint-Brieuc, and Saint-Malo aerodromes	
11: Night	Operations cancelled on account of weather	
12: Night	Oil plants, Cologne, Duisburg, Gelsenkirchen; rail centres near Cologne and in the Ruhr; Dunkirk and Flushing docks; Lorient; several aerodromes	1
13: Night	Berlin—railway stations and goods yards; railway yards at Düsseldorf and Rheine; oil refineries at Cologne, Gelsenkirchen, Hanover, Leuna; factories, Cologne, Geldern, Lintorf; docks at Bremerhaven, Calais, Dortmund, Duisburg, Wilhelmshaven; Haamstede, Kreuzbruch (north of Berlin), Lübeck, Norderney aerodromes. Weather bad	2
14: Night	Berlin—terminal railway stations and their goods yards; oil refinery, Hamburg; aeroplane factory, Bremen; harbours and shipping in ports from Stavanger (Norway) to Lorient; 26 aerodromes	10
15: Day	Coastal objectives from Norway to France; military stores and buildings at Rennes; aerodromes	} 2
15: Night	Hamburg—railways, shipyards, docks, public utility services; Kiel dockyards; Calais and Ostend ports; two German aircraft shot down	
16: Day	Oil plants, Bremen and Cologne; Dortmund-Ems canal	
16: Night	Hamburg—railway yards, electricity works, industrial establishments, oil refineries: Blohm und Voss shipyards; Antwerp and Dunkirk docks; several aerodromes	
17: Night	Oil refineries, Gelsenkirchen; industrial targets in Ruhr; rail and river communications in Western Germany; Lorient naval base; aerodromes in occupied territory	3
18: Night	Synthetic oil plant, Leuna—concentrated attack	
19: Night	Berlin—military objectives; shipyards and docks, Bremerhaven, Hamburg, Kiel; synthetic oil plants, Gelsenkirchen, Hamburg; power station, Hamborn; rail junctions and yards at Aurich, Bremen, Duisburg; Lorient naval base; Harfleur harbour	} 3
	Czechoslovakia—Skoda armament works, Pilsen	
20: Night	Duisburg-Ruhrort—inland port, extensively damaged; Cherbourg, Dunkirk, Lorient, Ostend ports; several aerodromes	1
21: Night	Operations cancelled owing to weather	
22: Day	Stavanger, Schiphol-Amsterdam, and Leeuwaarden (Holland) aerodromes; factory at Solingen (Ruhr)	

DATE	TARGET	AIR-CRAFT LOST
November		
22: Night	Merinac-Bordeaux aerodrome (enemy air base against Atlantic shipping); Cherbourg, Flushing, Le Havre, Lorient, Ostend ports; oil-storage tanks, Dortmund and Wanne-Eickel; goods yards, Dortmund and Duisburg-Ruhrort	
23: Day	Vikero (Norway) wireless station	
23: Night	Berlin—rail stations and goods yards; Leipzig—rail stations and goods yards; objectives in Duisburg-Ruhrort; Cologne—canal wharves; Krupps works, Essen; Dortmund rail sidings; oil tanks at Dortmund and Wanne-Eickel; a factory at Kastrop-Rauxel; Lorient submarine base; a power station at Brest; Boulogne harbour; several aerodromes	2
	Italy—military objectives in Turin	
24: Day	Kristiansand (Norway) aerodrome; Hook of Holland harbour; in conjunction with Fleet Air Arm, Boulogne port	
24: Night	Hamburg (main target); Altona gasworks; chemical factory, Harburg-Wilhelmsburg; Wilhelmshaven and Den Helder docks; Boulogne port; A.A. and search-light batteries; several aerodromes	1
25: Night	Kiel and Wilhelmshaven naval bases; Hamburg and Willemsoord docks; De Mok seaplane base; several aerodromes	1
26: Night	Cologne—armament factories and other military objectives; Berlin—rail targets; Antwerp, Boulogne, Calais, Flushing, Lorient, Rotterdam docks and shipping; shipping off Dutch coast; oil stores, Ghent; several aerodromes	5
	Italy—Turin Royal Arsenal	
27: Day	Supply ship and tanker off Frisian Islands	
27: Night	Cologne (main target); Antwerp, Boulogne, Le Havre docks	1
28: Night	Düsseldorf and Mannheim industrial areas (main target); Stettin—naval yards and oil plant: Antwerp, Boulogne, Cuxhaven, Le Havre ports and docks; military store-houses near Mainz; West German rail communications; Coblenz and Eindhoven aerodrome	2
29: Day	A Coastal Command aircraft sank a ship of 8000 tons sailing under escort off the Dutch coast	
29: Night	Cologne; Bremen naval shipyards (two main targets); Boulogne and Le Havre subsidiary targets; Lorient naval base before daylight of night 29/30	
30: Night	Operations cancelled owing to weather	
December		
1: Day	Lorient submarine base and naval docks (dawn attack); Esbjerg (Denmark) gasworks; Kristiansand (Norway) military camp; Brest dry docks, jetty, and power station (evening attack)	
1: Night	Wilhelmshaven naval shipyards. Weather bad	
2: Day	Supply ship off Norway coast	
2: Night	Shipping off Norway coast; wharves at Feje Island (40 miles north-west of Bergen); Lorient submarine base	
3: Day	Aerodromes in Northern France	
3: Night	Ludwigshaven and Mannheim; Essen—blast furnace; Dunkirk port. Attacks reduced by bad weather	1
4: Night	Düsseldorf; Antwerp and Calais ports; several aero-dromes, gun positions, searchlights	1
	Italy—industrial targets at Turin	
5: Day	Eindhoven electro-chemical factory; Haamstede and Rotterdam aerodromes; Lorient submarine base	
5: Night	Operations cancelled owing to weather	

APPENDIX III

FIGHTER COMMAND: PRE-WAR FIGHTER SQUADRONS

No. 11 Group			No. 12 Group		
Squadron No.	*Pre-war Station*	*Type of Aircraft*	*Squadron No.*	*Pre-war Station*	*Type of Aircraft*
1	Tangmere, Sussex	Hurricane	19	Duxford, Cambridge	Spitfire
3	Kenley, Surrey	Hurricane	23	Wittering, Northants	
17	Kenley, Surrey	Hurricane	41	Catterick, Yorks	Spitfire
25	Hawkinge, Kent	Blenheim	46	Digby, Lincoln	Hurricane
29	Debden, Essex		64	Church Fenton, Yorks	
32	Biggin Hill, Kent		66	Duxford, Cambridge	
43	Tangmere, Sussex	Hurricane	72	Church Fenton, Yorks	
54	Hornchurch, Essex	Spitfire	73	Digby, Lincoln	Hurricane
56	North Weald, Essex	Hurricane	213	Wittering, Northants	Hurricane
65	Hornchurch, Essex		504	Hucknall, Notts	Hurricane
74	Hornchurch, Essex	Spitfire	602	Abbotsinch, Renfrew	Spitfire
79	Biggin Hill, Kent	Hurricane	603	Turnhouse, Edinburgh	Spitfire
85	Debden, Essex	Hurricane	607	Usworth, Durham	Hurricane
87	Debden, Essex	Hurricane	608	Thornaby, Yorks	
111	Northolt, Mdx	Hurricane	609	Yeadon, Yorks	Spitfire
151	North Weald, Essex		610	Hooton Park, Cheshire	
501	Filton, Glos	Hurricane	611	Speke, Liverpool	Hurricane
600	Hendon, London		616	Doncaster, Yorks	
601	Hendon, London	Blenheim and Hurricane			
604	Hendon, London				
605	Castle Bromwich, Birmingham	Hurricane			
615	Kenley, Surrey	Hurricane			

Later Squadrons

No. 92	Hurricane and Spitfire	
145	Hurricane	
152		
229	Hurricane	
234		
238	Hurricane	
242	Hurricane	(Canadian personnel)
249		
253		
257	Hurricane	
261		
302	Hurricane	(Polish personnel)
303	Hurricane	(Polish personnel)
310	Hurricane	(Czech personnel)
1	R.C.A.F.	(Canadian personnel with Canadian-built Hurricane)
421	Flight	

APPENDIX IV

GERMAN AND BRITISH AIRCRAFT LOSSES IN THE BATTLE OF BRITAIN, AND OTHER STATISTICS

| | LUFTWAFFE | | | | | ROYAL AIR FORCE | |
| | NIGHT | | DAY | | | | |
DATE	A.A.	R.A.F.	A.A.	R.A.F.	TOTAL	AIRCRAFT	PILOTS
June 1940							
18	...	7	...	...	7	...	...
19	...	3	...	...	3	...	...
25	1½	3½	...	3 ¹	8	...	...
26	...	3	...	...	3	...	...
29	...	...	...	1	1	...	...
30	...	...	...	5 ¹	5	...	...
MONTHLY TOTAL	1½	16½	...	9	27	...	...
July 1940							
1	...	...	...	3	3	...	...
3	...	...	...	7	7	...	...
4	...	...	...	2	2	...	...
5	...	...	...	1	1	...	...
6	...	...	...	2	2	...	...
7	...	...	...	7	7	3	3
8	...	...	...	8	8	...	...
9	...	...	1	8	9	...	...
10	...	...	...	14	14	2	1
11	...	...	3	20	23	4	2
12	...	...	1	10 ²	11	2	2
13	...	...	...	12	12	1	1
14	...	...	1	6	7	1	1
16	...	...	...	3	3	...	...
18	...	...	...	1	1	...	...
19	...	...	3	9	12	5	5
20	...	1	3	17	21	2	1
21	...	...	...	3 ³	3	...	...
22	...	...	...	1	1	...	...
23	...	1	...	1	2	...	...
24	...	...	2	10	12	2	1
25	...	...	1	27	28	5	3
26	...	1	...	3	4	...	...
27	...	...	...	4	4	2	2
28	...	...	...	9 ⁴	9	2	1
29	1	...	...	21	22	2	2
30	...	...	...	2	2	...	...
31	...	...	...	1	1	2	2
MONTHLY TOTAL	1	3	15	212	231	35	27

¹ Aircraft shot down over France.
² Includes one Heinkel 111 shot down into the sea by an Anson aircraft of Coastal Command.
³ First Messerschmitt 110 fighter-bomber used.
⁴ First Messerschmitt 109 fighter-bomber used.

| | LUFTWAFFE | | | | | ROYAL AIR FORCE | |
| | NIGHT | | DAY | | | | |
DATE	A.A.	R.A.F.	A.A.	R.A.F.	TOTAL	AIRCRAFT	PILOTS
August 1940							
1	...	...	...	2	2	1	1
5	...	...	...	4	4	1	1
6	...	...	...	1	1	...	...
8	...	...	...	60	60 [1]	16	13
9	...	...	½	½	1	...	...
11	½	½	5	55	61 [2]	26	24
12	...	...	7	55	62 [3]	13	12
13	...	...	3	75	78	13	3
14	1	...	6	24	31	7	5
15	...	1	22	159 [4]	182	34	17
16	1	...	3	72	76	22	8
17	...	...	...	...	1	...	...
18	...	...	25	128 [5]	153	22	10
19	...	...	1	5	6	3	1
20	...	...	...	7	7	2	1
21	...	...	...	13	13	1	...
22	1	...	2	8	11	4	2
23	...	...	1	2	3	...	...
24	...	1	10	41	51	19	7
25	...	...	6	49	55	13	9
26	1	...	1	46	48	15	4 [6]
27	1	...	1	3	5	...	...
28	...	...	1	27	28	14	7 [7]
29	1	...	1	10	12	9	2
30	1	...	5	58	64	25	10
31	...	...	21	73	94	37	11
MONTHLY TOTAL	7½	2½	121½	977½	1109	297	148
September 1940							
1	...	...	4	25	29	15	6
2	...	...	22	43	65	20	8
3	...	...	...	25	25	15	7
4	...	2	12	52	66	17	5
5	...	...	2	37	39	20	11
6	...	...	1	45	46	19	7
7	...	...	28	75	103	22	13
8	...	...	6	5	11	3	2
9	...	...	3	49	52	13	7
10	...	...	...	2	2	...	...
11	2	...	9	84	95	24	17
12	...	...	...	1	1	...	...
13	1	...	...	1	3 [8]	...	...
14	...	...	2	16	18	9	3

[1] 24 bombers and 36 fighters. Target: Channel convoy.
[2] 13 bombers, 47 fighters and fighter-bombers, 1 seaplane.
[3] 26 bombers and 36 fighters.
[4] 127 bombers and 32 fighters.
[5] 89 bombers and 39 fighters.
[6] 4 pilots and 2 air gunners.
[7] 7 pilots and 3 air gunners.
[8] One aircraft destroyed by balloon barrage.

DATE	LUFTWAFFE					ROYAL AIR FORCE	
	NIGHT		DAY		TOTAL	AIRCRAFT	PILOTS
	A.A.	R.A.F.	A.A.	R.A.F.			
September 1940							
15	4	2	7	178	191 [1]	25	11
16	...	...	...	...	1 [2]	...	...
17	4	1	2	5	12	3	1
18	...	...	1	47	48	12	3
19	2	...	...	5	7	...	...
20	...	...	...	4	4	7	4
21	...	...	...	2	2	...	...
22	...	...	...	1	1	...	...
23	2	...	...	11	13	11	3
24	...	...	...	8	8	4	2
25	...	...	4	22	26	4	1
26	1	...	1	32	34	8	3
27	...	...	2	131	133	34	17
28	1	...	...	6	8 [2]	7	7
29	1	...	4	3	8	4	2
30	...	...	3	46	49	22	10
MONTHLY TOTAL	18	5	113	961	1100 [3]	318	150
October 1940							
1	1	...	...	4	5	3	3
2	...	1	1	9	11	1	1
3	...	...	1	...	1	...	...
4	...	...	1	2	3 [3]	1	1
5	1	...	...	23	24	9	2
6	...	...	...	1	1	...	...
7	...	...	...	27	27	16	6
8	...	...	1	7 [4]	8	2	2
9	...	...	...	4	4	1	...
10	...	...	...	5	5	5	3
11	...	...	...	8	8	9	3
12	...	...	...	11	11	10	4
13	...	...	...	2	2	2	...
15	2	...	...	17	19	15	6
16	4	...	...	1 [5]	5	...	...
17	...	...	...	4	4	3	3
19	...	...	...	2	2	...	...
20	4	...	...	8 [6]	12	3	...
21	...	...	...	1	1	...	...
22	...	...	...	3	3	6	4
23	1	...	...	...	1	...	...
24	...	...	...	2	2	...	...

[1] 131 bombers were destroyed by day and 6 by night.

[2] One aircraft destroyed by balloon barrage.

[3] German High Command communiqué admitted loss of 5 aircraft, and R.A.F. claimed two 'probables' that day; these are not included above.

[4] Two of these aircraft were Heinkel floatplanes shot down by aircraft of Coastal Command.

[5] The aircraft destroyed by R.A.F. was a floatplane shot down by a fighter of Coastal Command.

[6] Includes one aircraft shot down in the North Sea by a Hudson aircraft of Coastal Command.

| Date | LUFTWAFFE | | | | TOTAL | ROYAL AIR FORCE | |
| | NIGHT | | DAY | | | AIRCRAFT | PILOTS |
	A.A.	R.A.F.	A.A.	R.A.F.			
October 1940							
25	2	...	...	15	17	10	3
26	1	...	...	5	6	2	2
27	3	...	...	10	13	8	4
28	3	...	...	4	7	...	...
29	2	...	...	30	32	7	2
30	...	...	...	9	9	5	4
31	...	...	...	...	...	...	...
MONTHLY TOTAL	24	1	4	214	243	118	53
November 1940							
1	5 ...	...	1	10	16	7	5
2	1	...	...	9	10	...	...
3	...	...	½	½	1	1	1
5	...	...	...	7	7	5	2
6	1	...	...	5 [1]	6	4	3
7	...	...	...	7	7	5	2
8	...	...	...	20	20	6	3
9	3	...	...	4 [2]	7	5	2
11	...	...	...	12	12	2	2
11	...	...	...	13	(Italian aircraft)	...	...
12	...	...	...	1	1	...	...
13	2	...	...	4	6	...	...
14	2	...	2	17	21	2	...
15	5	...	...	18	23	2	1
16	1	...	...	...	1	...	...
17	...	...	1	12	13	5	1
18	...	...	...	2 [3]	2	...	...
19	5	...	...	...	5	...	...
20	...	...	...	1	1	...	...
21	...	...	...	1 [4]	1	1	1 [4]
22	...	...	...	2	2	...	...
23	...	...	...	4	4	...	...
23	...	...	...	7	(Italian aircraft)	...	...
24	3	...	...	3	6	...	...
25	...	...	...	1	1	...	...
26	...	...	1	3	4	...	...
27	1	...	...	11	12	2	...
28	...	...	...	5	5	7	6
29	...	...	...	5	5	2	...
30	...	...	...	5	5	2	...
MONTHLY TOTAL	29	...	5½	169½	204	58	27

[1] One aircraft shot down by Coastal Command included.
[2] At this date anti-aircraft guns had destroyed 400 enemy aircraft since the beginning of the war.
[3] Both these aircraft were destroyed by Coastal Command aircraft on North Sea patrol.
[4] Both German and British aircraft destroyed by collision in the air.

APPENDIX V

BRITISH AIR ACES OF FIGHTER COMMAND GAZETTED UP TO JANUARY 31, 1941

	ENEMY AIRCRAFT DESTROYED AND REMARKS
P/O Eric Stanley Lock, D.S.O., D.F.C. and bar (Shrewsbury) (No. 41 squadron)	22 at least
Sgt. Herbert James Lempriere Hallowes, D.F.M. and bar (Lambeth, London)	21. Reported missing June 7, 1940
S/L Archibald Ashmore McKellar, D.S.O., D.F.C. and bar (Paisley, Scotland) (Nos. 602 and 605 squadrons)	20. Killed in action November 1, 1940
Sgt. James Harry Lacey, D.F.M. and bar (Wetherby, Yorks) (No. 501 squadron)	19 at least
P/O Harbourne Mackay Stephen, D.S.O., D.F.C. and bar (Ballater, Scotland) (No. 74 squadron)	19
F/Lt. Mark Henry Brown, D.F.C. and bar (Portage La Prairie, Manitoba) (No. 1 squadron)	18 at least, mostly in Battle of France; later commanded the squadron as squadron leader
S/L Michael Nicholson Crossley, D.S.O., D.F.C. (Halford, Warwickshire) (No. 32 squadron)	18 and possibly 5 more
P/O Albert Gerald Lewis, D.F.C. and bar (Kimberley, South Africa)	18. Destroyed 6 in one day, 5 on another
S/L Adolph Gysbert Malan, D.S.O., D.F.C. and bar (Wellinglington, South Africa) (No. 74 squadron)	18 and possibly another 6. (Later score 32)
F/O Newell Orton, D.F.C. and bar (Warwick) (No. 73 squadron)	18. In France; unofficial score recorded by a contemporary
S/L Roland Robert Stanford Tuck, D.S.O., D.F.C. and bar (Catford, London) (No. 257 squadron)	18 at least. Score subsequently 22; second Bar to D.F.C. Prisoner of war
F/O Edgar James Kain, D.F.C. (Auckland, New Zealand) (No. 73 squadron)	17. In France; unofficial score recorded by a contemporary. Killed in France in a flying accident while stunting low over an aerodrome
F/Lt. Geoffrey Allard, D.F.C., D.F.M. and bar (York)	17, and shared in others in France and England as sergeant and later as commissioned officer; he destroyed 7 enemy aircraft in 3 days. Killed on active service in March 1941
P/O Robert Francis Thomas Doe, D.F.C. and bar (Reigate, Surrey) (No. 238 squadron)	14. On one occasion he dived vertically through a strong protective formation of fighters and attacked two 4-engined aircraft
Sgt. Andrew McDowall, D.F.M. and bar (Kirkinner, Wigtownshire, Scotland) (No. 602 squadron)	14 at least
F/Lt. John Wolferstan Villa, D.F.C. and bar (South Kensington, London) (No. 92 squadron)	13 and possibly 2 more

F/Sgt. George Cecil Unwin, D.F.M. and bar (Bolton-on-Dearne, Yorks) (No. 19 squadron)	13, and assisted in the destruction of others
F/Lt. Adrian Hope Boyd, D.F.C. and bar (No. 65 and No. 145 squadrons)	12
F/Lt. Robert Findlay Boyd, D.F.C. and bar (East Kilbride, Scotland) (No. 602 squadron)	12 at least
F/O Brian John George Carbury, D.F.C. and bar (Wellington, New Zealand) (No. 41 squadron)	12, and shared in 4 others
F/Lt. Stanley Dudley Pearce Connors, D.F.C. and bar (Calcutta)	12. Killed in action.
F/Lt. John Charles Dundas, D.F.C. and bar (Doncaster) (No. 609 squadron)	12 at least. Killed in action
F/Lt. Roy Gilbert Dutton, D.F.C. and bar (Hatton, Ceylon) (No. 111 squadron)	12. Over Belgium and in Battle of Britain
F/Lt. John Ignatius Kilmartin, D.F.C. (Dundalk, Eire) (No. 1 squadron)	12 in Battle of France
Sgt. Reginald Thomas Llewellyn, D.F.M. (Bristol)	12 and shared in others
Sgt. Gareth Leoffric Nowell, D.F.M. and bar (Wilmslow, Cheshire)	12 in one week
P/O William Dennis David, D.F.C. and bar (Surbiton, Surrey)	11
F/Lt. Alan Christopher Deere, D.F.C. and bar (Auckland, New Zealand)	11, probably one more, and assisted to destroy 2 others
P/O Thomas Francis Neil, D.F.C. and bar (Bootle, Lancs) (No. 249 squadron)	11 at least; 3 in one engagement
S/L Douglas Robert Stewart Bader, D.S.O., D.F.C. (London) (No. 242 squadron)	10, and damaged several more. Subsequent score 22½. Prisoner of war
F/Lt. James Michael Bazin, D.F.C. (Newcastle-on-Tyne) (No. 608 squadron)	10. Led two squadrons in head-on attack against 100/120 enemy aircraft; enemy fled
F/O Leslie Redford Clisby, D.F.C. (McLaren Vale, S. Australia) (No. 1 squadron)	10. Killed in action in France
F/Sgt. William Henry Franklin, D.F.M. and bar (Poplar, London) (Killed in action as pilot officer)	10, and assisted in destroying 2 more
P/O William Lidstone McKnight, D.F.C. and bar (Edmonton, Canada)	10. Killed in action August 1941
F/O Ian Bedford Nesbitt Russell, D.F.C. (Melbourne, Australia)	10, and probably 6 more
F/Lt. Percival Stanley Turner, D.F.C. (Ivybridge, Devon)	10. Over Dunkirk and England; shot down 2 with damaged aircraft
F/Lt. Ronald Derek Gordon Wight, D.F.C. (Skelmorlie, Ayrshire) (No. 213 squadron)	10, including 4 in France. Missing
P/O Frederick Carey, D.F.C. and bar (London) (No. 3 squadron)	9
P/O Peter Melvill Gardner, D.F.C. (Grimsby)	9 (4 in France); possibly more
S/L Joseph Robert Kayll, D.S.O., D.F.C. (Sunderland)	9
Sgt. Donald Ernest Kingaby, D.F.M. (Holloway, London) (No. 92 squadron)	9 at least; 4 in one day
S/L Aeness Ranald Donald MacDonell, D.F.C. (Baku, Russia)	9, and damaged 4 more
F/Lt. James Murray Strickland, D.F.C. (Iloilo, Philippine Islands)	9
P/O Timothy Ashmed Vigors, D.F.C. (Hatfield, Herts)	9
Sgt. Royce Clifford Wilkinson, D.F.M. and bar (Knaresborough, Yorks)	9
P/O Anthony Charles Bartley, D.F.C. (Dacca, India)	8 at least
F/Lt. Nicholas Gresham Cooke, D.F.C. (Blakeney, Norfolk) (No. 25 squadron) Cpl. Albert Lippett, D.F.M. (Yarmouth) (No. 25 squadron)	8 in two patrols in one day. Killed in action

Sgt. John Teasdale Craig, D.F.M. (Newcastle-on-Tyne)	8
Sgt. William Lawrence Dymond, D.F.M. (Twickenham)	8. In France and over England; probably 3 more
F/Lt. John Ellis, D.F.C. (Deal) (O.C. No. 610 squadron with rank of squadron leader from July 1940)	8. Over Dunkirk and England; 3 more by April 1941; No. 610 squadron had then destroyed at least 89 enemy aircraft; Bar to D.F.C.
F/O Thomas Arthur Francis Elsdon, D.F.C. (Broughty Ferry)	8. Six after August 31, 1940, over England
Sgt. Paul Caswell Powe Farnes, D.F.M. (Boscombe)	8
P/O John Albert Axel Gibson, D.F.C. (Brighton, New Zealand)	8. (Steered his aircraft when in flames away from Folkestone)
P/O Thomas Grier, D.F.C. (Glasgow)	8, and shared in others
P/O Dudley Trevor Jay, D.F.C. (London)	8, and damaged more
P/O John Blandford Latta, D.F.C. (Vancouver, British Columbia) (No. 242 squadron)	8. In France and England. Destroyed a second enemy aircraft after being himself hit
P/O Keith Temple Lofts, D.F.C. (Canterbury) (No. 615 squadron)	8. In Belgium, France, and England
Sgt. Donald Alastair Stewart McKay, D.F.M. (Pontefract, Yorks) (No. 421 flight)	8 at least, and valuable reconnaissances
S/L John Oliver William Oliver, D.S.O., D.F.C. (Chelsea)	8 at least (his squadron destroyed over 50)
F/Lt. John Colin Mungo Park, D.F.C. (Wallasey) (No. 74 squadron)	8, and half share in another. When posted missing in July 1941 had destroyed 12 at least
P/O Maurice Michael Stephens, D.F.C. and bar (Doranda, Ranchi, India)	8
P/O James Eric Storrar, D.F.C. (Ormskirk, Lancs)	8. Over Dunkirk and English Channel
S/L John Marlow Thompson, D.F.C. (Keynsham, Somerset) (No. 111 squadron)	8, and damaged at least 6
P/O John Ronald Urwin-Mann, D.F.C. (Victoria, British Columbia) (No. 238 squadron)	8 at least
P/O George Harman Bennions, D.F.C. (Burslem, Stoke-on-Trent)	7, possibly several more
F/Lt. Peter Malan Brothers, D.F.C. (Westerham, Kent) (No. 32 squadron)	7. Battle of Britain and before
F/Lt. George Patterson Christie, D.F.C. and bar (Westmount, Quebec) (No. 66 squadron)	7 at least
F/Lt. Walter Myers Churchill, D.S.O., D.F.C. (No. 605 squadron)	7. Commanded the squadron in France which shot down 62 enemy aircraft for the loss of four pilots
P/O John Churchin, D.F.C. (Hawthorn, Melbourne, Australia)	7 at least, and shared in others
F/O Gordon Neil Spencer Cleaver, D.F.C. (Stanmore, Middx.) (No. 601 squadron)	7, and possibly 2 more; in France, over Dunkirk and England
F/O John Reynolds Cock, D.F.C. (Renmark, S. Australia) (No. 87 squadron)	7. On one occasion he swam ashore
F/Lt. Christopher Frederick Currant, D.F.C. (Luton)	7, and damaged others
P/O Bryan Vincent Draper, D.F.C. (Barry, S. Wales) (No. 74 squadron)	7 since December 1939

F/O Anthony Eyre, D.F.C. (Lowestoft) (No. 615 squadron)	7. In France and Battle of Britain
F/O Henry Michael Ferriss, D.F.C. (Lee, London) (No. 111 squadron)	7. Later killed in action
F/Lt. Athol Stanhope Forbes, D.F.C. (London) (No. 303 squadron)	7. Awarded the Polish Virtuti Militari
F/Lt. Denys Edgar Gillam, D.F.C., A.F.C. (Tynemouth) (No. 616 squadron)	7, probably 4 more and 6 damaged; on one occasion shot down a Junkers 88 and landed within 11 minutes of taking off
F/Lt. Edward John Gracie, D.F.C. (Acton, London)	7, and damaged 5 more
F/O Leonard Archibald Haines, D.F.C. (Melcombe Regis, Weymouth) (Killed on active service)	7, and assisted in another; 2 pursued to France and shot down
Sgt. Ronald Fairfax Hamlyn, D.F.M. (Harrogate) (No. 610 squadron)	7, including 5 in one day
P/O Michael James Herrick, D.F.C. (Hastings, New Zealand)	7. 5 in France, and 2 on September 4, 1940, in night fighter action
Sgt. Harold Norman Howes, D.F.M. (Gillingham, Kent) (Killed in action)	7, and damaged several others in France and England
F/Lt. Paterson Clarence Hughes, D.F.C. (Sydney, Australia) (No. 64 squadron)	7. Later killed on active service
F/Lt. Anthony Desmond Joseph Lovell, D.F.C. (Ceylon) (No. 41 squadron)	7
F/Lt. James Henry Gordon McArthur, D.F.C. (Tynemouth)	7 at least
F/O Desmond Annesley Peter McMullen, D.F.C. (Godstone, Reigate)	7, and shared in others
F/O Howard Clive Mayers, D.F.C. (Sydney, Australia)	7, and possibly 3 more
F/O Richard Maxwell Milne, D.F.C. (Edinburgh) (No. 151 squadron)	7
F/Sgt. Percy Frederick Morfill, D.F.M. (Gosport)	7 at least
F/Lt. Thomas Frederick Dalton Morgan, D.F.C. and bar (Cardiff) (No. 43 squadron)	7. Score raised to 13 in May 1941 in night fighting; promoted squadron leader
F/O Peter William Olber Mould, D.F.C. (Hallaton, Uppingham) (No. 1 squadron)	7. In Battle of France
P/O Constantine Oliver Joseph Pegge, D.F.C. (Slough)	Wounded in one eye, and windscreen opaque by bullets, but returned and landed
F/Lt. John William Charles Simpson, D.F.C. (Ramsey St Mary's, Huntingdonshire) (No. 43 squadron)	7
F/Lt. John Eric James Sing, D.F.C. (Bristol) (No. 213 squadron)	7, and damaged others
F/O Wilfred Max Sizer, D.F.C. (Chelmsford) (No. 213 squadron)	7 at least, and shared in 4 others over France and England. On one patrol was shot down by 5 Me's and landed 2 miles outside La Panne; swam a canal, had face wounds dressed at Casualty Station, thence to England, and on patrol again after two days' sick leave
Sgt. Wilfred Malcolm Skinner, D.F.M. (Gloucester) No 74 squadron)	7

	Enemy Aircraft Destroyed and Remarks
F/O Thomas Paul Michael Cooper-Slipper, D.F.C. (Kinver, near Stourbridge) (No. 605 squadron)	7, and damaged 3 others. On one occasion he deliberately rammed and destroyed a hostile enemy aircraft after his own controls had been practically shot away
P/O Noel Karl Stansfield, D.F.C. (Edmonton, Alberta)	7. Over Dunkirk and England
F/O Frederic Frank Taylor, D.F.C. (Newbury, Berks) (No. 261 squadron)	7 at least, 2 in one engagement. Killed in action
Sgt. Thomas Young Wallace, D.F.M. (Johannesburg, South Africa)	7 and probably 4 more in three weeks
F/Lt. John Terrance Webster, D.F.C. (Liverpool) (No. 41 squadron)	7, and assisted in 2 more
Sgt. Cyril Frederick Babbage, D.F.M. (Ludlow, Shropshire)	6, probably 1 more
S/L John Vincent Clarence Badger, D.F.C. (Lambeth, London) (No. 43 squadron)	6
P/O Walter Beaumont, D.F.C. (Dewsbury, Yorks)	6. Since missing
P/O Ronald Berry, D.F.C. (Hull)	6, and assisted in others
Sgt. Michael Christopher Bindloss Boddington, D.F.M. (Hawkshead, Lancs) (No. 234 squadron)	6
P/O Crelin Arthur Walford Bodie, D.F.C. (Kirton, near Ipswich)	6, 3 in one day
Sgt. Horatio Herbert Chandler, D.F.M. (Bexhill)	6 since April 1940
Sgt. Arthur Victor Clowes, D.F.M. (New Sawley, Derbyshire) (No. 1 squadron)	6. Mostly in France; subsequently destroyed at least 11, promoted to flight lieutenant and awarded D.F.C.
F/Lt. John Hunter Coghlan, D.F.C. (Shanghai) (No. 56 squadron)	6. Killed in action
F/O Peter Collard, D.F.C. (London) (No. 615 squadron)	6. Missing
P/O David Moore Crook, D.F.C. (Huddersfield) (No. 609 squadron)	6, and damaged several more
F/O Carl Raymond Davis, D.F.C. (South Africa) (No. 601 squadron)	6 since the war began, and damaged several others. Killed in action
P/O Charles Trevor Davis, D.F.C. (Cardiff)	6
P/O Victor George Daw, D.F.C. (Portsmouth)	6
F/O Alan Francis Eckford, D.F.C. (Thame, Oxfordshire) (No. 253 squadron)	6. In France and England
F/O Anthony Douglas Forster, D.F.C. (Bishop Middleham, Durham) (No. 607 squadron)	6, including 4 in France
Sgt. Alfred Henry Basil Friendship, D.F.M. and Bar (St Albans, Herts)	6. In France
P/O George Ernest Goodman, D.F.C. (Haifa, Palestine) (No. 1 squadron)	6 at least
P/O Douglas Hamilton Grice, D.F.C. (Wallasey Village, Cheshire) (No. 32 squadron)	6. Escaped from enemy territory
Sgt. Glyn Griffiths, D.F.M. (Llandudno) (No. 17 squadron)	6 at least; 2 in one day
P/O Jack Royston Hamar, D.F.C. (Knighton, Radnor)	6. Since deceased
F/Lt. Robert Hugh Holland, D.F.C. (Ceylon) (No. 92 squadron)	6 at least
F/O John Bernard William Humpherson, D.F.C. (Enfield)	6. 2 in France, and possibly 3 more
F/Lt. Charles Brian Fabris Kingcome, D.F.C. (Calcutta) (No. 65 squadron)	6
P/O Kenneth Norman Thomson Lee, D.F.C. (Birmingham)	6 at least

F/Lt. James Archibald Findlay MacLachlan, D.F.C. and bar (Styal, Cheshire) (No. 261 squadron)	6 and possibly 7; 4 and possibly 5 in one day, up to February 5, 1941
P/O Eric Simcox Marrs, D.F.C. (Dover) (No. 152 squadron)	6 at least
F/O Brian Van Mentz, D.F.C. (Johannesburg)	6 and probably 3 more in France and England. Killed on active service
F/Lt. Stanley Charles Norris, D.F.C. (Tooting, London) (No. 29 squadron)	6, and damaged 2 more
P/O James Joseph O'Meara, D.F.C .(Barnsley, Yorks) (Nos. 64 and 91 squadrons)	6 by September 1940; 11 at least by March 12, 1941. Bar to D.F.C. and flying officer
F/Lt. Robert Wardlow Oxspring, D.F.C. (Hampstead, London) (No. 66 squadron)	6. One while acting as rear gunner
P/O Peter Lawrence Parrott, D.F.C. (Aylesbury)	6 at least destroyed or severely damaged
S/L Michael Lister Robinson, D.F.C. (Chelsea, London) (No. 609 squadron)	6 at least; twice destroyed 2 in one day
Sgt. William Thomas Edward Rolls, D.F.M. (London)	6 at least
S/L Philip James Sanders, D.F.C. (Brampton, Chesterfield) (No. 92 squadron)	6 at least; probably 1 more; in France and England
P/O Charles Anthony Woods-Scawen, D.F.C. (Karachi, India) (No. 43 squadron) (Killed in action)	6, and severely damaged several others; shot down 6 times; escaped from 25 miles inside French territory
P/O Patrick Philip Woods-Scawen, D.F.C. (Karachi, India) (No. 85 squadron)	6 Killed in action
F/Lt. Thomas Smart, D.F.C. (Broughton-in-Furness)	6 at least, including Dunkirk
F/Lt. Edward Brian Bretherton Smith, D.F.C. (Formby, Lancs) (No. 610 squadron)	6. Came down by parachute when his aircraft caught fire over the sea
F/O Rupert Frederick Smythe, D.F.C. (Killiney, Co. Dublin) (No. 29 squadron)	6
Sgt. Edward Rowland Thorn, D.F.M. (Portsmouth) (No. 25 squadron) / LAC Frederick James Barker, D.F.M. (Bow, London) (No. 25 squadron)	6 as team in Defiant
P/O James Arthur Walker, D.F.C. (Gleichen, Alberta) (No. 111 squadron	6
F/Lt. Peter Russell Walker, D.F.C. (Hacheston, Woodbridge, Suffolk) (No. 1 squadron)	6 in France
F/Lt. Percy Stevenson Weaver, D.F.C. (Bath)	6
Sgt. Alfred Whitby, D.F.M. (Liverpool)	6. 5 in Battle of France and 1 in England
F/O Harold Arthur Cooper Bird-Wilson, D.F.C. (Prestatyn, Wales) (No. 17 squadron)	6, and shared in the destruction of others
Sgt. Eric William Wright, D.F.M. (Cherry Hinton, Cambridge) (No. 605 squadron)	6 at least
P/O John Henry Ashton, D.F.C. (Newcastle-under-Lyme) (No. 145 squadron)	5 at least, 4 in Battle of France
F/O Roland Prosper Beamont, D.F.C. (Enfield) (No. 87 squadron)	5 at least
Sgt. John Maurice Bentley Beard, D.F.M. (Shoreham, Sussex)	5. In September destroyed 2 Me 109's which attacked him from rear when he was pursuing a bomber

S/L Minden Vaughan Blake, D.F.C. (Newman, New Zealand) (No. 234 squadron)	5
F/Lt. John Clifford Boulter, D.F.C. (Barnes, London) (No. 603 squadron)	5 at least, and shared in destruction of others. Died of wounds
P/O Wallace Cunningham, D.F.C. (Glasgow)	5
S/L John Scatliff Dewar, D.S.O., D.F.C. (Mussoori, Lahore, India) (Killed in action)	5. His squadron destroyed more than 60 enemy aircraft
Sgt. Alan Stuart Harker, D.F.M. (Bolton)	5 at least
F/Sgt. Frederick William Higginson, D.F.M. (Swansea)	5
P/O Petrus Hendrik Hugo, D.F.C. (Victoria West, Cape Province)	5
F/Lt. Caesar Barrand Hull, D.F.C. (Shangani, S. Rhodesia) (No. 223 squadron)	5. In Norway. Killed fighting in Battle of Britain
F/Lt. Robert Voase Jeff, D.F.C. and bar (Kuala Lumpur, F.M.S.) (No. 87 squadron)	5. In France. Killed in action
F/Sgt. Adrian Francis Laws, D.F.M. (East Dereham, Norfolk)	5 and damaged 2. Killed
F/Lt. Walter John Lawson, D.F.C. (Tunbridge Wells) (No. 19 squadron)	5 at least
P/O David Cooper Leary, D.F.C. (London) (No. 17 squadron)	5 at least; in November 1940, when his squadron was protecting two destroyers being attacked by enemy dive-bombers heavily escorted by fighters, he destroyed 2 bombers and assisted in the destruction of another. Killed in action
P/O John Keswick Ulick Blake McGrath, D.F.C. (Tonbridge, Kent)	5 and possibly 7 more
P/O Kenneth William McKenzie, D.F.C. (Belfast)	5. One of his victims was deliberately rammed
P/O Kenneth Manger, D.F.C. (Halifax) (No. 17 squadron) (Killed in action)	5. On one occasion landed near Dunkirk pier by parachute, was rescued by French craft and went on patrol next day
F/O Richard Frewen Martin, D.F.C. (Bournemouth) (No. 73 squadron)	5. In France. Escaped from internment in Luxemburg
P/O James Reginald Bryan Meaker, D.F.C. (Kinsale, Co. Cork)	5 at least, and damaged others
F/O William Henry Rhodes-Moorhouse, D.F.C. (London) (No. 601 squadron)	5. Killed in Battle of Britain; only son of Lt. W. B. Rhodes-Moorhouse, first air V.C. of the Great War
P/O Ian James Muirhead, D.F.C. (Leyton, London) (Killed in action)	5. Escaped from enemy-held territory
F/Lt. Charles Gordon Chaloner Olive, D.F.C. (Brisbane, Australia) (No. 65 squadron)	5. In France and England
Sgt. Peter Anthony Burnell-Phillips, D.F.M. (Richmond, Surrey)	5 at least; forced a Dornier to crash into sea although he had expended all his ammunition; destroyed 1 enemy aircraft after being wounded in foot

	Enemy Aircraft destroyed and Remarks
F/Lt. Alexander Coultate Rabagliati, D.F.C. (Durban, Natal)	5, and damaged others
F/O Blair Dalzo Russell, D.F.C. (Montreal) (No. 1 R.C.A.F.)	5, and assisted in another
P/O Donald Stuart Scott, D.F.C. (Hook-with-Warsash, Hants)	5, and severely damaged 3 more
F/O Peter James Simpson, D.F.C. (Hove) (No. 111 squadron)	5 at least, in France and England
Sgt. George Smythe, D.F.M. (Westminster, London)	5, and assisted in damaging others
F/Lt. Ian Scovil Soden, D.S.O. (London) (No. 56 squadron)	5 and possibly 2 more; on one occasion attacked 50 to 60 enemy aircraft single-handed. Killed in Battle of Britain
P/O Donald William Alfred Stones, D.F.C. (Norwich)	5. In France
F/O Hugh Norman Tamblyn, D.F.C. (Watrous, Sask.) (No. 242 squadron)	5 at least. Killed in action as flight lieutenant
P/O Archibald Nigel Charles Weir, D.F.C. (Missing)	5. Dunkirk and Channel; 3 in one day
P/O William Dudley Williams, D.F.C. (East Grinstead, Sussex) (No. 152 squadron)	5 at least
F/O Herbert John Woodward, D.F.C. (Harefield, Middx) (No. 64 squadron)	5
S/L The Hon. Maxwell Aitken, D.F.C. (No. 601 squadron)	4. One at night
P/O Harold Derrick Atkinson, D.F.C. (Wintringham, Yorks)	4
F/O Richard George Arthur Barclay, D.F.C. (Upper Norwood, Surrey) (No. 249 squadron)	4 at least
F/Lt. Robert Alexander Barton, D.F.C. (Kamloops, British Columbia) (No. 41 squadron)	4, and shared in others; on September 27 the squadron destroyed 20 enemy aircraft
W/C Francis Victor Beamish, D.S.O., D.F.C., A.F.C. (Dunmanway, Cork) (Station Commander)	4 and half of another, and possibly 7 more
Sgt. Samuel Leslie Butterfield, D.F.M. (Leeds) (Killed)	4. In one engagement
F/O James Alexander Campbell, D.F.C. (Nelson, British Columbia) (No. 87 squadron) (Killed in action)	4. In France. With 7 Hurricanes attacked 40 Me's
Sgt. Henry Cartwright, D.F.M. (Wigan) (Killed in action).	4. In France
F/Lt. Wilfred Greville Clouston, D.F.C. (Auckland, New Zealand) (No. 19 squadron)	4. France and Belgium
P/O William Dennis David, D.F.C. (Surbiton, Surrey) (No. 87 squadron)	4. Shot down 2 enemy aircraft when 7 Hurricanes attacked 40 Me's
S/L George Lovell Denholm, D.F.C. (Bo'ness, West Lothian) (No. 603 squadron)	4. His squadron destroyed 54 enemy aircraft in about six weeks
S/L Edward Mortlock Donaldson, D.S.O. (Negri Sembilan, F.M.S.) (No. 151 squadron)	4. His squadron destroyed 10 or 11 and possibly 5 more in their first two days in action
F/Lt. Billy Drake, D.F.C. (London) (No. 1 squadron and No. 421 flight)	4 at least; and a valuable reconnaissance
P/O John Connell Freeborn, D.F.C. (Middleton, near Leeds) (No. 74 squadron)	4. Over the Low Countries, Dunkirk, Channel, and S.E. England. By February 21, 1941, destroyed 12 at least and damaged many more; Bar to D.F.C. and flight lieutenant

F/Lt. Derek Pierre Aumale Boitel-Gill, D.F.C. (Thames Ditton)	4. In August 1940 during fight against 30 bombers and 90 fighters, when 5 enemy aircraft were destroyed, 3 were destroyed by this officer
F/O Richard Lindsay Glyde, D.F.C. (Perth, W. Australia) (No. 87 squadron)	4. In France. Missing
P/O Colin Falkland Gray, D.F.C. (Papanui, Christchurch, New Zealand)	4, and believed 4 more, and also assisted in 2
F/Lt. Peter Prosser Hanks, D.F.C. (York) (No. 1 squadron)	4. In France
S/L Sir Archibald Philip Hope, Bt., D.F.C. (No. 601 squadron)	4, and shared in others
F/Lt. Frank Jonathan Howell, D.F.C. (Golders Green, London)	4, and partly responsible for 5 more and has damaged several others
F/O Jerrard Jefferies, D.F.C. (Sutton Coldfield) (No. 17 squadron)	4, and severely damaged 2 more
P/O Desmond Hayward Sidley Kay, D.F.C. (London) (No. 25 squadron)	4. Over Low Countries; forced-landed near Zoute, holed in one tank
F/Lt. John Alexander Kent, D.F.C., A.F.C. (Winnipeg) (No. 303 squadron)	4 at least; attacked 40 Me 109's single-handed and shot down 2. Awarded Polish Virtuti Militari
F/Lt. William John Leather, D.F.C. (Sleaford, Lincs.) (No. 611 squadron)	4, including 1 over Dunkirk and 3 on convoy patrols
S/L Ernest Archibald McNab, D.F.C. (Regina, Sask.) (No. 1 squadron, R.C.A.F.)	4, and led No. 1 squadron, R.C.A.F., which destroyed 23 enemy aircraft at least
Sgt. Jack Mann, D.F.M. (Northampton) (No. 91 squadron)	4 at least
F/Lt. Peter Gerald High Matthews, D.F.C. (Hoylake, Cheshire) (No. 1 squadron)	4 at least
P/O Dennis Crowley-Milling, D.F.C. (St Asaph, Flintshire) (No. 242 squadron)	4 at least
P/O Norman Robert Norfolk, D.F.C. (Nottingham) (No. 72 squadron)	4 at least
F/Lt. William Barrington Royce, D.F.C. (No. 504 squadron)	4, and led his squadron in command
F/O Gordon Leonard Sinclair, D.F.C. (Eastbourne) (No. 19 squadron)	4
S/L Peter Wooldridge Townsend, D.F.C. and Bar (Rangoon) (No. 43 squadron)	4, and excellent squadron leadership; subsequently destroyed 11 at least, awarded D.S.O., promoted to W/C in command No. 85 squadron
F/Lt. Richard Macklow Trousdale, D.F.C. (Ahacawai, New Zealand) (No. 255 squadron)	4 at least, including 1 at night
Sgt. John White, D.F.M. (Motherwell, Lanarkshire) (No. 72 squadron)	4 and possibly 4 more
F/Lt. Peter William Dunning-White, D.F.C. (Hadley Wood, Middx.) (No. 615 squadron)	4 including 1 at night
Sgt. Clifford Whitehead, D.F.M. (Birmingham)	4 and possibly 3 more

	Enemy Aircraft destroyed and Remarks
P/O Allen Richard Wright, D.F.C. (Teignmouth, Devon)	4 including a Heinkel III at night, and 4 more aircraft badly damaged
P/O Richard Clare Whittaker, D.F.C. (Yoxford, Suffolk) (No. 17 squadron) (Killed in action)	4, and severely damaged 4 more
F/Lt. William Francis Blackadder, D.S.O. (No. 607 squadron)	3 and for leading patrols in France and making reconnaissances of roads and bridges
F/Lt. James Robert Maitland Boothby, D.F.C. (Yelverton, Devon) (No. 85 squadron)	3 in one day. In France
S/L Andrew Douglas Farquhar, D.F.C. (Renfrew) (No. 602 squadron)	3. In the North before the Battle of Britain
F/Lt. Lionel Manley Gaunce, D.F.C. (Lethbridge, Alberta) (No. 3 squadron)	3. In Battle of Britain
F/Lt. Sidney Robert Gibbs, D.F.C. (Calgary, Canada) (No. 204 squadron)	Heinkel 115 floatplanes shot down by Sunderland of Coastal Command. Located survivors of *Adania*
P/O Dorian George Gribble, D.F.C. (Hendon) (No. 54 squadron)	3, and damaged many more, over Low Countries, Dunkirk, and Channel
P/O William Henry Hodgson, D.F.C. (Dunedin, New Zealand) (Killed on active service)	3, and damaged several more. Landed his burning aircraft away from civilians
S/L Henry Algernon Vickers Hogan, D.F.C. (Rawalpindi, India)	3 and squadron leadership; squadron destroyed 69 enemy aircraft
S/L Philip Algernon Hunter, D.S.O. (Frimley, Hants) (No. 25 squadron) LAC Frederick Harry King, D.F.M. (Leicester) (No. 25 squadron)	3 In Defiant over the Low Countries and Dunkirk. Both killed in action
F/Lt. Patrick Geraint Jameson, D.F.C. (Wellington, New Zealand) (No. 46 squadron)	3. In Norway
F/O Alastair John Oswald Jeffrey, D.F.C. (Mussoorio, India) (No. 64 squadron)	3, and destroyed 4 enemy aircraft on the ground. Killed in action
S/L Ronald Gustave Kellett, D.S.O., D.F.C. (Tadcaster, Yorks) (No. 600 and No. 303 squadrons)	3. His squadron destroyed 33 enemy aircraft in one week and 113 in one month; awarded the Polish Virtuti Militari
S/L Duncan Stuart MacDonald, D.F.C. (Oban) (No. 213 squadron)	3 at least since September 1940
F/Lt. Gordon Roy McGregor, D.F.C. (Westmount, Quebec) (No. 1 squadron, R.C.A.F.)	3 at least, and damaged many others
F/Lt. Michael Alan Newling, D.F.C. (Barnes, Surrey) (No. 145 squadron)	3 at least, and assisted in destroying others since May 1940
W/C Thomas Geoffrey Pike, D.F.C. (Lewisham, London) (No. 219 squadron)	3 including 2 in one night and believed 1 more at night. Succeeded Little in command of 219 squadron
F/Lt. Robin Peter Reginald Powell, D.F.C. (Penang, Straits Settlements) (No. 111 squadron)	3 at least, in May 1940

	Enemy Aircraft Destroyed and Remarks
S/L Gerald Alfred Wellesley Saunders, D.F.C. (West Kensington, London) (No. 65 squadron)	3 at least; served in squadron from its formation and appointed to command in October 1940
F/Lt. James Gilbert Sanders, D.F.C. (Mortlake, Surrey) (No. 111 squadron)	3
F/O Ronald Nicholas Selley, D.F.C. F/O Hilton Aubrey Haarhoff, D.F.C. (Selley was born in Durban, Natal) (No. 220 squadron)	Pilot and rear gunner 2 in a Hudson of 1 Coastal Command, protecting shipping evacuating the B.E.F. from Dunkirk
F/Sgt. Harry Steere, D.F.M. (Wallasey, Cheshire)	3, and assisted in destroying 3 more
P/O Peter Charles Parker Stevenson, D.F.C. (Billinghay, Lincs)	3, and assisted in others
F/O Cedric Arthur Cuthbert Stone, D.F.C. (Amritsar, India) (No. 3 squadron)	3. Early in May in France
Sgt. Kenneth Norman Varwell Townsend, D.F.M. (Alexandria, Egypt)	3 and possibly 2 more in May 1940
F/Lt. Raymond Myles Beecham Duke-Woolley, D.F.C. (Manchester) (No. 253 squadron)	3 at least, and damaged several more
F/Lt. Bryan John Wicks, D.F.C. (Felixstowe) (No. 56 squadron)	3 at least, and shared in others. Escaped from German - occupied territory in disguise
F/O Derek Hurlstone Allen, D.F.C. (Leicester) (No. 85 squadron)	2. In May 1940, including 1 Junkers 89
S/L Robert Swinton Allen, D.F.C. (Manchester) Sgt. William Richard Williams, D.F.M. (Kansas, U.S.A.)	Crew of bomber who scored two night victories over 1 Heinkel 111 and 1 Junkers 87
P/O Charles Francis Ambrose, D.F.C. (Plumstead, London) (No. 46 squadron)	2, and damaged several others
F/O Kenneth Hughes Blair, D.F.C. (Heaton Moor, Stockport) (No. 85 squadron)	2. In France in May 1940 and patrol over Maastricht
F/Lt. John Cunningham, D.F.C. (Croydon) (No. 604 squadron)	2. Night fighting during last three months of 1940 over Britain, when he made 25 night sorties and 7 interceptions
F/Lt. James William Elias Davies, D.F.C. (Bernardsville, New Jersey, U.S.A.) (No. 79 squadron)	2, and badly damaged another. Killed in action
AC1 Jack Guest, D.F.M. (Barnsley, Yorks) (Killed in action)	2. As air gunner in Battle bomber
S/L Patrick John Handy Halahan, D.F.C. (Dublin) (No. 1 squadron)	2 and half share in another; led No. 1 squadron, A.A.S.F.
Sgt. Bernard James Jennings, D.F.M. (Luton). (No. 19 squadron)	2 and probably 6 more
P/O Richard John Jouault, D.F.C. (Amiens, France) (No. 220 squadron, Coastal Command)	2. With front gun of Hudson in attack against 40 Junkers 87's over Dunkirk
S/L Charles George Lott, D.S.O., D.F.C. (Southsea)	2. Possibly another, and assisted in destroying 3 more. Lost an eye
F/Lt. Christopher John Mount, D.F.C. (London). (No. 602 squadron)	2, and damaged 3

	Enemy Aircraft Destroyed and Remarks
S/L John Alexander Peel, D.F.C. (Boscombe, Hants) (No. 145 squadron)	2 at least. Shot down Dornier 17 when 25 miles from coast, then had to abandon his own aircraft; rescued by lifeboat when almost unconscious
P/O Phillip Walford Peters, D.F.C., pilot (Streatham) Sgt. Deryk Cobham Spencer, D.F.M., navigator (Southport, Lancs) Cpl. Lewis George Smith, D.F.M., air gunner (Canterbury) (Coastal Command)	And 2 more damaged during patrol over Dunkirk evacuation by section of 3 Hudson 2 aircraft of Coastal Command, when attacked by 9 Messerschmitts
F/Lt. John Sample, D.F.C. (No. 607 squadron)	2. During May 1940; himself shot down and forced to jump
P/O Richard Playne Stevens, D.F.C. (Tonbridge) (No. 151 squadron)	2. During night fighting; both enemy aircraft were shot down one night in January 1941, in one instance after a pursuit down from 30,000 ft. almost to ground-level. On two subsequent occasions shot down 2 enemy aircraft in one night; awarded Bar to D.F.C.
P/O Ernest Cecil John Wakeham, D.F.C. (Harberton, Totnes, Devon) (Missing)	2 and 2 others at least severely damaged, in May 1940; shot down and landed between Ostend and Dunkirk
F/O Adrian Warburton, D.F.C. (Middlesbrough) (No. 431 flight)	2. Night fighting
F/O Allen Benjamin Angus, D.F.C. (Winnipeg) (No. 85 squadron)	1 and half share in another and seriously damaged a third. Shot down to forced landing in Belgium but escaped and rejoined unit
F/Sgt. Frederick George Berry, D.F.M. (Calcutta) (No. 1 squadron) (Killed in action)	1. Bomber attacking troopship Lancastria at Saint-Nazaire
Sgt. James Douglas Culmer, D.F.M. (Walthamstow, London) (No. 25 squadron)	1 Heinkel 111 destroyed at night in November 1940 over Essex while rear gunner in Defiant
LAC Leslie Stewart Dillnutt, D.F.M. (London) (Coastal Command) (Missing as sergeant)	1 and possibly damaged 2 when air gunner of Hudson on patrol over Dunkirk during evacuation of B.E.F.
F/Lt. Henry Gordon Goddard, D.F.C. (No. 219 squadron)	1 Junkers 88 at night in November 1940
S/L James Hayward Little, D.F.C. (New Orleans, U.S.A.) (Nos. 601 and 219 squadrons)	1 Dornier 17 at night. Led 219 squadron from May 1940 for a year

		Enemy Aircraft destroyed and Remarks
P/O	Graham Herbert Russell, D.F.C. (Kuala Lumpur, F.M.S.) (No. 236 squadron, Coastal Command)	1 Dornier 24 flying boat after reconnaissance of Brest
G/C	Stanley Flamank Vincent, D.F.C., A.F.C. (Hampstead, London) (Station Commander)	1, and damaged another; wing organization and observation of patrols in flight

NUMERICALLY UNCLASSIFIED

S/L	John William Donaldson, D.S.O. (Kuala Lumpur, F.M.S.)	6. During operations at Aandalsnes, in Central Norway, in April 1940, No. 223 squadron destroyed 6 enemy aircraft and put 8 more out of action. Story in Vol. I, pp. 178–187. Sgt. Russell received the Military Medal for re-arming aircraft under bombing and machine-gun fire
F/Lt.	Randolph Stuart Mills, D.F.C. (London)	
P/O	Sidney Robert McNamara, D.F.C. (Ipswich)	
P/O	Philip Hannah Purdy, D.F.C. (St Stephen, New Brunswick)	
Sgt.	Ernest Frederick William Russell, M.M. (Hurst Green, Etchingham, Sussex) (All of No. 223 squadron)	
F/Lt.	Howard Peter Blatchford, D.F.C. (Edmonton, Alberta) (No. 257 squadron)	? In November 1940 led a squadron which destroyed 8 and damaged 5 Italian aircraft in one day; in this combat he destroyed at least 1 aircraft, rammed and damaged an enemy fighter when his ammunition was expended, and made two head-on feint attacks on enemy fighters and drove them off
F/O	Mark Medley Carter, D.F.C.	? In May 1940 led his flight against 60 Junkers 87's of which 11 were destroyed
F/O	William Pancoast Clyde, D.F.C. (Sevenoaks)	? In France in May 1940
Sgt.	William Ralph Crich, D.F.M. (Valletta, Malta)	? In France in May and June 1940
S/L	Horace Stanley Darley, D.S.O. (Wandsworth, London) (No. 609 squadron)	?
W/C	John Humphrey Edwardes-Jones, D.F.C. (No. 213 squadron)	?
F/O	William Ernest Gore, D.F.C. (No. 607 squadron)	? His section shot down 3 enemy aircraft in May 1940 in France. Gore escaped by parachute from burning aircraft. Killed in Battle of Britain
S/L	Barrie Heath, D.F.C. (Birmingham) (No. 611 squadron)	?
F/Lt.	Brian John Edward Lane, D.F.C. (No. 213 squadron)	?

	Enemy Aircraft Destroyed and Remarks
F/Lt. Richard Hugh Anthony Lee, D.S.O., D.F.C. (No. 85 squadron)	? In France with Air Component. In his last engagement he pursued a Junkers 89 over enemy territory at 200 ft. under intense fire from the ground. Escaped from behind German lines after being arrested.
F/Lt. Reginald Eric Lovett, D.F.C. (Hendon, London) (No. 73 squadron)	? Shot down in flames in France. Killed in Battle of Britain
F/Lt. James Eglington Marshall, D.F.C. (Tilbury) (No. 85 squadron)	?
F/O James Storrs Morton, D.F.C. (Blackheath, London) (No. 603 squadron)	?
S/L Joseph Somerton O'Brien, D.F.C. (No. 23 squadron)	? Killed in action
F/O Cyril Dampier Palmer, D.F.C. (Cleveland, Ohio, U.S.A.) (No. 1 squadron)	? With A.A.S.F. in France
F/O Harold George Paul, D.F.C. (Oxford) (No. 73 squadron)	? With A.A.S.F. in France
S/L Percy Charles Pickard, D.S.O., D.F.C. (Handsworth, Sheffield) (No. 311 (Czech) squadron)	? Led 311 squadron
Sgt. Lionel Sanderson Pilkington, D.F.M. (Hull)	?
F/O Paul Henry Mills Richey, D.F.C. (Chelsea) (No. 1 squadron)	? With A.A.S.F. in France. Wounded and shot down in France
F/Lt. John Evelyn Scoular, D.F.C. (No. 73 squadron)	?
F/Sgt. Francis Joseph Soper, D.F.M. (Devonport) (No. 1 squadron)	? With A.A.S.F. in France
F/O William Hector Stratton, D.F.C. (Hastings, New Zealand) (No. 1 squadron)	? With A.A.S.F. in France
F/O Hamilton Charles Upton, D.F.C. (Manchester) (No. 43 squadron)	?
F/Lt. Douglas Herbert Watkins, D.F.C. (Heswall, Cheshire) (No. 611 squadron)	?
Sgt. Raymond Arthur Cecil de Courcy White, D.F.M. (Chelsea)	? In France
S/L John Worrall, D.F.C. (Bombay)	? Assisted in destroying 3 enemy aircraft. His squadron destroyed 43 and possibly 22 more

GENERAL STATISTICS

No. of enemy aircraft destroyed over and around Great Britain from
    June 18 to November 30, 1940:   2914

No. destroyed from August 8 to October 31, 1940:   2445
    (Bombers and fighters fell in almost equal numbers; about 700
    were destroyed by Auxiliary Air Force squadrons)

No. of German aircraft destroyed in seven days ending August 15, 1940
    (of which 161 were Junkers 87 and 88 dive-bombers and 75 were
    heavy bombers: and including one seaplane):   475

Between August 8 and October 31:
    The Royal Air Force Fighter Command pilots' casualties were 375 killed
        and 358 wounded.
    Other casualties (mostly civilians) were:
        By day: 1700 killed and 3360 seriously wounded.
        By night: 12,581 killed and 16,965 seriously wounded.

Fighter Command day patrols:		*Daily Average*
From August 8 to September 5 inclusive	4,523	156
From September 8 to October 5 inclusive	3,291	$117\frac{1}{2}$
From October 6 to October 31 inclusive	2,786	107
TOTAL	10,600	122

Hurricanes of Air Component shot down more than 350 bombers and fighters in
    France, and by the end of the evacuation of Dunkirk fighters not included
    within the Air Component had shot down 450 bombers and fighters.

Scores of some of the squadrons:
    By December 26, 1940, No. 74 squadron had shot down 100 enemy aircraft
        while operating from one air station.
    No. 607 (County of Durham) squadron fought in France and shot down
        74 enemy aircraft between May 10 and May 20, 1940. By April 1,
        1941, the squadron had shot down 102 German aircraft.
    No. 609 (West Riding) squadron shot down its 100th enemy aircraft during
        the first week in November 1940.
    No. 303 (Polish) squadron destroyed $117\frac{1}{2}$ enemy aircraft during the
        Battle of Britain. The squadron destroyed 67 aircraft on five separate
        days: September 7 (14); September 11 (14); September 15 (16);
        September 26 (13); and September 27 (10).
    No. 604 (County of Middlesex) squadron had destroyed more than 30
        night raiders by June 1941.

Index

340

Badger, Squadron Leader J. V. C., D.F.C., 168, 169
Balbo, Marshal Italo, death of, 140
Baldwin of Bewdley, Earl, on parity with German Air Force, 40
Balloon Barrage Command, purpose of, 154
Balloon Barrage, breaking loose of balloons, instructions on, 163–164
Bapaume, district, 74
Barratt, Air Marshal Arthur S., dinner invitation to an R.A.F. crew, 111–112; headquarters of, 117
Battle bombers, 36–37, 39, 40, 41, 45, 46, 66, 70 *et seq.*, 83, 114
Baux, source of bauxite, 152
Beachy Head, 265, 268
Beamish, Wing Commander F. V., A.F.C., 238
Beaufort bombers, 23, 28
Beauraing road, attack on, 74
Beaverbrook, Maxwell Aitken, Lord, Minister of Aircraft Production, 70, 298 *n.*; appeal of, for aluminium, 152 *and n.*, 153; criticisms of, 153
Belgian Army, size of, 15; 7th Infantry Division, 33; capitulation of, 48, 91; equipment of, 53; German pressure against, 54; delaying action by, 58; Cavalry Corps and the Weygand plan, 88, 90
Belgian Army Air Force, 11, 50; losses of, 33; destruction of, 43; morale of crews, 50; pilots of, in defence of Britain, 50, 206
Belgian contingent, aid of, to Britain, 139
Belgium, seizure in, of German secret documents, 10, 12–13, 42–43; bombing of, 11; attack along German frontier, 11; appeal for help, 12; German pretext for invasion of, 14; neutrality of, 14; refusal of German demands, 14; entry of British troops, 15; Battle of, 16, 32–57, 65; British bombers over, 76; capitulation of, 118, 124; barges of, 143; aerodromes of, destruction of, 153; German losses in, 264
Beneš, Dr Eduard, 139, 231
Bergen aerodrome, 11
Bergeret, General, 125
Bergues-Furnes-Nieuport line, 93
Bergues-Mardyck line, 92, 93
Berkshire, air attack on, 256
Berlin, 136
Berneuil, 68

Berry-au-Bac aerodrome, 63, 114, 115
Besson, General, and the Riom trial, 63
Betheniville, 63
Bexhill, bombing of, 267
Bidassoa, river, 134
Biddell, Flight Lieutenant W. H., 96
Biggin Hill aerodrome, bombing of, 194, 199–200
Biggin Hill fighter wing, 85
Billotte, General, 48
Binche, 77
Bishop's Stortford, 279
Blanchard, Jean-Pierre, first parachutist, 51
Blanchard, General, 90
Blatchford, Flight Lieutenant H. P., D.F.C., 288–289
Blenheim bombers and fighters, 22–25, 28, 34, 41–42, 46, 49, 54, 66, 71, 74, 78, 83, 109, 117, 167, 199, 235; armour of, 131
Bloch, Marcel, and the Riom trial, 63
Blount, Air Vice-Marshal C. H. B., 14, 51, 53
Bois d'Epinoy, 90
Bomber Command, 16, 29, 65, 67; operations of, in France from British bases, 66, 68, 71 *et seq.*, 81–82; bombing, methods of, 73; operational exercises, 80–81 *and n.*; crews, training of, 83; growth of targets of, 142; form of attack initiated by, 148; night patrols, difficulties of, 235; operations, effect of weather on, 254; targets of, 304–319
Bordeaux, 120, 121, 142; 'the men of,' 122, 123
Boulogne, 54, 78, 82, 84; evacuation of, 86
Boyd, Flight Lieutenant A. H., D.F.C., 181 *and n.*, 182
Bozanville, 111
Brabant, 20, 29
Breda, 39
Bremen, targets at, 72, 74, 144
Brest, 54; German occupation of, effect of, on S.W. England, 132
Bridge of Waith, first British civilian killed at, by German bomb, 129
Briedgen bridge, 32, 33
Brighton, bombing of, 241
Bristol, attacks on, 260, 263
Bristol Aeroplane Company, Ltd., 260
Bristol Channel, 137, 161

345

349